DANIELS and WORTHINGHAM'S

Muscle Testing

Techniques of Manual Examination and Performance Testing

FIRST SOUTH ASIA EDITION

DANIELS and WORTHINGHAM'S

Muscle Testing

Techniques of Manual Examination and Performance Testing

Dale Avers | PT, DPT, PhD, FAPTA
Professor
Department of Physical Therapy Education
College of Health Professions
SUNY Upstate Medical University
Syracuse, New York

Marybeth Brown | PT, PhD, FAPTA, FACSM
Professor Emeritus
Physical Therapy Program, Biomedical Sciences
University of Missouri
Columbia, Missouri

ELSEVIER

ELSEVIER

RELX India Pvt. Ltd.

Registered Office: 818, 8th floor, Indraprakash Building, 21, Barakhamba Road, New Delhi-110001
Corporate Office: 14th Floor, Building No. 10B, DLF Cyber City, Phase II, Gurgaon-122002, Haryana, India

---

Notice

Practitioners and researchers must always rely on their own experience and knowledge in evaluating and using any information, methods, compounds, or experiments described herein. Because of rapid advances in the medical sciences, in particular, independent verification of diagnoses and drug diagnosis should be made. To the fullest extent of the law, neither the Publisher nor the authors, contributors, or editors, assume any liability for any injury and/or damage to persons or property as a matter of product liability, negligence or otherwise, or from any use or operation of any methods, products, instructions, or ideas contained in the material herein.

This publication is licensed for sale in India, Bangladesh, Bhutan, Maldives, Nepal, Pakistan and Sri Lanka only. Circulation of this version outside these territories is unauthorized and illegal.

Content Strategist: Udita Joseph
Content Project Manager: Shivani Pal
Cover Designer: Raman Kumar

Printed in India by Rajkamal Electric Press, Kundli, Haryana.

To my students and colleagues, who continue to challenge me to be the best I can be.

— Dale Avers

This book is dedicated to my wonderful colleagues, who are the true backbone of our profession, and to my students, for these are the men and women who have made my days tremendously fun and totally worthwhile. This book is also dedicated to Helen J. Hislop— friend, mentor, and incredible woman.

— Marybeth Brown

Helen J. Hislop, PT, PhD, FAPTA — A Tribute

In 2013 the physical therapy profession lost one of the brightest beacons it had ever known. Helen Hislop was an extraordinary woman who changed the course of our profession, in part by implementing heightened standards of academic success and by creating the DPT and PhD degrees during her tenure at the University of Southern California. She also took the editorship of *Physical Therapy*, the professional journal of the American Physical Therapy Association, and transformed it from an anecdotal "how to" magazine into a scientific journal with genuine credibility in the medical community. The sheer magnitude of her contributions is probably beyond that of any physical therapist in the history of our profession.

One of the most notable achievements in Helen's repertoire was her authorship of four editions of the classic text, *Daniels and Worthingham's Muscle Testing: Techniques of Manual Examination*. First published in 1946, the original Daniels, Williams, and Worthingham book was a "how to" manual for testing the patient with poliomyelitis. Although the book was modified to some extent over the next 30 years, the practice of physical therapy changed considerably during that time span and the earlier muscle testing book did not reflect the expansion of the profession to include the testing of neurological patients, the testing of men and women with orthopedic injuries and joint replacements, and contending with the burgeoning older adult population. Helen became involved in shepherding the book to a more contemporary text beginning with the 6th edition, and when the book was published in 1995, it reflected a sea change. Beautiful anatomical drawings produced under Helen's direction were incorporated, the testing of new patient populations was added, and there was the inclusion of new muscle tests that had evolved from clinical practice that were far more accurate than those described in previous texts,

such as the 25× heel rise. Although these changes were the product of Helen's vision, the contributions of her coauthor, Jacqueline Montgomery, MA, PT, were of tremendous importance as Jackie was a clinician with her finger on the pulse of clinical practice.

In 2010, Helen called to ask if I would become a contributor to the 9th edition, and I agreed. After multiple trips to Helen's home in North Carolina it became apparent that her declining health was going to preclude completion of the book without a great deal more help. We worked for another year, but with looming deadlines and the need for a move away from "manual" muscle testing, and the inclusion of functional testing, it became necessary to enlist additional help. Dale Avers, PT, DPT, PhD, FAPTA, was asked to be an author and edition 9 continued to evolve in response to changing practice.

Even with multiple hospitalizations and further declines in health, Helen continued to be a vital contributor to edition 9. At all times she was "in charge." Her fortitude was extraordinary; once a vision was planted in her brain, there was no dissuading her from the task at hand. She never saw the final completed copy of edition 9 but she contributed to each and every one of the enormous changes brought forth in the new book. Even though Helen is gone, her contributions will persist through many more iterations of this text.

Wherever Helen may be, there is no question she is lustily singing Gilbert and Sullivan tunes, engaging those around her in lively and insightful conversation, regaling anyone who will listen with tales of Scottish history, and making people laugh. Hopefully, too, she has caught the "big fish" that eluded her for her entire 84 years.

Rest in peace, dear friend.

— Mb

It gives me immense pleasure to write a foreword to this book. Personally I have been reading this book as a bachelor's student since I opted physical therapy as a career way back in 1990 (using it as a reference book thereafter as a professional and teacher). Also, I am highly convinced that it provides all the required information related to manual muscle testing.

First published in 1946, the book was a "how to" manual for testing of muscle strength of the post-polio residual paralysis patients. The book has certainly come a long way through nine editions in more than 70 years. Through these editions it has been constantly researched and revised to be presented currently as a plethora of the most updated knowledge.

Muscle strength testing is an integral part of physical therapy and is an essential tool for assessment, diagnosis and treatment of physical impairments. With the advancement of health science, health professionals like orthopedicians, neurologists, plastic surgeons, gynaecologists and paediatricians are also aspiring for the knowledge and practice of MMT. Even the athletic trainers find it essential for modern sports. This edition of the book has been designed and edited in such a way that it will fulfil the requirements of every health professional. Taking over the charge after the sad demise of Helen J. Hislop, Marybeth Brown and Dale Avers have done a magnificent job in adding new changes to this edition. This 10th edition presents a more practical way of strength testing as functional testing in place of manual muscle testing. The text is based on movement (e.g. elbow flexion) rather than tests of individual muscles (biceps brachii). The numerical grade represents the performance of all muscles contributing to that movement. Apart from the usual way of strength testing, this edition also presents a unique way of testing by a handheld muscle dynamometer and its procedure (Chapter 9). I would like to thank the authors for bringing back to the minds of the readers the alternative ways of testing, such as 1 RM and Multiple RM used for strength testing. These are equipment based, power testing, body weight testing, endurance testing, weight machinery, etc. For HHD and alternative test methods, normative values have been introduced for ready references. Here is a pickup point for researchers and scholars: 10th edition of the book is more evidence and research based. Strength testing methods are included for young adults to very old persons. Exercises for strengthening of muscles (actions) are added, which will give a boost to the beginners. Case studies and the readily available anatomical references are the key features of this edition.

The book is filled with concrete examples, fine drawings and careful guidelines, which make these strength testing techniques easy to grab and apply. It is up-to-date and serves equally as a reference book for the qualified physiotherapists, athletic trainers, other health professionals as well as for students. Overall, this book a must read for a physical therapist or an aspiring physical therapy student.

Dr. Raghunath Sahoo, BPT, MPT (Ortho), MIAP
Sr. Physiotherapist, PGIMER, Chandigarh
Former Lecturer,
Rajiv Gandhi Health University, Bengaluru

PREFACE

For more than 70 years, *Daniels and Worthingham's Muscle Testing* has been informing students and practitioners about the art and science of manual muscle testing. Over the past seven decades there have been nine editions of the text, not including this current edition.

So, why an Edition 10? *Muscle Testing* has evolved into a different entity during its lengthy history. Initially a primer on how to test muscles affected by poliomyelitis, *Daniels and Worthingham's Muscle Testing* book now reflects the muscle testing requirements for a far broader scope of practice. Additionally, muscle testing techniques are now appropriate for patients who range in age from young adults to those who have lived 100 or more years (material appropriate for children may be found in other sources). Building on manual testing, this edition includes power testing and endurance testing, as well as alternate testing using free-weights, weight machines, elastic bands, body weight, functional testing, and most recently, handheld dynamometry. The tests included in this edition are far more evidence-based than they have been in the past due to the contributions of numerous researchers who have advanced our understanding of assessment. In many instances, normative values now exist and they have been included in Edition 10. Finally, for the beginning practitioner, exercises have been added to help the new therapist in the design of appropriate treatment programs. Thus, as the health professions have evolved, so too has muscle testing. We believe this book is the most up-to-date muscle testing book available, with detailed "how to" information on hundreds of tests. Importantly, this new edition is evidence-based, an imperative in our contemporary health-care system.

For those of you with historical perspective, it is evident that a number of editors and contributors to *Muscle Testing* have come and gone over the years. The historical figures associated with the early editions of this text are long gone, but each made important contributions and passed the mantle to the next generation of scholars. Now, it is we who are the caretakers of the book and in due time we too will pass the torch to younger individuals with their fingers on the pulse of practice and scholarship. Why us? We were chosen because of a long and rich association with Helen Hislop, the previous author who was at the helm of the book for nearly 40 years. Helen valued our clinical expertise and anatomical knowledge and gave her blessing to this change of the book's leadership. We hope you will be pleased with our efforts.

We are enormously grateful to our forebears for the work that went into the creation of this text. We are grateful as well to the individuals who helped in the creation of the book, particularly our developmental editor, Linda Wood, who has skillfully guided the development of five editions of the book. We also thank Yoshi Miyake for the drawings of the new tests and Jeanne Robertson for the new anatomical drawings. For the original videos, we thank Judith Burnfield, whose work we have built upon in developing the new videos for this edition. Additional thanks go to the individuals who contributed to and reviewed sections of the book during its development: Richard Bohannan, PT, PhD, FAPTA, of Campbell University; Christopher Neville, PT, PhD, of Upstate Medical University; and Kevin Neville, PT, DPT, of Upstate Medical University. We are grateful for their valuable insights. We are also grateful for the four second-year DPT students from Upstate Medical University who were the models for many of the illustrations in the new edition: Melanie Chapman, Marissa Coppola, Kathryn Dziwulski, and Vanessa Sweet. And finally, we thank the team at Elsevier including Sarah Vora, Michael Fioretti, and many others whose behind-the-scenes work helped bring the book to fruition.

Dale Avers, PT, DPT, PhD, FAPTA
Marybeth Brown, PT, PhD, FAPTA

Chapter 10
Case Studies

This 10th edition presents manual muscle testing within the context of strength testing. Classic muscle testing is a fundamental skill of every physical therapist and is essential to the diagnosis and assessment of movement impairments. However, as manual muscle testing has come under scientific scrutiny, it is obvious that its use to evaluate and assess strength as a component of functional movement patterns and tasks is inadequate. Therefore, in addition to the classic presentation of manual muscle testing, this edition presents methods of strength testing that are valid, objective, and applicable across various settings.

A number of noteworthy changes have been made in the new edition. First and foremost, it is a modern 21st century text that has been thoroughly researched. Each test presented is backed by evidence, and the utility of each muscle testing approach is presented in context with alternative options. Throughout the text there are updated testing methods. Origins, insertions, and actions of key muscles for each manual muscle test are now included and precede the description of most test procedures. Additionally, for each specific muscle (e.g., serratus anterior, tibialis anterior), there are exercises that the therapist can use to strengthen weak muscles in patients. Each recommended exercise has been demonstrated, in most instances, to elicit at least 40% of maximum voluntary strength. Thus exercises are sufficiently rigorous to induce genuine strength increases in patients.

Chapter 7 presents a variety of strength testing methods using common equipment. Although this chapter was introduced in the previous edition, additional tests have been added to it and modifications to other tests were made. Additional normative values have been included and values for reliability, validity and specificity are now part of the text, when these values exist. Chapter 8 describes functional tests that have a significant strength component. Age-based norms are included when available, and patient scenarios are presented that provide the rationale for each recommended approach to strength testing. Finally, there is a new Chapter 9 on handheld dynamometry, an emerging technology that offers an additional means of distinguishing between limbs that have subtle strength differences and an opportunity for more precise testing. Normative values for handheld dynamometry have also been included when normative values exist. We believe that you will find this a very different text from Edition 9 and a welcome addition to your library.

Muscle strength is a critical component of functional movement. Assessment must include accurate measurement of the quantity of strength within the context of functional tasks and movement. Especially for the lower extremities, methods that allow the expansion of the findings of manual muscle testing from an impairment to a function level are needed. Quantitative assessment promotes accurate assessment of progress and patient performance within the context of age-based normative values. Although few "hard numbers" of threshold strength levels exist for specific functional movements, we have identified the known muscles that have been correlated with a specific task and, in some cases, have suggested values that may serve as a target for the minimum strength required for a specific functional task.

The manual muscle testing portion of this book, as in previous editions, directs its focus on manual procedures. For the most part, joint motions (e.g., hip flexion) rather than individual muscles (e.g., iliopsoas) are the focus of this text because of the contributions of more than one muscle to a movement. Although prime movers of a movement can be identified, secondary or accessory movers may be equally important and should not be overlooked or underestimated. Rarely is a prime mover the only active muscle, and rarely is it used under isolated control for a given movement. For example, knee extension is the prerogative of the five muscles of the quadriceps femoris, yet none of these five extend the knee in isolation from its synergists. Regardless, definitive activity of any muscle in a given movement can be precisely detected by electromyography, and such studies, when they exist, are now included as important pieces of evidence in this updated text.

Range of motion in this book is presented only to illustrate the range required to test a movement correctly. A consensus of typical ranges is presented with each test, but the techniques of measurement used are not within the scope of this text.

Brief History of Muscle Testing

Wilhelmine Wright and Robert W. Lovett, MD, Professor of Orthopedic Surgery at Harvard University Medical School, were the originators of the muscle testing system that incorporated the effect of gravity.[1,2] Janet Merrill, PT, Director of Physical Therapeutics at Children's Hospital and the Harvard Infantile Paralysis Commission in Boston, an early colleague of Dr. Lovett, stated that the tests were used first by Wright in Lovett's office gymnasium in 1912.[3] The seminal description of the tests used largely today was written by Wright and published in 1912[1]; this was followed by an article by Lovett and Martin in 1916[4] and by Wright's book in 1928.[5] Miss Wright was a precursor of the physical therapist of today, there being no educational programs in physical therapy in her time, but she headed Lovett's physical therapeutic clinic. Lovett credits her fully in his 1917 book, *Treatment of Infantile Paralysis*,[6] with developing the testing for polio. In Lovett's book, muscles were tested using a resistance-gravity system and graded on a scale of 0 to 6. Another early numerical scale in muscle testing was described by Charles L. Lowman, MD, founder and medical director of Orthopedic Hospital, Los Angeles.[7] Lowman's system (1927) covered the effects of gravity and the full range of movement on all joints and was particularly helpful for assessing extreme weakness. Lowman further described muscle testing procedures in the *Physiotherapy Review* in 1940.[8]

H.S. Stewart, a physician, published a description of muscle testing in 1925 that was very brief and was not anatomically or procedurally consistent with what is done today.[9] His descriptions included a resistance-based grading system not substantially different from current use: maximal resistance for a normal muscle, completion of the motion against gravity with no other resistance for a grade of fair, and so forth. At about the time of Lowman's book, Arthur Legg, MD, and Janet Merrill, PT, wrote a valuable small book on poliomyelitis in 1932. This book, which offered a comprehensive system of muscle testing, was used extensively in physical therapy educational programs during the early 1940s; muscles were graded on a scale of 0 to 5, and a plus or minus designation was added to all grades except 1 and zero.[10]

Among the earliest clinicians to organize muscle testing and support such testing with sound and documented kinesiologic procedures in the way they are used today were Henry and Florence Kendall. Their earliest published documents on comprehensive manual muscle testing became available in 1936 and 1938.[11,12] The 1938 monograph on muscle testing was published and distributed to all Army hospitals in the United States by the U.S. Public Health Service. Another early contribution came from Signe Brunnström and Marjorie Dennen in 1931; their syllabus described a system of grading movement rather than individual muscles as a modification of Lovett's work with gravity and resistance.[13]

The first comprehensive text on muscle testing was written by Lucille Daniels, MA, PT; Marian Williams, PhD, PT; and Catherine Worthingham, PhD, PT, published in 1946.[14] These three authors prepared a comprehensive handbook on the subject of manual testing procedures that was concise and easy to use. It remains one of the most used texts the world over and is the predecessor for all subsequent editions of *Daniels and Worthingham's Muscle Testing* including this edition.

The Kendalls (together and then Florence alone after Henry's death in 1979) developed and published work on muscle testing and related subjects for more than 6 decades[15-17] Their first edition of *Muscles: Testing and Function* appeared in 1949.[15] Earlier, the Kendalls had developed a percentage system ranging from 0 to 100 to express muscle grades as a reflection of normal; they reduced the emphasis on this scale, only to return to it in the latest edition (1993), in which Florence again advocated the 0 to 10 scale.[17] The contributions of the Kendalls should not be considered as limited to grading scales, however. Their integration of muscle function with posture and pain in two separate books[15,16] and then in one book[17] is a unique and extremely valuable contribution to the clinical science of physical therapy.

Muscle testing procedures used in national field trials that examined the use of gamma globulin in the prevention of paralytic poliomyelitis were described by Carmella Gonnella, Georgianna Harmon, and Miriam Jacobs, all physical therapists.[18] The later field trials for the Salk vaccine also used muscle testing procedures.[19] The epidemiology teams at the Centers for Disease Control were charged with assessing the validity and reliability of the vaccine. Because there was no other method of accurately "measuring" the presence or absence of muscular weakness, manual muscle testing techniques were used.

A group from the D.T. Watson School of Physiatrics near Pittsburgh, which included Jesse Wright, MD; Mary Elizabeth Kolb, PT; and Miriam Jacobs, PT, PhD, devised a test procedure that eventually was used in the field trials.[20] The test was an abridged version of the complete test procedure but did test key muscles in each functional group and body part. It used numerical values that were assigned grades, and each muscle or muscle group also had an arbitrary assigned factor that corresponded (as closely as possible) to the bulk of the tissue. The bulk factor multiplied by the test grade resulted in an "index of involvement" expressed as a ratio.

Before the trials, Kolb and Jacobs were sent to Atlanta to train physicians to conduct the muscle tests, but it was decided that experienced physical therapists would be preferable to maintain the reliability of the test scores.[20] Lucy Blair, then the Poliomyelitis Consultant in the American Physical Therapy Association, was asked by Catherine Worthingham of the National Foundation for Infantile Paralysis to assemble a team of experienced physical therapists to conduct the muscle tests for the field trials. Kolb and Jacobs trained a group of 67 therapists in the use of the abridged muscle test.[20] This work of determining the presence or absence of weakness and paralysis had enormous impact on the eventual approval of the Salk vaccine. A partial list of participants was appended to the Lilienfeld paper in the *Physical Therapy Review* in 1954.[19]

How to Use This Book

The general principles that govern manual muscle testing are described in Chapter 1. Chapter 2 describes the purposes and limitations of manual muscle testing, placing manual muscle testing in the context of strength testing across settings. Chapters 3 through 7 present traditional and updated techniques for testing motions of skeletal muscle groups in the body region covered by that chapter. Chapter 4 reflects additional changes to practice through the expansion of the trunk muscle strength testing section, particularly trunk endurance; the pelvic floor muscle testing section; and the respiratory muscle section. Chapter 7 describes methods of strength testing using equipment and instruments, and Chapter 8 is devoted to functional tests, which have become critical for successful documentation. Students should learn manual muscle testing within the context of strength testing to avoid some of the limitations described in Chapter 2. Chapter 9 is completely new and describes manual testing using a handheld dynamometer and includes normative values where they exist. Chapter 10 provides case studies to describe different methods of strength testing in various patient populations and settings.

For instant access to anatomical information without carrying a large anatomy text to a muscle testing session, see the Ready Reference Anatomy section on Evolve. This chapter is a synopsis of muscle anatomy, muscles as part of motions, muscle innervations, and myotomes.

To assist readers, each muscle has been assigned an identification number based on a regional sequence, beginning with the head and face and proceeding through the neck, thorax, abdomen, perineum, upper extremity, and lower extremity. This reference number is retained throughout the text for cross-referencing purposes. Two lists of muscles with their reference numbers are presented, one alphabetical and one by region, to assist readers in finding muscles in the Ready Reference section. These can also be found on the inside front and back covers of the book.

Names of the Muscles

Muscle names have conventions of usage. The most formal usage (and the correct form for many journal manuscripts) is the terminology established by the Federative International Committee on Anatomical Terminology (FCAT) in 1998. However, common usage often neglects these prescribed names in favor of shorter or more readily pronounced names. The authors of this text make no apologies for not keeping strictly to formal usage. Most of the muscles cited follow Terminologia Anatomica. Others are listed by the names in most common use. The alphabetical list of muscles (see the inside front cover of the book) gives the name used in this text and the correct Terminologia Anatomica term, when it differs, in parentheses.

Anatomical Authorities

The authors of this book relied on both the American and British versions of *Gray's Anatomy* as principal references for anatomical information, as well as Sabotta's *Atlas of Human Anatomy*. Because proficiency in muscle testing can only be achieved if the practitioner has a thorough understanding of anatomy, anatomical drawings are presented throughout the book, many in cross-section format, and descriptions of origins and insertions and functions are provided in multiple places, in detail and in abbreviated form.

The Convention of Arrows in the Text

Red arrows in the text denote the direction of movement of a body part, either actively by the patient or passively by the examiner. The length and direction of the arrow indicates the relative excursion of the part.

Black arrows in the text denote resistance by the examiner.

It is important to remind the reader that mastery of muscle testing, whether performed manually or using a strength-testing device, requires substantial practice. The only way to acquire proficiency in clinical evaluation procedures is to practice over and over again. As experience with patients matures over time, the nuances that can never be fully described for the wide variety of patients encountered by the clinician will become as much intuition

as science. Muscle testing continues to be among the most fundamental skills of the physical therapist and others who are concerned with abnormalities of human motion. The skill of manual muscle testing is a critical clinical tool that every physical therapist must not only learn but also master. A physical therapist who aspires to be recognized as a master clinician will not achieve that status without acquiring exquisite skills in manual muscle testing and precise assessment of muscle performance.

References

1. Wright WG. Muscle training in the treatment of infantile paralysis. *Boston Med Surg J*. 1912;167:567–574.
2. Lovett RW. Treatment of infantile paralysis. Preliminary report. *JAMA*. 1915;64:2118.
3. Merrill J. Personal letter to Lucille Daniels dated January 5, 1945.
4. Lovett RW, Martin EG. Certain aspects of infantile paralysis and a description of a method of muscle testing. *JAMA*. 1916;66:729–733.
5. Wright WG. *Muscle Function*. New York: Paul B. Hoeber; 1928.
6. Lovett RW. *Treatment of Infantile Paralysis*. 2nd ed. Philadelphia: Blakiston's Son & Co.; 1917.
7. Lowman CL. A method of recording muscle tests. *Am J Surg*. 1927;3:586–591.
8. Lowman CL. Muscle strength testing. *Physiotherap Rev*. 1940;20:69–71.
9. Stewart HS. *Physiotherapy: Theory and Clinical Application*. New York: Paul B. Hoeber; 1925.
10. Legg AT, Merrill J. Physical therapy in infantile paralysis. In: *Mock. Principles and Practice of Physical Therapy*. Vol. 2. Hagerstown, MD: W.F. Prior; 1932.
11. Kendall HO. Some interesting observations about the after care of infantile paralysis patients. *J Excep Child*. 1936;3: 107.
12. Kendall HO, Kendall FP. *Care During the Recovery Period of Paralytic Poliomyelitis. U.S. Public Health Bulletin No. 242*. Washington, D.C.: U.S. Government Printing Office; 1938.
13. Brunnstrom S, Dennen M. Round table on muscle testing. New York: Annual Conference of the American Physical Therapy Association, Federation of Crippled and Disabled, Inc. (mimeographed); 1931.
14. Daniels L, Williams M, Worthingham CA. *Muscle Testing: Techniques of Manual Examination*. Philadelphia: W.B. Saunders; 1946.
15. Kendall HO, Kendall FP. *Muscles: Testing and Function*. Baltimore: Williams & Wilkins; 1949.
16. Kendall HO, Kendall FP. *Posture and Pain*. Baltimore: Williams & Wilkins; 1952.
17. Kendall FP, McCreary EK, Provance PG. *Muscles: Testing and Function*. 4th ed. Baltimore: Williams & Wilkins; 1993.
18. Gonella C, Harmon G, Jacobs M. The role of the physical therapist in the gamma globulin poliomyelitis prevention study. *Phys Ther Rev*. 1953;33:337–345.
19. Lilienfeld AM, Jacobs M, Willis M. Study of the reproducibility of muscle testing and certain other aspects of muscle scoring. *Phys Ther Rev*. 1954;34:279–289.
20. Kolb ME. Personal communication, October 1993.

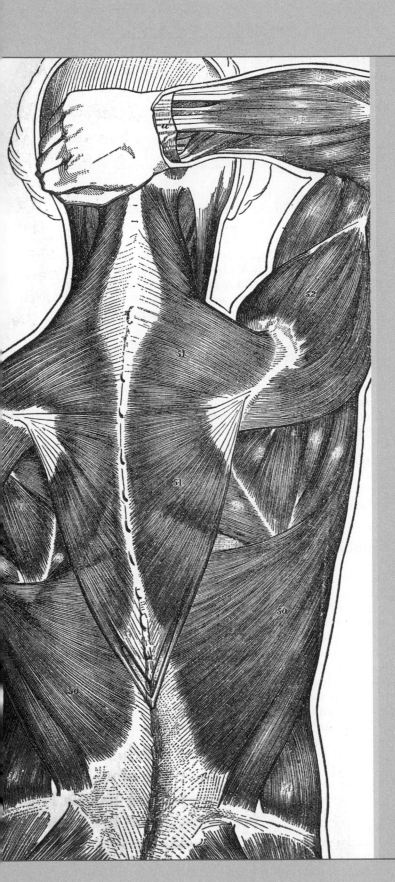

Principles of Manual Muscle Testing

GRADING SYSTEM

Grades for a manual muscle test are recorded as numeric ordinal scores ranging from zero (0), which represents no discernable muscle activity, to five (5), which represents a maximal or best-possible response or as great a response as can be evaluated by a manual muscle test. Because this text is based on actions (e.g., elbow flexion) rather than tests of individual muscles (e.g., biceps brachii), the grade represents the performance of all muscles contributing to that action.

The numeric 0 to 5 system of grading is the most commonly used muscle strength scoring convention across health care professions. Each numeric grade (e.g., 4) can be paired with a word grade (e.g., good) that describes the test performance in qualitative, but not quantitative, terms. (See table.) Use of these qualitative terms is an outdated convention and is not encouraged because these terms tend to misrepresent the strength of the tested action. For knee extension, forces that are less than 50% of average and therefore not "normal" are often graded 5.[1] Knee extension actions graded as 4 may generate forces as low as 10% of maximal expected force, a level clearly not described appropriately as "good." For this reason, the qualitative terms have largely been removed from this book. The numeric grades are based on several factors that will be addressed later in this chapter.

Numeric Score	Qualitative Score
5	Normal (N)
4	Good (G)
3	Fair (F)
2	Poor (P)
1	Trace activity (T)
0	Zero (no activity) (0)

OVERVIEW OF TEST PROCEDURES

Break Test

Manual resistance is applied to a limb or other body part after it has actively completed its test range of motion against gravity. The term *resistance* is always used to denote a concentric force provided by the tester that acts in opposition to contracting muscles. Manual resistance should always be applied opposite to the muscle action of the participating muscle or muscles. The patient is asked to hold the body segment at or near the end of the available range, or at the point in the range where the muscle is most strongly challenged. At this point, the patient is instructed to not allow the therapist to "break" the hold while the therapist applies manual resistance. For example, a seated patient is asked to flex the elbow to its end range (Grade 3); when that position is reached, the therapist applies resistance just proximal to the wrist, trying to "break" the muscle's hold and thus allow the forearm to move downward into extension. This is called a break test, and it is the procedure most commonly used in manual muscle testing nowadays. However, there are

alternatives to the break test for grading specific muscle actions.

As a recommended alternative procedure, the therapist may choose to place the muscle or muscle group to be tested in the end or test position, after ensuring that the patient can complete the available range (Grade 3), before applying additional resistance. In this procedure the therapist ensures correct positioning and stabilization for the test.

Make Test

An alternative to the break test is the application of manual resistance against an actively contracting muscle or muscle group (i.e., opposite the direction of the movement) that matches the patient's resistance but does not overcome it. During the maximum contraction, the therapist gradually, over approximately 3 seconds, increases the amount of manual resistance until it matches the patient's maximal level. The make test is not as reliable as the break test, therefore making the break test the preferred test.

Active Resistance Test

Resistance is applied opposite the actively contracting movement throughout the range, starting at the fully lengthened position. The amount of resistance matches the patient's resistance but allows the joint to move through the full range. This kind of manual muscle test requires considerable skill and experience to perform and is not reliable; thus its use is not recommended as a testing procedure but may be effective as a therapeutic exercise technique.

Application of Resistance

The principles of manual muscle testing presented here and in all published sources since 1921 follow the basic tenets of muscle length–tension relationships, as well as those of joint mechanics.[2,3] In the case of the elbow flexion, for example, when the elbow is straight, the biceps are long but the lever is short; leverage increases as the elbow flexes and becomes maximal at 90°, where it is most efficient. However, as flexion continues beyond that point, the biceps are short and their lever arm again decreases in length and efficiency.

In manual muscle testing, external force in the form of resistance is applied at the end of the range or after backing off slightly from the end of range in the direction opposite the actively contracting muscle. For some muscle actions (e.g., knee flexion), this backing off is considerable—to the point that the primary muscles tested are at what may be considered mid-range. Two-joint muscles are typically tested in mid-range where length-tension is more favorable. Ideally, all muscles and muscle groups should be tested at optimal length-tension, but there are many occasions in manual muscle testing where the therapist is not able to distinguish between Grades 5 and 4 without putting the patient at a mechanical disadvantage. Thus the one-joint brachialis, gluteus medius, and quadriceps muscles are tested at end range and the two-joint hamstrings and gastrocnemius muscles are tested in mid-range.

Critical to the accuracy of a manual muscle test are the location of the applied resistance and the consistency of application across all patients. The placement of resistance is typically near the distal end of the body segment to which the tested muscle attaches. There are exceptions to this rule. One exception is when resistance cannot be provided effectively without moving to a more distal body segment. In the case of shoulder and hip internal and external rotators, this involves applying resistance through the hand placed on the distal forearm or lower leg. Another exception involves patients with a shortened limb segment as in an amputation. Take for example a patient with a transfemoral amputation. Even if the patient could hold against maximum resistance while abducting the hip, the weight of the lower limb is so reduced and the therapist's lever arm for resistance application is so short, that a grade of 5 cannot be assumed regardless of the resistance applied. A patient holding against maximum resistance may still struggle with the force demands of walking with a prosthesis. If a variation is used, the therapist should make a note of the placement of resistance to ensure consistency in testing.

The application of manual resistance should never be sudden or uneven (jerky). The therapist should apply resistance with full patient awareness and in a somewhat slow and gradual manner, slightly exceeding the muscle's force as it builds over 2 to 3 seconds to achieve the maximum tolerable intensity. Applying resistance that slightly exceeds the muscle's force generation will more likely encourage a maximum effort and an accurate break test.

The therapist also should understand that the weight of the limb plus the influence of gravity is part of the test response. Heavier limbs and longer limb segments put a higher demand on the muscles that move them. Therefore lifting the lower limb against gravity can demand more than 20% of the "normal strength" of the hip muscles.[4] In contrast, lifting the hand against gravity requires less than 3% of the normal strength of the wrist muscles.[4] When the muscle contracts in a parallel direction to the line of gravity, it is noted as "gravity minimal." It is suggested that the commonly used term "gravity eliminated" be avoided because, of course, that can never occur except in a zero-gravity environment.

Weakened muscles are tested in a plane horizontal to the direction of gravity with the body part supported on a smooth, flat surface in such a way that friction force is minimal (Grades 2, 1, and 0). A powder board may be used to minimize friction. For stronger muscles that can complete a full range of motion in a direction against the pull of gravity (Grade 3), resistance is applied perpendicular to the line of gravity (Grades 4 and 5). Acceptable variations to antigravity and gravity-minimal positions are discussed in individual test sections.

Stabilization

Stabilization of the body or segment is crucial to assigning accurate muscle test grades. Patients for whom stabilization is particularly important include those with weakness in stabilizing muscles (e.g., scapular stabilizers) when testing the shoulder muscles and those who are particularly strong in the tested muscle action.

Numerous muscles, some seemingly remote, can contribute as stabilizers to the performance of tested muscle actions. However, muscle test performance is not meant to be dependent on muscles other than the prime movers. To give an extreme example, shoulder abduction on the left side should not be dependent on the trunk muscles on the right side. Therefore a patient with weak trunk muscles and limited sitting balance should be supported and stabilized either through patient positioning or by a stabilizing hand on the right shoulder.

A muscle or muscle group that is particularly strong may also require patient stabilization if the full capacity of a muscle group is to be accurately tested.[5] For example, a tester may not be able to break the knee extension action of a patient who is allowed to rise off of a support surface during the performance of a break test. However, the same patient, properly stabilized by the tester, an assistant, or a belt during testing, may not be able to hold against maximum tester resistance and thus break the muscle contraction, indicating that the patient has a muscle test grade of 4 rather than 5.

CRITERIA FOR ASSIGNING A MUSCLE TEST GRADE

The grade given on a manual muscle test comprises both subjective and objective factors. Subjective factors include the therapist's impression of the amount of resistance given during the actual test and then the amount of resistance the patient actually holds against during the test. Objective factors include the ability of the patient to complete a full range of motion or to hold the test position once placed there, the ability to move the part against gravity, or an inability to move the part at all. All these factors require clinical judgment, which makes manual muscle testing a skill that requires considerable practice and experience to master. An accurate test grade is important not only to establish the presence of an impairment but also to assess the patient's longitudinal status over time. Clinical reasoning is necessary for the therapist to determine the causes for the lack of ability to complete the full range or hold the position, ascertain which is most applicable, and decide whether manual muscle testing is appropriate.

Consistent with a typical orthopedic exam, the patient is first asked to perform the active movement of the muscle to be tested. Active movement is performed by the patient without therapist or mechanical assistance. This active movement informs the therapist of the patient's willingness and ability to move the body part, of the available range in the related joint(s), and whether there are limitations to full range, such as pain, excess tone, or weakness. Active movement without resistance is the equivalent of a Grade 3. Active movement is also called active range of motion and begins every muscle test to help determine the appropriate test position and amount of resistance to apply.

Grade 5 Muscle

A grade of 5 is assigned when a patient can complete full active range of motion (active movement) against gravity and hold the test position against maximum resistance. If the therapist can break a patient's hold, a grade of 5 should *not* be assigned. Overgrading will prevent the differentiation of a weak from a strong muscle and the identification of muscles that do, versus do not, get stronger over time.

The wide range of "normal" muscle performance typically leads to a considerable underestimation of a muscle's capability.[6] If the therapist has no experience in examining people who are free of disease or injury, it is unlikely that there will be any realistic or accurate assessment of what is Grade 5 and how much normality can vary. In general, a student learns manual muscle testing by practicing on classmates, but this provides only minimal experience compared with what is needed to master the skill. It should be recognized, for example, that the average therapist cannot "break" knee extension in a reasonably fit young man, even by doing a handstand on his leg! A therapist may not be aware of underestimation of a muscle contraction unless quantitative measures of strength are also used, such as in a sit-to-stand test. In addition, contributing to an underestimation of weakness is the inability of some therapists, particularly those who are women, to apply adequate resistance.[7]

Grade 4 Muscle

Grade 4 is assigned when the patient can complete the full active range of motion (active movement) against gravity but is not able to hold the test position against maximum resistance. The Grade 4 muscle "gives" or "yields" to some extent at the end of its test range with maximal or submaximal resistance. When maximal resistance results in a break or give, irrespective of age or disability, the muscle is assigned a grade of 4. However, if pain limits the ability to maximally resist the force applied by the therapist, evaluation of actual strength may not be realistic and should be documented as such. An example might be, "Elbow flexion appeared strong but painful."

The grade of 4 represents the true weakness in manual muscle testing procedures (pun intended). Sharrard counted remaining alpha motor neurons in the spinal cords of individuals with poliomyelitis at the time of autopsy.[8] He correlated the manual muscle test grades in the patient's chart with the number of motor neurons remaining in the anterior horns. His data revealed that more than 50% of motor neurons of a muscle group were absent when the muscle test grade was 4. Thus, when the muscle could withstand considerable but less than "normal" resistance, it had already been deprived of at least half of its innervation. Appropriate stabilization is critical to determine the true difference between a Grade 5 and Grade 4 muscle.

Grade 3 Muscle

The Grade 3 muscle test is based on an objective measure. The muscle or muscle group can complete a full range of motion against the resistance of gravity. This is also called "active range." Even if a tested muscle can move through the full range against gravity and tolerate a small or "mild" amount of resistance, the muscle is assigned a grade of 3.

Direct force measurements have demonstrated that the force level of the Grade 3 muscle is quite low (less than 5% of normal for knee extension), so that a much greater span of functional loss exists between Grades 3 and 5 than between Grades 3 and 1.[9] Beasley, in a study of children ages 10 to 12 years, reported the Grade 3 in 36 muscle tests as no greater than 40% of Grade 5 (one motion), the rest being 30% or below normal "strength," with the majority falling between 5% and 20% of a Grade 5.[10] A grade of 3 may represent a *functional threshold* for some muscle actions tested (e.g., elbow flexion during feeding); however, a grade 3 may fall far short of the functional requirements of many lower extremity muscles during weight-bearing activities, particularly for such muscle groups as the hip abductors and the ankle plantar flexors. The therapist must be sure that muscles given a grade of 3 are not in the joint "locked" position during the test (e.g., locked elbow when testing elbow extension).

Grade 2 Muscle

The Grade 2 is assigned to a muscle group that can move the body segment when gravity is minimized. This position is typically described as the horizontal plane of motion. Movement in this plane may be eased by use of a powder board or other such friction-eliminating surface.

Grade 1 Muscle

The Grade 1 is assigned when the therapist can detect visually or by palpation some contractile activity in one or more of the muscles that participate in the action being tested (provided that the muscle is superficial enough to be palpated). The therapist also may be able to see or feel a tendon pop up or tense as the patient tries to perform the movement. However, there is no movement of the part as a result of this contractile muscle activity.

Patient positioning is less important in Grade 1 testing because a Grade 1 muscle can be detected in almost any position. When a Grade 1 muscle is suspected, the therapist should passively move the part into the test position and ask the patient to hold the position and then relax; this will enable the therapist to palpate the muscle or tendon, or both, during the patient's attempts to contract the muscle and also during relaxation. Care should be taken to avoid substitution of other muscles.

Grade 0 Muscle

The Grade 0 muscle is assigned when palpation or visual inspection fail to provide evidence of contraction. This does not mean there is no muscle activation. In fact, electromyography may demonstrate that some activation is present. Thus the phrase "no discernable contraction" defines a Grade 0 in this text.

Plus (+) and Minus (−) Grades

Use of a plus (+) or minus (−) addition to a manual muscle test grade is discouraged. Avoiding the use of plus or minus signs restricts manual muscle test grades to those that are meaningful, defendable, and reliable. The use of pluses and minuses adds a level of subjectivity that lacks reliability, especially for grades of 3 or greater. However, in the case of Grade 2, described above, there is a considerable difference between the muscle that can complete full range in a gravity-minimized position (horizontal position) and the one that cannot complete full range but can achieve some joint movement. Therefore the grade of 2- is acceptable when the muscle can complete partial range of motion in the horizontal plane, gravity minimized. The difference between Grade 2 and Grade 1 muscles represents such a broad functional difference that a minus sign may be important in assessing even minor improvements in function. The therapist is encouraged to supplement the grade with descriptive documentation of the quality of movement.

Grade 4 Muscle Revisited

Historically, manual muscle testing has used two grading systems, one using numbers (5-0) and the other using descriptors (normal to zero). Although both systems convey the same information, the authors favor the numeric system because it avoids use of the vague and subjective term "good." As noted previously, there is no other term in muscle testing that is more problematic. Too often clinical practitioners, including therapists and physicians, construe the term in the literal sense, interpreting "good" to mean totally adequate. The assumption is that if strength is adequate, then the patient is not in need of rehabilitation.

However, an abundance of evidence demonstrates unequivocally that once the therapist discerns that strength is no longer normal, but "good" instead, the muscle being tested has already lost approximately half its strength.

Evidence of this has already been presented.[11] More recently, Bohannon found that force values for muscles that were graded as "normal" ranged from 80 to 625 Newtons,[6] an astronomic difference, further demonstrating how difficult it is to distinguish a "good" muscle from a "normal" muscle.

It is unclear how a grade of "good" became synonymous with achievement of a satisfactory end point of treatment. Certainly, the pressure from third-party payers to discharge patients as soon as possible does not help the therapist to fulfill the minimum goal of reaching "prior level of function." Nonetheless, the opportunity for patients to recover muscle forces to the fullest extent possible is a primary goal of an intervention. If this goal is not met, patients (especially aging individuals) may lose their independence or find themselves incapable of returning to a desired sport or activity because their weak muscles fatigue too quickly. Athletes who have not fully recovered their strength before returning to a sport are far more likely to suffer a reinjury, potentially harming themselves further.

There are numerous instances in which a Grade 4 muscle cannot meet its functional demands. When the gluteus medius is Grade 4, a patient will display a positive Trendelenburg sign. When the soleus is Grade 4, the heel rise fails to occur during the latter portion of the stance phase of gait, which reduces gait speed.[12] When the abdominals are Grade 4, there is difficulty stabilizing the pelvis while arising from bed or when sitting up, and this often results in back pain. Calling a muscle "good," rather than Grade 4 is simply is not "good" enough.

Repeatedly there is a disconnect between what patients can functionally accomplish and the manual muscle strength grade the therapist assigns, particularly in older adults. By the time a person reaches the age of 80 years, approximately 50% of their muscle mass and strength may be lost due to natural decline,[13] and yet therapists often assign a manual muscle test grade of "normal" or "within normal limits" to an 80-year-old, even though the individual's strength is half of what it used to be. Functionally, these same older adults with "normal strength" cannot get out of a chair without pushing on the arms or ascend stairs without pulling on the railing. Therefore assigning "within functional limits" is discouraged. Muscle grades that are inaccurate based on the patient's age, gender, and presumed strength or because the therapist cannot apply adequate resistance must be avoided.

In summary, a "good" muscle is not always "good." Everything must be done to ensure accuracy in manual muscle test grading and to provide the intervention necessary to fully restore strength and function to "normal." Substituting the numerical system of 5-0 for the subjective terms "good" or "normal" in manual muscle testing assessment is a start in the right direction.

Available Range of Motion

When muscle shortness ("tightness"), a contracture, or fixed joint limitation (e.g., total knee replacement) limits joint range of motion, the patient performs only within the range available. In this circumstance, the *available range* is the full passive range of motion for that patient at that time, even though it is not "normal." This is the range used to assign a muscle testing grade. For example, the normal knee extension range is 135° to 0°. A patient with a 20° knee flexion contracture is tested for knee extension strength at the end of available range or 20°. If this range (in sitting) can be completed with maximal resistance, the grade assigned would be a 5. If the patient cannot actively complete that range, the grade assigned MUST be less than 3. The patient then should be repositioned in the side-lying position to ascertain the correct grade.

SCREENING TESTS

In the interests of time and cost-efficient care, it is often unnecessary to perform a muscle test on each muscle of the body. As the strength of various muscle actions tend to be correlated and internally consistent,[6] a systematic testing of a limited number of muscle actions often will suffice. Three screening indexes warrant mentioning. Each was developed with a specific diagnostic group in mind and allows for the calculation of a total score. The first, the Motricity Index, was developed for patients with stroke and includes three muscle actions of the upper limb (shoulder elevation, elbow flexion, and hand grasp) and three muscle actions of the lower limb (hip flexion, knee extension, and ankle dorsiflexion).[9] The second, the Motor Index Score, was developed for patients with spinal cord injury and includes muscle actions representative of key nerve root levels in the upper and lower limbs (elbow flexion [C5], wrist extension [C6], elbow extension [C7], finger flexion [C8], small finger abduction [T1], hip flexion [L2], knee extension [L3], ankle dorsiflexion [L4], great toe extension [L5], ankle plantarflexion [S1]).[14] The final test, the Medical Research Council Sum Score, was produced to capture weakness in patients with Guillain-Barré but has since been used with other patients with dispersed weakness. It includes most of the actions included in the Motricity Index (shoulder abduction, elbow flexion, wrist extension, hip flexion, knee extension, ankle dorsiflexion).[15]

Never should the therapist use phrases such as "within normal limits" or "within functional limits" for a screening exam. If a nonspecific strength exam is performed (e.g., through observation of tasks), documentation is better served with terms like "patient demonstrated no difficulty performing task," rather than making a judgment about the degree of strength present.

To screen for muscles that need definitive testing, the therapist can use a number of maneuvers to identify movements that do and do not need testing. Observation of the patient before the examination will provide valuable clues to muscular weakness and performance deficits. For example, the therapist can do the following:

- Observe the patient as he or she enters the treatment area to detect gross abnormalities of gait or other aspects of mobility.
- Observe the patient doing other everyday activities such as rising from a chair, completing admission or history forms, or removing street clothing.
- Ask the patient to walk on the toes and then on the heels.
- Ask the patient to grip the therapist's hand.
- Perform gross checks of bilateral muscle groups: reaching toward the floor, overhead, and behind the back.

If evidence from the previous "quick checks" suggests a deficit in movement, manual muscle testing can quickly be focused to the region observed to be weak, in the interest of time and to optimize the patient's clinic visit.

PREPARING FOR THE MUSCLE TEST

The therapist and the patient must work in harmony if the test session is to be successful. This means that some basic principles and inviolable procedures should be second nature to the therapist.

1. The patient should be as free as possible from discomfort or pain for the duration of each test. It may be necessary to allow some patients to move or be positioned differently between tests.
2. The environment for testing should be quiet and nondistracting. The ambient temperature should be comfortable for the partially disrobed patient.
3. The testing surface must be firm to help stabilize the part being tested. The ideal is a firm surface, minimally padded or not padded at all. The firm surface will not allow the trunk or limbs to "sink in." Friction of the surface material should be kept to a minimum. When the patient is reasonably mobile, a plinth is fine, but its width should not be so narrow that the patient is afraid of falling or sliding off. Sometimes a low mat table is the more practical choice. The height of the table should be adjustable to allow the therapist to use proper leverage and body mechanics.
4. Patient position should be carefully organized so that position changes in a test sequence are minimized. The patient's position must permit adequate stabilization of the part or parts being tested by virtue of body weight or with help provided by the therapist.
5. All materials needed for the test must be at hand. This is particularly important when the patient is anxious for any reason or is too weak to be safely left unattended.

Materials needed include the following:
- Manual muscle test documentation forms (Fig. 1.1)
- Pen, pencil, or computer terminal
- Pillows, towels, pads, and wedges for positioning
- Sheets or other draping linen
- Goniometer
- Stopwatch
- Specific equipment for specific functional tests
- Test forms for functional tests

DOCUMENTATION OF MANUAL MUSCLE TESTS

Date of Examination				Examiner's Initials			

LEFT				RIGHT		
3	2	1		1	2	3
			CERVICAL			
			Capital extension			
			Cervical extension			
			Capital flexion (chin tuck)			
			Cervical flexion			
			Cervical rotation			
			TRUNK			
			Trunk extension combined			
			Lumbar			
			Thoracic			
			Elevation of the pelvis			
			Trunk flexion			
			Trunk rotation			
			Core tests			
			Prone plank			
			Side bridge endurance test			
			Timed partial curl up test			
			Isometric trunk flexor endurance test			
			Front abdominal power test			
			Unilateral supine bridge test			
			Maximal inspiratory pressure			
			Maximal expiratory pressure			
			Cough			
			Pelvic floor			
			UPPER EXTREMITY			
			Scapular abduction and upward rotation (serratus)			
			Scapular elevation			
			Scapular adduction (retraction)			
			Scapular depression and adduction			
			Scapular adduction (retraction) and downward rotation (rhomboids)			
			Latissimus dorsi			
			Shoulder flexion			
			Shoulder extension			
			Shoulder abduction			
			Shoulder horizontal abduction (posterior deltoid)			
			Shoulder horizontal adduction (pectoralis major)			
			Shoulder external rotation			
			Shoulder internal rotation (subscapularis)			
			Elbow flexion (combined)			
			Elbow extension			
			Forearm supination			
			Forearm pronation			
			Wrist flexion combined			
			Flexor carpi radialis			
			Flexor carpi ulnaris			

FIGURE 1.1 Documentation of manual muscle examination. *Continued*

MANUAL MUSCLE TESTS - Page 2

Date of Examination _____ Examiner's Initials _____

3	2	1		1	2	3
			LEFT / **RIGHT**			
			Wrist extension combined			
			Extensor carpi radialis longus and brevis			
			Extensor carpi radialis ulnaris			
			Hand			
			Finger proximal phalanges (PIP) and distal phalanges (DIP) flexion			
			Combined			
			Flexor digitorum superficialis (PIP)			
			Flexor digitorum profundus (DIP)			
			Finger MCP extension			
			Extensor digitorum			
			Extensor indicis			
			Extensor digiti minimi			
			Finger MCP flexion			
			Finger abduction			
			Dorsal interossei			
			Abductor digiti minimi			
			Finger adduction (palmar interossei)			
			Thumb MCP and IP flexion			
			Flexor pollicis brevis			
			Flexor pollicis longus			
			Thumb MCP and IP extension (extensor pollicis brevis and longus)			
			Thumb abduction			
			Abductor pollicis longus			
			Abductor pollicis brevis			
			Thumb adduction (adductor pollicis)			
			Opposition			
			Opponens pollicis			
			Opponens digiti minimi			
			Grip strength			
			LOWER EXTREMITY			
			Hip flexion			
			Hip flexion, abduction, and external rotation with knee flexion (sartorius)			
			Hip extension combined			
			Gluteus maximus			
			Supine hip extensor test			
			Hip abduction			
			Hip adduction			
			Hip external rotation			
			Hip internal rotation			
			Knee flexion combined			
			Medial hamstring test (semitendinosus and semimembranosus)			
			Lateral hamstring test (biceps femoris)			

FIGURE 1.1, cont'd

MANUAL MUSCLE TESTS - Page 3

Date of Examination				Examiner's Initials			

LEFT					RIGHT		
3	2	1			1	2	3
			Knee extension				
			Ankle plantar flexion combined				
			Soleus				
			Foot dorsiflexion and inversion				
			Foot inversion				
			Foot eversion with plantar flexion				
			Hallux and toe MP flexion				
			Hallus MP flexion				
			Toe MP flexion				
			Hallux and toe DIP and PIP flexion				
			Hallux and toe MP and IP extension				

Comments:

Diagnosis _____ Onset _____ Age _____ Birth date _____

Patient Name _____

last   first   middle   ID number

FIGURE 1.1, cont'd

- Interpreter (if needed)
- Assistance for turning, moving, or stabilizing the patient
- Emergency call system (if no assistant is available)
- Reference material

EXERCISES

Specific exercises have been included in the text where there is electromyographic evidence of isometric maximal voluntary contraction (MVC). Clinically, motions that evoke higher electromyographic activities (%MVC) have been interpreted to be more challenging to a muscle.[16] The following scale is used when interpreting %MVC:

Low	0%–20%
Moderate	21%–40%
High	41%–60%
Very high	>60%

An MVC of greater than 40% is considered necessary for strengthening.[17,18]

We have included higher-tier exercises as suggested exercises. These exercises should be considered challenging and used later in the rehabilitation process. The therapist should also be aware of the different types of contractions applied in muscle testing and exercise. See Box 1.1.

Box 1.1 Types of Contractions

Concentric contraction refers to the shortening of a muscle as it contracts, as in the bending flexion portion of a biceps curl or extension of the elbow when lifting an object overhead. Concentric activity is generally the primary motion of the muscle.

Eccentric contraction refers to the lowering phase of an exercise, when the muscle lengthens, as in lowering the weight to the chest during the bench press or lowering oneself into a chair. Eccentric muscle activity is seen in many mobility-related functional tasks such as stepping down a curb or in gait.

Isometric contraction refers to the creation of muscle tension without joint movement. Isometric contractions are often used when the limb is immobilized, such as post surgery. Isometric contractions are used with handheld dynamometry, discussed in Chapter 9.

PRIME MOVERS

Within each chapter are tables indicating the muscles involved in the action that is tested (e.g., shoulder flexion). When prime movers have been identified for a particular action, they are in **boldface** type. For example, the prime mover of shoulder flexion is the anterior deltoid muscle and therefore this muscle is bolded. In other instances, there is no distinct prime mover and thus no bolding. The movement of back extension, for example, involves a dozen muscles, none of which is a prime mover, and therefore there are no muscle names bolded. Our intent in highlighting the prime movers is to help the student more readily understand which muscles are critical for many important movements and to have a better understanding of which muscles to strengthen when weakness is present.

SUMMARY

From the foregoing discussion, it should be clear that manual muscle testing is an exacting clinical skill. Practice, practice, and more practice on a variety of patient types create the experience essential to building the skill to an acceptable level of clinical proficiency, to say nothing of clinical mastery.

REFERENCES

1. Bohannon RW. Measuring knee extensor muscle strength. *Am J Phys Med Rehabil*. 2001;80:13–18.
2. LeVeau BF. *Williams and Lissner's Biomechanics of Human Motion*. 3rd ed. Philadelphia: WB Saunders; 1992.
3. Soderberg GL. *Kinesiology: Application to Pathological Motion*. Baltimore: Williams & Wilkins; 1997.
4. Resnick JS, Mammel M, Mundale MO, et al. Muscular strength as an index of response to therapy in childhood dermatomyositis. *Arch Phys Med Rehabil*. 1981;62:12–19.
5. Magnusson SP, Geismar RA, Gleim G, et al. The effect of stabilization on isokinetic knee extension and flexion torque production. *J Athlet Train*. 1993;28:221–225.
6. Bohannon RW, Corrigan D. A broad range of forces is encompassed by the maximum manual muscle test grade of five. *Percept Mot Skills*. 2000;90:747–750.
7. Mulroy SJ, Lassen KD, Chambers SH, et al. The ability of male and female clinicians to effectively test knee extension strength using manual muscle testing. *J Orthop Sports Phys Ther*. 1997;26:192–199.
8. Sharrard WJW. Muscle recovery in poliomyelitis. *J Bone Joint Surg Br*. 1955;37:63–69.
9. Demeurisse G, Demol O, Roboye E. Motor evaluation in hemiplegia. *Eur Neurol*. 1980;19:382–389.
10. Beasley WC. Normal and fair muscle systems: Quantitative standards for children 10 to 12 years of age. Presented at 39th Scientific Session of the American Congress of Rehabilitative Medicine, Cleveland, Ohio; August 1961.
11. Beasley WC. Influence of method on estimates of normal knee extensor force among normal and post-polio children. *Phys Ther Rev*. 1956;36:21–41.
12. Perry J. *Gait Analysis: Normal and Pathological Function*. 2nd ed. Thorofare, NJ: Slack, Inc.; 2010.
13. Piering AW, Janowski AP, Moore MT, et al. Electromyographic analysis of four popular abdominal exercises. *J Athl Train*. 1993;28:120–126.
14. Lazar RB, Yarkony GM, Ortolano D, et al. Prediction of functional outcome by motor capability after spinal cord injury. *Arch Phys Med Rehabil*. 1989;70:819–822.
15. Hough CL, Lieu BK, Caldwell ES. Manual muscle strength testing of critically ill patients: feasibility and interobserver agreement. *Crit Care*. 2011;15(1):R43.
16. Smith J, Padgett DJ, Kaufman KR, et al. Rhomboid muscle electromyography activity during 3 different manual muscle tests. *Arch Phys Med Rehabil*. 2004;85(6):987–992.
17. Ayotte NW, Stetts DM, Keenan G, et al. Electromyographical analysis of selected lower extremity muscles during 5 unilateral weight-bearing exercises. *JOSPT*. 2007;37:48–55.
18. Escamilla RF, Lewis C, Bell D, et al. Core muscle activation during Swiss ball and traditional abdominal exercises. *JOSPT*. 2010;40:265–276.

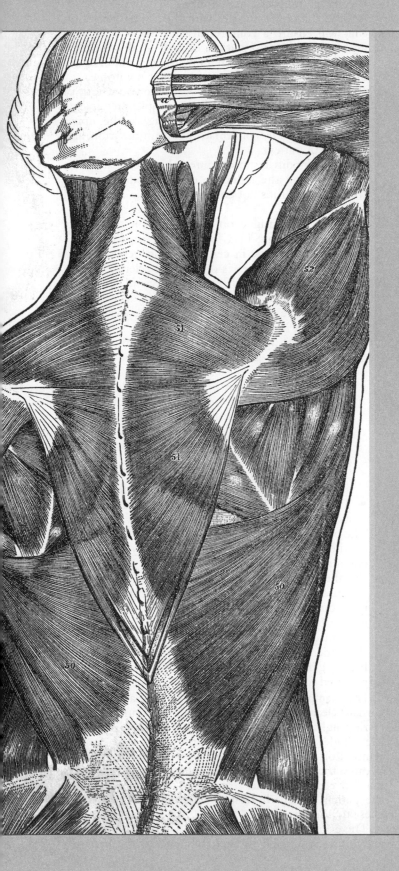

Relevance and Limitations of Manual Muscle Testing

INTRODUCTION

Manual muscle testing (MMT) is well recognized as the most common strength-testing technique in physical therapy and other health professions, having first appeared during the poliomyelitis epidemic in New England before World War I. A brief history of MMT is described elsewhere in this text. MMT serves unique purposes that can vary according to the setting in which it is practiced. Although MMT is an essential and foundational skill in a therapist's examination techniques, it also has its limitations. Appreciating these limitations and learning how to compensate for them helps to make MMT as relevant nowadays as it was when first conceptualized during the polio era.

THE EXAMINER AND THE VALUE OF THE MUSCLE TEST

The knowledge and skill of the examiner determine the accuracy and defensibility of a manual muscle test. Specific aspects of these qualities include the following:

- Knowledge of the location and anatomic features of the muscles in a test. In addition to knowing the muscle attachments, the examiner should be able to visualize the location of the tendon and its muscle in relationship to other tendons and muscles and other structures in the same area (e.g., the tendon of the extensor carpi radialis longus lies on the radial side of the tendon of the extensor carpi radialis brevis at the wrist).
- Knowledge of the direction of muscle fibers and their alignment in each muscle.
- Knowledge of the function of the participating muscles (e.g., synergist, prime mover, agonist, and antagonist).
- Consistent use of a standardized method for each test procedure.
- Consistent use of proper positioning and stabilization techniques for each test procedure. Stabilization of the proximal segment of the joint being tested is achieved in several ways. These include patient position (via body weight), the use of a firm surface for testing, patient muscle activation, manual fixation by the examiner, or external fixation such as with a belt.
- Ability to identify patterns of substitution in a given test and how they can be detected based on a knowledge of which other muscles can be substituted for the one(s) being tested.
- Ability to detect contractile activity during both contraction and relaxation, especially in the minimally active muscle.
- Sensitivity to differences in contour and bulk of the muscles being tested in contrast to the contralateral side or to normal expectations based on such things as body size, occupation, or leisure work.
- Awareness of any deviation from normal values for range of motion and the presence of any joint laxity or deformity.

- Understanding that the muscle belly must not be grasped at any time during a manual muscle test except specifically to assess muscle mass.
- Ability to identify muscles with the same innervation that will ensure a comprehensive muscle evaluation and accurate interpretation of test results (because weakness of one muscle in a myotome should require examination of all muscles within that myotome).
- Relating the diagnosis to the sequence and extent of the test (e.g., the patient with C7 complete tetraplegia will require definitive muscle testing of the upper extremity but only confirmatory tests in the trunk and lower extremities).
- Ability to modify test procedures when necessary while understanding the influence of the modification on the result and thus not compromising the accuracy of the test result.
- Knowledge of fatigue on the test results, especially muscles tested late in a long testing session, and a sensitivity to fatigue in certain diagnostic conditions such as myasthenia gravis or multiple sclerosis.
- Understanding of the effect of sensory and perceptual loss on movement. The examiner also may inadvertently *influence* the test results and should be especially alert when testing in the following situations:
  - The patient with open wounds or other conditions requiring gloves, which may blunt palpation skills.
  - The patient who must be evaluated under difficult conditions such as in an intensive care unit with multiple tubes and monitors or immediately after surgery, the patient in traction, the patient for whom turning is contraindicated, the patient on a ventilator, and the patient in shackles or restraints.
  - The patient with limited understanding of the test, such as in the presence of delirium or dementia.
  - The patient who cannot assume test positions, such as the prone position.
- The previous situations require careful documentation of the assessment of strength and any limitations encountered.
- The therapist must avoid the temptation to use shortcuts or "tricks of the trade" before mastering the basic procedures, lest such shortcuts become an inexact personal standard. One such pitfall for the novice tester is to inaccurately assign a lower muscle grade when the patient could not successfully perform a test at a higher grade without actually testing in the position required for the lower grade.

For example, when testing trunk flexion, a patient just partially clears the scapula from the surface, with the hands resting lightly on the side of the head (the position for the Grade 5 test), thus not earning a Grade 5. The temptation may exist to assign a grade of 4 to this test because the patient could not achieve a Grade 5, but this may "overrate" the true strength of trunk flexion unless the patient is actually tested with the arms across the chest to confirm Grade 4.

The good clinician never ignores a patient's comments and must be a good listener, not just to the patient's

Early Kendall Examination

Accuracy in giving examinations depends primarily on the examiner's knowledge of the isolated and combined actions of muscles in individuals with normal muscles, as well as in those with weak or paralyzed muscles.

The fact that muscles act in combination permits substitution of a strong muscle for a weaker one. For accurate muscle examinations, no substitutions should be permitted; that is, the movement described as a test movement should be done without shifting the body or turning the part to allow other muscles to perform the movement for the weak or paralyzed group. The only way to recognize substitution is to know normal function and realize the ease with which a normal muscle performs the exact test movement.

Kendall HO, Kendall FP

From Care During the Recovery Period in Paralytic Poliomyelitis. Public Health Bulletin No. 242. Washington, DC: U.S. Government Printing Office; 1939: 26.

questions but also to the meaning of the words the patient uses. This quality is an essential element of good communication and is the primary means of encouraging understanding and respect between therapist and patient. The patient is the best guide to a successful muscle test.

INFLUENCE OF THE PATIENT ON THE TEST

The intrusion of a living, breathing, feeling person into the testing situation may distort scoring for the unwary examiner. The following circumstances should be recognized:
- There may be variation in the assessment of the true effort expended by a patient in a given test (reflecting the patient's desire to do well or to seem more impaired than is actually the case).
- The patient's willingness to endure discomfort or pain may vary (e.g., the stoic, the complainer, the high competitor).
- The patient's ability to understand the test requirements may be limited in some cases because of cognitive impairments, comprehension, and language barriers.
- The motor skills required for the test may be beyond those possessed by some patients, making it impossible for them to perform as requested.
- Lassitude and depression may cause the patient to be indifferent to the test and the examiner.
- Cultural, social, and gender issues may be associated with palpation and exposure of a body part for testing.
- Size and available force differences between big and small muscles can cause considerable differences in grading, although not an individual variation (e.g., the gluteus medius versus a finger extensor). There is a huge variability in maximum torque between such muscles, and the examiner must use care not to assign a grade that is inconsistent with muscle size and architecture.

USE OF MANUAL MUSCLE TESTING IN VARIOUS CLINICAL SETTINGS

MMT is used in many different types of health care settings. In this section, we will discuss some of the more common applications of MMT in various clinical and therapeutic settings, with emphasis on the specific challenges often seen in each. The reader should be aware that the examples provided here are not limited to these settings only.

Acute Care Facilities

Often patients seen in acute care facilities are either acutely ill or are seen postoperatively. In the acutely ill patient, MMT may be used to assess the patient's mobility status to inform a discharge plan. A manual strength exam performed as part of a general assessment may provide information concerning the amount of assistance the patient requires and whether the patient will need an assistive device. Assessing the patient's strength to help ensure safe transfers from bed to chair, to a standing position, or on and off the toilet is an essential part of the acute-care patient management process. A strength assessment may also inform the therapist of the patient's ability to follow directions and/or to verbalize concerns such as following a stroke or in the presence of delirium or other cognitive loss.[1,2]

Strength assessment may also indicate the presence of pain. Identifying painful muscles before asking a patient to do an activity, such as transfers, will save time in the long run (and potential embarrassment). Strength assessment can take the form of active movement followed by resistance, such as in a manual muscle test or in a 10-repetition maximum such as in a seated shoulder dip.

Strength assessment in the postoperative patient informs the therapist of the integrity of the patient's nervous system. The therapist may be the first person requiring the patient to move actively after surgery and thus may be the first one to observe the patient's ability to contract a muscle. Although this scenario is rare, clearly the consequences of assuming an attitude of "all is well" and finding out during a transfer that the patient cannot use part of an extremity would have avoidable consequences. Strength testing in this scenario might take the form of isometric contractions, especially if there are contraindications to joint movement, suspected postsurgical pain as in a newly repaired fractured hip, or in restricted range of motion such as in a total hip arthroplasty. If testing is done in a manner that differs from the published directions, documentation should describe how the test was performed. For example, if isometric testing was done at the hip because the patient was not permitted to move the hip through full range after a hip arthroplasty, the therapist should document the test accordingly: "Patient's strength at the hip appeared to be under volitional control, but pain and postsurgical precautions prevented thorough assessment."

Key movements that should be assessed for viability and for the strength necessary to perform transfers or gait include elbow extension, grip, shoulder depression, knee extension, hip abduction, ankle plantar, and dorsiflexion. Functional tests that might be useful in assessing the patient include gait speed, chair stand, timed transfer, or the timed up-and-go test (see Chapter 8).

Special considerations for the acute care setting may include the patient's rapid fluctuations in response to medications, illness, or pain. Reassessment may be necessary when any changes in strength are documented along with therapist's insights into why the changes are occurring. Clearly, strength gains are not possible in the short time a typical patient is in acute care but rather should be attributed to increased confidence in moving, less pain, better understanding of the movement to be performed, motor learning, and so forth.

Acute Rehabilitation Facilities

Strength assessment in the acute rehabilitation setting may be performed as a baseline assessment to determine progress over time and to identify key impairments that affect the patient's mobility-related and other functional goals. Knowledge of community-based norms for mobility such as chair stands, distance walked, stair climbing speed, floor transfer ability, and gait speed will inform the therapist's clinical decision-making. (See Chapter 8 for a more complete description of these tests.) A standard manual muscle test and/or a 10-repetition maximum strength assessment are other methods used to assess relevant strength abilities.

As in the acute care setting, assessment of strength for mobility tasks is critical in the acute rehabilitation setting. Recognition of the importance of key muscle groups in specific mobility tasks, such as the plantar-flexors in gait speed, is key to informed clinical decision-making.

Special considerations for the acute rehabilitation setting often include rapid change over a short period. Positive changes may be attributed to increased comfort and less pain, less apprehension, neuroplasticity, and a change in medications. Negative changes may be attributed to, for example, a decline in medical status, pain, or depression. Muscle fatigue resulting from an extended inpatient stay, poor fitness, and excessive sedentary behavior or general body fatigue related to frailty or post–acute care implications may affect the perception of strength. The patient may not be able to assume a proper test position because of postsurgical restrictions or a lack of range of motion, requiring the therapist to do a strength-screen rather than a strength test. Although a screen may be appropriate, the screen cannot serve as an accurate baseline because of the lack of standardization. Functional testing may be more informative and accurate in these situations. The therapist should take special care to document any deviations from the standardized manual muscle test.

Long-Term Care Facilities

Strength testing and assessment approaches used in long-term care settings are similar to those used in acute rehabilitation. Strength assessment can serve as a baseline to identify key impairments that impact a patient's fall risk, mobility, and other functional goals as well as to determine the patient's progress over time. Strength screening can be part of a required annual assessment for long-term residents. Strength in the form of a chair stand test or grip strength is a key component of the diagnosis of frailty and therefore can inform prognosis.[3]

Frailty is a common geriatric syndrome, characterized by decreased reserve and increased vulnerability to adverse outcomes, including falls, hospitalization, institutionalization, and death.[4] The majority of residents in long-term care are considered frail.[5] A profound loss of strength is a significant cause of frailty and serves as a diagnostic criterion. Box 2.1 lists the diagnostic criteria for frailty. Based on these criteria, strength assessment and functional testing are essential in the examination and intervention of nursing home residents.[4]

Box 2.1 Diagnostic Criteria for Frailty

Diagnostic criteria for frailty include the presence of three or more of the following[4,10]:
1. Unintentional weight loss (>10 lb in past year)
2. General feeling of exhaustion on 3 or more days/week (self-report)
3. Weakness (grip strength in lowest 20%; <23 lb for women; <32 lb for men)
4. Slow walking speed (lowest 20%; ≤0.8 m/s)
5. Low levels of physical activity (in kcal/week lowest 20%; = 270 kcal/week for women; 383 kcal/week for men—equivalent to sitting quietly and/or lying down for the vast majority of the day)

The presence of one or two of these characteristics indicates prefrailty.

Box 2.2 Community Mobility Requirements

To be considered mobile, an individual should be able to: Walk 300 m minimum per errand[12] Perform multiple errands during one trip outside the home[13] Carry a package weighing 7.5 lb[13] Change direction while walking[14] Step onto and off of a curb without support	Achieve a gait speed of >0.8 m/s Make postural transitions including stooping, lifting, reaching, and reorientation of head—independent of change in direction[13] Climb stairs Navigate slopes and uneven surfaces[13] Step over objects

Although a natural consequence of aging is a gradual loss of strength and power, it should not be assumed that older adults are functionally weaker than younger adults.[6-8] Because MMT has a ceiling effect, the therapist should not have lower expectations or overestimate strength in frail older adults. *Criteria for grading remain the same for people of all ages and conditions.* Because the ceiling effect of a manual muscle test can be so profound, especially in regard to function, functional testing is a better option for strength testing and assessment in the long-term care setting.[9] Community criterion reference values exist that guide the long-term care therapist in establishing appropriate goals and expectations (Box 2.2). Older adults might be better served with strength training options such as a leg press or latissimus pull down rather than the cuff weights or a recumbent bicycle or cross-trainer that are commonly used in long-term care settings. The reader is referred to Chapter 7 for alternative strength measurement options.

Home Health Setting

Strength testing and assessment of home health patients for the purpose of comparison with community-based norms and for identification of impairments related to function are the primary purposes of MMT and alternative strength-testing methods in the home health setting. Returning a patient to community-based mobility may prevent frailty and increase the patient's quality of life. Lower-extremity strength is a primary component of these goals. Box 2.2 lists community mobility requirements that can be used as outcome goals for home health patients and serve to guide strength testing. In addition, for a homebound patient to receive home health services, the Centers for Medicare and Medicaid Services require patients to demonstrate "considerable and taxing effort in leaving the home," a criterion that has strength implications.[11]

Outpatient Clinics

Strength testing and assessment in outpatient clinics provide essential information, such as the (1) origin of the patient's pain, (2) quality of the contraction, (3) symmetry between sides and between the primary mover (agonist) and opposing muscles (antagonist), and (4) weakness within a kinetic chain (body segments linked by a series of joints).[15] This information aids in making a differential diagnosis. It can also provide a baseline assessment for changes over time, such as in the case of sciatica-induced weakness.[16] Challenges of MMT in the outpatient setting can include the presence of pain that prohibits a full, voluntary contraction and limitations of range of motion, such as with retraction and upward rotation of the scapula at the shoulder. Although a weak and painful or strong and painful contraction can be diagnostic, it can preclude the assessment of quantitative strength.[17] The ceiling effect of MMT often prevents an accurate assessment of strength quantity. Therefore we recommend that quantitative strength be assessed through a 1-RM or 10-RM strength assessment when pain permits (see Chapter 7). It is useful to assess the noninvolved side to ascertain asymmetry.

Careful differentiation is required to use strength assessment and testing for diagnostic (as opposed to quantification) purposes. For example, the Cyriax method (see Chapter 7) of maintaining the joint in a neutral, relaxed position while assessing the muscle's contraction in various directions can reveal the presence of a contractile lesion if pain is produced during a contraction, while keeping noncontractile (e.g., connective tissues) elements on slack.[17] Alternatively, if the contraction is not painful while the joint is in a neutral position, an inert lesion, such as a bone spur or capsular inflammation, may be implicated.

The presence of pain, joint restriction, or muscle tightness may prevent the patient from assuming the correct testing position for accurate assessment of muscle testing. Although this text advocates testing the muscle in a pain-free position, substitution patterns are more difficult to discern; thus specific muscle strength quantification may not be possible. However, the therapist can document asymmetric differences, points in the range where pain exists or does not exist, and the nature of the pain that may aid the therapist in making an accurate diagnosis.

Another challenge for therapists in outpatient settings is the variety of patients seen in a given day. For example, a therapist may see a college or professional athlete in the same afternoon as a frail older adult. Careful discernment of appropriate strength testing is critical to avoid overestimation or underestimation of strength limitations. Using alternative muscle strength assessments as described in Chapters 7, 8, and 9 may be useful to avoid biases.

Wellness Clinics

Muscle screening provides feedback to participants regarding their abilities relative to age-matched normative samples that may impact functional abilities such as gait speed and chair stands. Although individual MMT is not routinely done as part of a wellness screening, functional movements such as floor transfers, 30-second sit-to-stands, or hand grip tests are useful to ascertain individual fitness levels and risk of disability. The information gleaned from a wellness assessment may indicate the need for an individualized physical therapy assessment of strength to maintain age-based expectations of function.[18,19]

Summary

MMT has utility in all clinical settings. However, it is incumbent on the therapist to judiciously use MMT when and if appropriate and to choose alternative forms of testing (e.g., functional and instrumented tests) when the information obtained from MMT is inadequate.

Even though muscle testing has tremendous value, there are situations in which it is not particularly informative, nor even accurate. Some of the clinical scenarios in which muscle testing is not optimal have already been discussed (e.g., in the presence of pain), but more detail will be presented in the next section.

LIMITATIONS OF MANUAL MUSCLE TESTING

As alluded to in Chapter 1, MMT has significant limitations. When it was first developed, the majority of patients seen by physical therapists had polio. The current patient population has changed enormously, and therapists now see hundreds of patient types who range in age from infancy to 100-plus years. Muscle examination has changed concomitantly to more accurately reflect the needs of clients, and MMT is only one approach among many. Each form of testing has its advantages and disadvantages, as will be noted in this chapter and elsewhere in this book. The major limitations of MMT are discussed in the following section.

Population Variation

Many articles that report MMT results are based on studies of normal adults or specific subpopulations such as athletes, sedentary individuals, and aged adults. Children occupy a separate category. In addition, results of muscle testing values are reported in individuals with a wide variety of pathologies, including Parkinson disease, cerebral palsy, and muscular dystrophy. Because of this wide variation, it is necessary to modify grading procedures but not testing technique. Thus test grades are not consistent from one patient population to another. Some testers also erroneously believe that the assigned grade should be modified based on age or ability, which should not be the case. Rather, MMT interpretation requires knowledge of the strength requirements of the task.

Objectivity

MMT, as originally described, suffers from a lack of objectivity, where objectivity is defined as a test not dependent primarily on the judgment of the examiner.[20,21] As discussed in Chapter 1, the ordinal scale of 5-0 as used to assign muscle strength grades is not objective and the use of qualitative terms such as good and fair further reduces its objectivity. However, it does provide useful information in a physical therapy assessment. Although clinical judgment is inherently a subjective assessment and cannot be discounted, the examination aspect of the patient encounter should primarily consist of objective measures.

Validity and Reliability

Reliability in MMT varies considerably according to the muscle tested, the experience of the examiner, the age of the patient, and the particular condition being tested. For example, in a study of 102 boys ages 5 to 15 years with Duchenne muscular dystrophy, intrarater reliability ranged from 0.65 to 0.93, with the proximal muscles having the higher reliability values.[22] The muscles with gravity minimized also had higher reliability values. In another study of physical therapists comparing MMT to handheld muscle dynamometry in 11 patients, reliability was high and differentiated between grades at all levels.[23] Frese and colleagues performed a reliability study among therapists on the middle trapezius and gluteus medius muscles and found 28% to 45% agreement for the same grade and 89% to 92% agreement within one grade.[24] They found the reliability to be poor, as measured by Cohen-weighted Kappa. In muscles with grades less than 3, reliability declined.[24-27] Reliability also decreased for the muscles of the lower extremity.[27]

Clearly, the reliability of MMT is of concern, and yet MMT remains an important screening and diagnostic tool. Therapists, especially novices, must be cautious about their test procedures and make vigorous attempts to standardize their methods. Reliability is increased by adhering to the same procedure for each test (for one or several examiners), by providing clear instructions to the subject, by having a quiet and comfortable environment for the test, and by being conscious of age or gender biases. To further enhance the reliability of the manual muscle test, the following steps should be taken[28-30]:
• Ensure proper positioning so the test muscle is the prime mover
• Ensure adequate stabilization of regional anatomy
• Observe the way the patient or subject assumes and maintains the test position
• Use consistent timing, pressure, and position

- Avoid preconceived impressions regarding the test outcome
- Use nonpainful contact and provide for a nonpainful execution of the test

Sensitivity

MMT also lacks sensitivity. Years ago, Beasley reported that patients with various neurologic disorders who had Grade 4 knee extension forces were only approximately 43% of normal, rather than the traditionally defined 75% of normal.[25] The Grade 3 group generated force that was only 9% of Grade 5, rather than 50% of Grade 5 usually assigned with MMT.[25] Similarly, inadequate sensitivity was reported for detecting muscle force deficits when comparing compromised muscles to those that are normal.[26]

Because MMT as originally described is subjective, the historical and conventional acceptability for reliability is that, among examiners, and in successive tests with the same examiner, the results should be within one-half of a grade (or within a plus or minus of the base grade).[29] Others maintain that within the same grade is acceptable, pluses and minuses notwithstanding.[30] However, even if this historical convention is used, therapists are unreliable in differentiating between the grades of 4 and 5.[9,26]

Diagnostic Validity

MMT is useful in the assessment of weakness of muscles directly involved with pain, injury, and neuromusculo-skeletal disorders.[28] The Cyriax method of discerning between contractile and noncontractile tissue is an example of muscle testing on the painful limb (see Chapter 7). In a study to detect differences between sides using MMT, the test accuracy as measured by sensitivity ranged from 62.9% to 72.3%, increasing with more pronounced strength differences.[28]

Ceiling Effect

MMT has wide variability in the range of forces reported for a given grade, especially in the upper range of the scale, further reducing its sensitivity. For example, in a subset of four studies, men with an MMT grade of 5 (by a negative break test) for knee extension and tested with handheld muscle dynamometry concurrently demonstrated values ranging from 85.4 to 650.0 Newtons.[9] In addition, the four studies analyzed represented all settings with a variety of patient types. The Grade 5 represented 86% of the range of measurable forces (Grades 3 to 5). Knee extension forces of more than 800 Newtons are not unusual for young men.[28] Thus MMT suffers from a profound ceiling effect. Many patients may be classified as having Grade 5 (normal) strength when they may have strength deficits only appreciated through more objective means. This ceiling effect may mask changes in strength

that have functional and prognostic consequences. Thus it is not recommended that MMT be used as an objective measure of progress greater than the grade of 3 because it is not an accurate measure.

Another concern of the applicability of MMT is its lack of accuracy to identity impairments related to function, secondary to the curvilinear relationship. The curvilinear relationship suggests that strength gains are not apparent when greater than a relative threshold because the threshold of a strength demand for some lower level functional task (feeding oneself or standing from a chair) has been exceeded by the strength gain. Alternatively, traditional MMT may not reflect the great amount of strength needed to perform functional tasks such as getting up from the floor or throwing a baseball because they exceed what a therapist can manually resist. When a basic manual muscle test screen reveals test grades that are greater than Grade 3 and in particular, where there are side-to-side differences, the therapist should rely on instrumented or functional testing to further clarify deficiencies and to differentiate between Grades 4 and 5 (see Chapters 7 through 9).

Handheld dynamometry (HHD) may address some of the aspects of reliability. Because HHD records a number, it does not require the therapist to execute a judgment about a grade. However, other issues of MMT still hold true for HHD, such as tester strength, discussed later. HHD is further discussed in Chapter 9.

Tester Strength

A break test in MMT requires the tester to exert greater force than the patient in any given muscle. When testing a very strong individual, such as a weightlifter or football player, a great amount of force on the part of the tester is required. Women traditionally have 35% less upper body strength than men, and differences have been recorded in MMT forces between female and male testers, leading to an underestimation of the patient's quadriceps strength.[26,31] For example, Beasley found in a sample of female therapists testing the quadriceps in patients with polio that of those muscles graded a 5, the mean force generated was only 53% of normal subjects.[25] Mulroy and colleagues also found that female therapists overgraded the strength of the quadriceps in 14 of 19 patients, in part because of patient strength greater than the therapist's.[31] Male therapists assigned too high a grade in 2 of 19 patients.[31]

Summary

MMT appears to be both reliable and valid in the presence of profound weakness, such as that seen in neuromuscular diseases. However, when used in individuals with near-normal levels of strength, it is recommended that MMT be used as a screening tool that informs alternative forms of strength testing such as those described in Chapters 7 and 9.

REFERENCES

1. Bittner EA, Martyn JA, George E, et al. Measurement of muscle strength in the intensive care unit. *Crit Care Med.* 2009;37:S321–S330.
2. Andrews AW, Bohannon RW. Short-term recovery of limb muscle strength after acute stroke. *Arch Phys Med Rehabil.* 2003;84:125–130.
3. Vermeulen J, Neyens JC, van Rossum E, et al. Predicting ADL disability in community-dwelling elderly people using physical frailty indicators: a systematic review. *BMC Geriatr.* 2011;11:33.
4. Fried LP, Tangen CM, Walston J, et al. Frailty in older adults: evidence for a phenotype. *J Gerontol A Biol Sci Med Sci.* 2001;56A:M146–M156.
5. Fried TR, Mor V. Frailty and hospitalization of long-term stay nursing home residents. *J Am Geriatr Soc.* 1997;45: 265–269.
6. Bortz WM. A conceptual framework of frailty: a review. *J Gerontol.* 2002;57A:M283–M288.
7. Visser M, Kritchevsky SB, Goodpaster B, et al. Leg muscle mass and composition in relation to lower extremity performance in men and women aged 70-79: the health, aging and body composition study. *J Am Geriatr Soc.* 2002; 50:897–904.
8. Schwartz RS. Sarcopenia and physical performance in old age: introduction. *Muscle Nerve Suppl.* 1997;5:S10–S12.
9. Bohannon RW, Corrigan D. A broad range of forces is encompassed by the maximum manual muscle test grade of five. *Percept Mot Skills.* 2000;90:747–750.
10. Xue QL, Bandeen-Roche K, Varadhan R, et al. Initial manifestations of frailty criteria and the development of frailty phenotype in the women's health and aging study II. *J Gerontol A Biol Sci Med Sci.* 2008;63:984–990.
11. U.S. Department of Health and Human Services. Centers for Medicare & Medicaid Services, Medicare benefit policy manual; Home Health Services; 2011; ch 7; pp 61–64. http://www.cms.gov/Regulations-and-Guidance/Guidance/Manuals/downloads/bp102c07.pdf.
12. Chang M, Cohen-Mansfield J, Ferrucci L, et al. Incidence of loss of ability to walk 400 meters in a functionally limited older population. *J Am Geriatr Soc.* 2004;52:2094–2098.
13. Shumway-Cook A, Patla AE, Stewart A, et al. Environmental demands associated with community mobility in older adults with and without mobility disabilities. *Phys Ther.* 2002; 82:670–681.
14. Perry J, Garrett M, Gronley JK, et al. Classification of walking handicap in the stroke population. *Stroke.* 1995;26:982–989.
15. Maffiuletti NA. Assessment of hip and knee muscle function in orthopaedic practice and research. *J Bone Joint Surg Am.* 2010;92:220–229.
16. Balague F, Nordin M, Sheikhzadeh A, et al. Recovery of impaired muscle function in severe sciatica. *Eur Spine J.* 2001;10:242–249.
17. Cyriax JH. *Textbook of Orthopaedic Medicine: Diagnosis of Soft Tissue Lesions.* Vol. 1. 8th ed. London: Bailliere Tindall; 1982:14–21.
18. Rikli R, Jones J. Development and validation of a functional fitness test for community-residing older adults. *J Aging Phys Act.* 1999;7:129–161.
19. Rikli R, Jones J. Functional fitness normative scores for community-residing older adults, ages 60-94. *J Aging Phys Act.* 1999;7:162–181.
20. Knepler C, Bohannon RW. Subjectivity of forces associated with manual muscle test scores of 3+, 4-, and 4. *Percept Mot Skills.* 1998;87:1123–1128.
21. Bohannon RW. Objective measures. *Phys Ther.* 1989;69: 590–593.
22. Florence JM, Pandya S, King WM, et al. Intrarater reliability of manual muscle test (medical research council scale) grades in Duchenne's muscular dystrophy. *Phys Ther.* 1992;72: 115–122, discussion 122–126.
23. Wadsworth CT, Krishnan R, Sear M, et al. Intrarater reliability of manual muscle testing and hand-held dynametric muscle testing. *Phys Ther.* 1987;67:1342–1347.
24. Frese F, Brown M, Norton BJ. Clinical reliability of manual muscle testing: middle trapezius and gluteus medius muscles. *Phys Ther.* 1987;67:1072–1076.
25. Beasley WC. Quantitative muscle testing: principles and application to research and clinical services. *Arch Phys Med Rehabil.* 1961;42:398–425.
26. Wintz M. Variations in current manual muscle testing. *Phys Ther Rev.* 1959;39:466–475.
27. Cuthbert SCJ, Goodheart GJ. On the reliability and validity of manual muscle testing: a literature review. *Chiropr Osteopat.* 2007;15:4.
28. Bohannon RW. Manual muscle testing: does it meet the standards of an adequate screening test? *Clin Rehabil.* 2005;19:662–667.
29. Lamb R. Manual muscle testing. In: Rothstein JM, ed. *Measurement in Physical Therapy.* New York: Churchill-Livingstone; 1985:47–55.
30. Palmer ML, Epler ME. *Fundamentals of Musculoskeletal Assessment Techniques.* 2nd ed. Philadelphia: Lippincott Williams & Wilkins; 1998.
31. Mulroy SJ, Lassen KD, Chambers SH, et al. The ability of male and female clinicians to effectively test knee extension strength using manual muscle testing. *J Orthop Sports Phys Ther.* 1997;26:192–199.

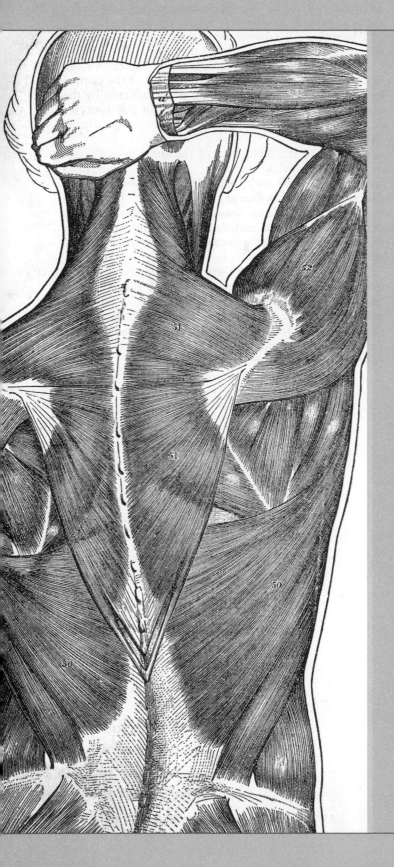

Testing the Muscles of the Neck

INTRODUCTION

The neck musculature contributes approximately 80% of the mechanical stability of the cervical spine.[1] Thus measurement of cervical muscle strength is important and relevant in many conditions. Trauma-related conditions such as whiplash or concussion, disease/disorder-related conditions such as rheumatoid arthritis and Guillain-Barré syndrome, and posture-ergonomic–related conditions make cervical muscle testing especially relevant.[2] A grade of 3 out of 5, the strength equivalent to moving against gravity, is sufficient for many functional activities but may not be sufficient to resist trauma such as concussion or a whiplash movement.[2] Because individuals with neck pain have reduced maximal isometric neck strength and endurance capacity, individuals with cervical pain should be manually muscle tested.[3]

Isometric measurement is the most common and reliable method of assessing cervical muscle strength and will be the only procedure discussed here. Because studies have shown the deep cervical flexors are inhibited more often in the presence of neck pain,[4] differentiation between the deep cervical flexors (longus capitus and colli), which are responsible for the chin tuck movement and which provide support of the cervical lordosis and the cervical joints,[5] and superficial cervical flexors (sternocleidomastoid and others), responsible for cervical flexion, is important.

Reliability of muscle testing of the cervical spine is affected by the lack of a fixed axis. This is particularly true with regard to the location of the thoracic support in prone extension. Significant torque differences were recorded (34 to 53 N) depending on the position of thoracic support.[6] Reliability is also affected by the lack of bilaterality for comparison purposes and the lack of reference values.

Cervical flexion muscle strength is influenced by the position of the neck and the maintenance of the normal lordosis. Cervical muscle strength is also affected by the position of the head over the thorax. In this text, we recommend resistance be placed at the mandible, below the chin.[2]

For testing the endurance of the short neck flexors, a systematic review recommended lifting the head with a slight chin tuck (page 36) as the most reliable (intercorrelation coefficient [ICC] >0.85).[3] Individuals with neck pain–related disorders have significantly less cervical strength and endurance.[3] Dvir and Prushansky found women's cervical spine strength to be approximately 40% that of men.[2]

As noted in Chapter 1, when obvious prime movers exist for a particular movement, they are bolded in the tables. However, in this chapter, there are no identifiable prime movers for capital extension, cervical extension, or capital flexion. It is the simultaneous contraction of a number of capital and cervical muscles that produces each of these three movements.

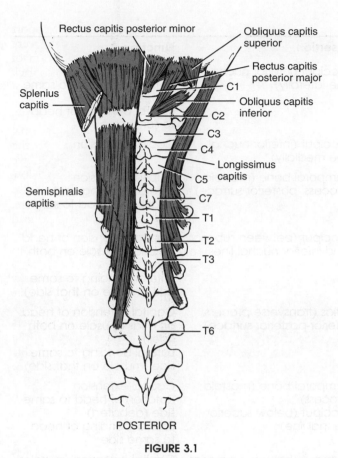

Rectus capitis posterior minor

Obliquus capitis superior

Rectus capitis posterior major

Splenius capitis

Obliquus capitis inferior

C1

C2

C3

C4

Longissimus capitis

C5

Semispinalis capitis

C7

T1

T2

T3

T6

POSTERIOR

FIGURE 3.1

Suboccipital nerve (n.)
To: Rectus capitis posterior major
Rectus capitis posterior minor
Obliquus capitis superior
Obliquus capitis inferior

C1

C2

Greater occipital n.
To: Semispinalis capitis
Longissimus capitis
Splenius capitis
Spinalis capitis

C3

C4

C5

Other capital extensors
receive innervation from
C3 down as far as T1

FIGURE 3.2

Range of Motion
0°–25°

Table 3.1 CAPITAL EXTENSION

I.D.	Muscle	Origin	Insertion	Function
56	Rectus capitis posterior major	Axis (spinous process)	Occiput (inferior nuchal line laterally)	Capital extension Rotation of head to same side Lateral bending of head to same side
57	Rectus capitis posterior minor	Atlas (tubercle of posterior arch)	Occiput (inferior nuchal line medially)	Capital extension
60	Longissimus capitis	T1-T5 vertebrae (transverse processes) C4-C7 vertebrae (articular processes)	Temporal bone (mastoid process, posterior surface)	Capital extension Lateral bending and rotation of head to same side
58	Obliquus capitis superior	Atlas (transverse process)	Occiput (between superior and inferior nuchal lines)	Capital extension of head on atlas (muscle on both sides) Lateral bending to same side (muscle on that side)
59	Obliquus capitis inferior	Axis (lamina and spinous process)	Atlas (transverse process, inferior-posterior surface)	Capital extension of head on atlas (muscle on both sides) Lateral bending to same side (muscle on that side)
61	Splenius capitis	Ligamentum nuchae C7-T4 vertebrae (spinous processes)	Temporal bone (mastoid process) Occiput (below superior nuchal line)	Capital extension Rotation of head to same side (debated) Lateral bending of head to same side
62	Semispinalis capitis (distinct medial part often named Spinalis capitis)	C7-T6 vertebrae (transverse processes) C4-C6 vertebrae (articular processes)	Occiput (between superior and inferior nuchal lines)	Capital extension (muscles on both sides) Rotation of head to opposite side (debated) Lateral bending of head to same side
63	Spinalis capitis	Medial part of Semispinalis capitis, usually blended inseparably	Occiput (between superior and inferior nuchal lines)	Capital extension

Grade 5 and Grade 4

Position of Patient: Prone with head off end of table. Arms at sides.

Instructions to Therapist: Stand at side of patient next to the head. Ask the patient to tilt the head up and look at the wall. If sufficient range is present, use one hand to provide resistance over the occiput (Fig. 3.3). Place the other hand beneath the overhanging head to support it should it give way with resistance. Resistance is applied directly opposite to the movement of the tilt of the head. Care should be made to test the head tilt, and not push the neck into flexion.

Test: Patient extends head by tilting chin upward. (Cervical spine is not extended.)

Instructions to Patient: "Look at the wall. Hold it. Don't let me push your head down."

Grading

Grade 5: Patient completes available range of motion without substituting cervical extension. Tolerates maximum resistance. (This is a strong muscle group.)

Grade 4: Patient completes available range of motion without substituting cervical extension. Tolerates strong to moderate resistance.

Grade 3

Position of Patient: Prone with head off end of table, with head supported by therapist. Arms at sides.

Instructions to Therapist: Stand at side of patient's head. One hand should remain under the head to support it should the muscles fail to hold position (Fig. 3.4).

Instructions to Patient: "Look at the wall."

Test: Patient completes available range without resistance.

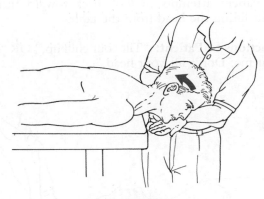

FIGURE 3.4

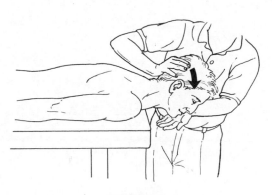

FIGURE 3.3

Grade 2, Grade 1, and Grade 0

Position of Patient: Supine with head on table. Arms at sides. Note: The gravity-minimized position (side-lying) is not recommended for any of the tests of the neck for Grades 2 and below because test artifacts are created by the therapist in attempting to support the head without aiding the motion.

Instructions to Therapist: Stand at end of table, facing patient. Support the head with two hands under the occiput. Place fingers just at the base of the occiput, lateral to the vertebral column to attempt to palpate the capital extensors (Fig. 3.5). Head may be slightly lifted off table to reduce friction.

Test: Patient attempts to look back toward therapist without lifting the head from the table.

Instructions to Patient: "Tilt your chin up," OR "Look back at me. Don't lift your head."

Grading

Grade 2: Patient completes limited range of motion.

Grade 1 and Grade 0: Palpation of the capital extensors at the base of the occiput just lateral to the spine may be difficult; the splenius capitis lies most lateral, and the recti lie just next to the spinous process.

Helpful Hint

Clinicians are reminded that the head is a heavy object suspended on thin support (neck). Whenever testing with the patient's head off the table, care should be used for the patient's safety and comfort, especially in the presence of suspected or known neck or trunk weakness or pain. Always place a hand under the head to be ready to support it should the muscles give way.

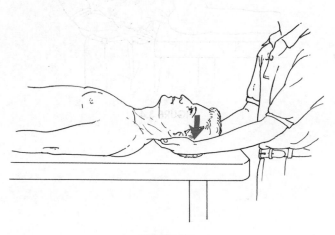

FIGURE 3.5

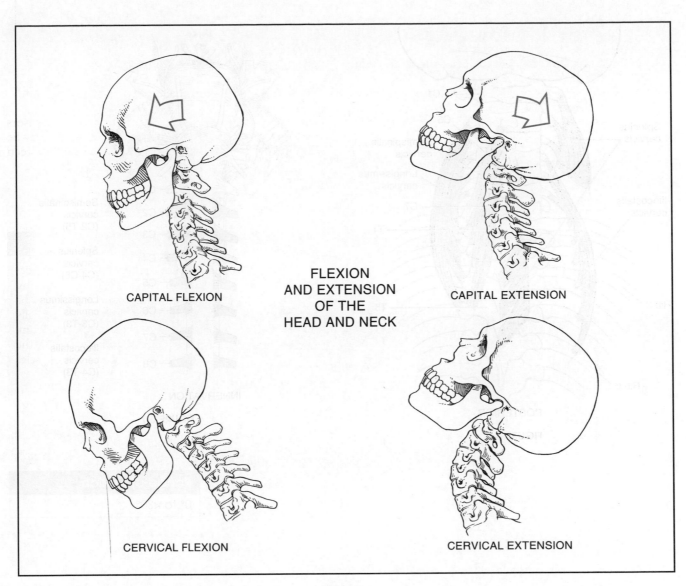

FLEXION
AND EXTENSION
OF THE
HEAD AND NECK

CAPITAL FLEXION

CAPITAL EXTENSION

CERVICAL FLEXION

CERVICAL EXTENSION

PLATE 1

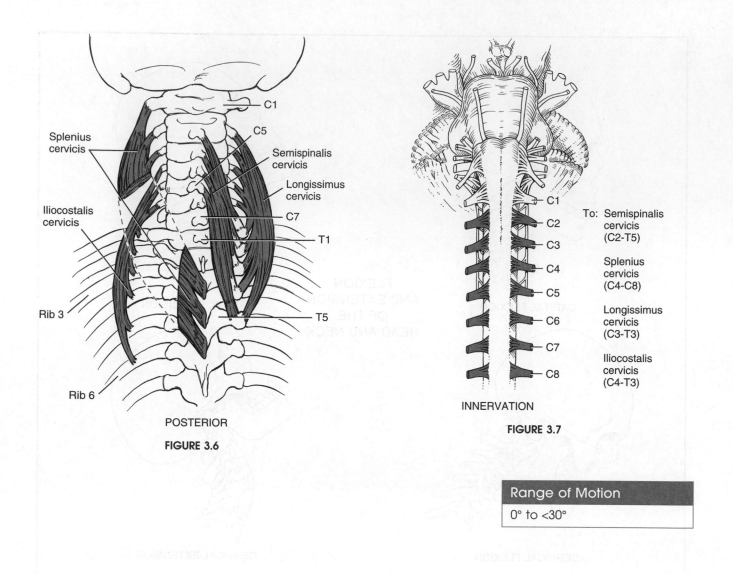

Splenius cervicis

Semispinalis cervicis

Longissimus cervicis

C1

C5

C7

T1

T5

Iliocostalis cervicis

Rib 3

Rib 6

POSTERIOR

FIGURE 3.6

C1
C2
C3
C4
C5
C6
C7
C8

To: Semispinalis
cervicis
(C2-T5)

Splenius
cervicis
(C4-C8)

Longissimus
cervicis
(C3-T3)

Iliocostalis
cervicis
(C4-T3)

INNERVATION

FIGURE 3.7

Range of Motion
0° to <30°

Table 3.2 CERVICAL EXTENSION

I.D.	Muscle	Origin	Insertion	Function
64	Longissimus cervicis	T1-T5 vertebrae (transverse processes) variable	C2-C6 vertebrae (transverse processes)	Extension of the cervical spine (both muscles) Lateral bending of cervical spine to same side (one muscle)
65	Semispinalis cervicis	T1-T5 vertebrae (transverse processes)	Axis (C2)-C5 vertebrae (spinous processes)	Extension of the cervical spine (both muscles) Rotation of cervical spine to opposite side (one muscle) Lateral bending to same side
66	Iliocostalis cervicis	Ribs 3-6 (angles)	C4-C6 vertebrae (transverse processes, posterior tubercles)	Extension of the cervical spine (both muscles) Lateral bending to same side (one muscle) Depression of ribs (accessory)
67	Splenius cervicis (may be absent or variable)	T3-T6 vertebrae (spinous processes)	C1-C3 vertebrae (transverse processes)	Extension of the cervical spine (both muscles) Rotation of cervical spine to same side (one muscle) Lateral bending to same side (one muscle) Synergistic with opposite sternocleidomastoid
124	Trapezius (upper)	Occiput (protuberance and superior nuchal line, middle 1/3) C7 (spinous process) Ligamentum nuchae T1-T12 vertebrae occasionally	Clavicle (posterior border of lateral ⅓)	Elevation of scapula and shoulder ("shrugging") (with levator scapulae) Rotation of head to opposite side (one) Capital extension (both) Cervical extension (both)
68	Spinalis cervicis (often absent)	C7 and often C6 vertebrae (spinous processes) Ligamentum nuchae T1-T2 vertebrae occasionally	Axis (spinous process) C2-C3 vertebrae (spinous processes)	Extension of the cervical spine

Others

I.D.	Muscle			
69	Interspinales cervicis			
70	Intertransversarii cervicis			
71	Rotatores cervicis			
94	Multifidi			
127	Levator scapulae			

CERVICAL EXTENSION

The cervical extensor muscles are limited to those that act only on the cervical spine with motion centered in the lower cervical spine.

Grade 5 and Grade 4

Position of Patient: Prone with head off end of table. Arms at sides.

Instructions to Therapist: Stand next to patient's head. Ask patient to lift head while looking at the floor. If sufficient range is present, place hand applying resistance over the parieto-occipital area (Fig. 3.8). Place the other hand below the chin, ready to support the head should it suddenly give way during resistance.

Test: Patient extends neck without tilting chin.

Instructions to Patient: "Push up on my hand but keep looking at the floor. Hold it. Don't let me push it down."

Grading

Grade 5: Patient holds test position against strong resistance. Therapist must use clinical caution because these muscles are not strong, and their maximum effort will not tolerate much resistance.

Grade 4: Patient holds test position against moderate resistance.

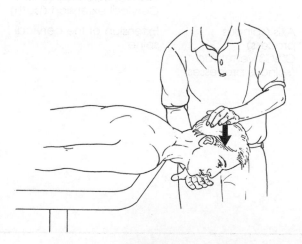

FIGURE 3.8

Grade 3

Position of Patient: Prone with head off end of table. Arms at sides.

Instructions to Therapist: Stand next to patient's head with one hand supporting (or ready to support) the forehead (Fig. 3.9).

Test: Patient extends neck without looking up or tilting chin.

Instructions to Patient: "Lift your forehead from my hand, and keep looking at the floor."

Grading

Grade 3: Patient holds test position but without resistance.

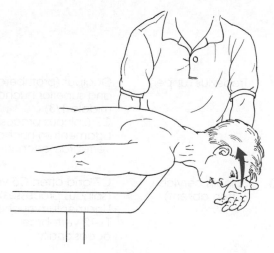

FIGURE 3.9

Alternate Test for Grade 3: This test should be used if there is known or suspected trunk extensor weakness. The therapist should always have an assistant participate to provide protective guarding under the patient's forehead. This test is identical to the preceding Grade 3 test except that stabilization is provided by the therapist to the upper back by the forearm placed over the upper back with the hand cupped over the shoulder (Fig. 3.10).

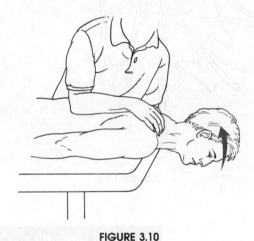

FIGURE 3.10

Grade 2, Grade 1, and Grade 0

Position of Patient: Supine with head fully supported by table. Arms at sides.

Instructions to Therapist: Stand at the patient's head, facing the patient. Place both hands under the patient's head. Fingers should be distal to the occiput at the level of the cervical vertebrae for palpation (Fig. 3.11). Ask patient to push head into therapist's hands without any tilt.

Test: Patient attempts to extend neck into table without tilt.

Instructions to Patient: "Try to push your head down into my hands."

Grading

Grade 2: Patient moves through small range of neck extension by pushing into therapist's hands.

Grade 1: Contractile activity palpated in cervical extensors.

Grade 0: No discernable palpable muscle activity.

Helpful Hint

Patients with a loss of cervical lordosis may have weak cervical extensors. Weak cervical extensors may be a risk factor for cervical kyphosis and dropped head syndrome.[7]

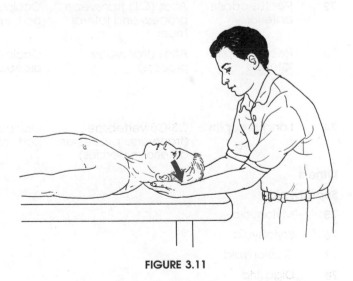

FIGURE 3.11

CAPITAL FLEXION (CHIN TUCK)

(Deep cervical flexors)

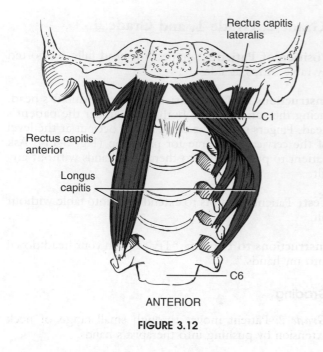

FIGURE 3.12

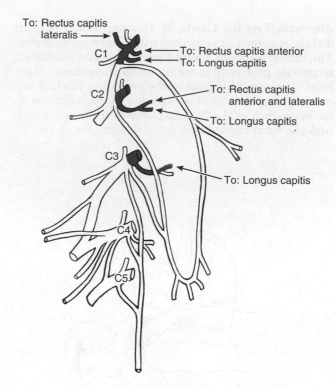

FIGURE 3.13

Range of Motion
0°–10°–15°

Table 3.3 CAPITAL FLEXION (CHIN TUCK)

I.D.	Muscle	Origin	Insertion	Function
72	Rectus capitis anterior	Atlas (C1) transverse process and lateral mass	Occiput (basilar part, inferior surface)	Capital flexion Stabilization of atlanto-occipital joint
73	Rectus capitis lateralis	Atlas (transverse process)	Occiput (jugular process)	Lateral bending of head to same side (obliquity of muscle) Assists head rotation Stabilizes atlanto-occipital joint (assists) Capital flexion
74	Longus capitis	C3-C6 vertebrae (transverse processes, anterior tubercles)	Occiput (basilar part, inferior surface)	Capital flexion Rotation of head to same side (muscle of one side)
Others				
Suprahyoids				
75	Mylohyoid			
76	Stylohyoid			
77	Geniohyoid			
78	Digastric			

(Deep cervical flexors)

The deep cervical flexors (longus capitus, rectus capitis, and colli) achieve capital flexion (nodding), called the chin tuck movement. Only the longus capitis can affect the cervical motion segments other than the atlanto-occiput joint (cranium-C1) because of its inferior attachment to the C6 vertebrae.[8] The weight of the head makes up $\frac{1}{7}$ of the body weight. Forward head posture (FHP) is the structural forward positioning of the head away from the centerline of the body. In FHP the upper cervical vertebrae are extended and the lower cervical vertebrae are flexed, increasing the force required to support the head by up to 3.6 times more than normal aligned posture.[9] In FHP, there is increased extension in the upper cervical joints and at the atlanto-occipital joint, causing the face to be directed upward (Fig. 3.14). FHP results in lengthening of the lower cervical flexors (sternocleidomastoid, scalenes, and upper cervical [capital] extensors) and results in weakness of the lower cervical extensors and upper capital flexors. FHP is commonly accompanied by thoracic kyphosis.

Starting Position of Patient: In all capital and cervical tests the patient is supine with head supported on table and arms at sides (Fig. 3.15). The therapist should be aware of and avoid the tendency of the patient to use the thoracic extensors to retract the head and cervical spine when exerting a maximal effort during the testing of capital flexion.

FIGURE 3.14

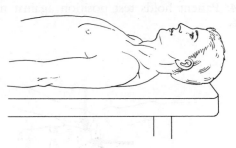

FIGURE 3.15

CAPITAL FLEXION (CHIN TUCK)

(Deep cervical flexors)

Grade 5 and Grade 4

Position of Patient: Supine with head on table. Arms at sides.

Instructions to Therapist: Stand at head of table, facing patient. Ask patient to tuck chin. If sufficient range is present, place cupped hands under the mandible to give resistance against chin tuck, in an upward direction (Fig. 3.16).

Test: Patient tucks chin into neck without raising head from table. No motion should occur at the cervical spine. This is the motion of nodding.

Instructions to Patient: "Tuck your chin and keep your eyes straight ahead. Don't lift your head from the table. Hold it. Don't let me lift up your chin."

Grading

Grade 5: Patient holds test position against maximum resistance. These are very strong muscles.

Grade 4: Patient holds test position against moderate resistance.

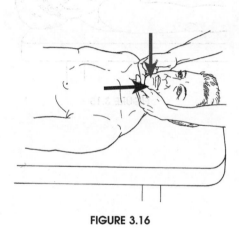

FIGURE 3.16

Grade 3

Position of Patient: Supine with head supported on table. Arms at sides.

Instructions to Therapist: Stand at head of table, facing patient.

Test: Patient tucks chin without lifting head from table (Fig. 3.17).

Instructions to Patient: "Tuck your chin into your neck. Do not raise your head from the table."

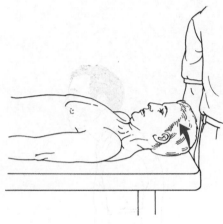

FIGURE 3.17

Grading

Grade 3: Patient completes available range of motion without resistance.

Grade 2, Grade 1, and Grade 0

Position of Patient: Supine with head supported on table. Arms at sides.

Instructions to Therapist: Stand at head of table, facing patient. Ask patient to tuck chin.

Test: Patient attempts to tuck chin (Fig. 3.18).

Instructions to Patient: "Try to tuck your chin into your neck."

Grading

Grade 2: Patient completes partial range of motion.

Grade 1: Contractile activity may be palpated in capital flexor muscles, but it is difficult and only minimal pressure should be used.

Grade 0: No discernable contractile activity.

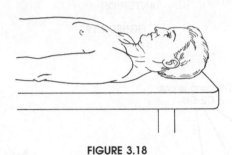

FIGURE 3.18

Helpful Hints

- Palpation of the small and deep muscles of capital flexion may be a difficult task unless the patient has severe atrophy. It is NOT recommended that much pressure be put on the neck when palpating. Remember that the ascending arterial supply (carotids) to the brain runs quite superficially in this region.
- In patients with lower motor neuron lesions that do not affect the cranial nerves, capital flexion is seldom lost. This can possibly be attributed to the suprahyoid muscles, which are innervated by cranial nerves. Activity of the suprahyoid muscles can be identified by control of the floor of the mouth and the tongue, as well as by the absence of impairment of swallowing or speech.[10]
- When capital flexion is impaired or absent, there usually is serious impairment of the cranial nerves, and other central nervous system (CNS) signs are present that may require further evaluation by the physical therapist.
- Endurance as assessed by the cervical flexion test (Grade 3) decreases approximately $\frac{1}{3}$ with neck pain (40 seconds compared with 23 seconds).[11]
- Forward head posture (FHP) is common in individuals who sit for long periods viewing a screen or who use bifocals (see Fig. 3.14).
- Capital flexors may be weak in the presence of FHP.
- For those patients with a thoracic kyphosis that is severe enough to prevent the head from lying flat or even reaching the table in a supine position, use pillows to support the cervical area so the head is in line with the trunk, before testing.

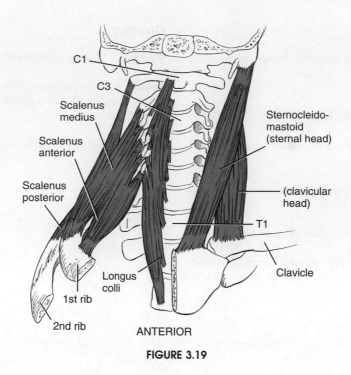

C1

C3

Scalenus
medius

Scalenus
anterior

Scalenus
posterior

1st rib

2nd rib

Longus
colli

Sternocleido-
mastoid
(sternal head)

(clavicular
head)

T1

Clavicle

ANTERIOR

FIGURE 3.19

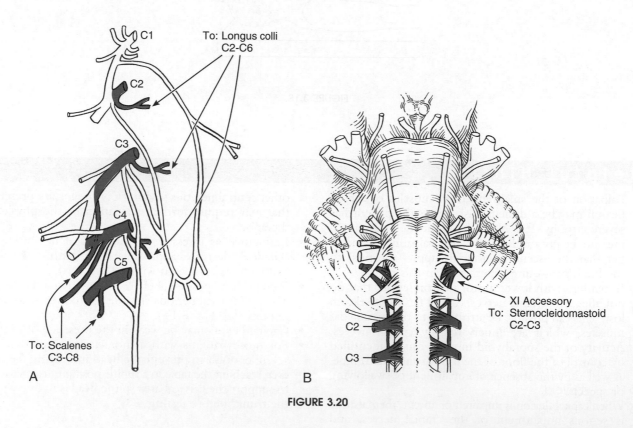

C1

C2

C3

C4

C5

To: Longus colli
C2-C6

To: Scalenes
C3-C8

A

C2

C3

XI Accessory
To: Sternocleidomastoid
C2-C3

B

FIGURE 3.20

Range of Motion
0°–35°–45°

Table 3.4 CERVICAL FLEXION

I.D.	Muscle	Origin	Insertion	Function
83	Sternocleidomastoid			Flexion of cervical spine (both muscles) Lateral bending of cervical spine to same side Rotation of head to opposite side Capital extension (posterior fibers) Raises sternum in forced inspiration
	Sternal head	Sternum (Manubrium, upper anterior aspect)	Two heads blend in middle of neck; occiput (lateral half of superior nuchal line)	
	Clavicular head	Clavicle (medial - ⅓ superior and anterior surfaces)	Temporal bone (mastoid process)	
79	Longus colli			Cervical flexion (weak) Cervical rotation to opposite side (inferior oblique head) Lateral bending (superior and inferior oblique heads) (debatable)
	Superior oblique head	C3-C5 vertebrae (transverse processes)	Atlas (anterior arch, tubercle)	
	Vertical intermediate head	T1-T3 and C5-C7 vertebrae (anterolateral bodies)	C2-C4 vertebrae (anterior bodies)	
	Inferior oblique head	T1-T3 vertebrae (anterior bodies)	C5-C6 vertebrae (transverse processes, anterior tubercles)	
80	Scalenus anterior	C3-C6 vertebrae (transverse processes, anterior tubercles)	First rib (scalene tubercle)	Flexion of cervical spine (both muscles) Elevation of 1st rib in inspiration Rotation of cervical spine to same side Lateral bending of neck to same side

Others

81	Scalenus medius	
82	Scalenus posterior	

Infrahyoids

84	Sternothyroid	
85	Thyrohyoid	
86	Sternohyoid	
87	Omohyoid	

The muscles of cervical flexion act only on the cervical spine with the center of motion in the lower cervical spine.[12,13] The chin tuck position should be gently maintained when testing the cervical flexors, avoiding an extended cervical position.

Grade 5 and Grade 4

Position of Patient: Supine, with knees bent and feet on the table (hook lying), arms at side.[3]

Instructions to Therapist: Stand next to patient's head. Ask patient to lift head from table while keeping chin tucked in with eyes towards ceiling. If sufficient range is present, place hand for resistance on patient's chin. Use two fingers only (Fig. 3.21). Other hand may be placed on chest, but stabilization is needed only when the trunk is weak.

Test: Patient lifts head straight up from the table while tucking the chin. This is a weak muscle group.

Instructions to Patient: "Lift your head from the table; keep your chin tucked in while looking at the ceiling. Do not lift your shoulders off the table. Hold it. Don't let me push your head down."

Grading

Grade 5 and Grade 4: Patient able to hold test position against moderate to mild two-finger resistance.

Grade 3

No resistance is used (Fig. 3.22).

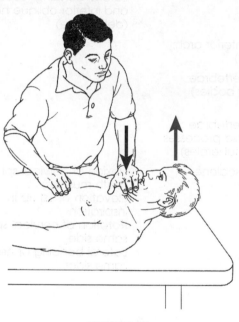

FIGURE 3.21

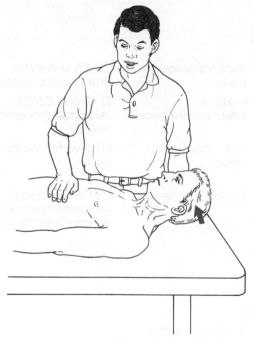

FIGURE 3.22

Grade 2, Grade 1, and Grade 0

Position of Patient: Supine with head supported on table. Arms at sides.

Instructions to Therapist: Stand at head of table, facing patient. Fingers of both hands (or just the index finger) are placed over the sternocleidomastoid muscles to palpate them during test (Fig. 3.23).

Test: Patient rolls head from side to side, keeping head supported on table.

Instructions to Patient: "Roll your head to the left and then to the right."

Grading

Grade 2: Patient completes partial range of motion. The right sternocleidomastoid produces the roll to the left side and vice versa.

Grade 1: No motion occurs, but contractile activity in one or both muscles can be detected.

Grade 0: No motion and no discernable contractile activity detected.

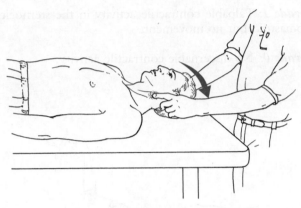

FIGURE 3.23

Substitution

The platysma may attempt to substitute for weak or absent sternocleidomastoid muscles during cervical or combined flexion. When this occurs, the corners of the mouth pull down; a grimacing expression or "What do I do now?" expression is seen. Superficial muscle activity will be apparent over the anterior surface of the neck, with skin wrinkling.

Range of Motion

0°–45°–55°

This test should be performed when there is suspected or known asymmetry of strength in these neck flexor muscles.

Grade 5, Grade 4, and Grade 3

Position of Patient: Supine with head supported on table and turned to the left (to test right sternocleidomastoid).

Instructions to Therapist: Stand at head of table, facing patient. Ask patient to raise head from table while keeping the head turned. If sufficient range is present, place hand applying resistance on the temporal area above the ear for resistance (Fig. 3.24).

Test: Patient raises head from table.

Instructions to Patient: "Lift up your head, keeping your head turned."

Grading

Grade 5: Patient holds test position and tolerates strong resistance. This is usually a very strong muscle group.

Grade 4: Patient holds test position and tolerates moderate resistance.

Grade 3: Patient completes available range of motion without resistance (Fig. 3.25).

Grade 2, Grade 1, and Grade 0

Position of Patient: Supine with head supported on table.

Instructions to Therapist: Stand at head of table, facing patient. Place fingers (or just the index finger) alongside the head and neck to palpate the sternocleidomastoid (see Fig. 3.23).

Test: Patient attempts to roll head from side to side.

Instructions to Patient: "Roll your head to the right and then to the left."

Grading

Grade 2: Patient completes partial range of motion.

Grade 1: Palpable contractile activity in the sternocleidomastoid but no movement.

Grade 0: No discernable contractile activity.

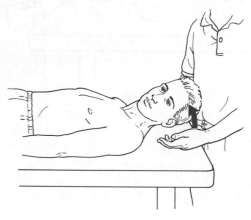

FIGURE 3.25

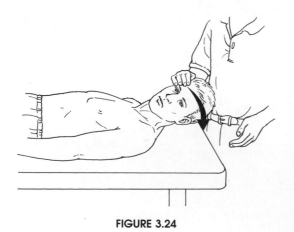

FIGURE 3.24

Fifty percent of the total neck rotation occurs between C1 and C2, before any rotation is noted throughout the remainder of the cervical spine.[14]

Grade 5, Grade 4, and Grade 3

Position of Patient: Supine with cervical spine in neutral (flexion and extension). Head supported on table with face turned as far to one side as possible. Sitting is an alternative position for all tests.

Instructions to Therapist: Stand at head of table, facing patient. Ask patient to turn head. If sufficient range exists, place hand for resistance over the side of the patient's head above the ear (Grades 5 and 4 only).

Test: Patient rotates head to neutral against maximum resistance. This is a strong muscle group. Repeat for rotators on the opposite side. Alternatively, have patient rotate from left side of face on table to right side of face on table.

Instructions to Patient: "Turn your head and face the ceiling. Hold it. Do not let me turn your head back."

Grading

Grade 5: Patient holds test position with maximum resistance.

Grade 4: Patient holds test position with moderate resistance.

Grade 3: Patient rotates head through full available range of motion to both right and left without resistance.

Grade 2, Grade 1, and Grade 0

Position of Patient: Sitting. Trunk and head may be supported against a high-back chair. Head posture neutral.

Instructions to Therapist: Stand directly in front of patient.

Test: Patient tries to rotate head from side to side, keeping the neck in neutral (chin neither down nor up).

Instructions to Patient: "Turn your head as far to the left as you can. Keep your chin level." Repeat for turn to right.

Grading

Grade 2: Patient completes partial range of motion.

Grade 1: Contractile activity in sternocleidomastoid or posterior muscles visible or evident by palpation. No movement.

Grade 0: No discernable palpable contractile activity.

Participating Muscles in Cervical Rotation (with reference numbers)

56. Rectus capitis posterior major	74. Longus capitis
59. Obliquus capitis inferior	79. Longus colli (Inferior oblique)
60. Longissimus capitis	80. Scalenus anterior
61. Splenius capitis	81. Scalenus medius
62. Semispinalis capitis	82. Scalenus posterior
65. Semispinalis cervicis	83. Sternocleidomastoid
67. Splenius cervicis	124. Trapezius
71. Rotatores cervicis	127. Levator scapulae

REFERENCES

1. Panjabi MM, Cholewicki J, Nibu K, et al. Critical load of the human cervical spine: an in vitro experimental study. *Clin Biomech (Bristol, Avon)*. 1998;13(1):11–17.
2. Dvir Z, Prushansky T. Cervical muscles strength testing: methods and clinical implications. *J Manipulative Physiol Ther*. 2008;31(7):518–524.
3. de Koning CH, van den Heuvel SP, Staal JB, et al. Clinimetric evaluation of methods to measure muscle functioning in patients with non-specific neck pain: a systematic review. *BMC Musculoskelet Disord*. 2008;19(9):142.
4. Jull GA, O'Leary SP, Falla DL. Clinical assessment of the deep cervical flexormuscles: the craniocervical flexion test. *J Manipulative Physiol Ther*. 2008;31(7):525–533.
5. Falla D, Jull G, Dall'Alba P, et al. An electromyographic analysis of the deep cervical flexor muscles in performance of craniocervical flexion. *Phys Ther*. 2003;83(10):899–906.
6. Rezasoltani A, Ylinen J, Bakhtiary AH, et al. Cervical muscle strength measurement is dependent on the location of thoracic support. *Br J Sports Med*. 2008;42(5):379–382.
7. Alpayci M, Şenköy E, Delen V, et al. Decreased neck muscle strength in patients with the loss of cervical lordosis. *Clin Biomech (Bristol, Avon)*. 2016;33:98–102.
8. Kamibayashi LK, Richmond FJ. Morphometry of human neck muscles. *Spine*. 1998;23(12):1314–1323.
9. Park SY, Yoo WG. Effects of the sustained computer work on upper cervical flexion motion. *J Phys Ther Sci*. 2014;26:441–442.
10. Perry J, Nickel VL. Total cervical spine fusion for neck paralysis. *J Bone Joint Surg Am*. 1959;41:37–60.
11. Harris KD, Heer DM, Roy TC, et al. Reliability of a measurement of neck flexor muscle endurance. *Phys Ther*. 2005;85:1349–1355.
12. Fielding JW. Cineroentgenography of the normal cervical spine. *J Bone Joint Surg Am*. 1957;39:1280–1288.
13. Ferlic D. The range of motion of the "normal" cervical spine. *Johns Hopkins Hosp Bull*. 1962;110:59.
14. Gray H. *Gray's Anatomy: The Anatomical Basis of Clinical Practice*. Elsevier Churchill Livingstone; 2005.

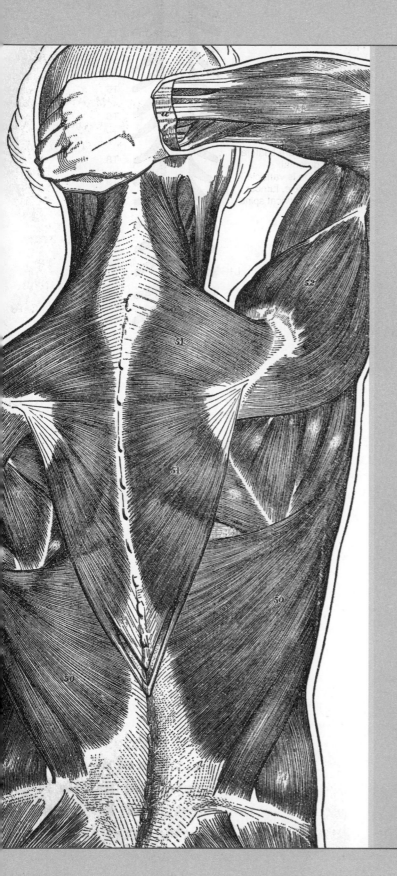

CHAPTER 4

Testing the Muscles of the Trunk and Pelvic Floor

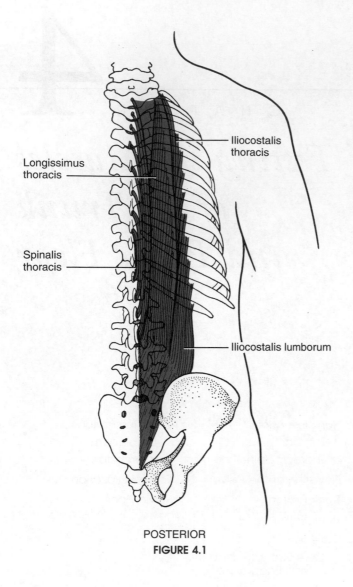

Iliocostalis
thoracis

Longissimus
thoracis

Spinalis
thoracis

Iliocostalis lumborum

POSTERIOR
FIGURE 4.1

T1

Longissimus thoracis
Iliocostalis thoracis
Spinalis thoracis
Semispinalis thoracis
Multifidus
Iliocostalis lumborum

All muscles are bilateral
and segmental;
Innervation is variable
along thoracic, lumbar,
and even cervical spine

L1

T1
T2
T3
T4
T5
T6
T7
T8
T9
T10
T11
T12
L1
L2
L3
L4
L5
S1
S2
S3

FIGURE 4.2

Range of Motion	
Thoracic spine: 0°–10°	
Lumbar spine: 0°–25°	

Table 4.1 TRUNK EXTENSION

I.D.	Muscle	Origin	Insertion	Function
89	Iliocostalis thoracis	Ribs 12 up to 7 (angles)	Ribs 6 up to 1 (angles) C7 vertebra (transverse processes)	Extension of the spine Lateral bending of spine to same side (muscles on one side) Depression of ribs
90	Iliocostalis lumborum	Tendon of erector spinae (anterior surface) Thoracolumbar fascia Sacrum (posterior surface)	Ribs 6–12 (angles)	Extension of spine Lateral bending of spine (muscles on one side) Depression of ribs (lumborum) Elevation of pelvis
91	Longissimus thoracis	Tendon of erector spinae Thoracolumbar fascia L1-L5 vertebrae (transverse processes)	T1-T12 vertebrae (transverse processes) Ribs 2–12 (between angles and tubercles)	Extension of the spine Lateral bending of spine to same side (muscles on one side) Depression of ribs
92	Spinalis thoracis (often indistinct)	Common tendon of erector spinae T11-L2 vertebrae (spinous processes)	T1-T4 vertebrae (or to T8, spinous processes) Blends with semispinalis thoracis	Extension of spine
93	Semispinalis thoracis	T6-T10 vertebrae (transverse processes)	C6-T4 vertebrae (spinous processes)	Extension of thoracic spine
94	Multifidi	Sacrum (posterior) Erector spinae (aponeurosis) Ilium (posterior superior iliac spine (PSIS)) and crest Sacroiliac ligaments L1-L5 vertebrae (mamillary processes) T1-T12 vertebrae (transverse processes) C4-C7 vertebrae (articular processes)	Spinous processes of higher vertebra (may span 2–4 vertebrae before inserting)	Extension of spine Lateral bending of spine (muscle on one side) Rotation to opposite side
95, 96	Rotatores thoracis and lumborum (11 pairs)	Thoracic and lumbar vertebrae (transverse processes; variable in lumbar area)	Next highest vertebra (lower border of lamina)	Extension of thoracic spine Rotation to opposite side
97, 98	Interspinales thoracis and lumborum	Thoracis: (3 pairs) between spinous processes of contiguous vertebrae (T1-T2; T2-T3; T11-T12) Lumborum: (4 pairs) lie between the 5 lumbar vertebrae; run between spinous processes	See origin	Extension of spine
99	Intertransversarii thoracis and lumborum	Thoracis: (3 pairs) between transverse processes of contiguous vertebrae T10-T12 and L1 Lumborum: medial muscles; accessory process of superior vertebra to mamillary process of vertebra below Lateral muscles: fill space between transverse processes of adjacent vertebrae	See origin	Extension of spine (muscles on both sides) Lateral bending to same side (muscles on one side) Rotation to opposite side

Continued

Table 4.1 TRUNK EXTENSION—cont'd

I.D.	Muscle	Origin	Insertion	Function
100	Quadratus lumborum	Ilium (crest and inner lip) Iliolumbar ligament	12th rib (lower border) L1-L4 vertebrae (transverse processes) T12 vertebra (body)	Elevation of pelvis (weak in contrast to lateral abdominals) Extension of lumbar spine (muscles on both sides) Inspiration (via stabilization of lower attachments of diaphragm) Fixation of lower portions of diaphragm for prolonged vocalization, which needs sustained expiration. Lateral bending of lumbar spine to same side (pelvis fixed) Fixation and depression of 12th rib
Other				
182	Gluteus maximus (provides stable base for trunk extension by stabilizing pelvis)			

The importance of the spinal extensors' muscle strength and endurance cannot be understated as they are implicated in back pain, posture, gait, and balance. For example, in older women with severely flexed posture (>8 cm from occiput to the wall), spinal extensors and abdominal muscles were found to be weaker than in those with mildly flexed posture.[1] Exaggerated posture such as extreme lumbar lordosis and pelvic tilt produce greater muscle activity than more optimal postures, and this has implications for physical therapists.[2] Muscle function in the neutral zone is important for stabilization of the lumbar spine.[3,4] Stabilization occurs through global and local stabilizers. The global stabilizers include the rectus abdominis and external oblique muscles. These muscles generate a large amount of muscle torque across multiple segments and thus control movement. The local stabilizers are the deeper muscles, having their origin or insertion directly or indirectly on the lumbar vertebrae. The transversus abdominis (TA) and lumbar multifidus (LM) are examples of local stabilizers. This system of global and local stabilizers is what provides lumbar stabilization.[5,6] The trunk flexors and extensors form the core, discussed later in this chapter.

The trunk extensor muscles are tonic or endurance-type muscles, whereas the trunk flexors are phasic or shorter acting. Therefore the maximum force generated per unit of muscle mass should be expected to be different (less for the extensors). Trunk extensor endurance has a role in upright posture and back pain, and therefore it may be informative to test the patient's hold time. Trunk extensors also control trunk flexion eccentrically.

Although there is no "gold standard" for the testing of spinal and abdominal muscles, this chapter includes methods from the best evidence as well as time-honored traditional methods.

LUMBAR SPINE

Grade 5 and Grade 4

Position of Patient: Prone with fingertips lightly touching the side of the head and shoulders in external rotation. The weight of the head and arms essentially substitutes for manual resistance by therapist.

Instructions to Therapist: Stand at side of patient to stabilize the lower extremities just above the ankles (Fig. 4.3). Ask patient to raise the head, shoulders, and chest off the table. Observe quality of motion and ability to hold the test position.

Alternate Instructions to Therapist: If the patient has hip extension weakness, stabilize the lower extremities by leaning firmly over the patient's body, placing both arms across the pelvis. Note it is very difficult to stabilize the pelvis adequately in the presence of significant hip weakness (Fig. 4.4).

Test: Patient extends the lumbar spine until the entire trunk is raised from the table (clears umbilicus).

Instructions to Patient: "Raise your head, shoulders, and chest off the table. Come up as high as you can."

Grading

Grade 5 and Grade 4: The therapist distinguishes between Grade 5 and Grade 4 muscles by observing the response (see Figs. 4.3 and 4.4). The Grade 5 muscle holds the test position like a lock; the Grade 4 muscle yields slightly because of an elastic quality at the end point. The patient with Grade 5 back extensor muscles can quickly come to the end position and hold that position without evidence of significant effort. The patient with Grade 4 back extensors can come to the end position but may waver or display some signs of effort.

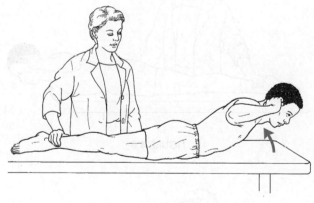

FIGURE 4.3

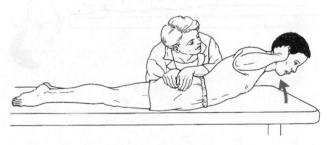

FIGURE 4.4

THORACIC SPINE

Grade 5 and Grade 4

Position of Patient: Prone with head and upper trunk extending off the table from about the nipple line (Fig. 4.5). Hands should be lightly touching the side of the head, with shoulders and elbows retracted (back).

Instructions to Therapist: Stand at side of patient to stabilize the lower limbs at the ankle. Ask patient to raise the head, shoulders, and chest to table level. (Note that this position does not require the same degree of stabilization as the lumbar extension tests.)

Test: Patient extends thoracic spine to the horizontal. This will be a small movement, and care should be made not to extend farther than horizontal because further movement will cause lumbar extension.

Instructions to Patient: "Raise your head, shoulders, and chest to table level."

Grading

Grade 5: Patient raises the upper trunk quickly from its forward flexed position to the horizontal with ease and no sign of exertion (Fig. 4.6).

Grade 4: Patient raises the trunk to the horizontal level but does so with obvious effort.

Grade 3

Note: Grades 3, 2, 1, and 0 tests involve the lumbar and thoracic spine.

Position of Patient: Prone with arms at sides.

Instructions to Therapist: Stand at side of table. Stabilize lower extremities just above the ankles.

Test: Patient extends spine, raising body from the table so that the umbilicus clears the table (Fig. 4.7).

Instructions to Patient: "Raise your head, arms, and chest from the table as high as you can."

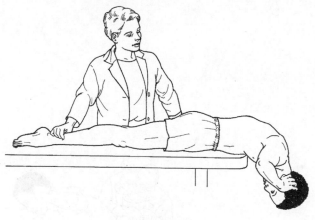

FIGURE 4.5

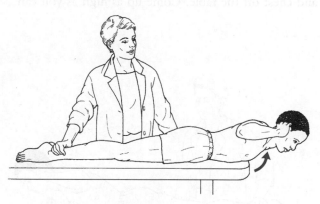

FIGURE 4.6

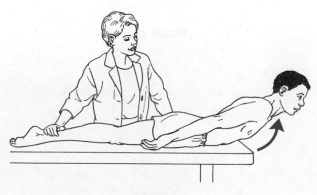

FIGURE 4.7

Grading

Grade 3: Patient completes the range of motion.

Grade 2, Grade 1, and Grade 0

These tests are identical to the Grade 3 test except that the therapist must palpate the lumbar and thoracic spine extensor muscle masses adjacent to both sides of the spine. The individual muscles cannot be isolated (Figs. 4.8 and 4.9).

Grading

Grade 2: Patient completes partial range of motion.

Grade 1: Contractile activity is detectable but no movement.

Grade 0: No discernable contractile activity.

- When the spinal extensors are strong and the hip extensors are weak, the patient can hyperextend the low back (increased lordosis) but will be unable to raise the trunk without very strong stabilization of the pelvis by the therapist.
- If the neck extensors are weak, the therapist may need to support the head as the patient raises the trunk.
- When the spinal extensors are weak and the hip extensors are strong, the patient will be unable to raise the upper trunk from the table. Instead, the pelvis will tilt posteriorly while the lumbar spine moves into flexion (low back flattens).
- If the hip extensor muscles are Grade 4 or better, it may be helpful to use belts to anchor hips to the table, especially if the patient is much larger or stronger than the testing therapist.
- If the patient is unable to provide stabilization through the weight of the legs and pelvis (such as in paraplegia or amputee), the test should be done on a mat table. Position the subject with both legs and pelvis off the mat. This allows the pelvis and limbs to contribute to stabilization, and the therapist holding the lower trunk has a chance to provide the necessary support. (If a mat table is not available, an assistant will be required, and the lower body may rest on a chair.)

FIGURE 4.8

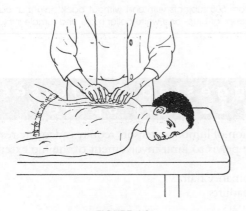

FIGURE 4.9

Sørensen Lumbar Spine Extension Test

The Biering-Sørensen test or Sørensen test is a measure of isometric endurance capacity of the back extensors and perhaps hip extensor muscles.[7,8] The modified Sørensen test is a similar test with patient arms at the side of the trunk, rather than across the chest, as in the original Biering-Sørensen test.

Position of Patient: Prone with the trunk flexed off the end of the table at a level between the anterior superior iliac spine (ASIS) and umbilicus. Until test begins, patient may stretch arms over a chair (in front of table) to provide support for the trunk (not shown).

Instructions to Therapist: Lean over patient to firmly stabilize the lower limbs and pelvis at the ankles. Ask patient to fold arms across the chest, then raise head, chest, and trunk so the trunk is straight. Use a stopwatch to time the effort, activating it at the "begin" command and stopping it when the patient shows obvious signs of fatigue and begins to falter.[9]

Test: Patient lifts the trunk to the horizontal and maintains the test position as long as possible (Fig. 4.10).

Instructions to Patient: "When I say 'begin,' lift your head, chest, and trunk from the table and hold the position as long as you can. I will be timing you."

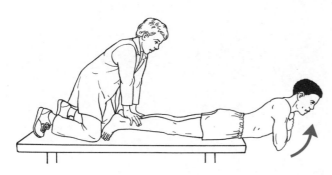

FIGURE 4.10

Helpful Hints

- The Sørensen test elicits no greater than 40%–52% of the maximal voluntary contractile force.[8]
- Back extensor strength declines approximately 40%–50% from the 3rd to 8th decades of life, markedly reducing endurance time (Table 4.2).[10-12]
- The Sørensen test has been validated as a differential diagnostic test for low back pain.[7,13]
- With a cutoff score of 28 s for men and 29 s for women, the Sørensen test had a sensitivity of 92.3% and specificity of 76.0% to predict low back pain in men and 84.3% sensitivity and 84.6% specificity for women.[14]

Table 4.2 AGE-BASED NORMS FOR MODIFIED SØRENSEN TEST

Age	Mean Hold Time in Seconds (SD)* Males	Mean Hold Time in Seconds (SD) Females
19-29	140[12]	130[15]
30-39	130[12]	120
35-39	97 (43)[15]	93 (55)[15]
40-44	101 (57)[15]	80 (55)[15]
40-49	120[12]	90[15]
45-49	99 (58)[15]	102 (64)[15]
50-54	89 (55)[15]	69 (60)[15]
50-59	90[12]	75[12]
60+	80[12]	90[12]

*Numbers in parentheses refer to standard deviation (SD). The standard deviation is only available for some age groups.

[12]Data from 561 healthy, nonsmoking subjects in Nigeria without low back pain.

[15]Data from 508 subjects with and without back pain that comprised equal groups of blue- and white-collar male and female subjects.

Suggested Exercises for Lumbar Spine[16]

Isolation of lumbar extensors requires adequate restraint of the pelvis to limit involvement of the hip extensors.

- Roman Chair
- Deadlifts
- Squats
- Extension-based resistance machines

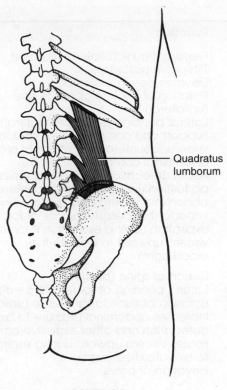

Quadratus
lumborum

POSTERIOR
FIGURE 4.11

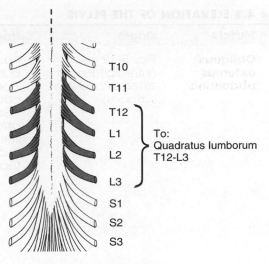

T10
T11
T12
L1
L2
L3
S1
S2
S3

To:
Quadratus lumborum
T12-L3

FIGURE 4.12

Range of Motion

Approximates pelvis to lower ribs; range not precise.

ELEVATION OF THE PELVIS

Table 4.3 ELEVATION OF THE PELVIS

I.D.	Muscle	Origin	Insertion	Function
110	**Obliquus externus abdominis**	Ribs 5–12 (interdigitating on external and inferior surfaces)	Iliac crest (outer border) Aponeurosis from 9th costal cartilage to ASIS; both sides meet at midline to form linea alba Pubic symphysis (upper border)	Flexion of trunk (bilateral muscles) Tilts pelvis posteriorly Elevates pelvis (unilateral) Rotation of trunk to opposite side (unilateral) Lateral bending of trunk (unilateral) Support and compression of abdominal viscera, counteracting effect of gravity on abdominal contents Assists defecation, micturition, emesis, and parturition (i.e., expulsion of contents of abdominal viscera and air from lungs) Important accessory muscle of forced expiration (during expiration it forces the viscera upward to elevate the diaphragm)
111	**Obliquus internus abdominis**	Iliac crest (anterior ⅔ of intermediate line) Thoracolumbar fascia Inguinal ligament (lateral ⅔ of upper aspect)	Ribs 9–12 (inferior border and cartilages by digitations that appear continuous with internal intercostals) Ribs 7–9 (cartilages) Aponeurosis to linea alba	Flexion of spine (bilateral) Lateral bending of spine (unilateral) Rotation of trunk to same side (unilateral) Increases abdominal pressure to assist in defecation and other expulsive actions Forces viscera upward during expiration to elevate diaphragm Elevation of pelvis
100	Quadratus lumborum	Ilium (crest and inner lip) Iliolumbar ligament	Rib 12 (lower border) L1-L4 vertebrae (transverse processes, apex) T12 vertebra (body; occasionally)	Elevation of pelvis (weak in contrast to lateral abdominals) Extension of lumbar spine (muscles on both sides) Inspiration (via stabilization of lower attachments of diaphragm) Fixation of lower portions of diaphragm for prolonged vocalization which needs sustained expiration. Lateral bending of lumbar spine to same side (pelvis fixed) Fixation and depression of 12th rib

Others

130	Latissimus dorsi (if arms are fixed)			
90	Iliocostalis lumborum			

ASIS, Anterior superior iliac spine.

Elevation of the pelvis is a critical component of gait because it allows the swing leg to clear the floor. The lateral abdominals, in conjunction with the quadratus, produce very strong pelvic elevation, and the therapist should not be able to break a Grade 5 muscle. The hip hike test described later was originally believed to isolate the quadratus lumborum, but a later study revealed the dominance of the abdominals. Even though hip hiking incorporates both the abdominals and quadratus,[17] it is still the best differentiation between quadratus and the abdominals that we have.

Grade 5 and Grade 4

Position of Patient: Supine or prone. The patient grasps edges of the table to provide stabilization during resistance (not illustrated).

Instructions to Therapist: Stand at foot of table, facing patient. Ask patient to hike pelvis. If sufficient range is present, grasp test limb with both hands, using a lumbrical grip just above the ankle, and pull caudally with a smooth, even pull (Fig. 4.13) to provide resistance. Resistance is given as in traction. The Grades 5 and 4 muscles tolerate a very large amount of resistance.

Test: Patient hikes the pelvis on one side, thereby approximating the pelvic rim to the inferior margin of the rib cage.

Instructions to Patient: "Hike your pelvis to bring it up to your ribs. Hold it. Don't let me pull your leg down."

Grading

Grade 5: Patient holds test position and limb does not move with maximal resistance.

Grade 4: Patient holds test position against very strong resistance. Testing this movement requires more than a bit of clinical judgment.

Grade 3 and Grade 2

Position of Patient: Supine or prone. Hip in extension; lumbar spine neutral or extended.

Instructions to Therapist: Stand at foot of table, facing patient. Use one hand to support the leg just above the ankle; keep the other hand under the knee so the limb is slightly off the table to decrease friction (Fig. 4.14).

Test: Patient hikes the pelvis on the test side to bring the rim of the pelvis closer to the inferior ribs.

Instructions to Patient: "Bring your pelvis up to your ribs."

Grading

Grade 3: Patient completes available range of motion.

Grade 2: Patient completes partial range of motion.

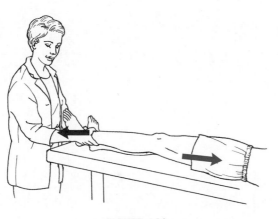

FIGURE 4.13

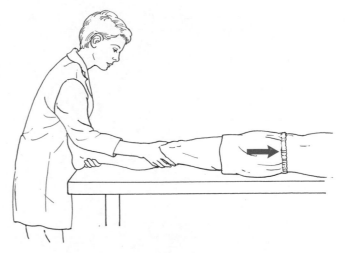

FIGURE 4.14

Grade 1 and Grade 0

These grades should be avoided to ensure clinical accuracy. The quadratus lumborum lies deep to the paraspinal muscle mass and can rarely be palpated. In people who have extensive truncal atrophy, paraspinal muscle activity may be palpated, and possibly, but not necessarily convincingly, the quadratus lumborum can be palpated.

Substitution

The patient may attempt to substitute with trunk lateral flexion, primarily using the abdominal muscles. The spinal extensors may be used without the quadratus lumborum. In neither case can manual testing detect an inactive quadratus lumborum.

Helpful Hint

It should be noted that the quadratus lumborum may have functions other than hip hiking, such as maintaining upright posture, although these functions have been less well studied. Quadratus lumborum strength has also been linked to low back pain and thus may deserve closer analysis.[18]

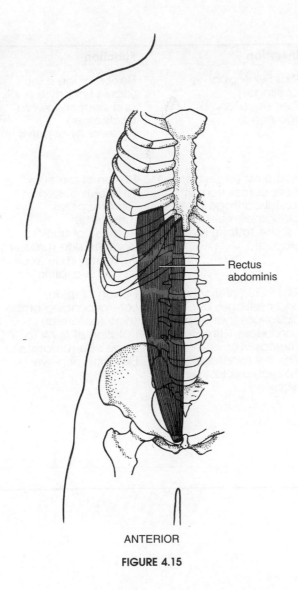

Rectus
abdominis

ANTERIOR

FIGURE 4.15

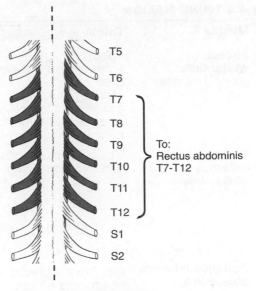

T5
T6
T7
T8
T9
T10
T11
T12
S1
S2

To:
Rectus abdominis
T7–T12

FIGURE 4.16

Range of Motion
0°–80°

Table 4.4 TRUNK FLEXION

I.D.	Muscle	Origin	Insertion	Function
113	**Rectus abdominis** (paired muscle)	Pubis Lateral fibers (tubercle on crest and pecten pubis) Medial fibers (ligamentous covering of symphysis attaches to contralateral muscle)	Ribs 5–7 (costal cartilages) Sternum (xiphoid ligaments)	Flexion of the spine (draws symphysis pubis and sternum toward each other) Posterior tilt of pelvis
110	**Obliquus externus abdominis**	Ribs 5–12 (interdigitating on external and inferior surfaces)	Iliac crest (outer border) Aponeurosis from 9th costal cartilage to ASIS; both sides meet at midline to form linea alba	Flexion of the trunk Tilts pelvis posteriorly Elevates pelvis (unilateral) Rotation of trunk to opposite side (unilateral) Accessory muscle of forced expiration
111	**Obliquus internus abdominis**	Iliac crest (anterior ⅔ of intermediate line) Thoracolumbar fascia Inguinal ligament (lateral ⅔ of upper aspect)	Ribs 9–12 (inferior border and cartilages by digitations that appear continuous with internal intercostals) Ribs 7–9 (cartilages) Aponeurosis to linea alba	Flexion of spine Lateral bending of the spine (unilateral) Rotation of trunk to same side (unilateral) Elevation of pelvis

Others

174	Psoas major
175	Psoas minor

ASIS, Anterior superior iliac spine.

Trunk flexion has multiple elements that include cervical, thoracic, and lumbar motion. Measurement is difficult at best and may be done in a variety of ways with considerable variability in results. The neck flexors should be eliminated as much as possible by asking the patient to maintain a neutral neck position with the chin pointed to the ceiling to avoid neck flexion. Legs should be straight to avoid hip flexor activation.[19]

Grade 5

Position of Patient: Supine, with legs straight and fingertips lightly touching the back of the head (Fig. 4.17).

Instructions to Therapist: Stand at side of table at level of patient's chest to ascertain whether scapulae clear table during test (Fig. 4.18). Ask patient to lift head, shoulders, and back off table, keeping the chin pointed to the ceiling. Observe motion for quality and effort. For a patient with no other muscle weakness, the therapist does not need to touch the patient. However, if the patient has weak hip flexors, the therapist should stabilize the pelvis by leaning across the patient on the forearms (see Fig. 4.18).

Test: Patient flexes trunk through range of motion, lifting the trunk until scapulae clear table. The neck should not flex.

Instructions to Patient: "Keep your chin pointed toward the ceiling and lift your head, shoulders, and back off the table."

Grading

Grade 5: Patient raises trunk until inferior angles of scapulae are off the table. (Weight of the arms serves as resistance.)

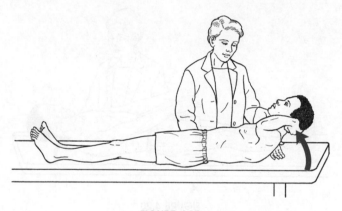

FIGURE 4.17

FIGURE 4.18

Grade 4

Position of Patient: Supine with arms crossed over chest (Fig. 4.19).

Test: Other than the patient's arm position, all other aspects of the test are the same as for Grade 5.

Grading

Grade 4: Patient raises trunk until scapulae are off the table. Resistance of arms is reduced in the cross-chest position.

Grade 3

Position of Patient: Supine with arms outstretched in full extension above plane of body (Fig. 4.20).

Test: Except for the patient's arm position, all other aspects of the test are the same as for Grade 5. Patient lifts trunk until inferior angles of scapulae are off the table. Position of the outstretched arms "neutralizes" resistance by bringing the weight of the arms closer to the center of gravity.

Instructions to Patient: "Keep your chin pointed to the ceiling as you raise your head, shoulders, and arms off the table."

Grading

Grade 3: Patient lifts trunk until inferior angles of scapulae are off the table.

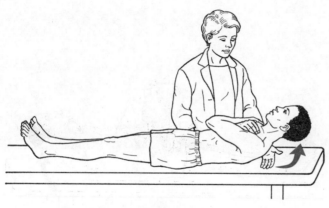

FIGURE 4.19

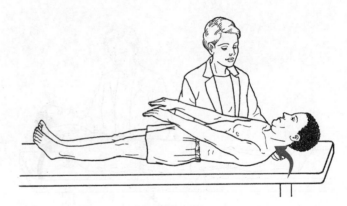

FIGURE 4.20

Grade 2, Grade 1, and Grade 0

Testing trunk flexion is rather clear-cut for Grades 5, 4, and 3. When testing Grade 2 and below, the results may be ambiguous, but observation and palpation are critical for defendable results. To determine Grades 2 to 0, the patient will be asked, in sequence, to raise the head, do an assisted forward lean, and cough.

Position of Patient: Supine with arms at sides. Knees flexed.

Instructions to Therapist: Stand at side of table. Place the hand used for palpation at the midline of the thorax over the linea alba, and use the four fingers of both hands to palpate the rectus abdominis (Fig. 4.21).

Note: The therapist tests for Grades 2, 1, and 0 in a variety of ways to make certain that muscle contractile activity that may be present is not missed.

Grading

Sequence 1: Head raise (Fig. 4.22): Ask the patient to lift the head from the table. If the scapulae do not clear the table, the Grade is 2. If the patient cannot lift the head, proceed to Sequence 2.

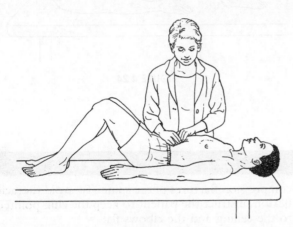

FIGURE 4.21

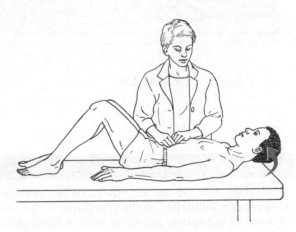

FIGURE 4.22

Sequence 2: Assisted forward lean (Fig. 4.23): The therapist cradles the upper trunk and head off the table and asks the patient to lean forward. If there is depression of the rib cage, the grade is 2. If there is no depression of the rib cage but visible or palpable contraction occurs, the grade assigned should be 1. If there is no activity, the grade is 0; proceed to Sequence 3.

Sequence 3: Cough (Fig. 4.24): Ask the patient to cough. If the patient can cough to any degree and depression of the rib cage occurs, the grade is 2. (If the patient coughs, regardless of its effectiveness, the abdominal muscles are automatically brought into play.) If the patient cannot cough but there is palpable rectus abdominis activity, the grade is 1. Lack of any discernable activity is Grade 0.

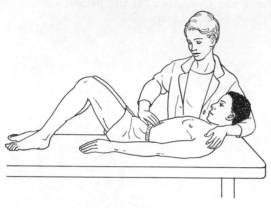

FIGURE 4.23

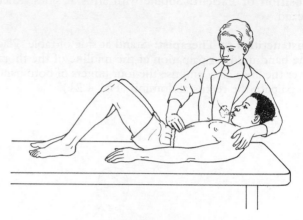

FIGURE 4.24

Helpful Hints

- In all tests, observe any deviations of the umbilicus. If there is a difference in the segments of the rectus abdominis in response to muscle testing, the umbilicus will deviate toward the stronger part (i.e., cranially if the upper parts are stronger, caudally if the lower parts are stronger, and laterally if one or more segments of *one* rectus is paralyzed).
- If the extensor muscles of the lumbar spine are weak, contraction of the abdominal muscles can cause posterior tilt of the pelvis. If this situation exists, tension of the hip flexor muscles would be useful to stabilize the pelvis; therefore the therapist should position the patient in hip and knee flexion.
- The thoracic flexion muscle test should be done absolutely correctly—that is, with the neck in neutral to avoid undue strain on the neck and in the presence of known or suspected osteoporosis. Care should be taken in the presence of osteoporosis because repeated trunk flexion can be related to increased risk of compression fractures of the spine. To avoid thoracic flexion, instruct the patient to keep the chin pointed to the ceiling and the elbows flat.
- To avoid cervical strain, have the patient avoid clasping the head with the hands. The hands should not carry any of the head's weight.
- Abdominal-strengthening exercises are performed with spine flexion and without hip flexion to reduce the role of hip flexors and undue disc compression.[19]
- Leg support during a pelvic tilt and fixed feet during spine and hip flexion exercises may decrease the intensity of rectus abdominis activity. Having the feet on the floor or fixed activates the hip flexors.[19]
- In summary, to ensure the patient's spine safety, remember these important guidelines.[19]
  a. Avoid active hip flexion or fixed feet.
  b. Do not allow the patient to pull the head up with the hands behind the head.

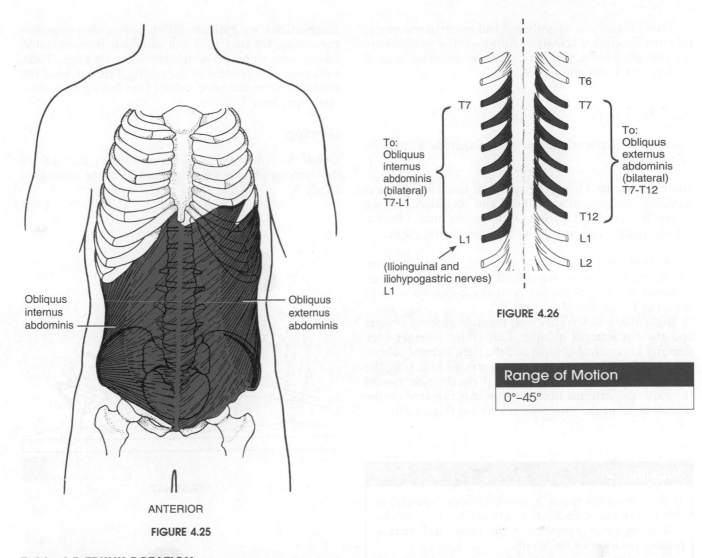

Obliquus internus abdominis

Obliquus externus abdominis

ANTERIOR

FIGURE 4.25

To:
Obliquus internus abdominis (bilateral)
T7–L1

T7

L1

(Ilioinguinal and iliohypogastric nerves)
L1

T6

T7

T12

L1

L2

To:
Obliquus externus abdominis (bilateral)
T7–T12

FIGURE 4.26

Range of Motion
0°–45°

Table 4.5 TRUNK ROTATION

I.D.	Muscle	Origin	Insertion	Function
110	**Obliquus externus abdominis**	Ribs 5–12 (interdigitating on external and inferior surfaces)	Iliac crest (outer border) Aponeurosis from 9th costal cartilage to ASIS; both sides meet at midline to form linea alba Pubic symphysis (upper border)	Flexion of trunk (bilateral muscles) Tilts pelvis posteriorly Elevates pelvis (unilateral) Rotation of trunk to opposite side (unilateral) Lateral bending of trunk (unilateral)
111	**Obliquus internus abdominis**	Iliac crest (anterior ⅔ of intermediate line) Thoracolumbar fascia Inguinal ligament (lateral ⅔ of upper aspect)	Ribs 9–12 (inferior border and cartilages by digitations that appear continuous with internal intercostals) Ribs 7–9 (cartilages) Aponeurosis to linea alba	Flexion of spine (bilateral) Lateral bending of spine (unilateral) Rotation of trunk to same side (unilateral) Elevation of pelvis

Other

Deep back muscles (1 side)

NOTE: Use caution with trunk rotation in patients with known or suspected osteoporosis.

ASIS, Anterior superior iliac spine.

Trunk rotation is a combined and essential movement of most functional activities. Although the obliques are the primary movers, trunk rotation also involves the small oblique extensors and flexors.

Grade 5

Position of Patient: Supine with fingertips to the side of the head.

Instructions to Therapist: Stand at the patient's waist level. Ask the patient to lift head and shoulders, moving elbow to opposite hip. Repeat for other side. Observe for adequate range, quality of movement and effort.

Test: With chin pointed to the ceiling, the patient flexes trunk and rotates to one side. This movement is then repeated on the opposite side so that the muscles on both sides can be examined.

Right elbow to left knee tests the right external oblique and the left internal oblique. Left elbow to right knee tests the left external oblique and the right internal oblique (Fig. 4.27). When the patient rotates to one side, the internal oblique muscle is palpated on the side toward the turn; the external oblique muscle is palpated on the side away from the direction of turning (Fig. 4.28).

Substitution

If the pectoralis major is active (inappropriately) in this test of trunk rotation at any grade, the shoulder will shrug or be raised from the table, and there is limited rotation of the trunk.

Instructions to Patient: "With your chin pointed to the ceiling, lift your head and shoulders from the table, taking your right elbow toward your left knee. Then, with your chin pointed to the ceiling, lift your head and shoulders from the table, taking your left elbow toward your right knee."

Grading

Grade 5: The scapula corresponding to the side of the external oblique function must clear the table for a Grade 5.

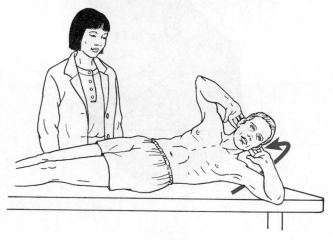

FIGURE 4.27

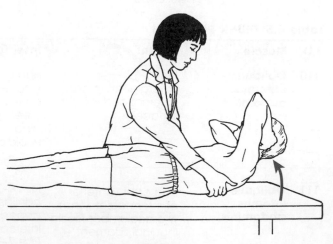

FIGURE 4.28

Grade 4

Position of Patient: Supine with arms crossed over chest.

Test: Other than patient's arm position, all other aspects of the test are the same as for Grade 5. The test is done first to one side (Fig. 4.29) and then to the other.

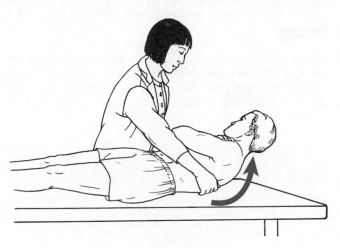

FIGURE 4.29

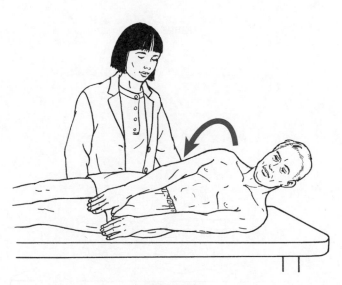

FIGURE 4.30

Grade 3

Position of Patient: Supine with arms outstretched above plane of body.

Test: Other than patient's arm position, all other aspects of the test are the same as for Grade 5. The test is done first to the left (Fig. 4.30) and then to the right (Fig. 4.31).

Grading

Grade 3: Patient raises the scapula off the table. The therapist may use one hand to check for scapular clearance (Fig. 4.32).

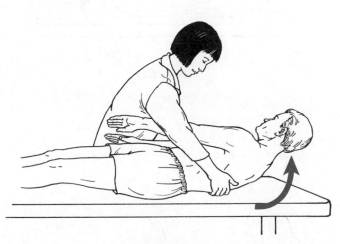

FIGURE 4.31

Grade 2

Position of Patient: Supine with arms outstretched above plane of body.

Instructions to Therapist: Stand at level of patient's waist. Palpate the external oblique first on one side and then on the other, with one hand placed on the lateral part of the anterior abdominal wall distal to the rib cage (see Fig. 4.32). Continue to palpate the muscle distally in the direction of its fibers until reaching the ASIS.

At the same time, palpate the internal oblique muscle on the opposite side of the trunk. The internal oblique muscle lies under the external oblique, and its fibers run in the opposite diagonal direction.

Therapists may remember this palpation procedure better if they think of positioning their two hands as if both hands were to be in the pants pockets or grasping the abdomen in pain. (The external obliques run from out to in; the internal obliques run from in to out.)

Instructions to Patient: "Keep your chin pointed to the ceiling while you lift your head, reach toward your right knee." (Repeat to left side for the opposite muscle.)

Test: Patient attempts to raise body and turn toward the right. Repeat toward left side.

Grading

Grade 2: Patient is unable to clear the inferior angle of the scapula from the table on the side of the external oblique being tested. However, the therapist must be able to observe depression of the rib cage during the test activity.

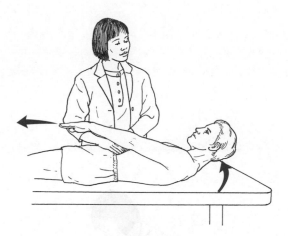

FIGURE 4.32

Grade 1 and Grade 0

Position of Patient: Supine with arms at sides. Hips flexed with feet flat on table.

Instructions to Therapist: Support patient's head as patient attempts to turn to one side (Fig. 4.33). (Turn to the other side in a subsequent test.) Under normal conditions, the abdominal muscles stabilize the trunk when the head is lifted. In patients with abdominal weakness the supported head permits the patient to recruit abdominal muscle activity without having to overcome the entire weight of the head.

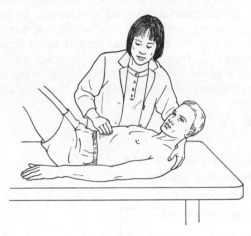

FIGURE 4.33

One hand palpates the internal oblique on the side toward which the patient turns (not illustrated) and the external oblique on the side away from the direction of turning (see Fig. 4.33). The therapist assists the patient to raise the head and shoulders slightly and turn to one side. This procedure is used when abdominal muscle weakness is profound.

Instructions to Patient: "Try to lift up and turn to your right." (Repeat for turn to the left.)

Test: Patient attempts to flex trunk and turn to either side.

Grading

Grade 1: The therapist can see or palpate muscular contraction.

Grade 0: No discernable muscle contraction from the obliquus internus or externus muscles.

Suggested Exercises for Abdominals[20]

- Abdominal slide (prone with hand roller)
- Torso Track®
- Ab roller (oblique)
- Crunch (straight and oblique)

CORE STRENGTH, STABILITY, AND ENDURANCE

Core strength and stability are important components of nearly every gross motor activity and, as such, deserve to be understood from the perspective of testing. Risk for injury is impacted by delays in core muscle activation, decreased muscle recruitment, muscle fatigue, neuromuscular imbalance, impaired proprioception, and delayed reflex responses.[21] The purpose of the core musculature is to provide trunk stability (stiffness) through intra-abdominal pressure and compression of the spinal segments and to allow movement in all directions.[22] Trunk stiffness is necessary to create anticipatory postural adjustments such as adjusting the center of gravity to affect balance and upper and lower extremity joint forces during upright tasks.[23,24] Cocontraction on the anterior and posterior aspect of the trunk increases intra-abdominal pressure and generates greater trunk stiffness.[22]

Core stability is defined as the ability to use muscular strength and endurance to control the spine over the pelvis and leg when performing functional and athletic activities.[25,26] Core stability requires coordination in addition to core strength and endurance.[27] No one muscle contributes more than 30% to the overall stability of the lumbar spine in a variety of loading conditions.[28] Therefore there is no one single most important stabilizing muscle.[29] The core muscles (Fig. 4.34) are composed of a mixture of fast and slow twitch muscle fibers, although slow twitch fibers dominate the lumbar paravertebral muscles.[30] The back extensors have more capillaries than nonpostural muscles, such as triceps brachii. The deep stabilizing muscles are also made up of slow twitch fibers. Endurance testing may be more appropriate than pure strength testing for these core muscles.[30] Although slow twitch muscles may be better suited to endurance-type testing, the combined core muscles are made up of both slow and fast twitch muscles, and thus there is no one endurance test for the core.[31] These muscles respond to changes in posture, external loading, and spinal intersegmental movement. The global superficial muscles, long muscles capable of generating large movements and torque, are made up of fast twitch fibers. Cocontraction of the internal oblique and transversus abdominis increases intra-abdominal

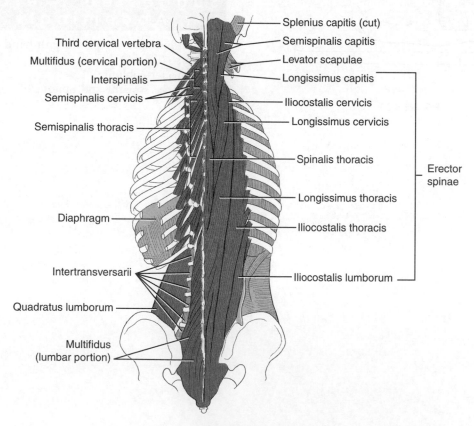

FIGURE 4.34

pressure and stiffness of the spinal segments, resulting in increased spinal stability.[32] It takes only 5% to 10% of maximal abdominal and multifidi contraction to stiffen the spine.

Endurance of the core musculature may be more important to function than pure strength.[33]

Some of the muscles that make up the core are not amenable to individual muscle testing and therefore are tested as *part* of the core. Others form individual and specific functions and can be tested individually (Fig. 4.35). However, when testing the core, all of these muscles are active (Table 4.6).

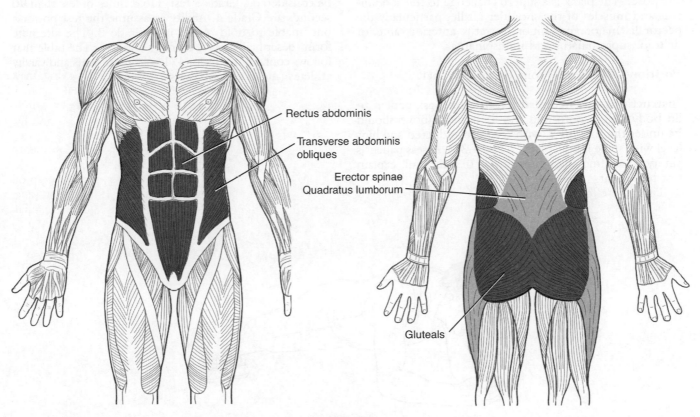

Rectus abdominis
Transverse abdominis
obliques
Erector spinae
Quadratus lumborum
Gluteals

FIGURE 4.35

Table 4.6 MUSCLES COMPRISING THE CORE[22]

Sagittal Plane	Contribution	Frontal Plane	Contribution
Rectus Abdominis	Active in trunk flexion and in combination with the hamstrings; rotates the pelvis posteriorly	Gluteus medius	Primary lateral stabilizer of the hip
Transversus abdominis	With assistance from the multifidus, increase spinal stiffness and raise intra-abdominal pressure	Gluteus minimus	Primary lateral stabilizer of the hip
Erector spinae		Quadratus lumborum	Stiffens the spine and may be active in all upright activities
Multifidus		Adductor magnus	All of the medial muscles maintain static alignment in the frontal plane
Gluteus maximus	Transfers forces from the lower extremity (LE) to the trunk	Adductor longus	
Hamstrings		Adductor brevis	
		Pectineus	

Prone Plank Test

The prone plank test activates core musculature. Correct form consists of maintaining the spine in a neutral position while maintaining scapular adduction and a posterior pelvic tilt.[34] An anterior pelvic tilt reduces EMG activation.[34]

Purpose: The plank is a superb challenge to the abdominals and muscles of the shoulder girdle, particularly the pectoralis major and minor, serratus anterior, anterior deltoid, supraspinatus and infraspinatus.

Position of Patient: Prone on floor or mat.

Instructions to Therapist: From prone, ask patient to lift body weight onto toes and forearms. Elbows should be under the shoulders, with scapulae adducted and hips level with spine like a "plank" (Fig. 4.36). Assess patient's ability to assume a plank position. If successful, explain test to patient.
Time the effort (Table 4.7).

Instructions to Patient: "Raise your yourself onto your forearms and toes. Keep your body completely straight. Suck your belly button into your spine" (see Fig. 4.36).

Scoring

A full plank position should be held for 120 seconds to be considered a Grade 5 test. Hold times of less than 90 seconds are Grade 4. Ability to assume the test position but unable to hold results in a Grade 3. The alternate form (described later) is scored a Grade 2. The table that follows contains norms for 471 college students and varsity athletes (mean age, 20 years):

FIGURE 4.36

Table 4.7 PERCENTILE SCORES BY SEX AND PERCENTILE SCORES BY SPORT STATUS[35]

Percentile	TIME TO FATIGUE IN THE PLANK TEST (SECONDS)			
	Male (*n* = 194)	Female (*n* = 275)	Non-Varsity (*n* = 109)	Varsity (*n* = 361)
90th	201	142	151	200
80th	157	108	123	178
70th	137	95	106	149
60th	122	84	94	123
50th	110	72	83	104
40th	97	63	71	92
30th	89	58	62	82
20th	79	48	53	66
10th	62	35	37	59

Alternate Form of Plank Testing

For a patient not able to do a full plank, ask the patient to flex the knees and hips and lift the body onto forearms and knees. The elbows should be in line below the shoulders. The patient must keep the buttocks in line with the spine, forming a straight line from neck to buttocks while on knees. Time the effort. This alternate form should be scored as a Grade 2. Hint: Make sure the pelvis and buttocks are not hiked but in line with the spine. The body must come forward onto the forearms to do this Grade 2 test properly.

Side Bridge Endurance Test

Purpose: Strength test for core. Quadratus lumborum oblique and transverse muscles are elicited without generating large compression forces on the lumbar spine.[36,37]

Position of Patient: Side-lying with legs extended, resting on the lower forearm with the elbow flexed to 90°. Upper arm is crossed over chest (Fig. 4.37).

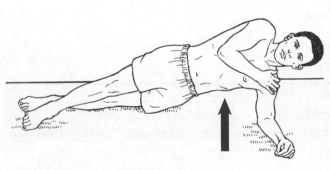

FIGURE 4.37

Instructions to Therapist: Stand or sit in front of patient. Ask patient to lift the hips off the table, keeping the body in a straight line with the contracted core. Time the effort, observing for quality and quantity of effort. Give patient feedback regarding posture; hips and trunk should be level throughout the test (see Fig. 4.37).

Test: Patient lifts hips off the table, holding the elevated position in a straight line with the body on a flexed elbow. This position is maintained until the patient loses form, fatigues, or complains of pain. The therapist times the effort.

Instructions to Patient: "When I say 'go!' lift your hips off the table, keeping them in a straight line with your body for as long as you can. I will be timing you."

Scoring: Record the best time of two trials.
Mean scores for men and women:[38]
Men: 95(±32)s
Women: 75(±32)s

Helpful Hints

- Despite the high reliability of the side bridge test, significant changes in hold times must be observed to confidently assess a true change in strength. Therefore the patient's rating of perceived exertion (RPE) would help to inform clinical decision-making.[33]
- Mean hold times ranged from 20 to 203 seconds (mean, 104.8 seconds) for the right side bridge test and from 19 to 251 seconds (mean, 103.0 seconds) for the left side bridge test.[33]
- Exercisers held the side bridge test nearly double the time nonexercisers did (64.9 vs. 31.8 seconds).[39]

Timed Partial Curl Up Test[40]

The timed partial curl up test is a standard in the fitness industry and is included here, even though it uses the hook lying position and thus encourages hip flexor activation.

Purpose: Strength test for abdominals.

Position of Patient: Supine in hook lying position on a mat with arms at sides, palms facing down, and the middle fingers touching a piece of tape affixed to the surface parallel to the hand. A second piece of tape is affixed 12 cm (4.7 in) further than the initial tape for those younger than 45 years and 8 cm (3.1 in) further for those 45 years and older (Fig. 4.38).

Instructions to Therapist: Stand to the side of patient. Ask patient to perform a slow, controlled sit up in time, lifting head and scapulae off the mat, while the middle finger reaches to the second tape. If successful, use a metronome set to 40 beats/min to time repetitions. Ask patient to curl up as many times as possible keeping time with the metronome. The low back should be flattened before curl up.

Test: The individual does as many curl ups as possible without pausing, to a maximum of 75.

Scoring: Refer to ACSM Norms for partial curl up (Table 4.8).

FIGURE 4.38

Table 4.8 ACSM NORMS For PARTIAL CURL UP

	AGE									
	20–29		30–39		40–49		50–59		60–69	
Sex	Male	Female	Male	Female	Male	Female	Male	F Female	Male	F Female
90th percentile	75	70	75	55	75	55	74	48	53	50
80	56	45	69	43	75	42	60	30	33	30
70	41	37	46	34	67	33	45	23	26	24
60	31	32	36	28	51	28	35	16	19	19
50	27	27	31	21	39	25	27	9	16	13
40	24	21	26	15	31	20	23	2	9	9
30	20	17	19	12	26	14	19	0	6	3
20	13	12	13	0	21	5	13	0	0	0
10	4	5	0	0	13	0	0	0	0	0

ACSM, The American College of Sports Medicine.

Data from Pescatello LS, Ross A, Riebe D, et al. *ACSM's Guidelines for Exercise Testing and Prescription.* 9 ed. Philadelphia: Wolters Kluwer/Lippincott Williams & Wilkins; 2014.

Isometric Trunk Flexor Endurance Test[22]

Purpose: Measure isometric core endurance.

Position of Patient: Sitting on table with wedge supporting the back at angle of 60° to the table. Hips and knees flexed to 90°, with feet stabilized with a strap. Arms are folded across the chest (Fig. 4.39).

Instructions to Therapist: Ask patient to hold test position when the wedge is pulled back 10 cm. Time effort as soon as wedge is pulled back. Terminate test when the patient can no longer maintain the 60° angle independently.

Scoring: Ages 18 to 55 years (mean, 30 years), mean hold time = 178 seconds.[39]
Exercisers held the test 3 times as long as nonexercisers (186 s vs. 68.25 s).[39]

Front Abdominal Power Test

Purpose: Assess the power component of core stability prestability and poststability training.

Position of Patient: Supine on a mat with arms at sides, feet shoulder width apart, and knees bent to 90° (Fig. 4.40A).

Instructions to Therapist: Place a 2-kg medicine ball into the patient's hands. Then ask patient to lift arms overhead and explosively project the medicine ball forward keeping the arms straight. Feet and buttocks should remain on the floor throughout the test. (Note: Feet may be secured manually or with a strap [not shown].) Measure the distance the ball was projected from the tips of the feet to the point where the ball landed. Patient should be sitting upright after the ball is thrown (Fig. 4.40B).

Scoring: 1.5 to 2 m was recorded in a group of 20-year-old men and women (standard error of the mean [SEM], 24 cm).[41,42]

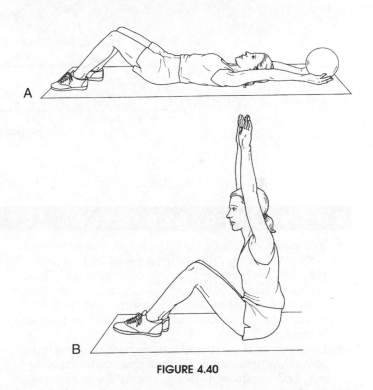

A

B

FIGURE 4.40

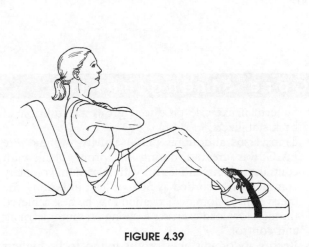

FIGURE 4.39

Unilateral Supine Bridge Test[43]

Purpose: The unilateral supine bridge test (USBT) assesses lumbopelvic neuromuscular control. This test was found to be correlated with lab-based biomechanical measures of isolated core stability.

Position of Patient: Supine with arms across chest with knees in hook lying.

Instructions to Therapist: Stand to side of patient. Ask patient to lift both hips into a double-leg bridge. When neutral spine and pelvis positions are achieved, ask patient to extend one knee so leg is straight and thighs parallel to one another (Fig. 4.41). Ask patient to hold position as long as possible, timing the effort. Test is terminated when patient is no longer able to hold a neutral pelvic position, as noted by a 10° change in transverse or sagittal plane alignment. Perform two trials, and average results.

Scoring: A sample of 20 healthy male volunteers (mean age, 25.7 years) held test position for an average of 23.0 seconds (16.5) with range of 3.1 to 59.5 seconds.[43]

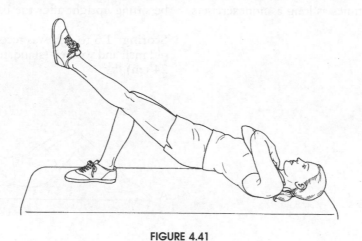

FIGURE 4.41

Suggested Exercises for Core Strengthening

- The side bridge, lateral step up, lunge, and quadruped with arm and leg lift have been found to be effective exercises for increasing overall core strength. These exercises have EMG amplitude greater than 45% maximum voluntary isometric contraction. 45%–50% of one repetition maximum correlates with an increase in strength.[44]
- Longissimus thoracis and lumbar multifidus are most active during bridging, side bridging, unilateral bridging, and quadruped opposite arm/lower extremity lift.[44]
- External oblique and rectus abdominis are most active during prone bridging and side bridging.[44]
- Side bridging was optimal for lower abdominal muscle activation.[44]

- Superman exercise produced greatest activation of back stabilizers.[44]
- Transversus abdominis (TrA) activity by fine wire EMG was greatest during the prone plank with contralateral arm and leg lift with maximum voluntary contractions recorded as 50% or less; indicating the transversus abdominis activation may be best achieved through low-load exercises focusing on motor learning and control.[45]
- Rectus abdominis activity was found to be highest in a curl up exercise on an unstable surface, such as a BOSU ball, with maximum voluntary contraction (MVC) of approximately 50%.[45]

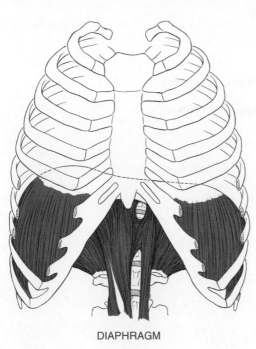

DIAPHRAGM

FIGURE 4.42

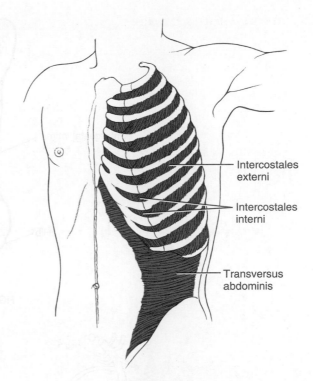

Intercostales externi

Intercostales interni

Transversus abdominis

FIGURE 4.43

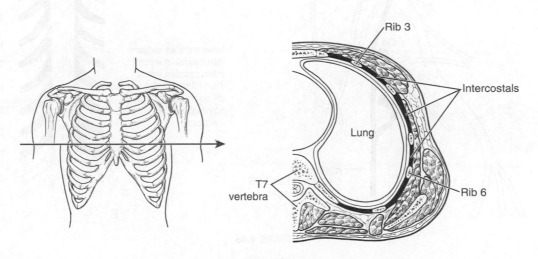

FIGURE 4.44

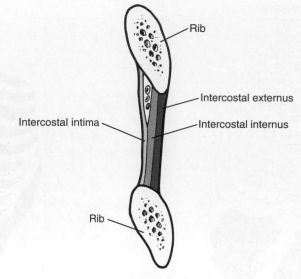

FIGURE 4.45

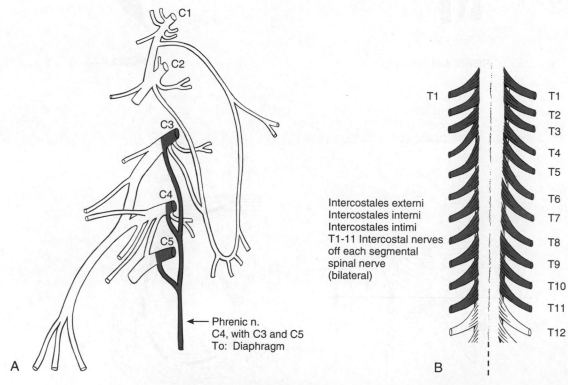

A

Phrenic n.
C4, with C3 and C5
To: Diaphragm

Intercostales externi
Intercostales interni
Intercostales intimi
T1-11 Intercostal nerves
off each segmental
spinal nerve
(bilateral)

B

FIGURE 4.46

Range of Motion

Normal range of motion of the chest wall during quiet inspiration is approximately 0.75 inches, with gender variations. Normal chest expansion in forced inspiration varies from 2.0 to 2.5 inches at the level of the xiphoid.[46]

Table 4.9 MUSCLES OF QUIET INSPIRATION

I.D.	Muscle	Origin	Insertion	Function
101	**Diaphragm**	Formed of 3 parts from the circumference of the thoracic outlet Sternal: Xiphoid Costal: Ribs 7–12 Lumbar: L1-L3 vertebrae	Fibers all converge on central tendon of diaphragm; middle of central tendon is below and partially blended with pericardium	*Inspiration:* Contraction of the diaphragm with the lower ribs fixed draws the central tendon downward and forward during inspiration This increases the vertical thoracic dimensions and pushes the abdominal viscera downward It also decreases the pressure within the thoracic cavity, forcing air into the lungs through the open glottis by the higher pressure of the atmospheric air These events occur along with intercostal muscle action, which elevates the ribs, sternum, and vertebrae, increasing the anteroposterior and transverse thoracic dimensions for the inspiratory effort The diaphragm adds power to expulsive efforts: lifting heavy loads, sneezing, coughing, laughing, parturition, and evacuation of bladder and bowels These activities are preceded by deep inspiration *Expiration:* Passive relaxation allows the half-dome to ascend, thus decreasing thoracic cavity volume and increasing its pressure
102	Intercostales externi (11 pairs)	Ribs 1–11 (lower borders and tubercles; costal cartilages)	Ribs 2–12 (upper margins of rib below; last 2 end in free ends of the costal cartilages) External intercostal membrane	The muscles of respiration are highly coordinated between abdominal and thoracic processes with the diaphragm being the major muscle of inspiration, accounting for about ⅔ of vital capacity The external intercostals are more active in inspiration than expiration but work closely with the internal intercostals to stiffen the chest wall, preventing paradoxical motion during descent of the diaphragm Elevation of ribs in inspiration There are data to support this claim for the upper four or five muscles, but the more dorsal and lateral fibers of the same muscles also are active in early expiration It is possible that the activity of the intercostals during respiration varies with the depth of breathing[47] Depression of the ribs in expiration (supporting data sparse) Rotation of thoracic spine to opposite side (unilateral) Stabilization of rib cage
103	Intercostales interni (11 pairs)	Sternum (anterior) Ribs 1–11 (ridge on inner surface) Costal cartilages of same rib Internal intercostal membrane	Upper border of rib below Fibers run obliquely to the external intercostals	Not as strong as the external intercostals Elevation of ribs in inspiration This may be true at least for the 1st to 5th muscles The more lateral muscle fibers run more obliquely inferior and posterior and are most active in expiration[47] Stabilization of rib cage

Continued

Table 4.9 MUSCLES OF QUIET INSPIRATION—cont'd

I.D.	Muscle	Origin	Insertion	Function
104	Intercostales intimi (innermost intercostals) Often absent	Ribs 1–11 (costal groove)	Rib below (upper margin) Fibers run in same pattern as internal intercostals	Presumed to be identical to intercostales interni
107	Levatores costarum (12 pairs)	C7-T11 vertebrae (transverse processes, tip)	Rib below vertebra of origin (external surface)	Elevation of ribs in inspiration (disputed) Lateral bending of spine
80	Scalenus anterior	C3-C6 vertebrae (transverse processes, anterior tubercles)	1st rib (scalene tubercle)	Flexion of cervical spine (both muscles) Elevation of 1st rib in inspiration Rotation of cervical spine to same side Lateral bending of neck to same side
81	Scalenus medius	C2 (axis)-C7 vertebrae (transverse processes, posterior tubercles) C1 (atlas) sometimes	1st rib (superior surface)	Cervical flexion (weak) Lateral bending of cervical spine to same side Elevation of 1st rib in inspiration Cervical rotation to same side
82	Scalenus posterior	C4-C6 vertebrae (transverse processes posterior tubercle, variable)	2nd rib (outer surface)	Cervical flexion (weak) Elevation of 2nd rib in inspiration Lateral bending of cervical spine to same side (accessory) Cervical spine rotation to same side
Others				
131	Pectoralis major (arms fixed)			

DIAPHRAGM

The diaphragm is under voluntary control via the efferent fibers of the left and right phrenic nerves. This voluntary control can be overridden by reflex activity. Contraction of the diaphragm causes the diaphragm to descend, increasing volume and decreasing pressure within the thoracic cavity. This pressure change creates a pressure gradient that results in movement of air into the airways. As the diaphragm descends, abdominal viscera are compressed and intraabdominal pressure increases. Once the viscera cannot be displaced further, additional contraction of the fibers of the diaphragm causes the lower ribs to move in a cephalad and lateral direction, producing a so-called bucket-handle motion.

Preliminary Examination

Uncover the patient's chest and abdominal area so that the motions of the chest and abdominal walls can be observed. Watch the normal respiration pattern and observe differences in the motion of the chest wall and (epigastric) area and note any contraction of the neck muscles and the abdominal muscles.

The epigastric rise and flaring of the lower margin of the rib cage during inspiration indicate that the diaphragm is active. During quiet inspiration, epigastric rise reflects the movement of the diaphragm descending over one intercostal space.[48,49] In deeper inspiratory efforts, the diaphragm may move across three or more intercostal spaces. The rise on both sides of the linea alba should be symmetric.

An elevation and lateral expansion of the rib cage are indicative of intercostal activity during inspiration. Exertional chest expansion measured at the level of the xiphoid process is 2.0 to 2.5 inches (the expansion may exceed 3.0 inches in more active young people and athletes).[50]

Measurement

Maximum inspiratory pressure (MIP) is the measurement of strength of inspiratory muscles.

Measurements of MIP and maximal expiratory pressure (MEP) may serve as a means of measuring ventilatory muscle strength, although not the strength of any single muscle. The MIP reflects the strength of the diaphragm and other inspiratory muscles, whereas the MEP reflects the strength of the abdominal muscles and other expiratory muscles.

Equipment: Either a manual pressure gauge (Fig. 4.47) or an electronic pressure gauge (Fig. 4.48) is used. Place a new cardboard mouthpiece or a clean rubber mouthpiece with flanges on the device for each patient use.

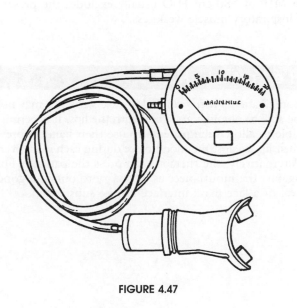

FIGURE 4.47

FIGURE 4.48

Maximal Inspiratory Pressure

Position of Patient: Seated in a chair, with a nose clip applied to the nose (Fig. 4.49).

Instructions to Therapist: Stand or sit in front of seated patient so as to read the gauge (see Fig. 4.49; therapist shown at side of patient to better illustrate procedure).

Test: Demonstrate the maneuver, and then have the patient repeat it. Patient first exhales completely then sucks in as hard as possible. The patient should maintain inspiratory pressure for at least 1.5 seconds; the largest negative pressure sustained for at least 1 second should be recorded. Allow the patient to rest for approximately 1 minute and then repeat the maneuver five times. Provide verbal or visual feedback after each maneuver, but do not allow trunk flexion or extension during the test. The goal is for the variability among measurements to be less than 10 cm H_2O. Measurements should be rounded to the nearest 5 cm H_2O.

FIGURE 4.49

Instructions to Patient: "Seal your lips firmly around the mouthpiece, exhale slowly and completely, and then pull in hard, like you are trying to suck up a thick milkshake."

Maximal Expiratory Pressure

Position of Patient: Seated in a chair, with a nose clip applied to the nose.

Instructions to Therapist: Stand or sit in front of seated patient so as to read the gauge.

Test: Demonstrate the maneuver, and have the patient repeat it. Patient first inhales completely, then blows out as hard as possible. The patient should maintain expiratory pressure for at least 1.5 seconds. The largest positive pressure sustained for at least 1 second should be recorded. Allow the patient to rest for approximately 1 minute and then repeat the maneuver five times. Provide verbal or visual feedback after each maneuver but do not allow trunk flexion or extension during the test. The goal is for the variability among measurements to be less than 10 cm H_2O. Measurements should be rounded to the nearest 5 cm H_2O.

Instructions to Patient: "I want you to inhale completely as you push the mouthpiece firmly against your lips and teeth and then push (or blow) as hard as possible, like you are trying to fill a very stiff balloon."

Grading

An MIP of ≥80 cm H_2O usually excludes the presence of inspiratory muscle weakness.[51]

Helpful Hint

Some patients with orofacial muscle weakness may not be able to obtain a good seal with the lips. It is permissible to allow such patients to use their hand to press their lips against the mouthpiece during each maneuver. Alternatively, the therapist can press the patient's lips against the mouthpiece as necessary to obtain a good seal or a face mask interface can be substituted.

INTERCOSTALS

There is no method of direct assessment of the strength of the intercostal muscles.

The scalene muscles, as assessed via needle EMG examination, are active with every inspiratory effort and should be considered a primary muscle of inspiration.[52]

Diaphragmatic function can also be measured through ultrasound. This is an examination technique that is not typically included in entry-level education. A machine with a microconvex, 2 to 4 MHz probe is used.[53] Two measurements can be used, both of which relate indirectly to the strength of the diaphragm. One is diaphragmatic excursion, measured using an anterior subcostal approach between the anterior axillary and midclavicular lines. A cutoff of less than 25 mm has been suggested as an indicator of severe diaphragmatic dysfunction.[54] The second is the thickening fraction (TF). Inspiratory and expiratory thicknesses are measured where the diaphragm is in contact with the rib cage in the eighth or ninth intercostal space between the mid and anterior axillary lines. The TF is measured as a percentage of the end-expiratory thickness. A TF less than 20% is likely to indicate severe dysfunction.[55]

Suggested Exercise for Inspiratory Training

Weak inspiratory muscles can be strengthened through targeted inspiratory muscle training (IMT). Training principles are similar to those used to increase the strength of any other muscle. Patients either inhale through a mouthpiece with an adjustable diameter opening or using a device with a spring-loaded valve that does not open to allow airflow until a threshold pressure is reached. This type of device, commonly referred to as threshold trainer, has the advantage of producing a load that is independent of the airflow rate generated by the user.[56] A typical training program would be performed for 15 minutes, twice daily, five to seven times per week, at an intensity of 30%-50% of MIP.[57]

Using abdominal weights to produce resistance can be effective.[58]

In this exercise the patient is supine and a predetermined weight is placed on the stomach. The goal is to have the patient elevate the weight with each inspiration.

FORCED EXPIRATION

The cough is an essential procedure to maintain airway patency and to clear the pharynx and bronchial tree when secretions accumulate. A cough may be a reflex or voluntary response to irritation anywhere along the airway downstream from the nose. The three phases of cough—inspiration, compression, and forced expiration—are mediated by the muscles of the thorax and abdomen, as well as those of the pharynx, larynx, and tongue. The deep inspiratory effort is supported by the diaphragm, intercostals, and arytenoid abductor muscles (the posterior cricoarytenoids), permitting inhalation of more than 1.5 L of air.[59] The palatoglossus and styloglossus elevate the tongue and close off the oropharynx from the nasopharynx. The compression phase requires the lateral cricoarytenoid muscles to adduct and close the glottis.

The strong expiratory movement is augmented by strong contractions of the thorax muscles, particularly the latissimus dorsi and the oblique and transverse abdominal muscles. The abdominal muscles raise intra-abdominal pressure, forcing the relaxing diaphragm up and drawing the lower ribs down and medially. Elevation of the diaphragm raises the intrathoracic pressure to approximately 200 mm Hg, and the explosive expulsion phase begins with forced abduction of the glottis.

Coughing often is used as the clinical test for forced expiration. An effective cough requires the use of all muscles of active expiration in contrast to quiet expiration, which is the passive relaxation of the muscles of inspiration. However, it must be recognized that a patient may not have an effective cough because of inadequate laryngeal control or low vital capacity.

Grading

The usual muscle test grades do not apply here; thus the following scale to assess the cough is used:

Functional: Normal or only slight impairment:
- Crisp or explosive expulsion of air
- Volume is sharp and clearly audible
- Able to clear airway of secretions

Weak Functional: Moderate impairment that affects the degree of active motion or endurance:
- Decreased volume and diminished air movement
- Appears labored
- May take several attempts to clear airway

Nonfunctional: Severe impairment:
- No clearance of airway
- No expulsion of air
- Cough attempt may be nothing more than an effort to clear the throat

Zero: Cough is absent.

Helpful Hints

- It is generally accepted that if an individual's forced vital capacity (FVC) is ≥60% of the predicted value, the inspired volume is sufficient to generate a functional, effective cough.[60]
- FVC can be measured with a simple spirometer (Fig. 4.50). A forced expiratory volume ≥60% of the individual's measured FVC should be adequate for sufficiently forceful expulsion.[61]
- A peak cough flow rate of 160 L/min is highly predictive of successful secretion clearance and subsequent extubation and decannulation in patients with neuromuscular disease.[62]

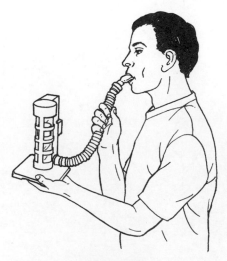

FIGURE 4.50

Table 4.10 MUSCLES OF FORCED EXPIRATION

I.D.	Muscle	Origin	Insertion	Function
110	**Obliquus externus abdominis**	Ribs 5–12 (interdigitating on external and inferior surfaces)	Iliac crest (outer border) Aponeurosis from 9th costal cartilage to ASIS; both sides meet at midline to form linea alba Pubic symphysis (upper border)	Flexion of trunk (bilateral muscles) Tilts pelvis posteriorly Elevates pelvis (unilateral) Rotation of trunk to opposite side (unilateral) Lateral bending of trunk (unilateral) Support and compression of abdominal viscera, counteracting effect of gravity on abdominal contents Assists defecation, micturition, emesis, and parturition (i.e., expulsion of contents of abdominal viscera and air from lungs) Important accessory muscle of forced expiration (during expiration it forces the viscera upward to elevate the diaphragm)
111	**Obliquus internus**	Iliac crest (anterior ⅔ of intermediate line) Thoracolumbar fascia Inguinal ligament (lateral ⅔ of upper aspect)	Ribs 9–12 (inferior border and abdominis cartilages by digitations that appear continuous with internal intercostals) Ribs 7–9 (cartilages) Aponeurosis to linea alba Pubic crest and pecten pubis	
112	Transversus abdominis	Inguinal ligament (lateral ⅓) Iliac crest (anterior ⅔, inner lip) Thoracolumbar fascia Ribs 7–12 (costal cartilages interdigitate with diaphragm)	Linea alba (blends with broad aponeurosis) Pubic crest and pecten pubis (to form falx inguinalis)	Constricts (flattens) abdomen, compressing the abdominal viscera and assisting in expelling their contents Forced expiration
113	Rectus abdominis	Arises via 2 tendons: Lateral: pubic crest (tubercle) and pecten pubis Medial: symphysis pubis (ligamentous covering)	Ribs 5–7 (costal cartilages) Costoxiphoid ligaments	Flexion of spine (draws symphysis and sternum toward each other) Posterior tilt of pelvis With other abdominal muscles, compresses abdominal contents
103	Intercostales interni	Ribs 111 (inner surface) Sternum (anterior) Internal intercostal membrane	Ribs 2–12 (upper border of rib below rib of origin)	Not as strong as the external intercostals Elevation of ribs in inspiration This may be true at least for the 1st to 5th muscles The more lateral muscle fibers run more obliquely inferior and posterior and are most active in expiration[47] Stabilization of rib cage

Continued

Table 4.10 MUSCLES OF FORCED EXPIRATION—cont'd

I.D.	Muscle	Origin	Insertion	Function
130	Latissimus dorsi	T6-T12 and all lumbar and sacral vertebrae (spinous processes via supraspinous ligaments) Iliac crest (posterior) Thoracolumbar fascia Ribs 9–12 (interdigitates with external abdominal oblique)	Humerus (floor of intertubercular sulcus) Deep fascia of arm	Extension, adduction, and internal rotation of shoulder Hyperextension of spine (muscles on both sides), as in lifting The muscle is most powerful in overhead activities (such as swimming (downstroke) and climbing), crutch walking (elevation of trunk to arms, i.e., shoulder depression), or swinging Adducts raised arm against resistance (with pectoralis major and teres major) It is very active in strong expiration, as in coughing and sneezing, and in deep inspiration Elevation of pelvis with arms fixed

Other

106	Transversus thoracis			

ASIS, Anterior superior iliac spine.

The pelvic floor muscles form the "floor" of the pelvis and perform four important functions:

Supportive: by counteracting passive gravitational pull and dynamic intra-abdominal pressures impacting the pelvic viscera in conjunction with the inner core muscles forming the canister of core stabilization.[63]

Sphincteric: by shortening in an anterosuperior direction, these muscles squeeze off the urethra, vagina, and anorectal junction to maintain urinary and fecal continence.[64]

Sexual: by rhythmically contracting during orgasm to enhance sexual satisfaction.

Postural stabilizer: by working with the transversus abdominis, multifidi, and pulmonary diaphragm, the pelvic floor creates the bottom of the inner core "canister" (Fig. 4.51).

Poor pelvic floor strength is associated with pelvic organ prolapse and urinary or fecal incontinence. Ninety-seven percent of women will experience some level of supportive dysfunction in their lifetime, leading to "falling" of the bladder, rectum, uterus, or small intestine.[65] Urinary or fecal incontinence is experienced by as many as 72% of women of all ages.[66] Fecal incontinence is thought to be grossly underreported because of the associated social stigma. However, urinary incontinence is amenable to treatment, with reports of an 84% success rate using the Kegel exercise (controlled voluntary contractions used to strengthen the pelvic floor).[67]

Sexual dysfunction may be related to weak pelvic floor musculature and urinary incontinence.[68,69] Thirty-one percent of men and 43% of women between the ages of 18 and 59 years report concerns during physical intimacy, some of which are related to urinary incontinence and a weak pelvic floor.[70] Up to 80% of aging women have similar concerns.[71]

The pelvic floor muscles can become weakened from childbirth,[72] poor patterns of muscle recruitment, medical comorbidities such as diabetes, abdominopelvic surgical procedures, constipation, abdominal obesity, chronic cough, hormonal changes, and loss of muscle mass with aging. Because of the frequency of pelvic floor weakness, pelvic floor muscle strength should be routinely assessed to rule out muscle weakness, spasm, or dyscoordination in the presence of lumbopelvic, urologic, gynecologic, sexual, or gastrointestinal dysfunction.

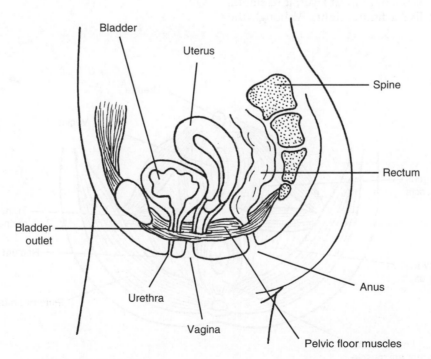

FIGURE 4.51 Pelvic floor muscles serve as a sling for the female organs.

Methods used to assess the strength and function of the pelvic floor muscles include the following:

- Presence of pelvic floor muscle activation: clinical observation, external perineal palpation, vaginal or rectal digital palpation, EMG, and pressure gauges.
- Quantification of pelvic floor muscle strength: manual muscle testing with rectal or vaginal palpation, vaginal cones,[73] and vaginal squeeze pressure.[74]
- Additional visualization of the pelvic floor musculature may be done with abdominal or pelvic two-dimensional ultrasound,[75] ultrasound, and magnetic resonance imaging.[76]

Anatomy of the Pelvic Floor

Muscles of the pelvic floor are difficult to visualize, particularly because most students do not have the opportunity to dissect this region in anatomy class. In both males and females, there are five muscles of the urogenital region that differ in size and disposition in relation to the male and female external genitalia. These five muscles are grouped into superficial and deep layers. Superficial muscles include three portions of the levator ani (puborectalis, pubococcygeus, iliococcygeus) and the ischiococcygeus. Connective tissue and the deep transverse perinei comprise the deep layer (Fig. 4.52).

The superficial layer is the outermost layer; it resembles a sling and is shaped like a figure eight. Although the superficial layer is relatively thin in terms of mass, it is highly sensitive. This area is responsible for controlling the anal and urethral sphincters, so these muscles play an important role in continence. To work effectively, the sphincters need the support of the rest of the pelvic floor, particularly the connective tissue elements. In addition, because the abdominals share the same connective tissue attachments as the pelvic floor musculature, in many women they too need to be strengthened, along with the pelvic floor musculature.

The deep layer of the pelvic floor is the real workhorse of the pelvic floor. The deep pelvic floor muscles have the highest resting muscle tone in the body and play a vital role in movement, posture, and breathing. These muscles must continuously support the weight of the pelvic and abdominal organs when the person is upright (see Fig. 4.51). The deep pelvic floor is sometimes called the pelvic diaphragm. Like its companion, "the roof" or the pulmonary diaphragm, it has minimal sensory innervation and its movement is not felt directly. When it works well, the pelvic floor functions like a well-balanced trampoline and has amazing tensile strength and elasticity. It plays a crucial role in ensuring spinal stability and free locomotion. Deep abdominal muscles in front, the multifidi around the spine, and the pulmonary diaphragm all must work together synergistically with the pelvic diaphragm. Thus "there is no core without the floor" (Table 4.11).

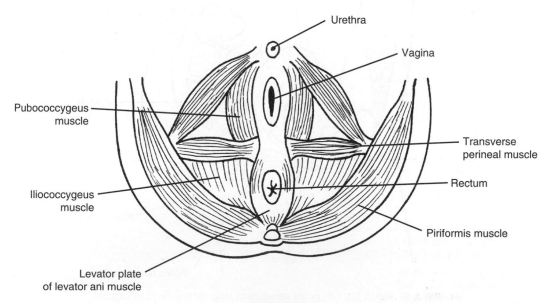

FIGURE 4.52

PELVIC FLOOR

Table 4.11 MUSCLES OF THE PELVIC FLOOR (PERINEUM)

I.D.	Muscle	Origin	Insertion
120	Bulbocavernosus	Surrounds the orifice of the vagina	Blends with sphincter ani externus
121	Ischiococcygeus	Inner surface of the ischial tuberosity	Tendinous aponeurosis attached to the sides and under surface of the crus clitoridis
118	Transversus perinei superficialis (indistinct, often missing)	Medial/anterior ischial tuberosity	Perineal body
119	Transversus perinei profundus	Inner surface ramus of the ischium	Blends into perineal body and vaginal wall
122	Sphincter urethrae	Superior: encircle lower end of the urethra Inferior: transverse perineal ligament	Interlace with fibers from the opposite side
Others			
115	Puborectalis		
115	Levator ani: Puborectalis Iliococcygeus Pubococcygeus		

Testing the Muscles of the Pelvic Floor

Test Description and Procedure

In a separate treatment room the therapist should explain the pelvic exam in total detail. It is not uncommon for therapists to have patients sign a consent form prior to beginning the exam. The patient should be advised that she can stop the exam at any time for any reason. After the patient thoroughly understands the exam, the therapist instructs her to disrobe from the waist down, cover herself with a sheet provided by the therapist, and lie supine on a plinth. The therapist leaves the room while the patient is preparing for the test. After the therapist returns, the patient is asked to roll her legs into external rotation and abduction (hook lying). After the patient is relaxed, the therapist dons sterile gloves that contain no allergens or other potentially irritating material to the patient. The therapist may apply a nonallergenic lubricant to the gloves for patient comfort. While standing slightly to the side of the patient, the therapist moves the sheet drape aside to locate needed landmarks, replaces the drape, and then slowly inserts the middle finger, index and middle finger, or middle and ring finger, into the vagina. If a patient has complaints of pelvic pain, usually only one finger is used. Once fingers are in place, the patient is asked to "pull my fingers up and in" a total of three to four times. Contractions are maintained for 1 to 2 seconds (Fig. 4.53).

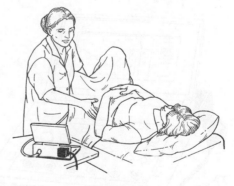

FIGURE 4.53

Grading

There are several grading scales, but the scale used most commonly is the Modified Oxford Scale.[77] The Modified Oxford Scale is a 6-point scale in which half numbers of + and − can be added when a contraction is considered to fall between two full grades, so that the scale expands to a 15-point scale (when both + and − are used):
0 = No contraction detected
1 = Flicker
2 = Weak (the patient contracts the pelvic floor muscles well enough to partially encircle the therapist's fingers)

3 = Moderate (the patient fully encircles the therapist's fingers)

4 = Good (the patient fully encircles the therapist's fingers and partially pull the fingers further into the vaginal cavity)

5 = Strong (the patient fully encircles the therapist's fingers with a *strong* contraction *and* pull the fingers fully up and into the vaginal canal)

The Modified Oxford Scale has fair reliability among experienced therapists.[78] Test accuracy may be enhanced with visual examination during the actual manual muscle test. Visual observation can confirm perineal tightening and whether the fingers are drawn up and in, but most therapists do not observe the movement for various reasons.

PERINEOMETER

The perineometer was developed to specifically determine the amount of contractile force a woman can generate with the pelvic floor musculature (Fig. 4.54). The portion of the perineometer that is inserted into the vagina is typically approximately 28 mm in diameter with an active measurement length of approximately 55 mm. Different types of perineometers are available, and each works on the same principle as a blood pressure monitor.

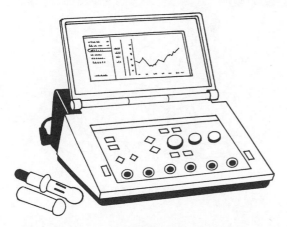

FIGURE 4.54

Perineometer Test

Purpose: Many women experience incontinence and/or sexual dysfunction, both of which may be a consequence of pelvic floor weakness. The perineometer is a device that was specifically developed to determine the amount of contractile force a woman can generate with the pelvic floor musculature (see Fig. 4.54). Many types of perineometer devices are available and each works on the same principle as a blood pressure monitor.

Position of Patient: Supine on a plinth with the knees flexed and the hips in some abduction.

Test Procedure: The perineometer is first covered with a sterile sheath and then inserted into the vagina. A sterile hypoallergenic gel may be used on the sheath. The patient is then asked to perform a Kegel exercise, exerting as much force against the probe as possible (squeezing it). The therapist must make sure the patient is *not* holding her breath while performing the pelvic contraction. The patient performs three contractions with a 10-second rest between each contraction; the therapist records the highest force output or the average of the three. One advantage of the perineometer over manual muscle testing (MMT) is that duration of contraction hold can be determined. The reliability of the perineometer is comparable to that of MMT. Interrater and intrarater reliability have been established.[79]

Instructions to Therapist: Cover the perineometer with a sterile sheath. A sterile hypoallergenic gel may be used on the sheath. Drape the patient. Explain procedure to patient. With patient supine and hips and knees flexed, insert perineometer into the vagina. After the probe is in place, patient is asked to perform a Kegel exercise, exerting as much force against the probe as possible (squeezing it). Patient should not hold breath during contraction. The patient performs three contractions with a 10-second rest between each contraction.

Instructions to Patient: "Squeeze as hard as you can against the probe, and hold it. Rest, now repeat."

Scoring
Record the highest force output or the average of the three contractions.

Helpful Hints

One advantage of the perineometer over a manual muscle test is that the duration of the contraction hold can be objectively determined. The reliability of the perineometer is comparable to that of manual muscle testing. Interrater and intrarater reliability have been established.[48]

The Kegel (pronounced KAY-gull) exercise is named after Dr. Arnold Kegel, who designed the exercise to strengthen the pelvic floor muscles, especially the pubococcygeal muscles. The exercise consists of tightening the pelvic floor muscles to stop a stream of urine. Strengthening the pelvic floor muscles increases vaginal tone, thus improving sexual response and limiting involuntary urine secondary to stress incontinence. Kegel exercises are often prescribed following childbirth or during or after menopause.

Risk Management Considerations

Vaginal, rectal, and instrumented testing of the pelvic floor is typically taught at the post-entry level. Given the sensitivity of this examination, there should be a compelling reason to perform it based on the patient's subjective complaint or previous test findings. An appropriate level of patient education to ensure informed consent should also be provided. Before engaging in this new area of practice, therapists should review their state's practice laws to ensure that pelvic floor examination is included within the physical therapist's scope of practice. In addition, each therapist must be able to demonstrate competence through evidence of training specific to pelvic floor rehabilitation, including internal assessment and treatment, before entering this new area of practice.

REFERENCES

1. Balzini L, Vannucchi L, Benvenuti F, et al. Clinical characteristics of flexed posture in elderly women. *J Am Geriatr Soc.* 2003;51(10):1419–1426.
2. Shirazi-Adl A, Sadouk S, Parnianpour M, et al. Muscle force evaluation and the role of posture in human lumbar spine under compression. *Eur Spine J.* 2002;11(6):519–526.
3. Panjabi MM. The stabilizing system of the spine. Part I. Function, dysfunction, adaptation, and enhancement. *J Spinal Disord.* 1992;5:383–389, discussion 397.
4. Panjabi MM. The stabilizing system of the spine. Part II. Neutral zone and instability hypothesis. *J Spinal Disord.* 1992;5:390–396, discussion 397.
5. Okubo Y, Kaneoka K, Imai A, et al. Electromyographic analysis of transversus abdominis and lumbar multifidus using wire electrodes during lumbar stabilization exercises. *J Orthop Sports Phys Ther.* 2010;40(11):743–750.
6. Bergmark A. Stability of the lumbar spine. A study in mechanical engineering. *Acta Orthop Scand Suppl.* 1989;230: 1–54.
7. Biering-Sørensen F. Physical measurements as risk indicators for low-back trouble over a one-year period. *Spine.* 1984;9:106–119.
8. Demoulin C, Vanderthommen M, Duysens C, et al. Spinal muscle evaluation using the Sørensen test: a critical appraisal of the literature. *Joint Bone Spine.* 2006;73(1):43–50.
9. Moreau CE, Green BN, Johnson CD, et al. Isometric back extension endurance tests: a review of the literature. *J Manip Physiol Ther.* 2001;24:110–122.
10. Singh DKA, Bailey M, Lee R. Decline in lumbar extensor muscle strength in older adults: correlation wht age, gender, and spine morphology. *BMC Muscuolskelet Disor.* 2013; 14(1):215.
11. Sinaki M, Nwaogwugwu NC, Phillipls BE, et al. Effect of gender, age, and anthropometry on axial and appendicular muscle strength. *Am J Phys Med Rehabi.* 2001;80(5):330–338.
12. Adedoyin RA, Mbada CE, Farotimi AO, et al. Endurance of low back musculature: normative data for adults. *J Back Musculoskelet Rehabil.* 2011;24:101–109.
13. Luoto S, Heliovaara M, Hurri H, et al. Static back endurance and the risk of low-back pain. *Clin Biomech (Bristol, Avon).* 1995;10:323–324.
14. Arab AM, Salavati M, Ebrahimi I, et al. Sensitivity, specificity and predictive value of the clinical trunk muscle endurance tests in low back pain. *Clin Rehabil.* 2007;21(7):640–647.
15. Alaranta H, Hurri H, Heliovaara M, et al. Non-dynamometric trunk performance tests: reliability and normative data. *Scand J Rehabil Med.* 1994;26:211–215.
16. Steele J, Bruce-Low S, Smith D. A review of the specificity of exercises designed for conditioning the lumbar extensors. *Br J Sports Med.* 2015;49:291–297.
17. Kendall FP, McCreary EK, Provance PG. *Muscles, Testing and Function: With Posture and Pain.* Baltimore, Md: Williams & Wilkins; 1993.
18. Ng JFK, Richardson C, Jull GA. Electromyographic amplitude and frequency changes in the iliocostalis lumborum and multifidus muscles during a trunk holding test. *Phys Ther.* 1997;77:954–961.
19. Monfort-Pañego M, Vera-García FJ, Sánchez-Zuriaga D, et al. Electromyographic studies in abdominal exercises: a literature synthesis. *J Manipulative Physiol Ther.* 2009;32(3): 232–244.
20. Escamilla RF, McTaggart MSC, Fricklas EJ, et al. An electromyographic analysis of commercial and common abdominal exercises: Implications for rehabilitation and training. *J Orthop Sports Phys Ther.* 2006;36(2):45–57.
21. Cholewicki J, Silfies SP, Shah RA, et al. Delayed trunk muscle reflex responses increase the risk of low back injuries. *Spine.* 2005;30(23):2614–2620.
22. Willson JD, Dougherty CP, Ireland ML, et al. Core stability and its relationship to lower extremity function and injury. *J Am Acad Orthop Surg.* 2005;13(5):316–325.
23. Brown SH, Haumann ML, Potvin JR. The responses of leg and trunk muscles to sudden unloading of the hands: implications for balance and spine stability. *Clin Biomech (Bristol, Avon).* 2003;18(9):812–820.
24. Hodges PW, Cresswell AG, Daggfeldt K, et al. Three dimensional preparatory trunk motion precedes asymmetrical upper limb movement. *Gait Posture.* 2000;11(2):92–101.
25. Bliss LS, Teeple P. Core stability: the centerpiece of any training program. *Curr Sports Med Rep.* 2005;4:179e83.
26. Kibler WB, Press J, Sciascia A. The role of core stability in athletic function. *Sports Med.* 2006;36(3):189–198.
27. Liemohn WP, Baumgartner TA, Gagnon LH. Measuring core stability. *J Strength Cond Res.* 2005;19(3):583–586.
28. Cholewicki J, VanVliet JJ 4th. Relative contribution of trunk muscles to the stability of the lumbar spine during isometric exertions. *Clin Biomech (Bristol, Avon).* 2002;17(2):99–105.
29. McGill SM, Grenier S, Kavcic N, et al. Coordination of muscle activity to assure stability of the lumbar spine. *J Electromyogr Kinesiol.* 2003;13(4):353–359.
30. Jørgensen K. Human trunk extensor muscles physiology and ergonomics. *Acta Physiol Scand Suppl.* 1997;637:1–58.
31. Akuhota V, Ferreiro A, Moore T, et al. Core stability exercise principles. *Curr Sports Med Rep.* 2008;7(1):39–40-44.
32. Stokes IAF, Gardner-Morse MG, Henry SM. Abdominal muscle activation increases lumbar spinal stability: analysis of contributions of different muscle groups. *Clin Biomech (Bristol, Avon).* 2011;26:797–798-803.
33. Evans K, Refshauge K, Adams R. Trunk muscle endurance tests: reliability, and gender differences in athletes. *J Sci Med Sport / Sports Med Aus.* 2007;10(6):447–455.
34. Cortell-Tormo JM, García-Jaén M, Chulvi-Medrano I, et al. Influence of scapular position on the core musculature activation in the prone plank exercise. *J Strength Cond Res.* 2017;31(8):2255–2262.
35. Strand SL, Hjelm J, Schoepe TC, et al. Norms for an isometric muscle endurance test. *J Hum Kinet.* 2014; 40:93–102.
36. Kavcic N, Grenier S, McGill SM. Determining the stabilizing role of individual torso muscles during rehabilitation exercises. *Spine.* 2004;29:1254–1265.
37. Juker D, McGill S, Kropf P, et al. Quantitative intramuscular myoelectric activity of lumbar portions of psoas and the abdominal wall during a wide variety of tasks. *Med Sci Sports Exerc.* 1998;30:301–310.
38. McGill SM, Childs A, Liebenson C. Endurance times for low back stabilization exercises: clinical targets for testing and training from a normal database. *Arch Phys Med Rehabil.* 1999;80(8):941–944.
39. Anderson D, Barthelemy L, Gmach R, et al. Core strength testing: developing normative data for three clinical tests. Doctor of Physical Therapy Research Papers. 2013;http://sophia.stkate.edu/dpt_papers/21.
40. Haff GG, Triplett NT, eds. *Essentials of Strength Training and Conditioning.* 4th ed. Champaign IL: Human Kinetics; 2016.
41. Cowley P, Swensen T. Development and reliability of two core stability field tests. *JSCR.* 2008;22(2):619–624.
42. Cowley P, Fitzgerald S, Sottung K, et al. Age, weight, and the front abdominal power test as predictors of isokinetic

trunk strength and work in young men and women. *JSCR.* 2009;23(3):915–925.

43. Butowicz CM, Ebaugh DD, Noehren B, et al. Validation of two clinical measures of core stability. *Int J Sports Phys Ther.* 2016;11(1):15–23.

44. Ekstrom RA, Donatelli RA, Carp KC. Electromyographic analysis of core trunk, hip, and thigh muscles during 9 rehabilitation exercises. *J Orthop Sports Phys Ther.* 2007; 37(12):754–755, 762.

45. Imai A, Kaneoka K, Okubo Y, et al. Trunk muscle activity during lumbar stabilization exercises on both a stable and unstable surface. *J Orthop Sports Phys Ther.* 2010;40(6): 369–375.

46. Carlson B. Normal chest excursion. *Phys Ther.* 1973;53:10–14.

47. Leech JA, Ghezzo H, Stevens D, et al. Respiratory pressures and function in young adults. *Am Rev Respir Dis.* 1983;128:17.

48. Wade OL. Movements of the thoracic cage and diaphragm in respiration. *J Physiol (Lond).* 1954;124:193–212.

49. Stone DJ, Keltz H. Effect of respiratory muscle dysfunction on pulmonary function. *Am Rev Respir Dis.* 1964;88:621–629.

50. Reid WD, Dechman G. Considerations when testing and training the respiratory muscles. *Phys Ther.* 1995;75:971–982.

51. American Thoracic Society/European Respiratory Society. ATS/ERS statement on respiratory muscle testing. *Am J Respir Crit Care Med.* 2002;166(4):518–624.

52. DeTroyer A, Estenne M. Coordination between rib cage muscles and diaphragm during quiet breathing in humans. *J Appl Physiol.* 1984;57:899–906.

53. Le Niendre A, Mongodi S, Philippart F. Bouhemad B. Thoracic ultrasound: potential new tool for physiotherapists in respiratory management. A narrative review. *J Crit Care.* 2016;31:101–109.

54. Lerolle N, Guérot E, Dimassi S, et al. Ultrasonographic diagnostic criterion for severe diaphragmatic dysfunction after cardiac surgery. *Chest.* 2009;135:401–407.

55. Summerhill EM, El-Sameed YA, Glidden TJ, et al. Monitoring recovery from diaphragmatic paralysis with ultrasound. *Chest.* 2008;133:737–743.

56. Gosselink R, Wagenaar RC, Decramer M. The reliability of a commercially available threshold loading device in healthy subjects and in patients with chronic obstructive pulmonary disease. *Thorax.* 1996;51:601–605.

57. Gosselink R, Dal Corso S. Respiratory muscle training. In: Frownfelter D, Dean E, eds. *Cardiovascular and Pulmonary Physical Therapy: Evidence to Practice.* 5th ed. St. Louis, MO: Mosby Elsevier; 2012:419–430.

58. Derrickson J, Ciesla N, Simpson N, et al. A comparison of two breathing exercise programs for patients with quadriplegia. *Phys Ther.* 1992;72:763–769.

59. Starr JA. Manual techniques of chest physical therapy and airway clearance techniques. In: Zadai CC, ed. *Pulmonary Management in Physical Therapy.* New York: Churchill-Livingstone; 1992:142–148.

60. Konrad D. Hillegrass E, ed. *Essentials of Cardiopulmonary Physical Therapy.* 4th ed. St. Louis, MO: Elsevier; 2017.

61. Evans JA, Whitelaw WA. The assessment of maximal respiratory mouth pressures in adults. *Respir Care.* 2009;54:1348.

62. Bach JR, Saporito LR. Criteria for extubation and tracheostomy tube removal for patients with ventilatory failure: a different approach to weaning. *Chest.* 1996;110:1566–1571.

63. Neumann P, Grimmer-Somers KA, Gill V, et al. Rater reliability of pelvic floor muscle strength. *Aust N Z Continence J.* 2007;13:9–14.

64. Retzky SS, Rogers RM. Urinary incontinence in women. *Ciba Clin Symp.* 1995;47(3):2–32.

65. Swift SE. The distribution of pelvic organ support in a population of female subjects seen for routine gynecologic health care. *Am J Obstet Gynecol.* 2000;183:277–285.

66. Hunskaar S, Burgio K, Diokno A, et al. Epidemiology and natural history of urinary incontinence (UI). In: Abrams P, Cardozo L, Khoury S, et al, eds. *Incontinence.* Plymouth, UK: Plymbridge Distributors Ltd; 2002:165–201.

67. Kegel AH. Progressive resistance exercise in the functional restoration of the perineal muscles. *Am J Obstet Gynecol.* 1948;56:238–249.

68. Lewis RW, Fugl-Meyer KS, Corona G, et al. Definitions/epidemiology/risk factors for sexual dysfunction. *J Sex Med.* 2010;7(4 Pt 2):1598–1607.

69. Knoepp LR, Shippey SH, Chen CC, et al. Sexual complaints, pelvic floor symptoms, and sexual distress in women over forty. *J Sex Med.* 2010;7:3675–3682.

70. Laumann EO, Paik A, Rosen RC. Sexual dysfunction in the United States: prevalence and predictors. *JAMA.* 1999;281:537-544. *Erratum in JAMA.* 1999;281(13):1174.

71. Dennerstein L, Randolph J, Taffe J, et al. Hormones, mood, sexuality, and the menopausal transition. *Fertil Steril.* 2002;77(suppl 4):S42–S48.

72. Dietz HP, Schierlitz L. Pelvic floor trauma in childbirth—myth or reality? *Aust N Z J Obstet Gynaecol.* 2005;45:3–11.

73. Plevnik S. A new method for testing and strengthening of pelvic floor muscles [abstract]. In: *Proceeding of the 15th Annual Meeting of the International Continence Society.* London, UK; September 1985.

74. Bø K, Sherburn M. Evaluation of female pelvic-floor muscle function and strength. *Phys Ther.* 2005;85:269–282.

75. Dietz H, Jarvis S, Vancaillie T. The assessment of levator muscle strength: a validation of three ultrasound techniques. *Int Urogynecol J Pelvic Floor Dysfunct.* 2002;13:156–159.

76. Bø K, Lilleås F, Talseth T, et al. Dynamic MRI of pelvic floor muscles in an upright sitting position. *Neurourol Urodyn.* 2001;20:167–174.

77. Laycock J. Clinical evaluation of the pelvic floor. In: Schussler B, Laycock J, Norton P, et al, eds. *Pelvic Floor Re-education.* London, UK: Springer-Verlag; 1994:42–48.

78. Ferreira CH, Barbosa PB, de Oliveira Souza F, et al. Inter-rater reliability study of the modified Oxford Grading Scale and the Peritron manometer. *Physiotherapy.* 2011;97(2): 132–138.

79. Hundley AF, Wu JM, Visco AG. A comparison of perineometer to brink score for assessment of pelvic floor muscle strength. *Am J Obstet Gynecol.* 2005;192:1583–1591.

REFERENCES

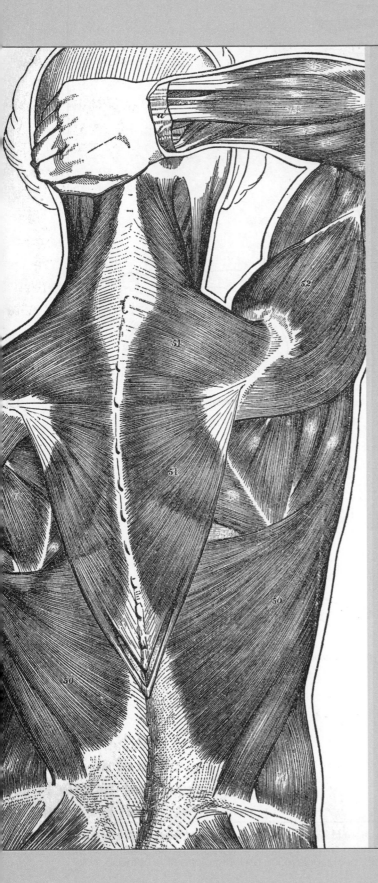

 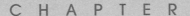
Testing the Muscles of the Upper Extremity

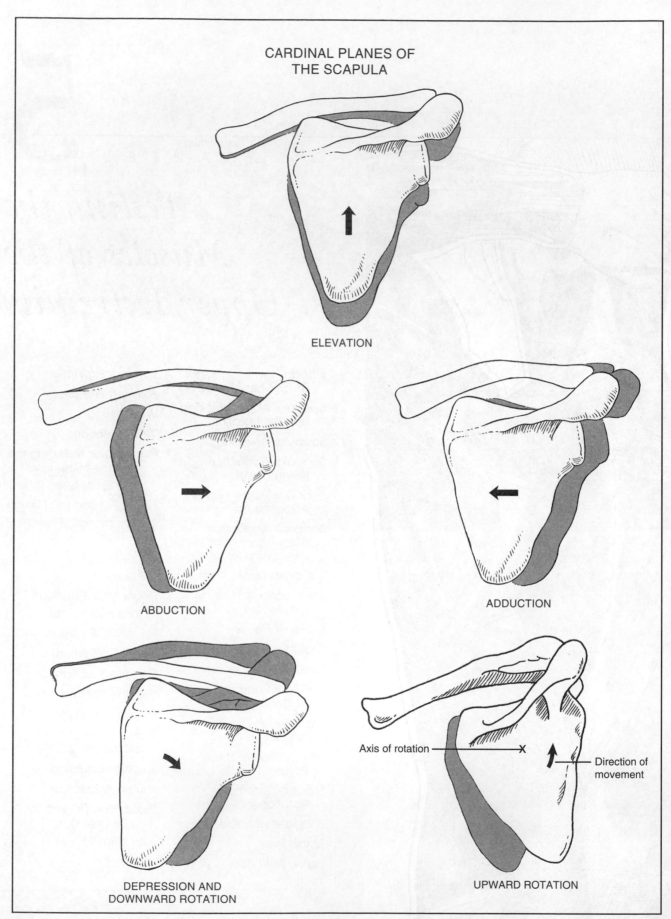

CARDINAL PLANES OF
THE SCAPULA

ELEVATION

ABDUCTION

ADDUCTION

DEPRESSION AND
DOWNWARD ROTATION

UPWARD ROTATION

Axis of rotation — X

Direction of
movement

PLATE 2 Elevation (as in shrugging the shoulders). Abduction (protraction) forward movement occurring in pushing, thrusting, or reaching. Adduction (retraction) (as in bracing the shoulders). Depression and downward rotation (medial rotation)—returning scapula to rest position. Upward rotation (lateral rotation) occurs with shoulder elevation and with protraction of the scapula

The shoulder girdle is a complex system comprised of five distinct joints and at least 16 muscles, many of which have multiple parts and actions. The purpose of scapulohumeral motion is the appropriate positioning of the glenohumeral (G-H) joint in space, while the purpose of scapular stability is to provide a foundation for G-H motion.[1]

The chief muscles that act upon the G-H joint are the deltoid (three parts), the pectorales (two parts), the latissimus dorsi, teres major, and the four rotator cuff muscles (subscapularis, supraspinatus, infraspinatus and teres minor).[2] The primary muscles acting upon the scapula to properly position the humerus are the serratus anterior and upper and lower trapezius.[3]

Shoulder elevation is the preferred term used in this text. Shoulder elevation is any combination of humeral abduction and flexion occurring at the glenohumeral joint. The most efficient shoulder elevators are the anterior and middle deltoid and the supraspinatus (initially).[1] Shoulder elevation is not to be confused with shoulder girdle elevation, the motion of shrugging the shoulders.

Preliminary Examination

Observation of posture in sitting and standing is important prior to strength testing, noting the natural variability between sides and between individuals. First examine the sitting patient (with hands in the lap) from the back (posterior view), noting the position of the scapulae at rest, any asymmetry of shoulder height, muscular bulk, position of the G-H joint, and any scapular winging (Figs. 5.1 and 5.2). Some scapular asymmetry is common and has many causes. Handedness, habitual stretch weakness (e.g., rounded shoulders that can accompany the forward head posture (see Fig. 3.14), and carrying purses or briefcases habitually on one side can all contribute to normal scapular asymmetry.

Position and Symmetry of Scapulae: The normal scapula lies close to the rib cage with the vertebral border nearly parallel to and from 1 to 3 inches lateral to the spinous processes. The inferior angle is on the chest wall.

The most prominent abnormal posture of the scapula is "winging," in which the vertebral border tilts away from the rib cage, a sign of probable serratus anterior weakness (see Fig. 5.2).

Scapulohumeral Rhythm: Next, observe scapulohumeral rhythm. Scapulohumeral rhythm consists of integrated movements of the G-H, scapulothoracic, acromioclavicular, and sternoclavicular joints that occur simultaneously. It occurs in sequential fashion to allow full functional motion of the shoulder complex. Although there is normal variability in scapulohumeral rhythm, the overall ratio of G-H to scapulothoracic motion is approximately 2:1 to complete 180° of shoulder elevation, but varies throughout the range.[3,4] Thus, for 180° of shoulder elevation, approximately 120° comes from the G-H joint and the other 60° from upward rotation of the scapula.

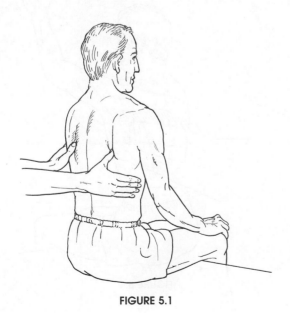

FIGURE 5.1

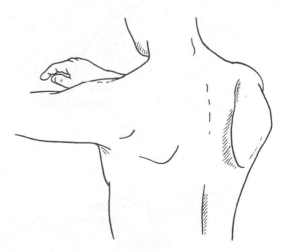

FIGURE 5.2

Preliminary Examination Continued

Scapular Range of Motion: Total scapular motion increases over the arc of shoulder elevation. G-H and scapular movements occur not as separate motions, but as synchronous motions throughout the range. Specifically:

a. The scapula sits against the thorax (T) during the first phase of shoulder abduction and flexion to provide initial stability as the humerus (H) abducts and flexes to 30°. During this first 30°, the scapula's contribution to G-H movement is minimal.

b. From 30° to 90° of elevation, the G-H joint contributes another 30° of motion, as the scapula upwardly rotates 30°. During this range, the scapulohumeral rhythm is typically greater than 2 : 1.[4] The upward rotation is accompanied by clavicular elevation through the sternoclavicular and acromioclavicular joints (Fig. 5.3).

c. The second phase (90° to 120°) is made up of 60° of G-H abduction and flexion and an additional 30° of scapular upward rotation. During this portion of the range, scapulohumeral rhythm declines to approximately 1 : 1.[4] Scapular rotation is associated with 5° of elevation at the sternoclavicular joint and 25° of rotation at the acromioclavicular joint (see Fig. 5.3).

d. After 120° of shoulder elevation, the scapula rotates approximately 1° for every 1° of shoulder elevation until maximal shoulder elevation is achieved for a total of approximately 35–55° of scapular upward rotation.[5]

Observe that the scapula basically remains in its rest position at ranges of less than 30° of shoulder elevation (the position is variable among subjects). To feel upward rotation, palpate the vertebral borders of both scapulae with the thumbs, placing the web of the thumb below the inferior angle and the extended fingers around the axillary borders (see Fig. 5.1), and ask the patient to lift the arm to 180° of shoulder elevation.

If the scapula moves a lot as the G-H joint moves through a range from 0° to 60°—that is, if in this range they move as a unit—there is limited G-H motion. Above 30° and to about 150° or 160° in both active and passive motions, the scapula moves in concert with the humerus in about a 2 : 1 ratio.

After assessing the scapular position at rest, ask the patient to raise the test arm above the head in the sagittal plane. If the arm can be raised well above 90° (G-H muscles must be at least Grade 3 to do this), observe the direction and amount of scapular motion that occurs. Normally, the scapula rotates upward in a motion that is controlled by the serratus, and if erratic or "uncoordinated" motion occurs, the serratus is most likely weak. The normal amount of motion from the vertebral border is about the breadth of two fingers (Fig. 5.4). If the patient can raise the arm with simultaneous rhythmical scapular upward rotation, proceed with the test sequence for Grades 5 and 4.

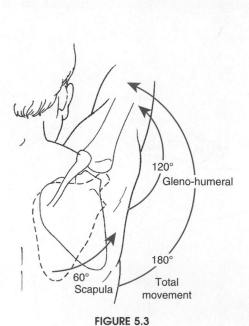

FIGURE 5.3

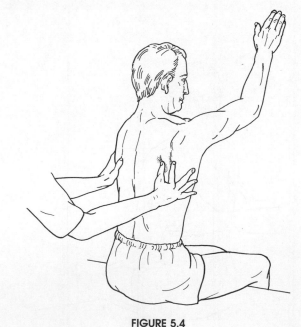

FIGURE 5.4

Preliminary Examination Continued

Scapula Abnormal Position at Rest: If the scapula is positioned abnormally at rest (i.e., downwardly rotated, abducted, or winging), the patient will not be able to elevate the arm above 90°. Proceed to serratus muscle tests described for Grades 2, 1, and 0. The serratus anterior never can be graded higher than the grade given to shoulder flexion. If the patient has a weak deltoid, the lever for testing is gone, and the arm cannot be used to apply resistance.

Helpful Hint

Thoracic spine extension is necessary to achieve full shoulder elevation. If a person is kyphotic, shoulder elevation will be sacrificed and a 10° to 20° deficit of shoulder elevation will be noted.

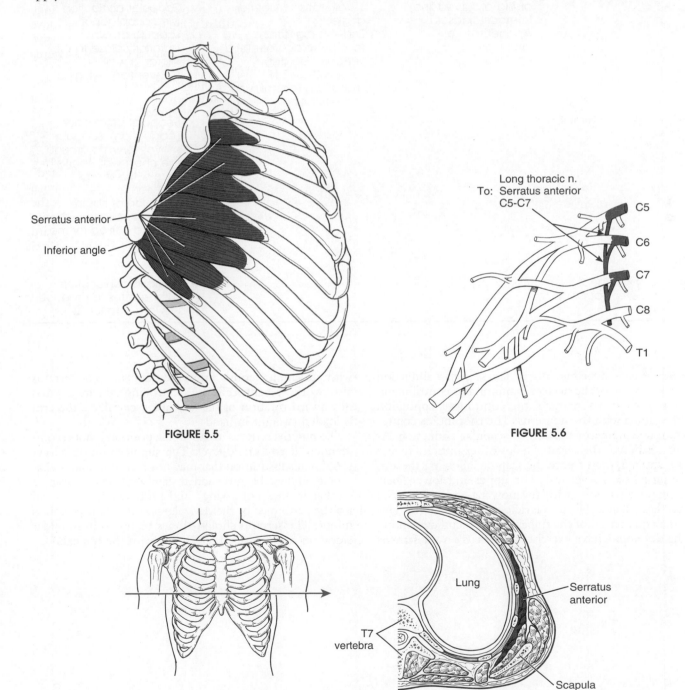

Serratus anterior

Inferior angle

FIGURE 5.5

Long thoracic n.
To: Serratus anterior
C5-C7

C5
C6
C7
C8
T1

FIGURE 5.6

Lung

Serratus anterior

T7 vertebra

Scapula

FIGURE 5.7 Arrow indicates level of cross section.

SCAPULAR ABDUCTION AND UPWARD ROTATION

(Serratus anterior)

Range of Motion
Reliable values not available

Table 5.1 SCAPULAR ABDUCTION AND UPWARD ROTATION

I.D.	Muscle	Origin	Insertion	Function
128	**Serratus anterior**	Ribs 1–8 and often 9 and 10 (by digitations along a curved line) Intercostal fascia Aponeurosis of intercostals	Scapula (ventral surface of vertebral border) 1st digitation (superior angle) 2nd–4th digitations (costal surface of entire vertebral border) Lower 4th or 5th digitations (costal surface of inferior angle)	Upward rotation of the scapula (glenoid faces up) • Scapular abduction • Medial border of scapula drawn anteriorly close to the thoracic wall (preventing "winging")
129	Pectoralis minor			• Scapular protraction (abduction): scapula moves forward around the chest wall. Works here with serratus anterior • Elevation of ribs in forced inspiration when scapula is fixed by the levator scapulae
Other				
124	Upper and lower trapezius			• Works in conjunction with serratus to produce upward rotation

The serratus is a prime mover for scapular abduction (protraction), with the pectoralis minor also contributing. Their purpose is to maintain the continuous apposition of the scapula with the humerus. The rhomboids control the rate and range of motion of scapular abduction. As the arm is raised, the serratus helps other muscles to first fix the scapula, then rotate the scapula, allowing the arm to be raised to the vertical. The upper and lower fibers of the trapezius assist with the upward and medial pull of the lateral end of the clavicle and acromion.[1] This simultaneous action of the trapezius has focused attention on the development of exercises that focus on the serratus without simultaneously firing the trapezius. The serratus also works eccentrically in controlling gravity-assisted downward rotation of the scapula, especially if the arm is loaded (weight in hand).

Testing the serratus in the supine position is not recommended at any grade level. The supine position allows too much substitution that may not be noticeable. Lying supine on the table gives added stabilization to the scapula so that it does not "wing" and protraction of the arm may be performed by the clavicular portion of the pectoralis minor. The serratus should always be tested in shoulder elevation to minimize the synergy with the trapezius.

Grade 5, Grade 4, and Grade 3

Position of Patient: Short sitting with arm forward flexed to about 130° and then protracted in that plane as far as it can move.

Instructions to Therapist: Stand at test side of patient. Ask patient to protract arm, to assess available range and the patient's ability to achieve the test position. If successful, position arm as noted above. Hand used for resistance grasps the upper arm just above the elbow and gives resistance in a backward direction. The other hand stabilizes the trunk just below the scapula on the same side, thus preventing trunk rotation (Fig. 5.8).

The therapist should select a spot on the wall or ceiling that can serve as a target for the patient to reach toward when the shoulder is at 130° of elevation.

Test: Therapist resists protraction and elevation the arm at about 130° of flexion. The patient holds against maximal resistance.

Instructions to Patient: "Hold your arm here. Don't let me move it."

Grading

Grade 5: Scapula maintains its abducted and rotated position against maximal resistance (see Fig. 5.8).

Grade 4: Scapular muscles "give" or "yield" against maximal resistance. The G-H joint is normally held rigid in the presence of a strong deltoid, but if the serratus yields, the scapula moves in the direction of adduction and downward rotation.

Grade 3: Scapula moves through full range of motion without winging, and without resistance other than the weight of the arm (Fig. 5.9).

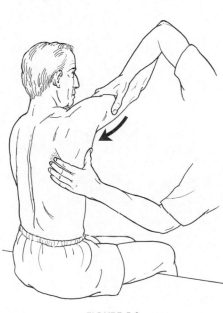

FIGURE 5.8

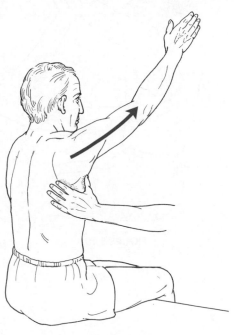

FIGURE 5.9

(Serratus anterior)

Grade 2

Position of Patient: Short sitting with arm flexed above 90° and supported by therapist.

Instructions to Therapist: Stand at test side of patient. One hand supports the patient's arm at the elbow, maintaining it above the horizontal (Fig. 5.10). The other hand is placed at the inferior angle of the scapula with the thumb positioned along the axillary border and the fingers along the vertebral border (see Fig. 5.10).

Test: Therapist monitors scapular motion by using a light grasp on the scapula at the inferior angle. Therapist must be sure not to restrict or resist motion. The scapula is observed to detect winging.

Instructions to Patient: "Hold your arm in this position" (i.e., above 90°). "Let it relax. Now hold your arm up again. Let it relax."

Grading

Grade 2: If the scapula abducts and rotates upward as the patient attempts to hold the arm in the elevated position, the weakness is in the G-H muscles. If the scapula does not smoothly abduct and upwardly rotate without the weight of the arm or if the scapula moves toward the vertebral spine, the weakness is in the serratus and should be graded a 2.

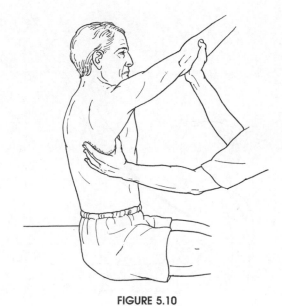

FIGURE 5.10

Grade 1 and Grade 0

Position of Patient: Short sitting with arm forward flexed to above 90° (supported by therapist).

Instructions to Therapist: Stand in front of and slightly to one side of patient. Support the patient's arm at the elbow, maintaining it above 90° (Fig. 5.11). Use the other hand to palpate the serratus with the tips of the fingers just in front of the inferior angle along the axillary border (see Fig. 5.11).

Test: Patient attempts to hold the arm in the test position.

Instructions to Patient: "Try to hold your arm in this position."

Grading

Grade 1: Muscle contraction is palpable.

Grade 0: No discernable palpable contraction.

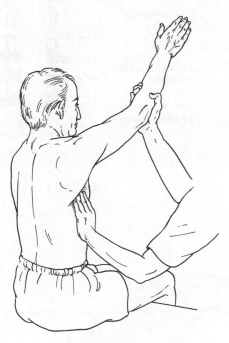

FIGURE 5.11

Helpful Hints

- The highest level of serratus anterior electromyography (EMG) activity is achieved below 90° of humeral elevation.[6]
- If a patient has a painful elbow (e.g., tennis elbow or epicondylitis) resistance may be applied above the painful joint, on the proximal arm.

Suggested Exercises for Serratus Anterior

- Push up progression
  - Least muscle demand: wall push up
  - Moderate muscle demand: pushup on knees
  - Highest muscle demand: pushup with feet elevated.[7]
- Push up plus*,[8] (produces minimal upper trapezius activation and maximum activation of the serratus)
- Dynamic hug[8]
- Diagonal exercise flexion (D1[7,9] and D2[7], D2 diagonal pattern extension)[7]
- Bench press, seated (using a weight machine) with upper trapezius[9]
- Isometric low row (with lower trapezius)[8]
- Lawnmower rows (with lower trapezius)[8]

*Push up plus is a classic pushup with extended arms and a narrow hand width. On fully extended arms, lift the back toward the ceiling. Then drop the trunk down, bending elbows 30°, then raising trunk again, lifting the back toward the ceiling at the end of the movement (it is a small movement, just a couple of inches).

SCAPULAR ELEVATION

(Trapezius, upper fibers and Levator scapula)[10]

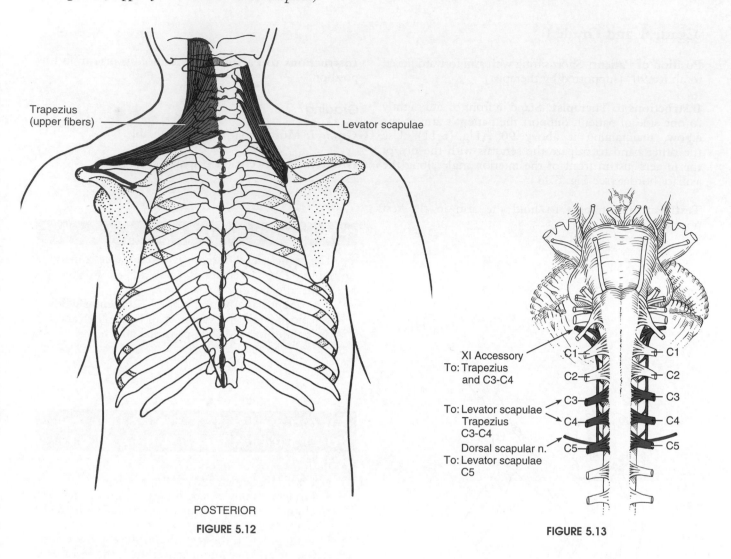

Trapezius
(upper fibers)

Levator scapulae

POSTERIOR

FIGURE 5.12

XI Accessory
To: Trapezius
and C3-C4

To: Levator scapulae
Trapezius
C3-C4

Dorsal scapular n.
To: Levator scapulae
C5

C1
C2
C3
C4
C5

C1
C2
C3
C4
C5

FIGURE 5.13

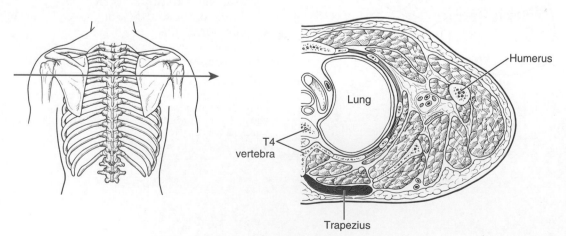

Humerus

Lung

T4
vertebra

Trapezius

FIGURE 5.14 Arrow indicates level of cross section.

(Trapezius, upper fibers and Levator scapula)[10]

Range of Motion
Reliable data not available

Table 5.2 SCAPULAR ELEVATION

I.D.	Muscle	Origin	Insertion	Function
124	**Trapezius (upper fibers)**	Occiput (external protuberance and superior nuchal line, medial ⅓) Ligamentum nuchae C7 vertebra (spinous process)	Clavicle (posterior border of lateral ⅓)	Upper: • Elevation of shoulder girdle ("shrugging") (with levator scapulae) • Rotation of head to opposite side (one) • Capital extension (both) Upper and Lower: • Rotation of the scapula so glenoid faces up (inferior angle moves laterally and forward); occurs only if contracting in conjunction with serratus anterior • Cervical extension (both)
127	Levator scapulae	C1-C4 vertebrae (transverse processes)	Scapula (vertebral border between superior angle and root of scapular spine)	• Elevates and adducts scapula • Scapular downward rotation (glenoid faces down) • Lateral bending of cervical spine to same side (one) • Cervical rotation to same side (one) • Cervical extension (both assist)
Others				
125	Rhomboid major	See Table 5.3		
126	Rhomboid minor	See Table 5.5		

Elevation of the scapula and point of the shoulder, as in shrugging the shoulders, is generated by the trapezius acting on the lateral clavicle, acromion and spine of the scapula, with some assistance from the levator scapula. If the trapezius is weak the therapist may see some scapular downward rotation due to the action of the levator. If the levator is weak, elevation may be accompanied by some scapular upward rotation.[1] In the intact muscle, elevation should be a straight "up" movement.

Grade 5, Grade 4, and Grade 3

Position of Patient: Short sitting over end or side of table in erect posture. Hands relaxed in lap.

Instructions to Therapist: Stand behind patient. Ask the patient to elevate (shrug) the shoulders (Grade 3). If range is full and symmetrical, apply resistance. Contour hands over top of both shoulders to give resistance in a downward direction. This muscle is quite strong, so the therapist's arms should be nearly straight, transferring the therapist's body weight through the arms to provide enough resistance. If unilateral weakness is suspected (rare), testing each side separately may be indicated.

Test: Patient elevates (shrugs) shoulders. The test is almost always performed on both sides simultaneously (Fig. 5.15).

Instructions to Patient: "Shrug your shoulders." OR "Raise your shoulders toward your ears. Hold it. Don't let me push them down."

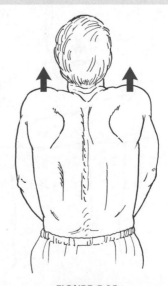

FIGURE 5.15

SCAPULAR ELEVATION

(Trapezius, upper fibers and Levator scapula)[10]

Grade 5, Grade 4, and Grade 3 Continued

Grading

Grade 5: Holds test position against maximal resistance (Fig. 5.16).

Grade 4: Patient holds test position against strong to moderate resistance. The shoulder muscles may "give" at the end point.

Grade 3: Elevates shoulders through full available range without resistance.

Grade 2, Grade 1, and Grade 0

Position of Patient: Prone, fully supported on table. Head may be turned away from test side for patient comfort and to reduce the potential contribution of the levator scapulae (Fig. 5.17).

Instructions to Therapist: Stand at test side of patient. Support test shoulder in palm of one hand. The other hand palpates the upper trapezius near its insertion above the clavicle. A second site for palpation is the upper trapezius just adjacent to the cervical vertebrae.

Test: With the therapist supporting the shoulder, the patient elevates the shoulder (usually done unilaterally) toward the ear.

Instructions to Patient: "Raise your shoulder toward your ear (shrug)."

Grading

Grade 2: Patient completes full range of motion in gravity-minimized position.

Grade 1: Upper trapezius fibers can be palpated at clavicle or neck. The levator muscle lies deep and is more difficult to palpate in the neck (between the sternocleidomastoid and the trapezius). It can be felt at its insertion on the vertebral border of the scapula superior to the scapular spine when the head is turned towards the side being tested.

Helpful Hints

- If the patient cannot assume the sitting position for testing for any reason, the tests for Grade 5 and Grade 4 in the supine position will be quite inaccurate. If the Grade 3 test is done in the supine position, it will require manual resistance because gravity is neutralized.
- If the prone position is not comfortable, the tests for Grades 2, 1, and 0 may be performed with the patient supine, but palpation in such cases will be less than optimal.

Suggested Exercises for Upper Trapezius

- Shoulder shrug[7]
- Abduction to 45°, 90° and 120° (decreases middle trapezius activity)
- Low row (decreases serratus anterior activity)
- Prone horizontal abduction at 135° with ER (thumb up) (optimizes upper trapezius and decreases serratus anterior activity)[7]

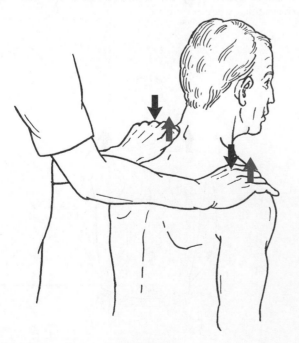

FIGURE 5.16

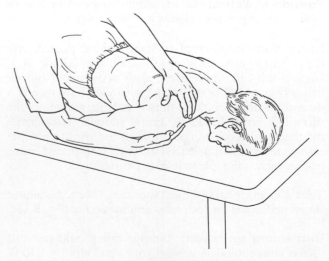

FIGURE 5.17

SCAPULAR ADDUCTION (RETRACTION)

(Trapezius, middle fibers and Rhomboid major and minor)

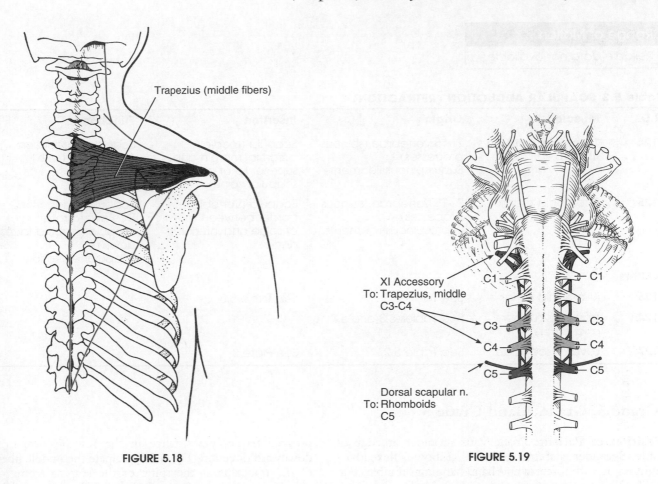

Trapezius (middle fibers)

FIGURE 5.18

XI Accessory
To: Trapezius, middle
C3-C4

Dorsal scapular n.
To: Rhomboids
C5

C1   C1
C3   C3
C4   C4
C5   C5

FIGURE 5.19

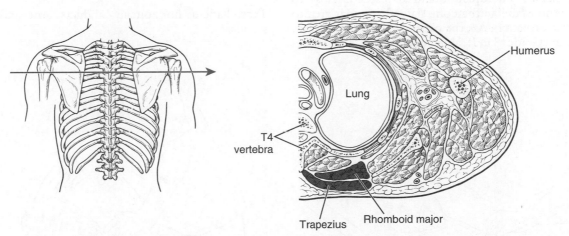

Humerus

Lung

T4
vertebra

Trapezius   Rhomboid major

FIGURE 5.20 Arrow indicates level of cross section.

SCAPULAR ADDUCTION (RETRACTION)

(Trapezius, middle fibers and Rhomboid major and minor)

Range of Motion
Reliable data not available

Table 5.3 SCAPULAR ADDUCTION (RETRACTION)

I.D.	Muscle	Origin	Insertion	Function
124	**Trapezius (middle fibers)**	T1-T5 vertebrae (spinous processes) Supraspinous ligaments	Scapula (medial acromial margin and superior lip of crest on scapular spine)	Scapular adduction (retraction) (with rhomboids)
125	Rhomboid major	T2-T5 vertebrae (spinous processes) Supraspinous ligaments	Scapula (vertebral border between root of spine and inferior angle)	Scapular adduction Downward rotation of scapula (glenoid faces down) Scapular elevation
Others				
126	Rhomboid minor	See Table 5.5	See Table 5.5	
124	Trapezius (upper and lower)	See Tables 5.3 and 5.4		
127	Levator scapulae	See Table 5.2	See Plate 3	

Grade 5, Grade 4, and Grade 3

Position of Patient: Prone with shoulder at edge of table. Shoulder is abducted to 90°. Elbow is flexed to a right angle with forearm and hand hanging off table (Fig. 5.21). Head may be turned to either side for comfort.

Instructions to Therapist: Stand at test side close to patient's arm. Stabilize the contralateral scapular area to prevent trunk rotation. Ask the patient to lift elbow toward the ceiling (Grade 3). If able to complete full range,

proceed to apply resistance in the test position in a downward direction (Fig. 5.22). Palpate the middle fibers of the trapezius at the spine of the scapula from the acromion to the vertebral column with the fingers of the other hand, as necessary.

Test: Patient horizontally abducts arm and adducts scapula.

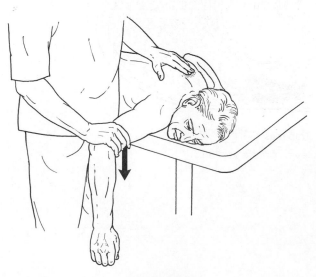

FIGURE 5.21

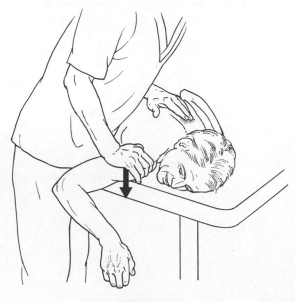

FIGURE 5.22

Grade 5, Grade 4, and Grade 3 Continued

Instructions to Patient: "Lift your elbow toward the ceiling. Hold it. Don't let me push it down."

Grading

Grade 5: Holds test position against maximal resistance.

Grade 4: Holds test position against strong to moderate resistance.

Grade 3: Completes available range without manual resistance (Fig. 5.23).

Grade 2, Grade 1, and Grade 0

Position of Patient and Therapist: Same as for Grade 5 test except that the therapist uses one hand to cradle the patient's shoulder and arm, thus supporting the arm's weight (Fig. 5.24), and the other hand for palpation.

Test: Same as that for Grades 5 to 3.

Instructions to Patient: "Try to lift your elbow toward the ceiling."

Grading

Grade 2: Completes full range of motion without the weight of the arm.

Grade 1 and Grade 0: A Grade 1 muscle exhibits contractile activity or slight movement. There will be neither motion nor discernable palpable contractile activity in the Grade 0 muscle.

Substitutions

By the rhomboids: The rhomboids can partially substitute for the middle trapezius in adduction of the scapula but if that should happen, adduction occurs simultaneously with scapular downward rotation.

Helpful Hint

When the posterior deltoid muscle is weak, support the patient's shoulder with the palm of one hand and allow the patient's elbow to flex. Passively move the scapula into adduction via horizontal abduction of the arm (see Fig. 5.24). Have the patient hold the scapula in adduction as the therapist slowly releases the shoulder support. Observe whether the scapula maintains its adducted position. If it does, it is Grade 3.

Suggested Exercises for Middle Trapezius

- Prone external rotation (ER)[9]
- Side-lying ER[9]
- Row with elbows extended

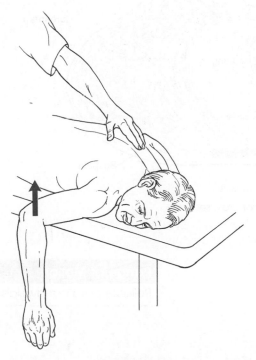

FIGURE 5.23

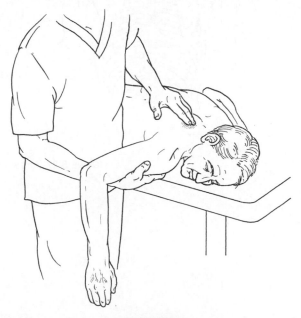

FIGURE 5.24

SCAPULAR DEPRESSION AND ADDUCTION

(Trapezius, lower and middle fibers)

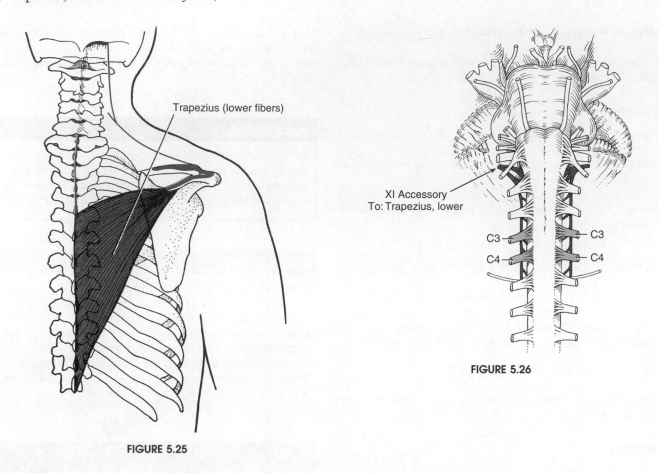

Trapezius (lower fibers)

FIGURE 5.25

XI Accessory
To: Trapezius, lower

C3   C3
C4   C4

FIGURE 5.26

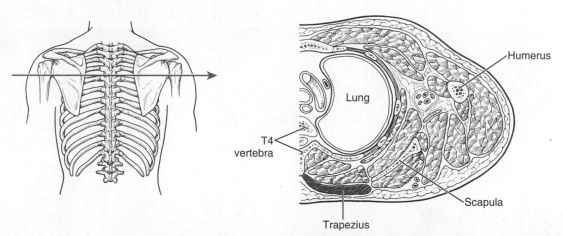

Humerus

Lung

T4
vertebra

Scapula

Trapezius

FIGURE 5.27 Arrow indicates level of cross section.

Range of Motion

Reliable data not available

Table 5.4 SCAPULAR DEPRESSION AND ADDUCTION

I.D.	Muscle	Origin	Insertion	Function
124	**Trapezius (middle and lower fibers)**	T1-T5 vertebrae (spinous processes) Supraspinous ligaments T6-T12 vertebrae (spinous processes)	Scapula (spine, medial end, and tubercle at lateral apex via aponeurosis)	*Middle:* • Scapular adduction (retraction) (with rhomboids) *Lower:* • Scapular adduction and depression
130	Latissimus dorsi	Spines of the 6 lower thoracic vertebrae, thoracolumbar fascia, crest of the ilium, lowest 4 ribs	Anterior humerus, lower margin of the intertubercular sulcus	• Scapular depression if the arms are fixed • Extension, adduction, and internal rotation of shoulder • Hyperextension of spine (muscles on both sides), as in lifting • The muscle is most powerful in overhead activities (such as swimming (downstroke) and climbing), crutch walking, elevation of trunk to arms, i.e., shoulder depression, or swinging[11]
Others				
131	Pectoralis major	Sternal half of clavicle, entire anterior surface of the sternum	Lateral lip of the intertubercular sulcus of anterior humerus	
129	Pectoralis minor	Ribs 3–5, intercostal cartilage	Coracoid process	

Grade 5, Grade 4, and Grade 3

Position of Patient: Prone with test arm over head to about 145° of shoulder elevation and abduction (in line with the fibers of the lower trapezius). Forearm is in mid position (neutral rotation) with the thumb pointing toward the ceiling. Head should be turned to the test side.

Instructions to Therapist: Stand at test side. Ask patient to raise the arm from the table as high as possible (Grade 3) (Fig. 5.28). If full range is present, provide resistance. Hand giving resistance is contoured over the distal forearm, just above wrist (Fig. 5.29). Resistance will be given straight downward (toward the floor). Fingertips of the

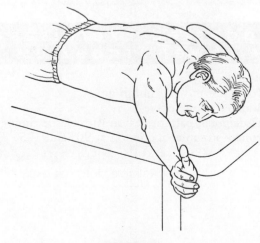

FIGURE 5.28

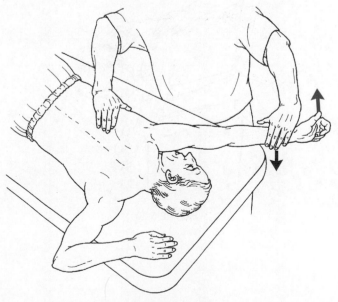

FIGURE 5.29

(Trapezius, lower and middle fibers)

Grade 5, Grade 4, and Grade 3 Continued

opposite hand palpate below the spine of the scapula and across to the thoracic vertebrae, following the muscle as it curves down to the lower thoracic vertebrae. If patient cannot hold the test position with resistance given on the forearm, apply resistance over distal humerus, above elbow (Grade 4).

Instructions to Patient: "Hold your arm. Don't let me push it down."

Grading

Grade 5: Holds test position against strong resistance applied over the forearm.

Grade 4: Holds test position against strong resistance applied over the distal humerus or light resistance over the forearm.

Grade 3: Patient raises arm from the table in test position against gravity, but patient cannot tolerate manual resistance (see Fig. 5.28).

Grade 2, Grade 1, and Grade 0

Position of Patient: Same as for Grade 5.

Instructions to Therapist: Stand at test side. Support patient's arm under the elbow (Fig. 5.30).

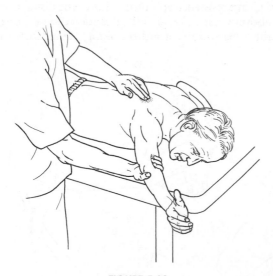

FIGURE 5.30

Test: Patient attempts to lift the arm from the table. If the patient is unable to lift the arm because of a weak posterior and middle deltoid, the examiner should lift and support the weight of the arm. In the presence of a weak lower trapezius, the patient may substitute the middle trapezius and rhomboids, causing a lowering of the arm into an abducted position.

Instructions to Patient: "Try to lift your arm from the table past your ear."

Grading

Grade 2: Completes full scapular range of motion without the weight of the arm.

Grade 1: Contractile activity can be palpated in the triangular area between the root of the spine of the scapula and the lower thoracic vertebra (T7-T12), that is, the course of the fibers of the lower trapezius.

Grade 0: No discernable palpable contractile activity.

Helpful Hints

- The lower trapezius will not be active with shoulder elevation of less than 120°, so if the patient does not have sufficient G-H range to assume the test position, the lower trapezius is nearly impossible to test as the scapulae adduct and the rhomboids take over. If the patient cannot isolate this test or substitutes away from test position, the grade is 0 (zero) or therapist should document, "unable to assume test position."
- Examiners are reminded of the test principle that the same lever arm must be used in sequential testing (over time) for valid comparison of results.

Suggested Exercises for Lower Trapezius

- Prone rowing[7]
- Prone flexion with thumb up[9]
- Modified prone cobra[12]
- D2 diagonal pattern flexion with elastic tubing[7]
- Prone horizontal abduction at 90° and 125°[7]

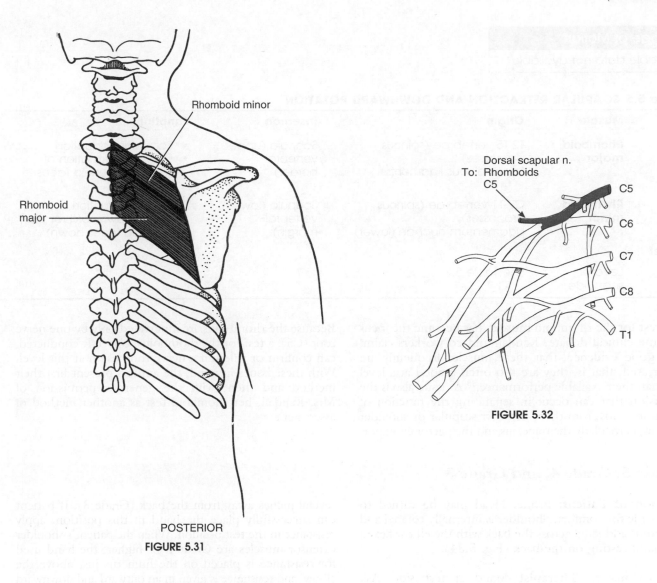

Rhomboid minor

Rhomboid major

POSTERIOR

FIGURE 5.31

Dorsal scapular n.
To: Rhomboids
C5

C5

C6

C7

C8

T1

FIGURE 5.32

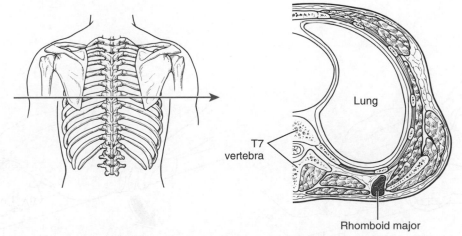

Lung

T7 vertebra

Rhomboid major

FIGURE 5.33 Arrow indicates level of cross section.

SCAPULAR ADDUCTION (RETRACTION) AND DOWNWARD ROTATION

(Rhomboids)

Range of Motion

Reliable data not available

Table 5.5 SCAPULAR RETRACTION AND DOWNWARD ROTATION

I.D.	Muscle	Origin	Insertion	Function
125	**Rhomboid major**	T2-T5 vertebrae (spinous processes) Supraspinous ligaments	Scapula (upper vertebral border)	• Scapular adduction • Downward rotation of scapula (glenoid faces down)
126	**Rhomboid minor**	C7-T1 vertebrae (spinous processes) Ligamentum nuchae (lower)	Scapula (lower vertebral margin)	Scapular adduction Scapular downward rotation (glenoid faces down)
Other				
127	Levator scapulae	See Table 5.2		

The test for the rhomboid muscles has become the focus of some clinical debate. Kendall and co-workers claim, with good evidence, that these muscles frequently are underrated; that is, they are too often graded at a level less than their available performance.[13] At issue also is the confusion that can occur in separating the function of the rhomboids from those of other scapular or shoulder muscles, particularly the trapezius and the pectoralis minor.

Because the rhomboids are innervated only by one nerve root (C5), a test for the rhomboids, correctly conducted, can confirm or rule out a nerve root lesion at this level. With these issues in mind, the authors present first their method and then, with the generous permission of Mrs. Kendall, her rhomboid test as another method of assessment.

Grade 5, Grade 4, and Grade 3

Position of Patient: Prone. Head may be turned to either side for comfort. Shoulder is internally rotated and the arm is adducted across the back with the elbow flexed and hand resting on the back (Fig. 5.34).

Instructions to Therapist: Stand at test side. Ask patient to place hand at the small of the back and lift it

several inches away from the back (Grade 3). If patient can successfully place the hand in this position, apply resistance in the test position. When the patient's shoulder extensor muscles are Grade 3 or higher, the hand used for resistance is placed on the humerus just above the elbow, and resistance is given in an outward and downward direction (Fig. 5.35).

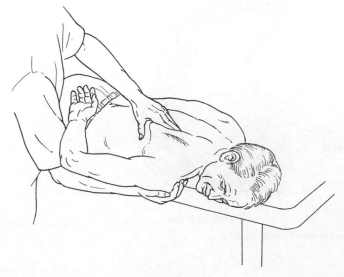

FIGURE 5.34

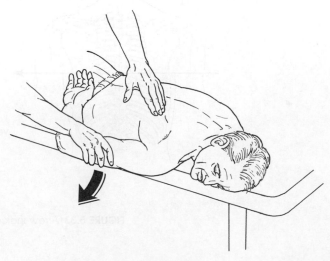

FIGURE 5.35

SCAPULAR ADDUCTION (RETRACTION) AND DOWNWARD ROTATION

(Rhomboids)

Grade 5, Grade 4, and Grade 3 Continued

When the shoulder extensors are weak, place the hand for resistance along the axillary border of the scapula (Fig. 5.36). Resistance is applied in a downward and outward direction.

The fingers of the hand used for palpation are placed deep under the vertebral border of the scapula.

Test: Patient lifts the hand off the back, maintaining the arm position across the back. At the same time the examiner is applying resistance above the elbow in an outward direction. With strong muscle activity, the therapist's fingers will "pop" out from under the edge of the scapular vertebral border (see Fig. 5.34.)

Instructions to Patient: "Lift your hand. Hold it. Don't let me push it down."

Grading

Grade 5: Completes available range and holds against maximal resistance (Fig. 5.37). The fingers will "pop out" from under the scapula when strong rhomboids contract.

Grade 4: Completes range and holds against strong to moderate resistance. Fingers usually will "pop out."

Grade 3: Completes range but tolerates no manual resistance at either the humerus or scapula (Fig. 5.38).

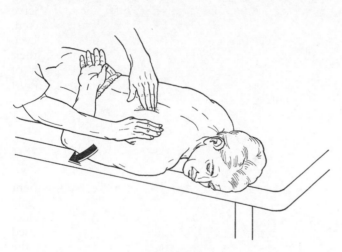

FIGURE 5.36

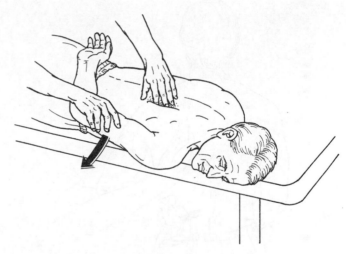

FIGURE 5.37

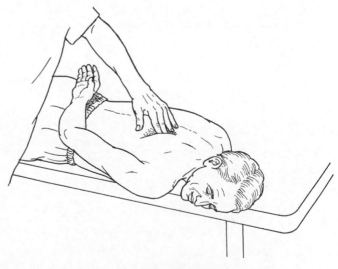

FIGURE 5.38

SCAPULAR ADDUCTION (RETRACTION) AND DOWNWARD ROTATION

(Rhomboids)

Grade 2, Grade 1, and Grade 0

Position of Patient: Short sitting with shoulder internally rotated and arm extended and adducted behind back (Fig. 5.39).

Instructions to Therapist: Stand at test side; support arm by grasping the wrist. The fingertips of one hand palpate the muscle under the vertebral border of the scapula.

Test: Patient attempts to move hand away from back.

Instructions to Patient: "Try to move your hand away from your back."

Grading

Grade 2: Completes range of scapular motion.

Grade 1 and Grade 0: A Grade 1 muscle has palpable contractile activity. A Grade 0 muscle shows no discernable palpable contractile activity.

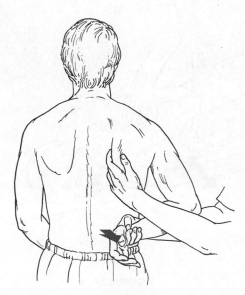

FIGURE 5.39

SCAPULAR ADDUCTION (RETRACTION) AND DOWNWARD ROTATION

(Rhomboids)

Alternate Rhomboid Test After Kendall[13]

As a preliminary to this rhomboid test, the shoulder adductors should be tested and found sufficiently strong to allow the arm to be used as a lever.

Position of Patient: Prone with head turned to side of test. Non-test arm is abducted with elbow flexed. Test arm is near the edge of the table. Arm (humerus) is fully adducted and held firm to the side of the trunk in external rotation (ER) and some extension with elbow fully flexed. In this position, the scapula is in adduction, elevation, and downward rotation (glenoid down).

Instructions to Therapist: Stand at test side. Hand used for resistance is cupped around the flexed elbow. The resistance applied by this hand will be in the direction of scapular abduction and upward rotation (out and up; Fig. 5.40). The other hand is used to give resistance simultaneously. It is contoured over the shoulder joint and gives resistance caudally in the direction of shoulder depression.

Test: Examiner tests the ability of the patient to hold the scapula in its position of adduction, elevation, and downward rotation (glenoid down).

Instructions to Patient: "Hold your arm as I have placed it. Do not let me pull your arm out and forward." OR "Hold the position you are in; keep your shoulder blade against your spine as I try to pull it away."

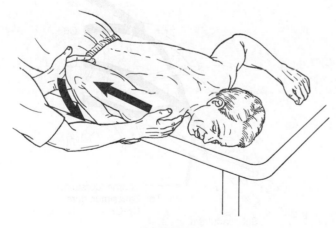

FIGURE 5.40

This large, broad muscle is anatomically complex, contributing to many movements at the humerus, scapula, and pelvis. It is the only muscle connecting the arms to the spine. Literally, it was our "swinging from the trees" muscle. It does not have a singular prime action. Rather its actions are dependent on the fixation of the humerus or pelvis. For example, when the humerus is fixed, the latissimus dorsi can lift the pelvis, which occurs during pressure relief in a wheelchair and during a sliding transfer (see Fig. 5.45). It is the main muscle used when we participate in the chin up/pull up exercise. When the pelvis is fixed, the latissimus dorsi acts on the arm in three ways:

1. Shoulder extension
2. Shoulder adduction
3. Shoulder medial rotation

The latissimus can also depress the humerus and internally rotate, adduct, and extend the shoulder, particularly from a position of flexion. The student will find the latissimus dorsi mentioned in other parts of this chapter as a participant in multiple muscle actions, further supporting the importance and complexity of this muscle.

The latissimus dorsi also assists with breathing with the forced expiration as well as deep inspiration of breath from the lungs.

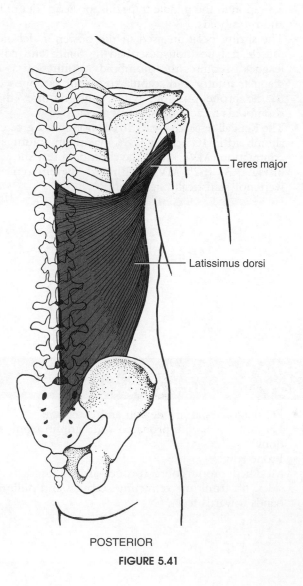

Teres major

Latissimus dorsi

POSTERIOR

FIGURE 5.41

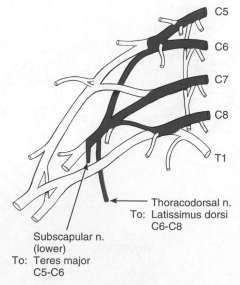

C5
C6
C7
C8
T1

Thoracodorsal n.
To: Latissimus dorsi
C6-C8

Subscapular n.
(lower)
To: Teres major
C5-C6

FIGURE 5.42

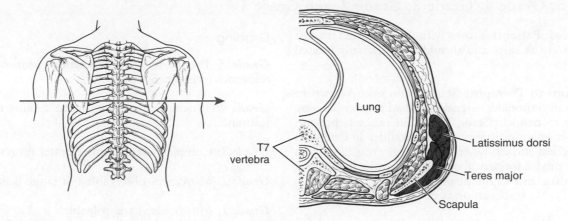

FIGURE 5.43

Table 5.6 LATISSIMUS DORSI

I.D.	Muscle	Origin	Insertion	Function
130	Latissimus dorsi	Spines of the 6 lower thoracic vertebrae, thoracolumbar fascia, crest of the ilium, lowest 4 ribs	Anterior humerus, lower margin of the intertubercular sulcus	Shoulder extension, adduction and internal (medial) rotation Hyperextension of the spine Strong expiration and deep inspiration Elevation of the pelvis with arms fixed

Grade 5, Grade 4, Grade 3, Grade 2, and Grade 1

Position of Patient: Prone with head turned to test side; arms are at sides and shoulder is internally rotated (palm up).

Instructions to Therapist: Stand at test side. Ask patient to lift arm into shoulder extension and adduction (keeping arm close to trunk) (Grade 3). If full range is present, apply appropriate resistance. With shoulder in extension and adduction and elbow extended, apply resistance with hand over medial forearm above patient's wrist in direction of abduction and slight flexion (outwards and down) (Fig. 5.44). No stabilization is needed because of prone position.

Test: Patient lifts arm into extension and adduction (close to trunk).

Instructions to Patient: "Hold your arm. Don't let me move it."

Grading

Grade 5: Patient holds test position against maximal resistance (see Fig. 5.44).

Grade 4: Patient holds test position against moderate resistance.

Grade 3: Completes range but tolerates no resistance.

Grade 2: Movement observable but range is limited.

Grade 1: Muscle activity is palpable.

Grade 0: No movement and no discernable muscle contraction is occurring.

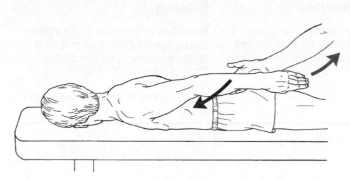

FIGURE 5.44

Alternate Test for Latissimus Dorsi

As explained above, with the upper limb fixed, elevation of the trunk and pelvis are possible through the action of the latissimus dorsi, such as in crutch walking or buttock pressure releases in sitting.

Position of Patient: Short sitting, arms adducted to trunk with hands flat on table adjacent to hips (Fig. 5.45).

If the patient's arms are too short to assume this position, provide a push-up block for each hand.

Instructions to Therapist: Stand behind patient. Fingers are used to palpate fibers of the latissimus dorsi on the lateral aspect of the thoracic wall (bilaterally) just above the waist (see Fig. 5.45).

Test: Patient pushes down on hands (or blocks) and lifts buttocks from table (see Fig. 5.45).

Instructions to Patient: "Lift your bottom off the table. Keep your arms into your sides."

Grading

Grade 3, Grade 4 and Grade 5: Patient can lift buttocks clear of table.

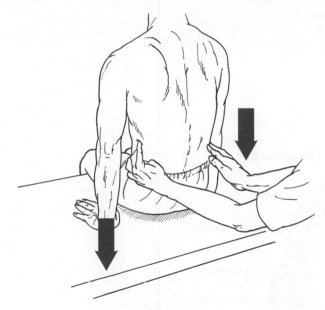

FIGURE 5.45

Suggested Exercises for the Latissimus Dorsi

- Pull ups[17]
- Latissimus pull downs[17]
- Inverted row[17]
- Press up[7]
- Standing extension from 90°-0° with elastic tubing[7]

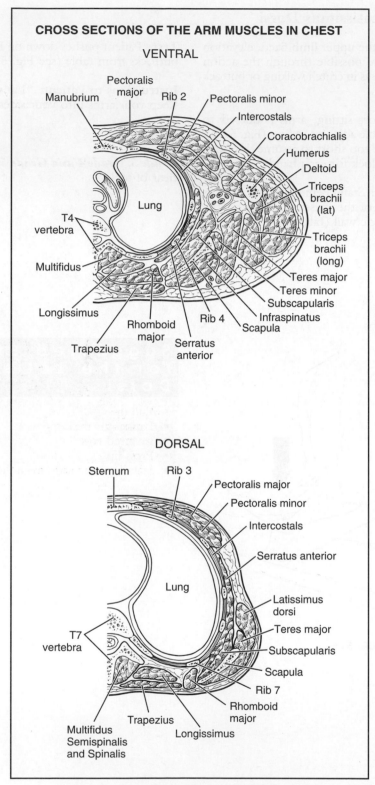

PLATE 3 Cross Sections of the arm muscles in chest.

The deltoid muscle, made of three parts (anterior, middle and posterior), has multiple functions of mobility and stabilization of the head of the humerus into the glenoid fossa. The deltoid can act in part or as a whole. Together, the three parts allow swinging of the arm, and preventing downward dislocation of the humeral head when carrying an object in the hanging hand.[18] The three parts work together to produce abduction of the shoulder joint. The anterior part has a flexion and internal rotation (IR) function and the posterior part has an extension and ER function.[1] The anterior part acts with the rotator cuff to raise the arm in both flexion and abduction. The middle part is a strong shoulder abductor while the posterior part is a strong extensor (with the latissimus dorsi and teres major) and to a lesser degree, a horizontal abductor. The deltoid is capable of extending the humerus beyond the midline whereas the latissimus dorsi is not.

(Anterior deltoid, Rotator cuff, Clavicular portion of pectoralis major, and Coracobrachialis*)

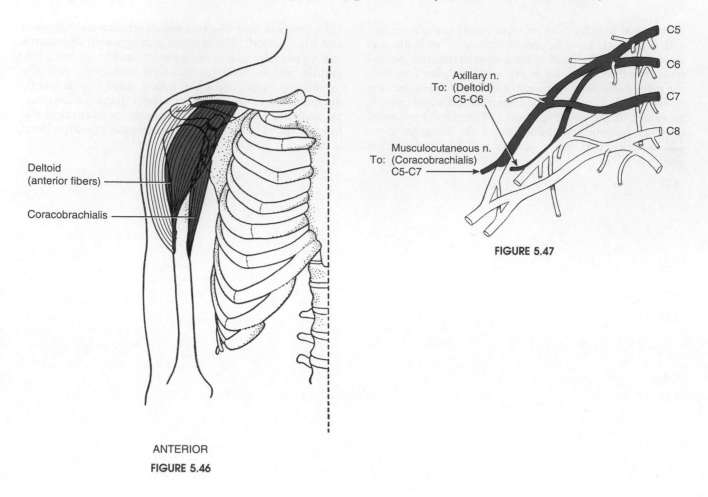

Deltoid
(anterior fibers)

Coracobrachialis

Axillary n.
To: (Deltoid)
C5-C6

Musculocutaneous n.
To: (Coracobrachialis)
C5-C7

C5
C6
C7
C8

FIGURE 5.47

ANTERIOR
FIGURE 5.46

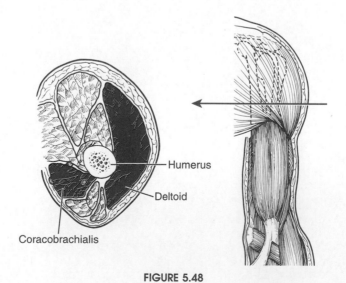

Humerus

Deltoid

Coracobrachialis

FIGURE 5.48

*The coracobrachialis muscle cannot be isolated, nor is it really palpable. It has no unique function. It is included here because classically it is considered a shoulder flexor and adductor.

(Anterior deltoid, Rotator cuff, Clavicular portion of pectoralis major, and Coracobrachialis)

Range of Motion
0°–180°

Table 5.7 SHOULDER FLEXION

I.D.	Muscle	Origin	Insertion	Function
133	**Deltoid (anterior)**	Clavicle (anterior superior border of lateral ⅓ of shaft)	Humerus (deltoid tuberosity on shaft)	Flexion and internal rotation of shoulder (anterior fibers) The deltoid tends to displace the humeral head upward Shoulder horizontal adduction (anterior fibers)
139	Coracobrachialis	Scapula (coracoid process at apex)	Humerus (shaft, medial surface at middle ⅓)	Flexion of arm Adduction of shoulder
131	Pectoralis major (clavicular fibers)	See Table 5.4		*Clavicular fibers:* Flexion of shoulder Horizontal shoulder adduction Internal rotation of shoulder
Others				
135	Supraspinatus	Scapula (supraspinous fossa, medial ⅔) Supraspinatus fascia	Humerus (greater tubercle, highest facet) Articular capsule of glenohumeral (G-H) joint	Maintains humeral head in glenoid fossa (with other rotator cuff muscles) Shoulder flexor Abduction of shoulder External rotation of shoulder
	Long and short head of biceps	See table 5.13		

SHOULDER FLEXION

(Anterior deltoid, Rotator cuff, Clavicular portion of pectoralis major, and Coracobrachialis)

Due to increasing moment arm with abduction, the anterior deltoid is more effective as a shoulder abductor in higher abduction angles (120°), with its greatest force production above the horizontal,[19] in contrast to the supraspinatus, which is a more effective shoulder abductor at lower abduction ranges. The supraspinatus has a role as a humeral head depressor during shoulder flexion.[20] The middle deltoid also provides G-H stabilization with greater amounts of shoulder flexion.

Grade 5, Grade 4, and Grade 3

Position of Patient: Short sitting with arms at sides, elbow slightly flexed, forearm pronated.

Instructions to Therapist: Stand at test side. Ask patient to raise arm forward to shoulder height (90°), keeping elbow straight. If full range is present (Grade 3), position arm in test position (90°) and apply appropriate resistance. Therapist's hand giving resistance is contoured over the distal humerus just above the elbow. The other hand may stabilize the shoulder (Fig. 5.49).

Test: Patient flexes shoulder to 90° with elbow straight without rotation or horizontal movement (see Fig. 5.49). The scapula should be allowed to abduct and upwardly rotate.

Instructions to Patient: "Hold your arm. Don't let me push it down."

Grading

Grade 5: Holds test position (90°) against maximal resistance.

Grade 4: Holds test position against strong to moderate resistance.

Grade 3: Completes test range (90°) without resistance (Fig. 5.50)

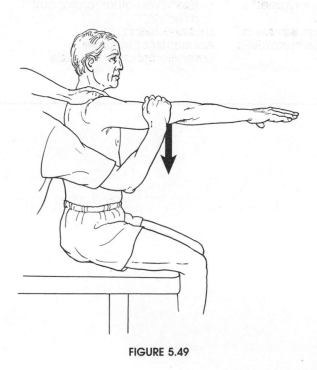

FIGURE 5.49

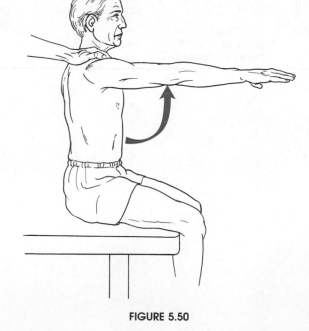

FIGURE 5.50

(Anterior deltoid, Rotator cuff, Clavicular portion of pectoralis major, and Coracobrachialis)

Grade 2, Grade 1, and Grade 0

Position of Patient: Side-lying position (test side up).

Instructions to Therapist: With patient side-lying to minimize gravity, stand behind patient and cradle the test arm at the elbow. Then ask patient to flex the shoulder. (A powder board may also be used.)

Test: Patient attempts to flex shoulder.

Instructions to Patient: "Try to raise your arm."

Grade 1 and Grade 0

Instructions to Therapist: Stand behind patient. Fingers used for palpation are placed over the superior and anterior surfaces of the deltoid over the shoulder joint (Fig. 5.51).

Grading

Test for Grade 2, Grade 1, and Grade 0:
Grade 2: Completes full range of motion in gravity-minimized position.

Grade 1: Therapist feels or sees contractile activity in the anterior deltoid, but no motion occurs.

Grade 0: No discernable palpable contractile activity.

Substitutions

- In the absence of a deltoid, the patient may attempt to flex the shoulder with the biceps brachii by first externally rotating the shoulder (Fig. 5.52). To avoid this, the arm should be kept in the mid position between internal and external rotation.
- Attempted substitution by the upper trapezius results in shoulder elevation.
- Attempted substitution by the pectoralis major results in horizontal adduction. It should be noted that substitution by the pectoralis major as a shoulder flexor can only occur up to about 70°.
- The patient may lean backward or try to elevate the shoulder girdle to assist in flexion.

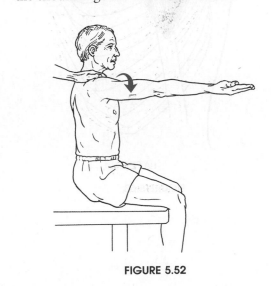

FIGURE 5.52

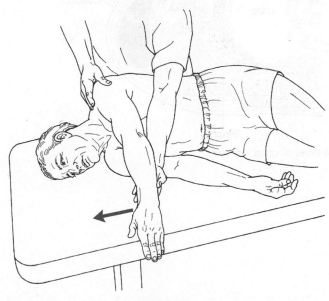

FIGURE 5.51

Suggested Exercises for Anterior Deltoid and Supraspinatus

- Push up (40%–50% MVC)[21]
- Pressing incline activities between 28° and 90°[22,23] such as dumbbell press
- Plyometric push-up (clapping) (60%–70% MVC)[21]
- Full and empty can.[8,24,25] Full can produces less deltoid activity.
- Slow, controlled shoulder flexion at 90° and 125°[24]
- Prone horizontal abduction at 100° with external rotation[8]
- Upright row[26]

SHOULDER EXTENSION

(Posterior deltoid, Latissimus dorsi, Teres major, and Long head of triceps)

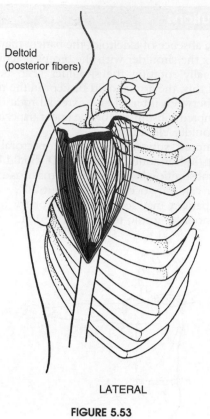

Deltoid
(posterior fibers)

LATERAL

FIGURE 5.53

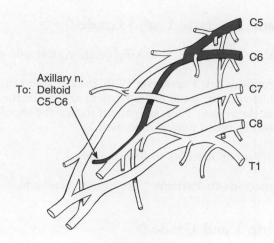

Axillary n.
To: Deltoid
C5-C6

C5
C6
C7
C8
T1

FIGURE 5.54

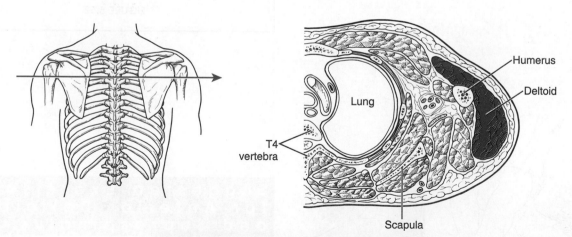

Humerus

Deltoid

Lung

T4
vertebra

Scapula

FIGURE 5.55 Arrow indicates level of cross section.

(Posterior deltoid, Latissimus dorsi, Teres major, and Long head of triceps)

Range of Motion
0°–45° (up to 60°)

Table 5.8 SHOULDER EXTENSION

I.D.	Muscle	Origin	Insertion	Function
133	**Deltoid (posterior)**	Scapula (spine on lower lip of lateral and posterior borders)	Humerus (deltoid tuberosity on mid shaft via humeral tendon)	Extension and external rotation. The posterior fibers of the deltoid tends to displace the humeral head upward Shoulder horizontal abduction
130	Latissimus dorsi	T6-T12, L1-L5, and sacral vertebrae (spinous processes) Supraspinous ligaments Ribs 9–12 (by slips interdigitating with obliquus abdominis externus) Ilium (crest, posterior) Thoracolumbar fascia	Humerus (intertubercular sulcus, floor) Deep fascia of arm	Shoulder extension (from a position of flexion) adduction, and internal rotation
138	Teres major	Scapula (dorsal surface of inferior angle)	Humerus (intertubercular sulcus, medial lip)	Extension of shoulder from a flexed position Internal rotation of shoulder Adduction and extension of shoulder
Other				
142	Triceps brachii (long head)			

SHOULDER EXTENSION

(Posterior deltoid, Latissimus dorsi, Teres major, and Long head of triceps)

The posterior deltoid is a stronger extensor throughout the range with the greatest contribution with the arms below horizontal. Its peak moment arm is at 30° of flexion (arm pointing down). The posterior deltoid is the primary shoulder hyper-extensor because neither the pectoralis major nor the latissimus dorsi extends the shoulder beyond anatomical neutral. This hyper-extension function allows the patient to reach behind the body to the gluteal area and beyond.[18] The posterior deltoid opposes the anterior deltoid in the sagittal (flexion) plane and acts as a strong external rotator (up to 80% when elevated into the plane of the scapula).[1]

Grade 5, Grade 4, Grade 3, and Grade 2

Position of Patient: Prone with arms at sides and shoulder internally rotated (palm up) (Fig. 5.56).

Instructions to Therapist: Stand at test side. Ask patient to lift arm as high as possible. If full range is available (Grade 3), position arm in test position near end range and apply appropriate resistance. The hand used for resistance is contoured over the posterior arm just above the elbow (Fig. 5.57).

Test: Patient raises arm off the table, keeping the elbow straight (Fig. 5.58).

Instructions to Patient: "Lift your arm as high as you can. Hold it. Don't let me push it down."

Grading

Grade 5: Holds test position against maximal resistance.

Grade 4: Holds test position against strong resistance.

Grade 3: Completes available range of motion with no manual resistance (see Fig. 5.58).

Grade 2: Completes partial range of motion.

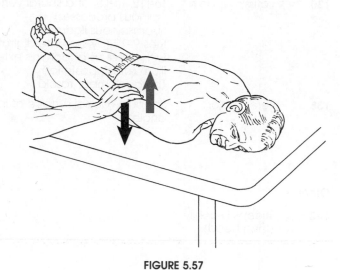

FIGURE 5.57

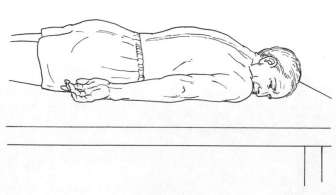

FIGURE 5.56

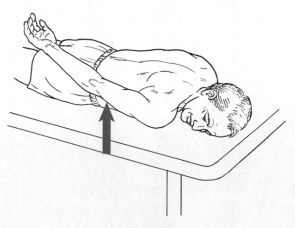

FIGURE 5.58

(Posterior deltoid, Latissimus dorsi, Teres major, and Long head of triceps)

Grade 1 and Grade 0

Position of Patient: Prone with arms at sides and shoulder internally rotated (palm up).

Instructions to Therapist: Stand at test side. Fingers for palpation are placed on the posterior aspect of the upper arm (posterior deltoid) (Fig. 5.59).

Palpate over the posterior shoulder just superior to the axilla for posterior deltoid fibers. Palpate the teres major on the lateral border of the scapula just below the axilla. The teres major is the lower of the two muscles that enter the axilla at this point; it forms the lower posterior rim of the axilla.

Test and Instructions to Patient: Patient attempts to lift arm from table.

Grading

Grade 1: Palpable contractile activity in any of the participating muscles but no movement of the shoulder.

Grade 0: No palpable contractile response in participating muscles.

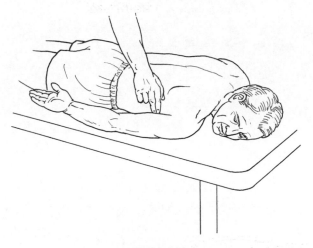

FIGURE 5.59

Suggested Exercises for the Middle and Posterior Deltoid

- D1 diagonal pattern extension[7]
- D2 diagonal pattern flexion[7]
- Push up exercises[7]
- Prone shoulder elevation (arm raised overhead in line with lower trapezius fibers)[7,24]
- Extension with internal rotation[24] shoulder abduction 30° with elbow extended. Arm extended and IR
- Side-lying ER at 0° abduction[7]
- Empty can[24]
- 45° incline row

SHOULDER ABDUCTION

(Middle deltoid and Supraspinatus)

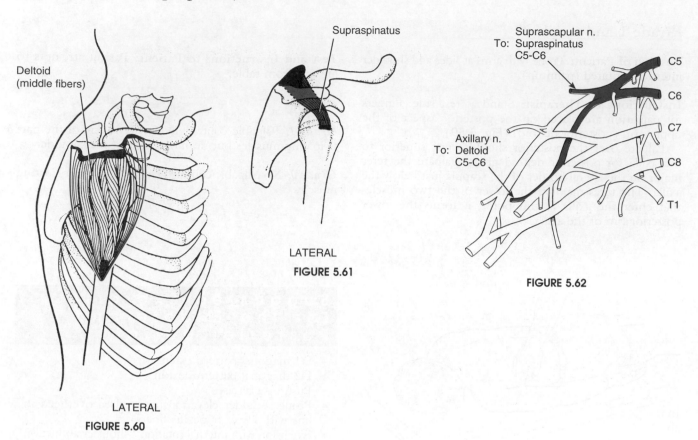

Deltoid
(middle fibers)

Supraspinatus

LATERAL

FIGURE 5.61

Suprascapular n.
To: Supraspinatus
C5-C6

C5

C6

C7

C8

T1

Axillary n.
To: Deltoid
C5-C6

FIGURE 5.62

LATERAL

FIGURE 5.60

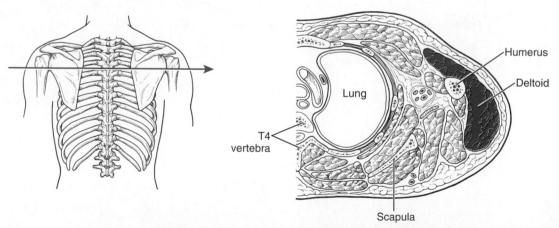

Humerus

Deltoid

Lung

T4
vertebra

Scapula

FIGURE 5.63 Arrow indicates level of cross section.

Range of Motion

0°–180°

Table 5.9 SHOULDER ABDUCTION

I.D.	Muscle	Origin	Insertion	Function
133	**Deltoid (middle fibers)**	Scapula (acromion, lateral margin, superior surface, and crest of spine)	Humerus (deltoid tuberosity on shaft via humeral tendon)	Abduction of shoulder (glenohumeral (G-H) joint): primarily the acromial middle fibers. The anterior and posterior fibers in this motion stabilize the limb in its cantilever position
135	Supraspinatus	Scapula (supraspinous fossa, medial ⅔) Supraspinatus fascia	Humerus (greater tubercle, highest facet) Articular capsule of glenohumeral (G-H) joint	Maintains humeral head in glenoid fossa (with other rotator cuff muscles) Abduction of shoulder External rotation of shoulder
	Long head of biceps (if humerus externally rotated			
Other				
	Remaining cuff muscles: Infraspinatus, teres minor, subscapularis			Depresses head of humerus

In the frontal plane, the middle deltoid performs shoulder abduction. It also performs horizontal abduction with the posterior deltoid. It has the largest cross-sectional area of the three deltoids. The supraspinatus and other rotator cuff muscles stabilize the humeral head against the elevating effect of the middle deltoid.[27]

Testing the Supraspinatus

Much controversy exists regarding the diagnosis of supraspinatus pathology. Two tests used to examine the supraspinatus muscle are the empty can test (also known as the Jobe test) and the full can test. In the full can test, the arm is externally rotated (thumb pointed up); in the empty can test the arm is internally rotated (thumb pointed down). In both tests the shoulder is in abduction but with 30° of flexion included. In a meta-analysis of the full and empty can tests,[28] the empty can or Jobe test had insufficient sensitivity and specificity to be clinically useful in diagnosing supraspinatus tendonitis or impingement but performed better in identifying a full-thickness or massive tear, especially in the presence of weakness (sensitivity = 41%; specificity = 70%).[29] Furthermore, the empty can (thumb pointed down) and full can (thumb pointed up) positions were not statistically different in their performance of identifying pathology, probably because the supraspinatus generates abduction torque in neutral rotation.[30]

SHOULDER ABDUCTION

(Middle deltoid and Supraspinatus)

Grade 5, Grade 4, and Grade 3

Position of Patient: Short sitting with arm at side and elbow slightly flexed.

Instructions to Therapist: Stand behind patient. Ask patient to lift arm out to the side to shoulder level (test position) with arm in neutral rotation and elbow straight. If sufficient range is present, proceed to test Grade 5. Therapist's hand giving resistance is contoured over arm just above elbow (Fig. 5.64). Resistance is given in a downward direction.

Test: Patient abducts arm to 90°.

Instructions to Patient: "Lift your arm out to the side to shoulder level. Hold it. Don't let me push it down."

Grading

Grade 5: Holds test position against maximal resistance.

Grade 4: Holds test position against strong resistance.

Grade 3: Completes range of motion to 90° without resistance (Fig. 5.65).

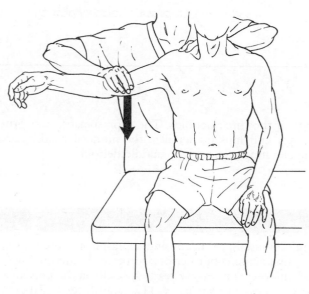

FIGURE 5.64

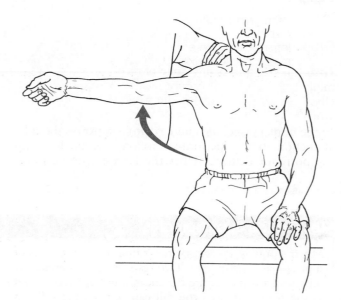

FIGURE 5.65

Grade 2

Position of Patient: Supine. Arm at side supported on table in neutral rotation (thumb pointed outward) (Fig. 5.66).

Instructions to Therapist: Stand at test side of patient (therapist is shown on opposite side of test in figure to clearly illustrate test procedure). Hand used for palpation is positioned over the middle deltoid, lateral to acromial process on the superior aspect of the shoulder.

Test: Patient attempts to abduct shoulder by sliding arm on table without rotating it (see Fig. 5.66). A powder board or towel under the arm may be used to decrease friction.

Instructions to Patient: "Take your arm out to the side."

Grading

Grade 2: Completes full range of motion in this gravity-minimized position or cannot raise shoulder to 90° with elbow straight (cannot lift the weight of the extended arm)

Grade 1 and Grade 0

Position of Patient: Supine with arm at side and elbow slightly flexed.

Therapist Instructions: Stand at side of table at a place where the deltoid can be reached. Palpate the deltoid on the lateral surface of the upper one third of the arm (Fig. 5.67).

Grade 1: Palpable or visible contraction of deltoid with no movement.

Grade 0: No discernable palpable contractile activity.

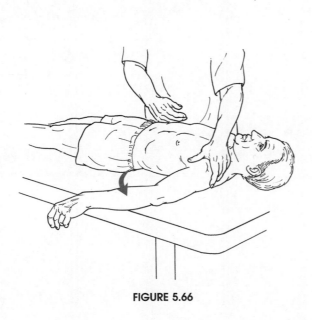

FIGURE 5.66

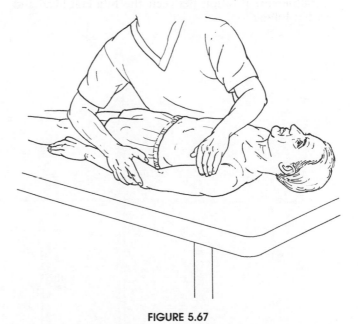

FIGURE 5.67

SHOULDER ABDUCTION

(Middle deltoid and Supraspinatus)

Substitution by Biceps Brachii

When a patient uses the biceps to substitute, the shoulder will externally rotate and the elbow will flex. The arm will be raised but not by the action of the abductor muscles. To avoid this substitution begin the test with the arm in a few degrees of elbow flexion, but do not allow active contraction of the biceps during the test.

Suggested Exercises for Middle Deltoid and Supraspinatus (Combined)

- Flexion at 125°[24]
- Prone horizontal abduction at 100° with full external rotation[8,25]
- Standing external rotation[25]

Helpful Hints

- Turning the face to the opposite side and extending the neck will put the trapezius on slack and make the supraspinatus more accessible for palpation.
- The deltoid and supraspinatus work in tandem; when one is active in abduction, the other also will be active. Only when supraspinatus weakness is suspected is it necessary to palpate.
- Do not allow shoulder elevation or lateral flexion of the trunk to the opposite side because these movements can create an illusion of abduction.
- The tendon of the supraspinatus is the most frequently injured of all the rotator cuff muscles because of its vulnerable position between the humeral head and acromion.[29]

- The supraspinatus is activated first when the patient abducts the arm from a neutral position of hanging at the side.[20] It functions to prevent the deltoid from superiorly translating the humeral head during abduction.[31]
- Peak activation of the supraspinatus is at 90° of abduction which corresponds with the largest shoulder joint compressive loads, when the forces of gravity and weight of the upper extremity are the greatest.[20,32]
- The predicted supraspinatus force during maximum effort isometric plane abduction (scaption) at the 90° position was 175N.[32]

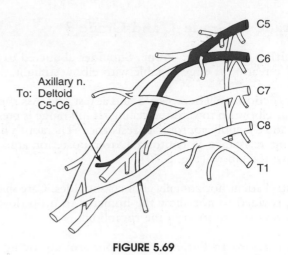

FIGURE 5.69

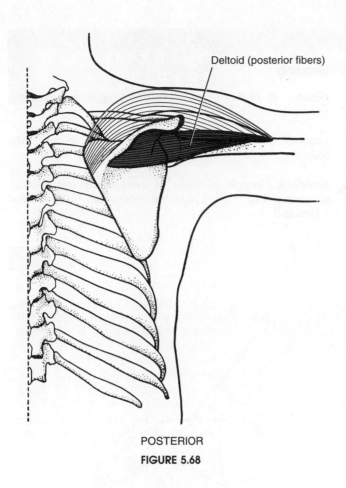

POSTERIOR
FIGURE 5.68

Range of Motion
0°–90° (range, 90°) when starting from a position of 90° of forward flexion
–40° to 90° (range, 130°) when starting with the arm in full horizontal adduction

Table 5.10 SHOULDER HORIZONTAL ABDUCTION

I.D.	Muscle	Origin	Insertion	Function
133	**Deltoid (posterior fibers)**	Scapula (spine on lower lip of crest)	Humerus (deltoid tuberosity via humeral tendon)	Shoulder horizontal abduction Extension and external rotation: posterior fibers
	Deltoid (middle fibers)	See Table 5.9		
Others				
136	Infraspinatus			
137	Teres minor			
125	Rhomboid major			
124	Trapezius (middle)			

SHOULDER HORIZONTAL ABDUCTION

(Posterior deltoid)

Grade 5, Grade 4, and Grade 3

Position of Patient: Prone. Shoulder abducted to 90° and forearm off edge of table with elbow straight.

Instructions to Therapist: Stand at test side. Ask patient to lift elbow up toward the ceiling. If full range is present (Grade 3), apply appropriate resistance. Therapist's hand giving resistance is contoured over posterior arm just above the elbow (Fig. 5.70).

Test: Patient horizontally abducts shoulder. Care should be provided to not allow the humerus to drop (lower), allowing substitution of the rhomboids.

Instructions to Patient: "Lift your arm up toward the ceiling. Hold it. Don't let me push it down."

Grading

Grade 5: Holds test position against maximal resistance.

Grade 4: Holds test position against strong to moderate resistance.

Grade 3: Completes range of motion without manual resistance (Fig. 5.71). Note the elbow can be flexed for a Grade 3.

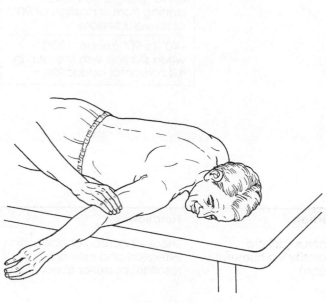

FIGURE 5.70

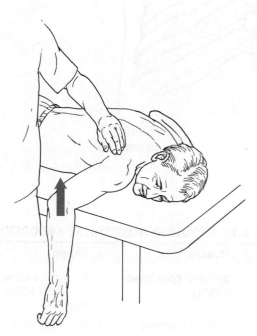

FIGURE 5.71

Grade 2, Grade 1, and Grade 0

Position of Patient: Short sitting.

Instructions to Therapist: Stand at test side. Support forearm under volar aspect (Fig. 5.72) and palpate over the posterior surface of the shoulder just superior to the axilla.

Test: Patient attempts to horizontally abduct the shoulder. Be careful not to allow the patient to drop the arm, substituting the rhomboids.

Instructions to Patient: "Try to move your arm backward."

Alternate Test for Grade 2, Grade 1, and Grade 0

Position of Patient: Short sitting with arm supported on table (smooth surface) in 90° of abduction; elbow partially flexed. A powder board can be used.

Instructions to Therapist: Stand behind patient. Stabilize by contouring one hand over the superior aspect of the shoulder and the other over the scapula (Fig. 5.73). Palpate the fibers of the posterior deltoid below and lateral to the spine of the scapula and on the posterior aspect of the proximal arm adjacent to the axilla.

Test: Patient slides (or tries to move) the arm across the table in horizontal abduction.

Instructions to Patient: "Slide your arm backward."

Grading

Grade 2: Moves through full range of motion.

Grade 1: Palpable contraction; no motion.

Grade 0: No discernable palpable contractile activity.

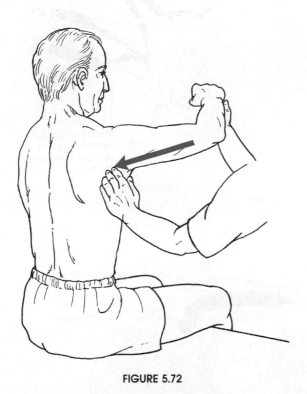

FIGURE 5.72

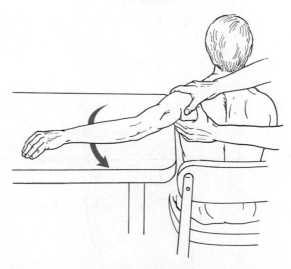

FIGURE 5.73

Helpful Hint

If the scapular muscles are weak, the therapist must manually stabilize the scapula to avoid scapular abduction.

Substitution by Triceps Brachii (Long Head)

Maintain the elbow in flexion to avoid substitution by the long head of the triceps.

Suggested Exercises for Posterior Deltoid

- Bent over rear deltoid raise
- Prone rear deltoid raise
- Prone horizontal abduction at 100° with full external rotation[25]
- Prone external rotation at 90° of abduction[25]

(Pectoralis major)

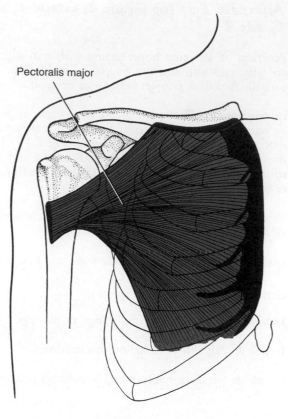

Pectoralis major

FIGURE 5.74

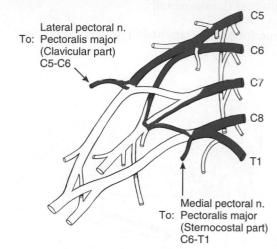

Lateral pectoral n.
To: Pectoralis major
(Clavicular part)
C5-C6

C5
C6
C7
C8
T1

Medial pectoral n.
To: Pectoralis major
(Sternocostal part)
C6-T1

FIGURE 5.75

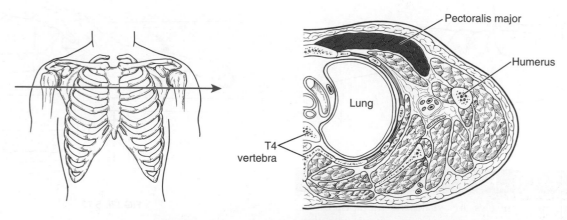

Pectoralis major

Humerus

Lung

T4
vertebra

FIGURE 5.76 Arrow indicates level of cross section.

Range of Motion
0°–130°
When starting from a position of 90° of forward flexion: 0° to −40° (range, 40°)
When starting with the arm in full horizontal abduction: 0° passing across the midline to −40° (range, 130°)

Table 5.11 SHOULDER HORIZONTAL ADDUCTION

I.D.	Muscle	Origin	Insertion	Function
131	**Pectoralis major**			
	Clavicular part	Clavicle (sternal half of anterior surface)	Humerus (intertubercular sulcus, lateral lip)	Internal rotation of shoulder Flexion of shoulder Horizontal shoulder adduction
	Sternal part	Sternum (anterior surface down to rib 6) Ribs 2–7 (costal cartilages) Aponeurosis of obliquus externus abdominis	Both parts converge on a bilaminar common tendon	Horizontal shoulder adduction Extension of shoulder Draws trunk upward and forward in climbing
Other				
133	Deltoid (anterior fibers)	See Table 5.7		

The two parts of the pectoralis major muscle can work separately or together. Together they adduct the arm across the body and medially rotate the shoulder. It swings the extended arm forwards and medially.[1] If the arm is fixed, such as gripping a branch overhead, the pectoralis major draws the trunk up and forwards.[1]

Grade 5 and Grade 4

Position of Patient:
Whole Muscle: Supine. Shoulder abducted to 90°; elbow flexed to 90°.

Clavicular Head: Patient begins test with shoulder in 60° of abduction with elbow flexed. Patient then is asked to horizontally adduct the shoulder in a slightly upward diagonal direction.

Sternal Head: Patient begins test with shoulder in about 120° of abduction with elbow flexed. Patient is asked to horizontally adduct the shoulder in a slightly downward diagonal direction.

Instructions to Therapist: Stand at side of shoulder to be tested. Ask the patient to move the arm with elbow flexed in horizontal adduction, keeping it parallel to the floor without rotation, checking the range of motion. If the arm moves across the body in a diagonal motion, test the sternal and clavicular heads of the muscle separately. If full range is present in a horizontal adducted direction (Grade 3), test the whole muscle together.

Therapist's hand used for resistance is contoured around upper arm, just proximal to elbow, allowing the forearm to hang free. Resistance is applied in the direction opposite the trunk in the transverse plane.

SHOULDER HORIZONTAL ADDUCTION

(Pectoralis major)

Grade 5 and Grade 4 Continued

Clavicular Head: Resistance is applied above the elbow in a downward direction (toward floor) and outward (i.e., opposite to the direction of the fibers of the clavicular head, which moves the arm diagonally up and inward) (Fig. 5.77).

Sternal Head: Resistance is applied above the elbow in an up and outward direction (Fig. 5.78) (i.e., opposite to the motion of the sternal head, which is diagonally down and inward).

Test: When the *whole muscle* is tested, the patient horizontally adducts the shoulder in the transverse plane through the available range of motion (Fig. 5.79).

When the *clavicular head is tested*, the patient's motion begins at 60° of abduction and moves up and in across the body.

When the *sternal head is tested*, the motion begins at 120° of shoulder abduction and moves diagonally down and in toward the patient's opposite hip.

Instructions to Patient:
Both Heads: "Move your arm across your chest. Hold it. Don't let me pull it back."

Clavicular Head: "Move your arm up and in."

Sternal Head: "Move your arm down and in."

Grading

Grade 5: Holds test position against maximal resistance.

Grade 4: Holds test position with strong to moderate resistance, but muscle exhibits some "give" at end of range.

Grade 3: Completes available range of motion in all three tests (if appropriate) with no resistance other than the weight of the extremity.

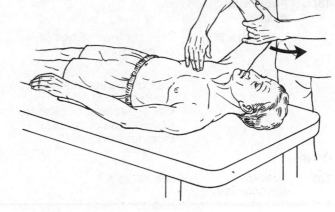

FIGURE 5.78

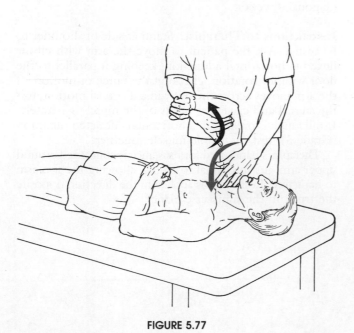

FIGURE 5.77

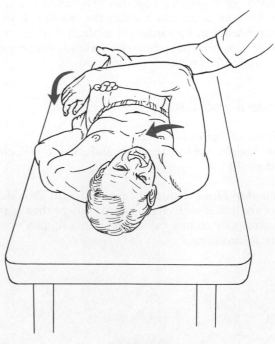

FIGURE 5.79

Grade 2, Grade 1, and Grade 0

Position of Patient: Supine. Arm is supported in 90° of abduction with elbow flexed to 90°.

Alternate Position: Patient is seated with test arm supported on table (at level of axilla) with arm in 90° of abduction midway between flexion and extension and elbow slightly flexed (Fig. 5.80). Friction of the table surface should be minimized (as with a powder board).

Instructions to Therapist: Stand at side of shoulder to be tested or behind the seated patient. If the patient is supine, support the full length of the forearm and hold the limb at the wrist (see Fig. 5.77).

For both tests palpate the pectoralis major muscle on the anterior aspect of the chest medial to the shoulder joint (Fig. 5.81.)

Test: Patient attempts to horizontally adduct the shoulder. The use of the alternate test position, in which the arm moves across the table, precludes individual testing for the two heads.

Instructions to Patient: "Try to move your arm across your chest." In seated position: "Move your arm in towards your body."

Grading

Grade 2: Patient horizontally adducts shoulder through available range of motion with the weight of the arm supported by the therapist or the table.

Grade 1: Palpable contractile activity.

Grade 0: No discernable palpable contractile activity.

Helpful Hint

Testing both heads of the pectoralis major separately should be routine in any patient with cervical spinal cord injury because of their different nerve root innervation.

Suggested Exercises for Pectoralis Major, Pectoralis Major and Teres Major

- Push up with narrow hand placement[33]
- Push up plus[34]
- D2 diagonal[34]

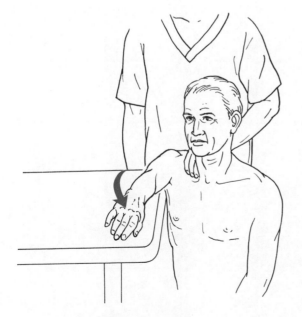

FIGURE 5.80

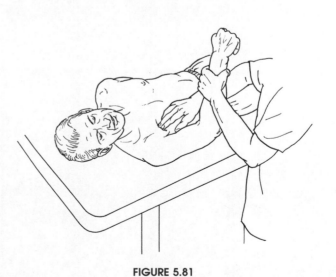

FIGURE 5.81

INTRODUCTION TO THE ROTATOR CUFF

The rotator cuff is made up of the four tendons of the subscapularis, supraspinatus, infraspinatus, and teres minor muscles. However the teres minor, parts of the infraspinatus, and most of the subscapularis do not have tendons, so rotator cuff is a misnomer.[1] However, it is a familiar term and will be used in this discussion. The teres major has an important role in stabilizing the head of the humerus into the glenoid when the arm is elevated over 90° and is often considered a part of the rotator cuff.[1] The rotator cuff functions to provide a compressive force in all positions of the arm at the shoulder. The infraspinatus and teres minor act as an external rotator and the subscapularis and teres major act as an internal rotator. The supraspinatus initiates and assists with abduction. The supraspinatus assists with external rotation when the shoulder is abducted. The shoulder with a poorly performing rotator cuff is quite impaired because of the importance of humeral stabilization.[1]

Resistance applied in tests of shoulder rotation should be administered gradually and carefully because of the inherent instability of the shoulder and in the presence of pain, muscle tears, or instability.

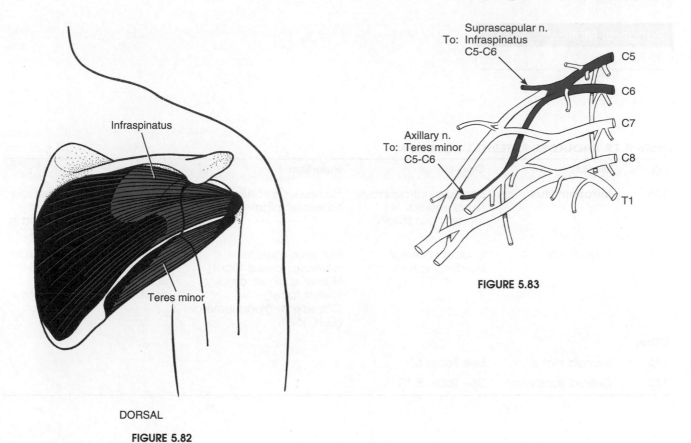

Infraspinatus

Teres minor

DORSAL

FIGURE 5.82

Suprascapular n.
To: Infraspinatus
C5-C6

C5

C6

C7

C8

T1

Axillary n.
To: Teres minor
C5-C6

FIGURE 5.83

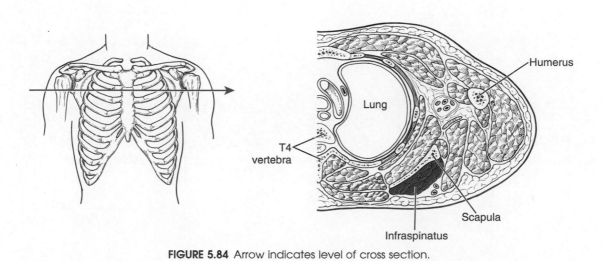

Humerus

Lung

T4
vertebra

Scapula

Infraspinatus

FIGURE 5.84 Arrow indicates level of cross section.

SHOULDER EXTERNAL ROTATION

(Infraspinatus and Teres minor)

Range of Motion
0°–80°

Table 5.12 SHOULDER EXTERNAL ROTATION

I.D.	Muscle	Origin	Insertion	Function
136	**Infraspinatus**	Scapula (infraspinous fossa, medial ⅔) Infraspinous fascia	Humerus (greater tubercle, middle facet)	External rotation of shoulder Stabilizes shoulder joint by depressing humeral head in glenoid fossa
137	Teres minor	Scapula (lateral border, superior ⅔)	Humerus (greater tubercle, lowest facet) Humerus (shaft, distal to lowest facet) Capsule of glenohumeral (G-H) joint	External rotation of shoulder Maintains humeral head in glenoid fossa, thus stabilizing the shoulder joint
Other				
135	Supraspinatus	See Table 5.9		
133	Deltoid (posterior)	See Table 5.10		

Grade 5, Grade 4, and Grade 3

Position of Patient: Short sitting, with elbow flexed to 90° and forearm in neutral rotation, perpendicular with the patient's trunk.

Instructions to Therapist: Stand in front of patient. Ask patient to move the forearm away from the trunk. If full range is available (Grade 3), apply appropriate resistance. One hand stabilizes the medial aspect of the elbow and the other hand provides resistance at the dorsal (extensor) surface of the forearm, just proximal to the wrist to avoid eliciting the wrist extensors (Fig. 5.85). Resistance is given on the outside of the forearm towards the trunk. Because this is not an anti-gravity position, maximal resistance should be used, if appropriate.

Test: Patient externally rotates arm, pushing forearm away from trunk.

Instructions to Patient: "Push your forearm away. Hold it. Don't let me move it."

Grade 3 Instructions to Patient: "Move your forearm away from your stomach" (Fig. 5.86).

Grading

Grade 5: Holds test position against maximal resistance.

Grade 4: Holds test position against strong resistance with some yield.

Grade 3: Completes available range of motion without manual resistance.

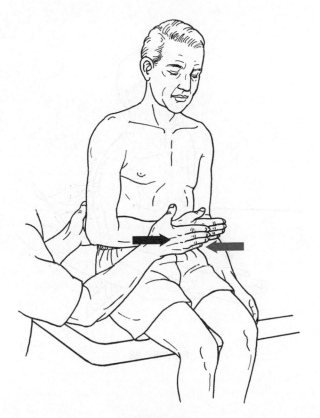

FIGURE 5.85

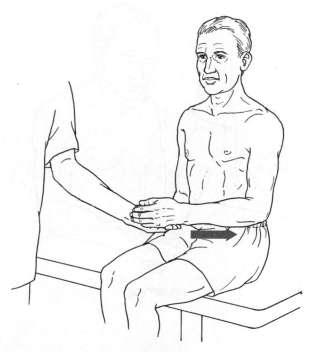

FIGURE 5.86

SHOULDER EXTERNAL ROTATION

(Infraspinatus and Teres minor)

Grade 2, Grade 1, and Grade 0

Position of Patient: Short sitting with elbow flexed to 90° and forearm in neutral rotation with hand facing forward, supported on table with friction minimized by therapist (Figs. 5.87 and 5.88), powder board or other means (see Fig. 5.87).

Instructions to Therapist: Sit or stand on a low stool at test side of patient at shoulder level (picture shows therapist on opposite side to avoid obstructing view). One hand stabilizes the outside of the flexed elbow while the other hand palpates for the tendon of the infraspinatus over the body of the scapula below the spine in the infraspinous fossa. Palpate the teres minor on the inferior margin of the axilla and along the axillary border of the scapula (see Fig. 5.88). Supination may occur instead of the requested external rotation during the testing of Grades 2 and 1. This motion can be mistaken for external rotation.

Test: Patient attempts to move forearm away from the trunk (see Fig. 5.88).

Instructions to Patient: "Try to push your forearm away from your stomach."

Grading

Grade 2: Completes available range in this gravity-eliminated position.

Grade 1: Palpation of either or both muscles reveals contractile activity but no motion.

Grade 0: No discernable palpable contractile activity.

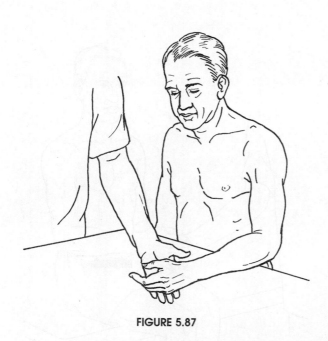

FIGURE 5.87

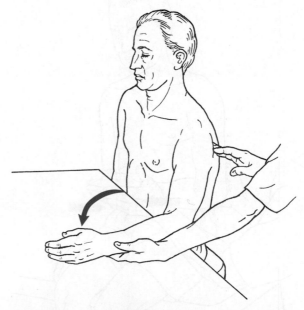

FIGURE 5.88

Alternate Position for Grade 5, Grade 4, and Grade 3

Position of Patient: Prone with head turned toward test side. Shoulder abducted to 90° with arm fully supported on table; forearm hanging vertically over edge of table. Place a folded towel under the arm or use the therapist's hand to cushion the arm if the table has a sharp edge (Fig. 5.89).

Instructions to Therapist: Stand at test side at level of patient's waist (see Fig. 5.89). Use one hand to give resistance over the forearm, as near the wrist as possible, for Grades 5 and 4. The other hand supports the elbow to provide some counter-pressure at the end of the range. NOTE: resistance will be much less than in the sitting position and care should be taken in this vulnerable position.

Test: Patient moves forearm upward through the range of external rotation.

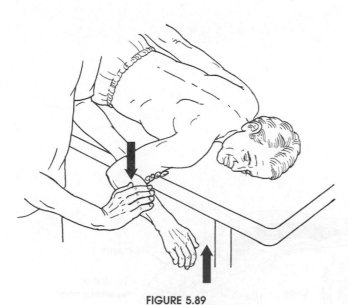

FIGURE 5.89

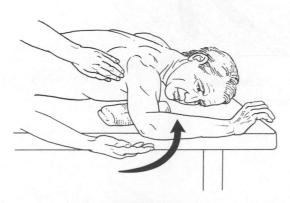

FIGURE 5.90

Instructions to Patient: "Raise your arm to the level of the table. Hold it. Don't let me push it down." Therapist may need to demonstrate the desired motion.

Grading

Grade 5: Holds test position against strong resistance.

Grade 4: Holds test position, but end range yields or gives way with strong resistance.

Grade 3: Completes available range of motion without manual resistance (Fig. 5.90).

Helpful Hints

- External rotation (ER) at 0° abduction has been shown to be the most optimal position to isolate the infraspinatus muscle.[30] The teres minor generates a relatively constant ER torque throughout arm abduction movement.
- The optimal manual muscle test (MMT) position for the infraspinatus has the least activation of the supraspinatus muscle (see Fig. 5.85).[30,35]
- Range of motion for 60+ year old individuals is less than younger adults and averages 71–72° for men and women.[36]
- Range of motion averages for children and adolescents are 93°–99°.[36]

Suggested Exercises for the Infraspinatus

- Prone horizontal abduction at 100° with ER and IR
- Side-lying ER with 0° abduction[7,25] (minimizes upper trapezius activity)
- D1 and D2 diagonal pattern flexion (may elicit upper trapezius)
- Standing EsR at 90° abduction (full can)[7]

Suggested Exercises for the Teres Minor

- Flexion above 120° with ER (thumb up)[7]
- Standing scapular rows at various degrees of flexion (45°, 90° and 135°)[7]
- Side-lying ER at 0° abduction[7]
- Prone horizontal abduction at 90°[7]
- Abduction with ER (thumb up and down)[7]

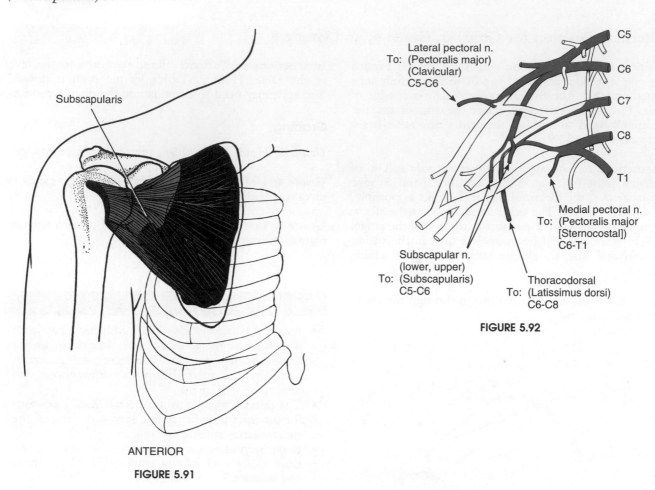

Subscapularis

Lateral pectoral n.
To: (Pectoralis major)
(Clavicular)
C5-C6

C5
C6
C7
C8
T1

Subscapular n.
(lower, upper)
To: (Subscapularis)
C5-C6

Medial pectoral n.
To: (Pectoralis major
[Sternocostal])
C6-T1

Thoracodorsal
To: (Latissimus dorsi)
C6-C8

FIGURE 5.92

ANTERIOR

FIGURE 5.91

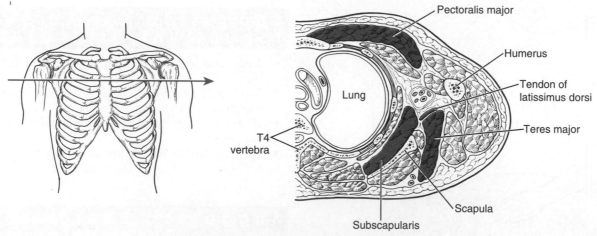

Pectoralis major

Humerus

Lung

Tendon of
latissimus dorsi

Teres major

T4
vertebra

Scapula

Subscapularis

FIGURE 5.93 Arrow indicates level of cross section.

Range of Motion
0°–60°

Table 5.13 SHOULDER INTERNAL ROTATION

I.D.	Muscle	Origin	Insertion	Function
134	**Subscapularis**	Scapula (fills fossa on costal surface) Intermuscular septa Aponeurosis of subscapularis	Humerus (lesser tubercle) Capsule of glenohumeral (G-H) joint (anterior)	Internal rotation of shoulder Maintains humeral head in glenoid fossa (with other rotator cuff muscles) Abduction of shoulder
138	Teres major	Scapula (dorsal surface of inferior angle)	Humerus (intertubercular sulcus, medial lip)	Internal rotation of shoulder Adduction and extension of shoulder Extension of shoulder from a flexed position
131	Pectoralis major	Sternal half of clavicle, entire anterior surface of the sternum	Lateral lip of the intertubercular sulcus of anterior humerus	
	Clavicular part	Clavicle (sternal half of anterior surface)	Humerus (intertubercular sulcus, lateral lip)	*Clavicular fibers:* Internal rotation of shoulder Flexion of shoulder Horizontal shoulder adduction
130	Latissimus dorsi	T6-T12, L1-L5, and sacral vertebrae (spinous processes) Supraspinous ligaments Ribs 9–12 (by slips that interdigitate with obliquus externus abdominis) Ilium (crest, posterior) Thoracolumbar fascia	Humerus (floor of intertubercular sulcus) Deep fascia of arm	Internal rotation of shoulder

(Subscapularis)

Grade 5, Grade 4, and Grade 3

Position of Patient: Short sitting with elbow flexed to 90°, forearm in neutral rotation, perpendicular to the trunk.

Instructions to Therapist: Stand in front of patient and ask patient to pull forearm toward the trunk. If full range is present (Grade 3), apply resistance. Stabilize the outside of the elbow with one hand while the other hand provides resistance at the volar (flexor) surface of the forearm, just proximal to the wrist (Fig. 5.94) so as not to elicit wrist flexors. Resistance is given on the volar surface in the direction away from the trunk. As in the tests for ER, this is a gravity-minimized position, so maximal resistance is used, if appropriate.

Test: Patient internally rotates arm, pulling forearm toward trunk.

Instructions to Patient: "Pull your forearm toward your stomach. Hold it. Don't let me pull it out."

Grading

Grade 5: Holds test position against maximum resistance.

Grade 4: Holds test position against strong resistance. Some yield is felt.

Grade 3: Completes available range without manual resistance.

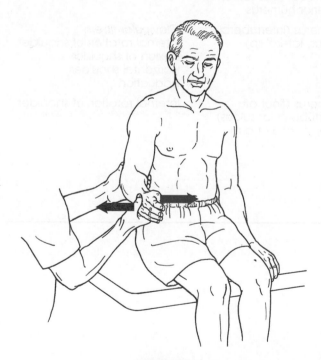

FIGURE 5.94

Grade 2, Grade 1, and Grade 0

Position of Patient: Short sitting or sitting at a table, with elbow flexed and forearm in neutral rotation.

Instructions to Therapist: Stand at test side or sit on low stool. One hand stabilizes the forearm while the other hand palpates for the tendon of the subscapularis, deep in the axilla (Fig. 5.95). NOTE: The hand of the therapist under the patient's hand will eliminate friction in the Grade 2 test if a flat surface is being used (Fig. 5.96). Alternatively, a powder board can be used.

Test: Patient attempts to internally rotate arm, pulling forearm toward trunk.

Instructions to Patient: "Try to pull your forearm toward your stomach."

Grading

Grade 2: Is not able to complete available range.

Grade 1: Palpable contraction occurs.

Grade 0: No discernable palpable contractile activity.

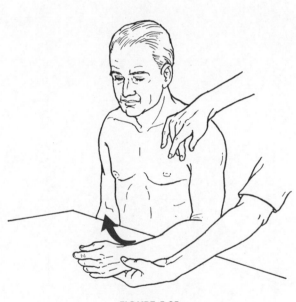

FIGURE 5.95

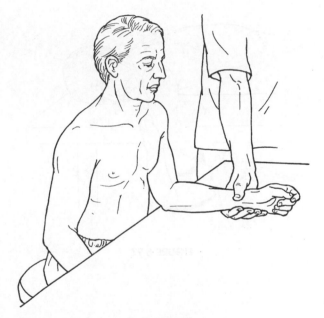

FIGURE 5.96

SHOULDER INTERNAL ROTATION

(Subscapularis)

Alternate Test for Grade 5, Grade 4, and Grade 3

Used if patient cannot sit.

Position of Patient: Prone with head turned toward test side. Shoulder is abducted to 90° with folded towel placed under distal arm and forearm hanging vertically over edge of table.

Instructions to Therapist: Stand at test side. Hand giving resistance is placed on the volar side of the forearm just above the wrist. The other hand provides counterforce at the elbow (Fig. 5.97). The resistance hand applies resistance in a downward and forward direction; the counterforce is applied backward and slightly upward. Stabilize the scapular region if muscles are weak or perform test in the supine position. NOTE: resistance will be much less than in the sitting position.

Test: Patient moves arm through available range of internal rotation (backward and upward).

Instructions to Patient: "Move your forearm up and back. Hold it. Don't let me push it down." Demonstrate the desired motion to the patient.

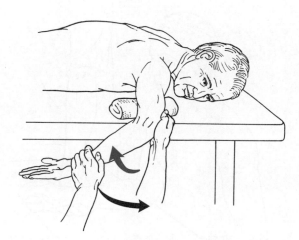

FIGURE 5.97

Alternate Test for Grade 5, Grade 4, and Grade 3 Continued

Grading

Grade 5: Holds test position firmly against strong resistance.

Grade 4: Holds test position, but there is a give against strong resistance.

Grade 3: Completes available range with no manual resistance (Fig. 5.98).

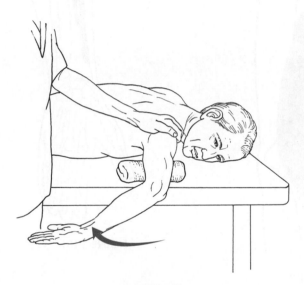

FIGURE 5.98

Helpful Hints

- Internal rotation is a stronger motion than external rotation. This is largely a factor of muscle mass.
- The movement most optimal for isolation and activation of the subscapularis muscle is the lift-off test against resistance, the clinical diagnostic test for subscapularis tears.[37] This movement can also be used as an exercise for the subscapularis.
- The belly press test is an alternative test to the lift-off test, useful when pain or limited motion prevents the shoulder from getting into the lift-off position.[38] It is performed in sitting or standing with the palm of the hand placed against the belly, just below the level of the xiphoid process. The patient is instructed to maximally push the hand into the belly by internally rotating the shoulder. A positive test is indicated when the patient drops the elbow toward the torso (shoulder adduction and extension), and inability to internally rotate the shoulder indicating a torn subscapularis tendon.
- The belly-press test was found to activate the upper subscapularis muscle more than the lift-off test, whereas the lift-off test was found to activate the lower subscapularis muscle more than the belly-press test.[38]
- The upper portion (innervated by the upper subscapularis nerve) is a more effective internal rotator at lower abduction angles compared with higher abduction angles. The lower subscapularis muscle activity (innervated by the lower subscapularis nerve) is unaffected by abduction angle.
- Performing internal rotation (IR) at 0° abduction produces similar amounts of upper and lower subscapularis activity.[39]

Suggested Exercises for the Subscapularis

- Pushup or palm press[7,24]
- Internal rotation at 0°[24,34]
- Standing high, mid, and low scapular rows
- Flexion above 120° with ER (thumb up).[7]
- Pushup plus exercise[34]
- D2 diagonal[34]
- Dynamic hug[34]

(Biceps, Brachialis, and Brachioradialis)

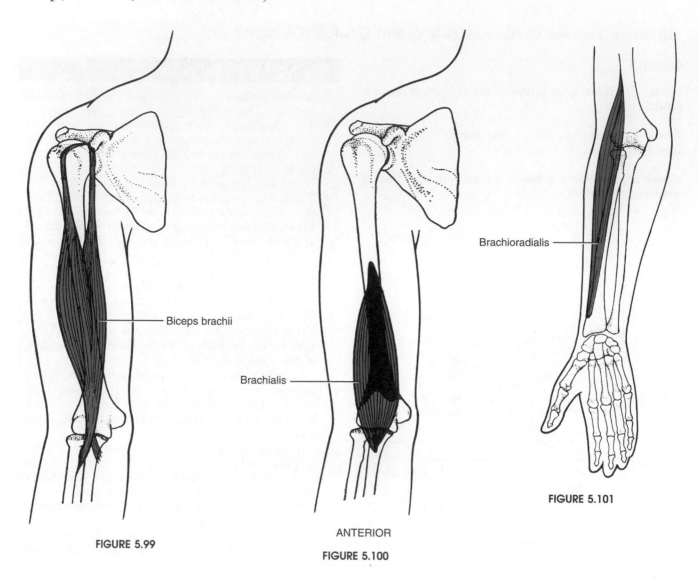

Biceps brachii

FIGURE 5.99

Brachialis

ANTERIOR

FIGURE 5.100

Brachioradialis

FIGURE 5.101

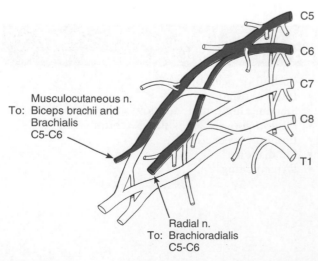

C5

C6

C7

C8

T1

Musculocutaneous n.
To: Biceps brachii and
Brachialis
C5-C6

Radial n.
To: Brachioradialis
C5-C6

FIGURE 5.102

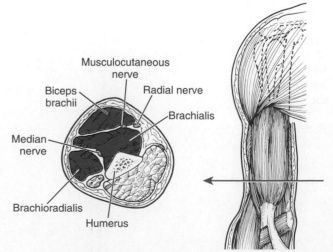

Musculocutaneous
nerve

Biceps
brachii

Radial nerve

Brachialis

Median
nerve

Brachioradialis

Humerus

FIGURE 5.103 Arrow indicates level of cross section.

Range of Motion
0°–150°

Table 5.14 ELBOW FLEXION

I.D.	Muscle	Origin	Insertion	Function
141	**Brachialis**	Humerus (shaft anterior, distal ½) Intermuscular septa (medial)	Ulna (tuberosity and coronoid process)	Flexion of elbow, forearm supinated or pronated
140	Biceps brachii Short head Long head	Scapula (coracoid process, apex) Scapula (supraglenoid tubercle) Capsule of glenohumeral (G-H) joint and glenoid labrum	Radius (radial tuberosity) Bicipital aponeurosis	*Both heads:* Flexion of elbow Supination of forearm (powerful) *Long head:* Stabilizes and depresses humeral head in glenoid fossa during deltoid activity
143	Brachioradialis	Humerus (lateral supracondylar ridge, proximal ⅔) Lateral intermuscular septum	Radius (distal end just proximal to styloid process)	Flexion of elbow
Others				
146	Pronator teres	See Table 5.17		
148	Extensor carpi radialis longus	See Table 5.19		
151	Flexor carpi radialis	See Table 5.18		
153	Flexor carpi ulnaris	See Table 5.18		

The two heads of the biceps work together to accomplish flexion of the elbow. As in the three heads of the triceps, the multiple heads are considered reserves, as both work together to flex the elbow.

Grade 5, Grade 4, and Grade 3

Position of Patient: Short sitting with arms at sides. The following are the positions of choice, but it is doubtful whether the individual muscles can be separated when strong effort is used. The brachialis is independent of forearm position.

Biceps Brachii: Forearm in supination (Fig. 5.104).

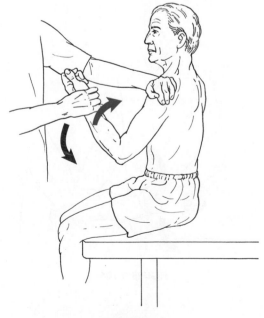

FIGURE 5.104

(Biceps, Brachialis, and Brachioradialis)

Grade 5, Grade 4, and Grade 3 Continued

Brachialis: Forearm in pronation (Fig. 5.105).

Brachioradialis: Forearm in mid position between pronation and supination (Fig. 5.106).

Instructions to Therapist: Stand in front of patient toward the test side. Ask patient to bend elbow. If full range is present (Grade 3), apply appropriate resistance. Therapist's hand giving resistance is contoured over the volar (flexor) surface of the forearm proximal to the wrist (see Fig. 5.104). The other hand is placed over the anterior surface of the shoulder and applies counterforce by resisting any upper arm movement.

No resistance is given in a Grade 3 test. The test elbow is cupped by the therapist's hand for support (Fig. 5.107, biceps illustrated at end range).

Test (All Three Forearm Positions): Patient flexes elbow through range of motion.

Instructions to Patient (All Three Tests):
Grade 5 and Grade 4: "Bend your elbow. Hold it. Don't let me pull it down."

Grade 3: "Bend your elbow."

Grading

Grade 5: Holds test position against maximal resistance.

Grade 4: Holds test position against strong to moderate resistance, but the end point may not be firm.

Grade 3: Completes available range with each forearm position.

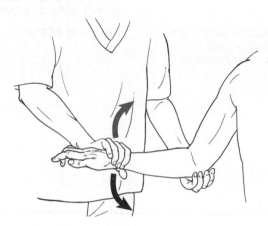

FIGURE 5.105

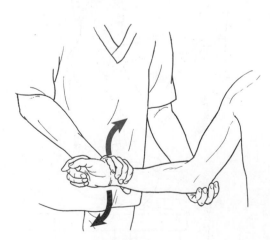

FIGURE 5.106

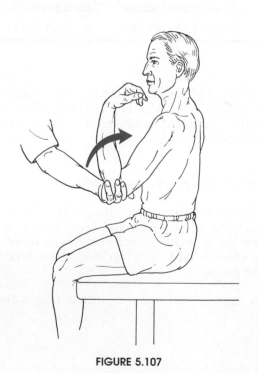

FIGURE 5.107

(Biceps, Brachialis, and Brachioradialis)

Grade 2

Position of Patient:

All Elbow Flexors: Short sitting with arm flexed to 90° and internally rotated (to minimize gravity) and supported by therapist (Fig. 5.108). Forearm is supinated (biceps), pronated (brachialis), and in mid position (brachioradialis).

Alternate Position for Patients Unable to Sit: Patient is side-lying with arm supported at the elbow in 90° flexion to minimize gravity. Elbow is flexed to about 45° with forearm supinated, pronated (for brachialis), and in mid position (for brachioradialis; Fig. 5.109, biceps illustrated).

Instructions to Therapist:

All Three Flexors: Stand in front of patient and support flexed arm under the elbow and wrist if necessary. Palpate the tendon of the biceps in the antecubital space (see Fig. 5.108). On the arm, the muscle fibers may be felt on the anterior surface of the middle two thirds of the biceps with the short head lying medial to the long head.

Palpate the brachialis in the distal arm medial to the tendon of the biceps. Palpate the brachioradialis on the lateral surface of the neutrally positioned forearm, where it forms the lateral border of the cubital fossa.

Test: Patient attempts to flex the elbow.

Instructions to Patient: "Try to bend your elbow."

Grading

Grade 2: Completes range of motion with gravity minimized (in each of the muscles tested).

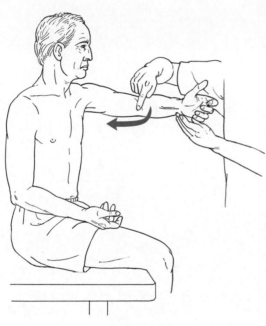

FIGURE 5.108

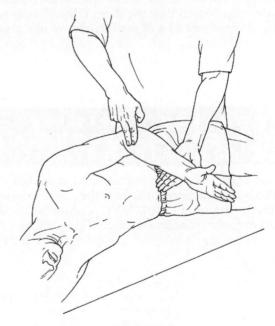

FIGURE 5.109

ELBOW FLEXION

(Biceps, Brachialis, and Brachioradialis)

Grade 1 and Grade 0

Positions of Patient and Therapist: Side-lying for all three muscles with therapist standing at test side. All other aspects are the same as for the Grade 2 test.

Test: Patient attempts to bend elbow with hand supinated, pronated, and in mid position.

Grading

Grade 1: Therapist can palpate a contractile response in each of the three muscles for which a Grade 1 is given.

Grade 0: No discernable palpable contractile activity.

Helpful Hints

- The patient's wrist flexor muscles should remain relaxed throughout the test because strongly contracting wrist flexors may assist in elbow flexion. Recall that the wrist flexors originate above the elbow joint axis on the distal humerus.
- Only the brachioradialis contributes to pronation with elbow flexion.[40]
- During resisted shoulder flexion with the elbow straight, both heads of the biceps are always active.[2]
- Basmajian[2] noted that the three elbow flexors work together without a lot of predictability of one muscle's action over the others when lifting a load. Generally, they are stronger in elbow flexion with supination than pronation.
- The brachialis is considered the workhorse of the elbow flexors as it is active in isometric flexion and eccentric extension. The other two flexors are not as active in eccentric extension.[2]
- The biceps brachii is composed of 60% type II fibers.[41]

Suggested Exercises for Biceps, Brachialis and Brachioradialis

- Dumbbell biceps curl and inclined dumbbell curl (shoulder extended) elicited the same maximal muscle activation (>40% MVC) concentrically and eccentrically throughout range.[42]

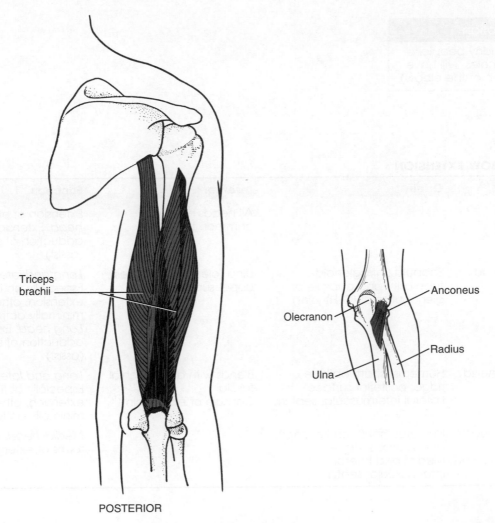

Triceps
brachii

Olecranon

Anconeus

Ulna

Radius

POSTERIOR

FIGURE 5.110

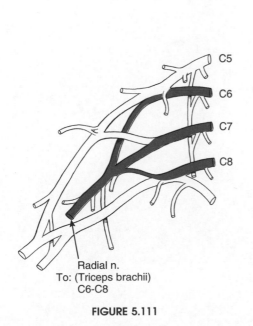

C5

C6

C7

C8

Radial n.
To: (Triceps brachii)
C6-C8

FIGURE 5.111

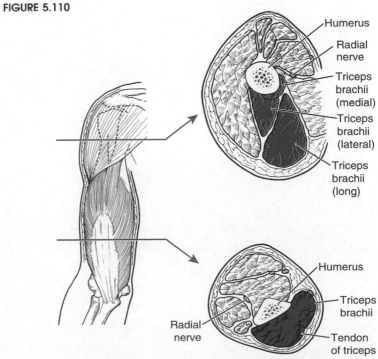

Humerus

Radial
nerve

Triceps
brachii
(medial)

Triceps
brachii
(lateral)

Triceps
brachii
(long)

Humerus

Triceps
brachii

Radial
nerve

Tendon
of triceps

FIGURE 5.112 Arrows indicates level of cross sections.

ELBOW EXTENSION

(Triceps brachii)

Range of Motion

150° to −5° (many people, especially females, will have hyperextension of the elbow)

Table 5.15 ELBOW EXTENSION

I.D.	Muscle	Origin	Insertion	Function
142	**Triceps brachii**		All heads have a common tendon to:	Extension of elbow *head*: Extension and adduction of shoulder (assist)
	Long head	Scapula (infraglenoid tuberosity and capsule of glenohumeral (G-H) joint)	Ulna (olecranon process, upper surface)	*Long and lateral heads*: Especially active in resisted extension, otherwise minimally active[24] *Long head*: Extension and adduction of shoulder (assist)
	Lateral head	Humerus (shaft: oblique ridge, posterior surface) Lateral intermuscular septum	Blends with antebrachial fascia Capsule of elbow joint	*Long and lateral heads*: Especially active in resisted extension, otherwise minimally active
	Medial head	Humerus (shaft: entire length of posterior surface) Medial and lateral intermuscular septa		*Medial head*: Active in all forms of extension

As in the biceps, all heads of the triceps brachii work together to extend the elbow. The triceps can fixate the elbow joint when the forearm and hand are used for fine movement (e.g., when writing). The triceps have a greater proportion of type II muscle fibers. The lateral head is used for movements requiring occasional high-intensity force, while the medial head enables precise, low-force movements.

Grade 5, Grade 4, and Grade 3

Position of Patient: Prone on table. The patient starts the test with the shoulder in 90° of abduction and the elbow flexed to 90° and in neutral rotation (forearm hanging over the side of the table) (Fig. 5.113).

Instructions to Therapist: Stand to the side of the patient. Ask patient to straighten the elbow. If full range is present (Grade 3), apply appropriate resistance. Provide support with one hand underneath the arm, just above the elbow. The other hand is used to apply downward resistance on the distal dorsal surface of the extended forearm just proximal to the wrist (Fig. 5.114 illustrates end position). Be sure to have the elbow in minimal flexion, so as not to allow the patient to "lock out" the elbow. This is especially important if hyperextension exists.

Test: Patient straightens elbow

Instructions to Patient: "Hold it. Don't let me bend it."

Grading

Grade 5: Holds test position firmly against maximal resistance.

Grade 4: Holds test position against strong resistance, but there is a "give" to the resistance at the end range.

Grade 3: Completes available range with no manual resistance (Fig. 5.115).

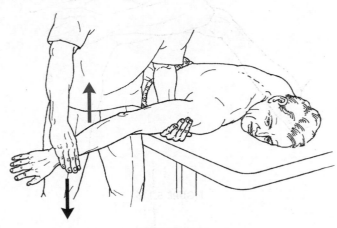

FIGURE 5.114

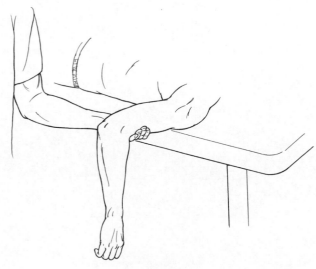

FIGURE 5.113

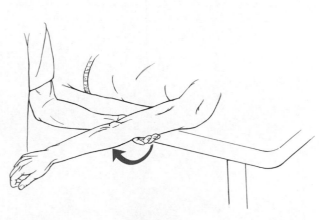

FIGURE 5.115

ELBOW EXTENSION

(Triceps brachii)

Grade 2, Grade 1, and Grade 0

Position of Patient: Short sitting. The shoulder is abducted to 90° and neutral rotation with the elbow flexed to about 45° to minimize gravity. The entire limb is parallel to the floor (Fig. 5.116).

Instructions to Therapist: Stand at test side of patient. For the Grade 2 test, support the limb at the elbow. For a Grade 1 or 0 test, support the limb under the forearm and palpate the triceps on the posterior surface of the arm just proximal to the olecranon process (Fig. 5.117).

Test: Patient attempts to extend the elbow.

Instructions to Patient: "Try to straighten your elbow."

Grading

Grade 2: Completes available range with gravity minimized.

Grade 1: Therapist can feel tension in the triceps tendon just proximal to the olecranon (see Fig. 5.117) or contractile activity in the muscle fibers on the posterior surface of the arm.

Grade 0: No discernable palpable muscle activity.

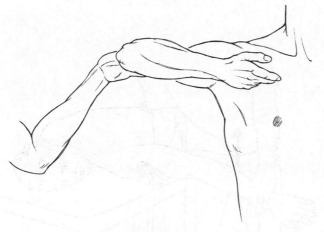

FIGURE 5.116

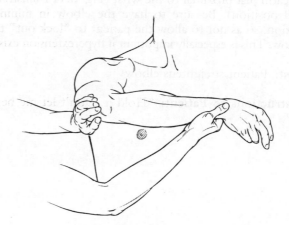

FIGURE 5.117

Substitutions

- Via external rotation. When the patient is sitting with the arm abducted, elbow extension can be accomplished with a Grade 0 triceps (Fig. 5.118) when the patient externally rotates the shoulder, thus dropping the arm below the forearm. As a result, the elbow literally falls into extension. This can be prevented by using a table or powder board to support the arm.
- Via horizontal adduction. This substitution can accomplish elbow extension and is done purposefully by patients with a cervical cord injury and a Grade 0 triceps. With the distal segment fixed (as when the therapist stabilizes the hand or wrist), the patient horizontally adducts the arm and the thrust pulls the elbow into extension (Fig. 5.119). The therapist, therefore, should provide support at the elbow for testing purposes rather than at the wrist.

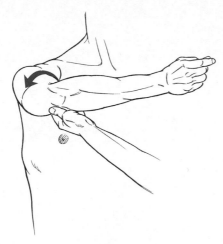

FIGURE 5.118

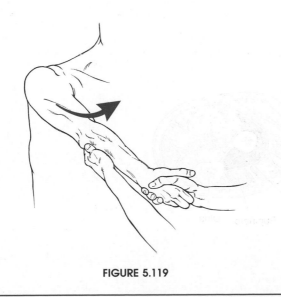

FIGURE 5.119

Helpful Hints

- Give resistance in Grade 5 and Grade 4 tests with the elbow slightly flexed to avoid enabling the patient to "lock" the elbow joint by hyperextending it.
- Although elbow extension is tested in the prone position, the therapist must be aware that with the shoulder horizontally abducted the two-joint muscle is less effective, and the test grade may be lower than it should be.[13]
- An alternate position for Grades 5, 4, and 3 is with the patient short sitting. The therapist stands behind the patient, supporting the arm in 90° of abduction just above the flexed elbow (Fig. 5.120). The patient straightens the elbow against the resistance given just proximal to the wrist.
- Triceps strength is usually the limiting factor in pressing-type movements such as pushups.

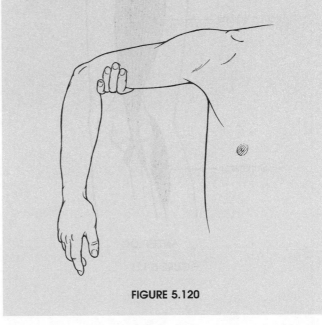

FIGURE 5.120

Suggested Exercises for Triceps Brachii

- Exercises that challenge the triceps close to full extension (lock outs) are likely to be highly beneficial.
- Close grip bench press
- Suspended pushups elicited more activity than conventional pushups[43]
- Standard pushups with narrow base hand position[44]
- Dips
- Triceps extension overhead
- Triceps press down using rope

FOREARM SUPINATION

(Supinator and Biceps brachii)

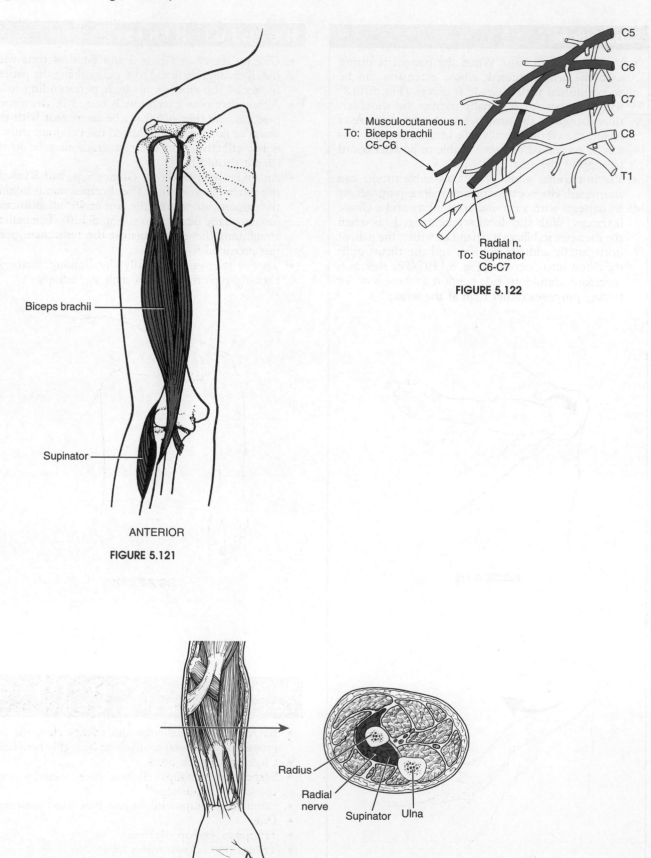

Biceps brachii

Supinator

ANTERIOR

FIGURE 5.121

Musculocutaneous n.
To: Biceps brachii
C5-C6

C5
C6
C7
C8
T1

Radial n.
To: Supinator
C6-C7

FIGURE 5.122

Radius

Radial
nerve

Supinator   Ulna

FIGURE 5.123 Arrow indicates level of cross section.

Range of Motion
0°–80°

Table 5.16 FOREARM SUPINATION

I.D.	Muscle	Origin	Insertion	Function
140	**Biceps brachii** **Both heads**			Flexion of elbow Supination of forearm (powerful) if combined with elbow flexion
145	**Supinator**	Humerus (lateral epicondyle) Ulna (supinator crest) Radial collateral ligament of elbow joint Annular ligament of radioulnar joint Aponeurosis of supinator	Radius (shaft, lateral aspect of proximal ⅓)	Supination of forearm (pure)

Grade 5, Grade 4, Grade 3, and Grade 2

Position of Patient: Short sitting; arm at side and elbow flexed to 90°; forearm in full pronation to neutral. Alternatively, patient may sit at a table with elbow supported.

Instructions to Therapist: Stand at side or in front of patient. Ask patient to turn the palm up as if holding soup in the hand. If sufficient range is present, proceed to apply resistance. One hand supports the elbow. Apply resistance with the heel of the therapist's hand over the dorsal (extensor) surface at the wrist, being careful not to grip the flexor surface of the forearm (Fig. 5.124).

Test: Patient begins in pronation and supinates the forearm until the palm faces the ceiling. Therapist resists motion in the direction of pronation.

Alternate Test: Grasp patient's hand as if shaking hands; cradle the elbow and resist via the hand grip (Fig. 5.125). This test is used if the patient has Grade 5 or 4 wrist and hand strength. It should not be used if there is wrist instability.

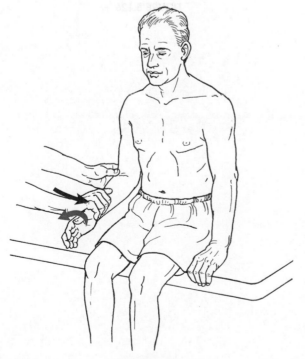

FIGURE 5.124

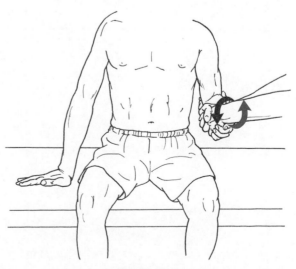

FIGURE 5.125

FOREARM SUPINATION

(Supinator and Biceps brachii)

Grade 5, Grade 4, Grade 3, and Grade 2 Continued

Instructions to Patient: "Turn your palm up. Hold it. Don't let me turn it down. Keep your wrist and fingers relaxed."

For Grade 3: "Turn your palm up."

Grading

Grade 5: Holds test position against maximal resistance.

Grade 4: Holds test position against strong to moderate resistance.

Grade 3: Completes available range of motion without resistance (Fig. 5.126, showing end range).

Grade 2: Completes partial range of motion.

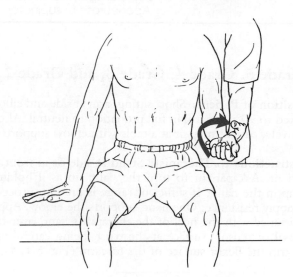

FIGURE 5.126

Grade 1 and Grade 0

Position of Patient: Short sitting. Arm and elbow are flexed as for the previous tests.

Instructions to Therapist: Support the forearm just distal to the elbow. Palpate the supinator distal to the head of the radius on the dorsal aspect of the forearm (Fig. 5.127).

Test: Patient attempts to supinate the forearm.

Instructions to Patient: "Try to turn your palm so it faces the ceiling."

Grading

Grade 1: Slight contractile activity but no limb movement.

Grade 0: No discernable palpable contractile activity.

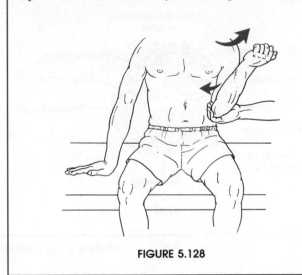

Substitution

Patient may externally rotate and adduct the arm across the body (Fig. 5.128) as forearm supination is attempted. When this occurs, the forearm rolls into supination with no activity of the supinator muscle.

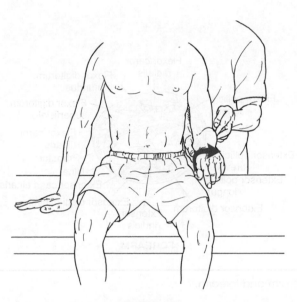

FIGURE 5.127

FIGURE 5.128

Helpful Hints

- It is controversial whether supination is stronger than pronation. Some studies report no difference and others report supination torque is more than pronation torque.[45]
- Biceps brachii activity is highest in mid-supination, when the length of the muscle is shorter.[45]
- The supinator is considered the prime mover of supination by some authorities, as supination is the

only movement it performs, and forearm position is irrelevant. The biceps however, is a far stronger supinator as its mass is 5× that of the supinator, but the biceps performs optimally when elbow flexion and supination are combined.[2,45]

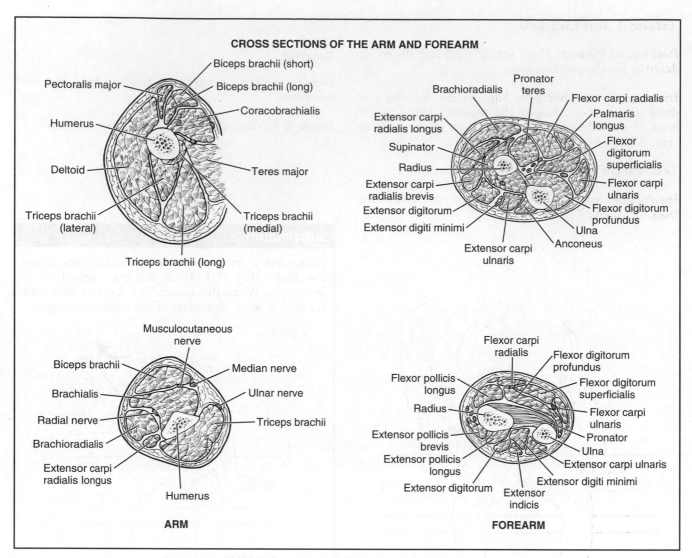

CROSS SECTIONS OF THE ARM AND FOREARM

Biceps brachii (short)

Pectoralis major

Biceps brachii (long)

Coracobrachialis

Humerus

Deltoid

Teres major

Triceps brachii (lateral)

Triceps brachii (medial)

Triceps brachii (long)

Brachioradialis

Pronator teres

Flexor carpi radialis

Extensor carpi radialis longus

Palmaris longus

Supinator

Flexor digitorum superficialis

Radius

Extensor carpi radialis brevis

Flexor carpi ulnaris

Extensor digitorum

Flexor digitorum profundus

Extensor digiti minimi

Ulna

Extensor carpi ulnaris

Anconeus

Musculocutaneous nerve

Biceps brachii

Median nerve

Brachialis

Ulnar nerve

Radial nerve

Triceps brachii

Brachioradialis

Extensor carpi radialis longus

Humerus

Flexor carpi radialis

Flexor digitorum profundus

Flexor pollicis longus

Flexor digitorum superficialis

Radius

Flexor carpi ulnaris

Extensor pollicis brevis

Pronator

Extensor pollicis longus

Ulna

Extensor carpi ulnaris

Extensor digitorum

Extensor digiti minimi

Extensor indicis

ARM

FOREARM

PLATE 4 Cross sections of the arm and forearm.

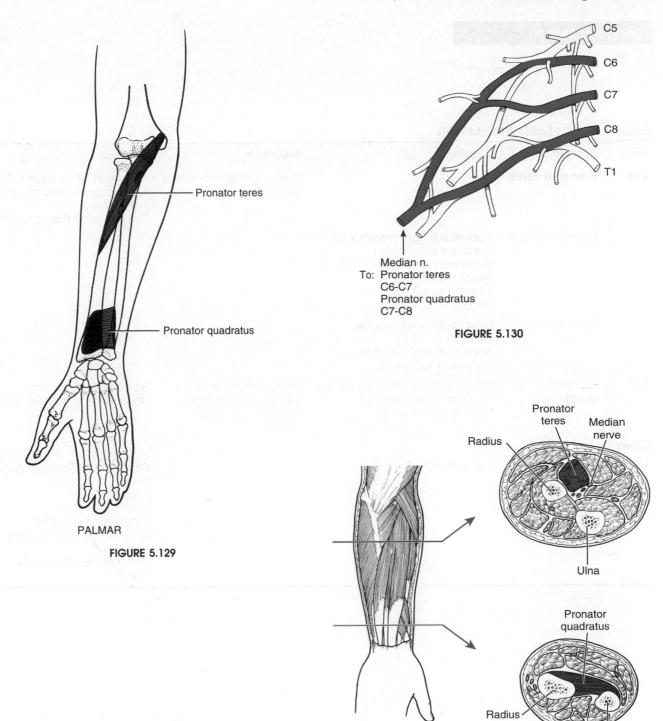

Pronator teres

Pronator quadratus

PALMAR

FIGURE 5.129

C5
C6
C7
C8
T1

Median n.
To: Pronator teres
C6-C7
Pronator quadratus
C7-C8

FIGURE 5.130

Pronator
teres

Median
nerve

Radius

Ulna

Pronator
quadratus

Radius

Ulna

FIGURE 5.131 Arrows indicate level of cross section.

FOREARM PRONATION

(Pronator teres and Pronator quadratus)

Range of Motion
0°–80°

Table 5.17 FOREARM PRONATION

I.D.	Muscle	Origin	Insertion	Function
146	**Pronator teres**		Radius (midshaft, lateral surface)	Pronation of forearm with resisted pronation or rapid pronation Elbow flexion (accessory)[2,45]
	Humeral head	Humerus (shaft proximal to medial epicondyle) Common tendon of origin of flexor muscles Intermuscular septum Antebrachial fascia		
	Ulnar head	Ulna (coronoid process, medial) Joins humeral head in common tendon		
147	Pronator quadratus	Ulna (oblique ridge on distal $\frac{1}{4}$ of anterior surface) Muscle aponeurosis	Radius (shaft, anterior surface distally; also area above ulnar notch)	Pronation of forearm Elbow flexion (accessory)
Other				
151	Flexor carpi radialis	See Table 5.18		*Pronation of forearm (weak assist)* Flexion of wrist Radial deviation (abduction) of wrist Extends fingers (tenodesis action) Flexion of elbow (weak assist)

Grade 5, Grade 4, and Grade 3

Position of Patient: Short sitting or may sit at a table. Arm at side with elbow flexed to 90° and forearm in supination.

Instructions to Therapist: Stand at side or in front of patient. Ask patient to turn palm down from supinated position. If sufficient range is present, proceed to apply resistance in test position. Support the elbow. Hand used for resistance applies resistance with hypothenar eminence over radius on the volar (flexor) surface of the forearm at the wrist (Fig. 5.132). Avoid pressure on the head of the radius and gripping the forearm for patient comfort.

Test: Patient attempts to pronates the forearm. Therapist resists motion at the wrist in the direction of supination for Grades 4 and 5.

Alternate Test: Grasp patient's hand as if to shake hands, cradling the elbow with the other hand and resisting pronation via the hand grip. This alternate test may be used if the patient has Grade 5 or 4 wrist and hand strength. This alternate test should not be used in the presence of wrist instability.

Instructions to Patient: "Turn your palm down. Hold it. Don't let me turn it up. Keep your wrist and fingers relaxed."

Grading

Grade 5: Holds test position against maximal resistance.

Grade 4: Holds test position against strong to moderate resistance.

Grade 3: Completes available range without resistance (Fig. 5.133, showing end range).

Grade 2: Complete partial range of motion

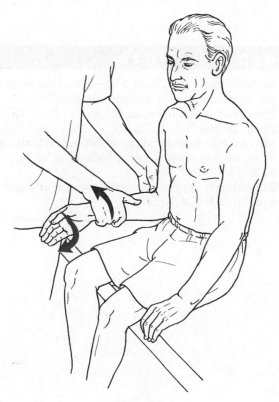

FIGURE 5.132

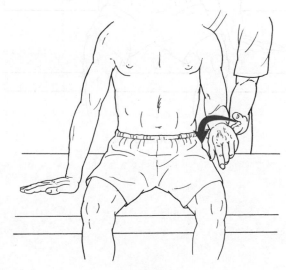

FIGURE 5.133

FOREARM PRONATION

(Pronator teres and Pronator quadratus)

Grade 1 and Grade 0

Instructions to Therapist: Stand to the side of the patient. Support the forearm just distal to the elbow. The fingers of the other hand are used to palpate the pronator teres over the upper third of the volar (flexor) surface of the forearm on a diagonal line from the medial condyle of the humerus to the lateral border of the radius (Fig. 5.134).

Test: Patient attempts to pronate the forearm.

Instructions to Patient: "Try to turn your palm down."

Grading

Grade 1: Visible or palpable contractile activity with no motion of the part.

Grade 0: No discernable palpable contractile activity.

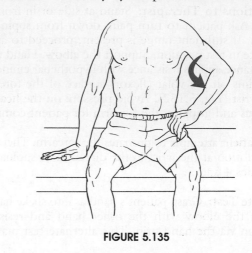

Patient may internally rotate the shoulder or abduct it during attempts at pronation (Fig. 5.135). When this occurs, the forearm rolls into pronation without the benefit of activity by the pronator muscles.

FIGURE 5.135

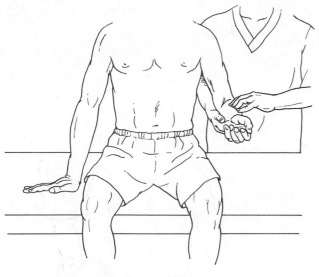

FIGURE 5.134

Helpful Hints

- Nondominant arm elicits 81%–95% of the force of the dominant arm in forearm rotation.[46]
- Pronation is strongest in the position of 45° of elbow flexion.[47]
- Men are 63% stronger in pronation and 68% stronger in supination than women, measuring as high as 12.6–14.8 Nm.[48]
- In isokinetic studies, women's forearm strength is equal to 5.0–5.4 Nm.[48]

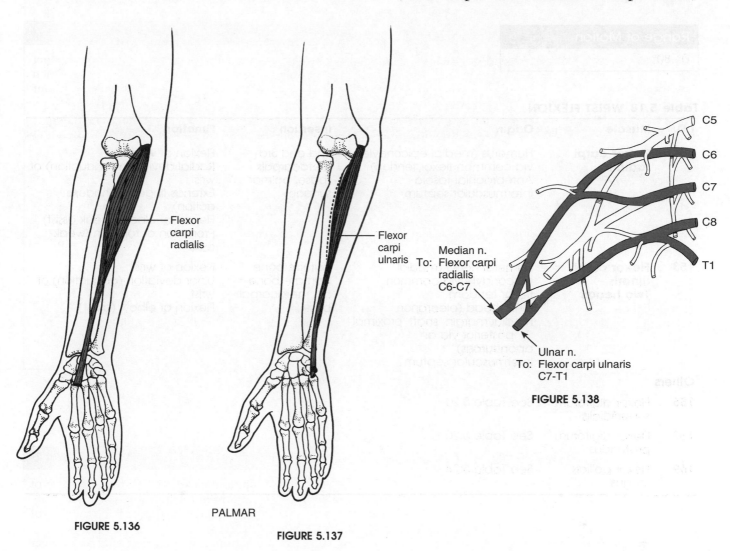

Flexor carpi radialis

FIGURE 5.136

PALMAR

Flexor carpi ulnaris

FIGURE 5.137

Median n.
To: Flexor carpi radialis
C6-C7

Ulnar n.
To: Flexor carpi ulnaris
C7-T1

FIGURE 5.138

C5
C6
C7
C8
T1

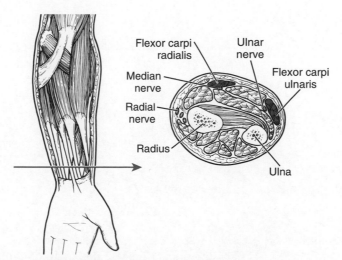

Flexor carpi radialis

Ulnar nerve

Median nerve

Flexor carpi ulnaris

Radial nerve

Radius

Ulna

FIGURE 5.139 Arrow indicates level of cross section.

WRISTT FLEXION

(Flexor carpi radialis and Flexor carpi ulnaris)

Range of Motion
0°–80°

Table 5.18 WRIST FLEXION

I.D.	Muscle	Origin	Insertion	Function
151	**Flexor carpi radialis**	Humerus (medial epicondyle via common flexor tendon) Antebrachial fascia Intermuscular septum	2nd and 3rd metacarpals (base, palmar surface)	Flexion of wrist Radial deviation (abduction) of wrist Extends fingers (tenodesis action) Flexion of elbow (weak assist) Pronation of forearm (weak assist)
153	**Flexor carpi ulnaris Two heads**	Humeral head (medial epicondyle via common flexor tendon) Ulnar head (olecranon, medial margin; shaft, proximal ⅔ posterior via an aponeurosis) Intermuscular septum	Pisiform bone Hamate bone 5th metacarpal, base	Flexion of wrist Ulnar deviation (adduction) of wrist Flexion of elbow (assist)
Others				
156	Flexor digitorum superficialis	See Table 5.20		
157	Flexor digitorum profundus	See Table 5.20		
169	Flexor pollicis longus	See Table 5.24		

(Flexor carpi radialis and Flexor carpi ulnaris)

Grade 5 and Grade 4

Position of Patient (All Tests): Short sitting. Forearm is supinated (Fig. 5.140). Wrist is in neutral position or slightly extended.

Test: Patient flexes the wrist, keeping the digits and thumb relaxed.

Instructions to Therapist: Sit or stand in front of the patient and ask the patient to bend the wrist (Grade 3). If sufficient range is present, proceed to test strength by placing the hand in the test position. One hand supports the patient's forearm under the wrist (see Fig. 5.140) while the other hand applies resistance over the volar (palmar) surface of the hand (Fig. 5.141).

To Test Both Wrist Flexors: Apply resistance to the palm of the test hand using four fingers or hypothenar eminence (see Fig. 5.141). Resistance is given evenly across the hand in a straight-down direction into wrist extension.

To Test the Flexor Carpi Radialis: Place the patient's wrist in radial deviation and slight wrist extension. Resistance is applied with the index and long fingers over the first and second metacarpal (radial side of the hand) in the direction of extension and ulnar deviation (Fig. 5.142).

To Test the Flexor Carpi Ulnaris: Place the wrist in ulnar deviation and slight wrist extension. Resistance is applied over the fifth metacarpal (ulnar side of the hand) in the direction of extension and radial deviation (Fig. 5.143).

Instructions to Patient (All Tests): "Hold it. Don't let me pull it down. Keep your fingers relaxed."

Grading

Grade 5: Holds test position of wrist flexion against maximal resistance.

Grade 4: Holds test position of wrist flexion against strong to moderate resistance.

FIGURE 5.140

FIGURE 5.141

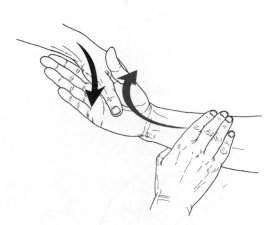

FIGURE 5.142

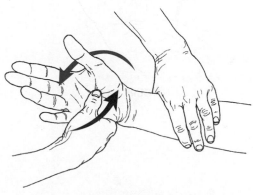

FIGURE 5.143

Chapter 5 | Testing the Muscles of the Upper Extremity **171**

WRIST FLEXION

(Flexor carpi radialis and Flexor carpi ulnaris)

Grade 3:

Both Wrist Flexors: Patient flexes the wrist through full range without resistance and without radial or ulnar deviation.

Flexor Carpi Radialis: Patient flexes the wrist in radial deviation through full range without resistance. This is a small movement as compared with ulnar deviation described below (Fig. 5.144).

The illustration is shown from the extensor surface to better illustrate the small movement.

Flexor Carpi Ulnaris: Patient flexes the wrist in ulnar deviation through full range without resistance (Fig. 5.145).

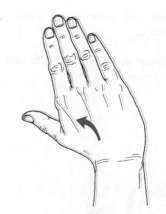

FIGURE 5.144

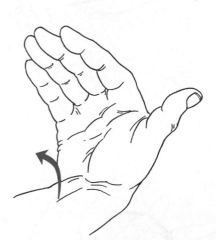

FIGURE 5.145

Grade 2

Position of Patient: Sitting with elbow supported on table. Forearm in mid position with hand resting on ulnar side (Fig. 5.146).

Instructions to Therapist: Support patient's forearm proximal to the wrist.

Test: Patient flexes wrist with the ulnar surface gliding across or not touching the table (see Fig. 5.146, end position). To test the two wrist flexors separately, hold the forearm so that the wrist does not lie on the table and ask the patient to perform the flexion motion while the wrist is in ulnar and then radial deviation.

Instructions to Patient: "Bend your wrist, keeping your fingers relaxed."

Grading

Grade 2: Completes available range of wrist flexion with gravity minimized.

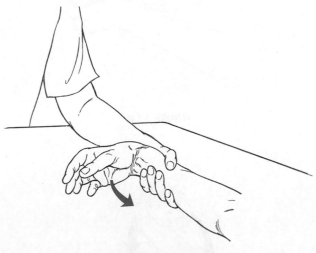

FIGURE 5.146

Grade 1 and Grade 0

Position of Patient: Supinated forearm supported on table.

Instructions to Therapist: Support the wrist in flexion; the index finger of the other hand is used to palpate the appropriate tendons.

Palpate the tendons of the flexor carpi radialis (Fig. 5.147) and the flexor carpi ulnaris (Fig. 5.148) in separate tests.

The flexor carpi radialis lies on the lateral palmar aspect of the wrist (see Fig. 5.141) lateral to the palmaris longus.

The tendon of the flexor carpi ulnaris (see Fig. 5.147) lies on the medial palmar aspect of the wrist (at the base of the fifth metacarpal).

Test: Patient attempts to flex the wrist.

Instructions to Patient: "Try to bend your wrist. Relax. Bend it again." Patient should be asked to repeat the test so the therapist can feel the tendons during both relaxation and contraction.

Grading

Grade 1: One or both tendons may exhibit visible or palpable contractile activity, but the part does not move.

Grade 0:

No discernable palpable contractile activity.

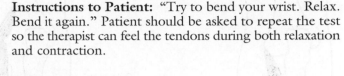

Helpful Hint

Flexor carpi ulnaris contributes to adduction (ulnar deviation) most strongly in the supinated position as compared with the pronated and neutral positions.[49]

Suggested Exercises

• Wrist curls with resistance

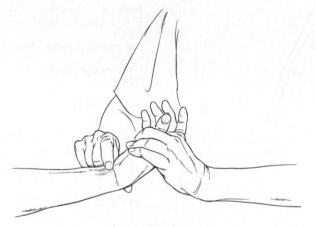

FIGURE 5.147

FIGURE 5.148

WRIST EXTENSION

(Extensor carpi radialis longus, Extensor carpi radialis brevis, and Extensor carpi ulnaris)

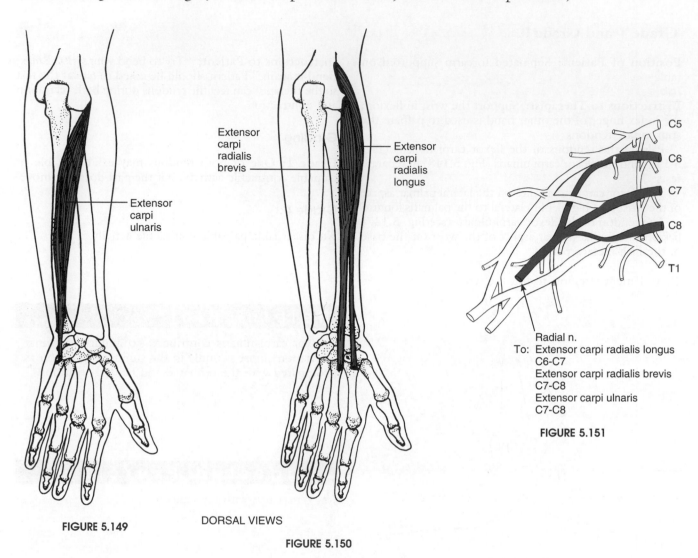

Extensor carpi ulnaris

Extensor carpi radialis brevis

Extensor carpi radialis longus

C5
C6
C7
C8
T1

Radial n.
To: Extensor carpi radialis longus
C6-C7
Extensor carpi radialis brevis
C7-C8
Extensor carpi ulnaris
C7-C8

FIGURE 5.151

FIGURE 5.149

DORSAL VIEWS

FIGURE 5.150

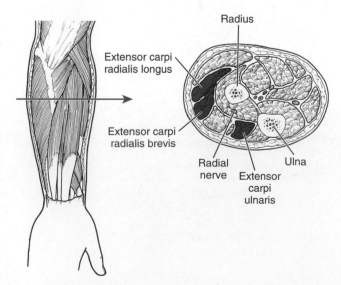

Radius

Extensor carpi radialis longus

Extensor carpi radialis brevis

Radial nerve

Extensor carpi ulnaris

Ulna

FIGURE 5.152 Arrow indicates level of cross section.

(Extensor carpi radialis longus, Extensor carpi radialis brevis, and Extensor carpi ulnaris)

Range of Motion
0°–70°

Table 5.19 WRIST EXTENSION

I.D.	Muscle	Origin	Insertion	Function
148	**Extensor carpi radialis longus**	Humerus (lateral supracondylar ridge, distal ⅓) Common forearm extensor tendon Lateral intermuscular septum	2nd metacarpal bone (base on radial side of dorsal aspect)	Extension and radial deviation of wrist Synergist for finger flexion by stabilization of wrist Elbow flexion (accessory)
149	Extensor carpi radialis brevis	Humerus (lateral epicondyle via common forearm extensor tendon) Radial collateral ligament of elbow joint Aponeurosis of muscle	3rd metacarpal bone (base of dorsal surface on radial side) 2nd metacarpal (occasionally)	Extension of wrist Radial deviation of wrist (weak) Finger flexion synergist (by stabilizing the wrist)
150	Extensor carpi ulnaris	Humerus (lateral epicondyle via common extensor tendon) Ulna (posterior border by an aponeurosis)	5th metacarpal bone (tubercle on medial side of base)	Extension of wrist Ulnar deviation (adduction) of wrist
Others				
154	Extensor digitorum	See Table 5.20		
158	Extensor digiti minimi	See Table 5.20		
155	Extensor indicis	See Table 5.20		

The ability to extend the wrist is an essential function for most hand activity. A minimum of 25° of wrist extension is necessary for optimal grip strength.[50]

The radial wrist extensors are considerably stronger than the ulnar wrist extensor. The extensor carpi radialis brevis' muscle belly is 5× larger than the extensor carpi radialis longus.[51] Wrist extensor strength of the dominant side is approximately 10% stronger than the non-dominant side.[52] There is a strong correlation between grip strength and wrist extension strength. Lateral epicondylitis (tennis elbow), most often affects the extensor carpi radialis brevis at its insertion on the lateral epicondyle, resulting in painful wrist extension.

Grade 5, Grade 4, and Grade 3

Position of Patient: Short sitting. Elbow is flexed, forearm is fully pronated, and forearm is supported on the table.

Instructions to Therapist: Sit or stand at a diagonal in front of patient. Ask the patient to lift hand (Grade 3). If sufficient range is available, proceed to apply resistance by placing the patient's hand in the test position of full extension (Fig. 5.153). The hand used for resistance is placed over the dorsal (extensor) surface of the metacarpals.

To test all three muscles, the patient extends the wrist without deviation. Resistance is given with four fingers or hypothenar eminence in a forward and downward

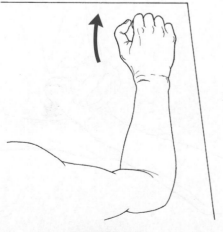

FIGURE 5.153

WRIST EXTENSION

(Extensor carpi radialis longus, Extensor carpi radialis brevis, and Extensor carpi ulnaris)

Grade 5, Grade 4, and Grade 3 Continued

direction over the second to fifth metacarpals for Grades 4 and 5 (Fig. 5.154).

To test the extensor carpi radialis longus and brevis (extension with radial deviation), position wrist in extension and radial deviation. Resistance is given on the dorsal (extensor) surface of the second and third metacarpals (radial side of hand) in the direction of flexion and ulnar deviation (Fig. 5.155).

To test the extensor carpi ulnaris (extension and ulnar deviation), position wrist in extension and ulnar deviation. Patient extends (lifts) the wrist, leading with the ulnar side of the hand. Resistance is given on the dorsal (extensor) surface of the fifth metacarpal (ulnar side of hand) in the direction of flexion and radial deviation (Fig. 5.156).

Test: For the combined test of the three wrist extensor muscles, the patient extends the wrist (lifts the hand) through the full available range. Do not permit extension of the fingers.

To test the two radial extensors, the patient extends the wrist, leading with the thumb side of the hand. The wrist may be prepositioned in some extension and radial deviation to direct the patient's motion.

To test the extensor carpi ulnaris, the patient extends the wrist, leading with the ulnar side of the hand. The therapist may preposition the wrist to direct the movement toward the ulna.

Instructions to Patient: "Hold it. Don't let me push it down."

For Grade 3: "Bring your hand up." (Add "to the side" when testing for radial or ulnar deviation.)

Grading

Grade 5: Holds test position against maximal resistance. Full extension is not required for the tests of radial and ulnar deviation.

Grade 4: Holds test position of wrist extension against strong to moderate resistance when all muscles are being tested. When testing the individual muscles, full wrist extension range of motion will not be achieved.

Grade 3: Completes full range of motion without resistance in the test for all three muscles. In the separate tests for the radial and ulnar extensors, the deviation required precludes full range of motion.

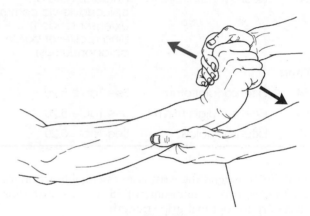

FIGURE 5.155

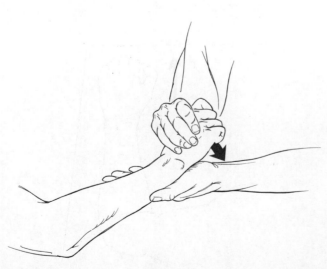

FIGURE 5.154

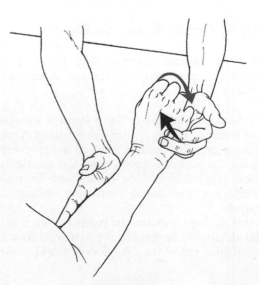

FIGURE 5.156

(Extensor carpi radialis longus, Extensor carpi radialis brevis, and Extensor carpi ulnaris)

Grade 2

Position of Patient: Forearm supported on table in neutral position.

Instructions to Therapist: Support the patient's wrist. This elevates the hand from the table and removes friction (Fig. 5.157).

Test: Patient extends the wrist.

Instructions to Patient: "Bend your hand back."

Grading

Grade 2: Completes full range with gravity minimized.

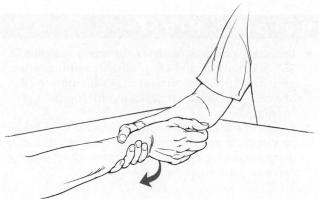

FIGURE 5.157

WRIST EXTENSION

(Extensor carpi radialis longus, Extensor carpi radialis brevis, and Extensor carpi ulnaris)

Grade 1 and Grade 0

Position of Patient: Hand and forearm supported on table with forearm fully pronated.

Instructions to Therapist: Support the patient's wrist in extension. The other hand is used for palpation. Use one finger to palpate one muscle in each test.

Extensor Carpi Radialis Longus: Palpate the tendon on the dorsum of the wrist in line with the second metacarpal (Fig. 5.158).

Extensor Carpi Radialis Brevis: Palpate the tendon on the dorsal surface of the wrist in line with the third metacarpal bone (Fig. 5.159).

Extensor Carpi Ulnaris: Palpate the tendon on the dorsal wrist surface proximal to the fifth metacarpal and just distal to the ulnar styloid process (Fig. 5.160).

Test: Patient attempts to extend the wrist.

Instructions to Patient: "Try to lift your hand."

Grading

Grade 1: For any given muscle, there is visible or palpable contractile activity, but no wrist motion ensues.

Grade 0: No discernable contractile activity.

Substitution

The most common substitution occurs when the finger extensors are allowed to participate. This can be avoided to a large extent by ensuring that the patient's fingers are relaxed and are not permitted to extend.

Helpful Hints

- Preferred position of the wrist when gripping is 35° of extension and 7° of ulnar deviation, where grip strength is the strongest. A minimum of 25° of wrist extension is necessary for optimal grip strength.[50]
- A patient with complete quadriplegia at C5-C6 will have only the radial wrist extensors remaining. Radial deviation during extension is therefore the prevailing extensor motion at the wrist.

Suggested Exercises for Wrist Extensors

- Wrist curls in pronated position
- Gripping/squeezing a ball or putty
- Wrist radial and ulnar deviation

FIGURE 5.158

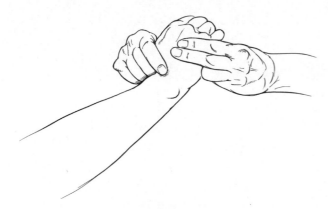

FIGURE 5.159

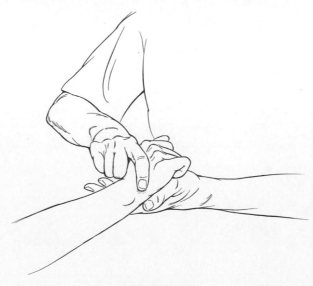

FIGURE 5.160

Evaluating the hand following a nerve injury is the primary reason single muscles or movements are tested. Because of the innervation pattern of the hand, grading of movements may be more appropriate than grading specific muscles. Because the hand muscles have multiple functions and can be active in combined movements, the therapist should incorporate knowledge of function, anatomy and kinesiology to master strength testing of the hand. For example, the only muscles of the hand that can be purely isolated are the first dorsal interosseous (radial abduction of the index finger) and the flexor pollicis longus (flexion of the thumb interphalangeal [IP] joint).[53] Alternatively, grip strength is considered a gross, functional measure of hand strength. Asking the patient to make a fist and straighten out the fingers will provide a general idea of active range of motion of the digits and help to provide focus of the muscular exam.

When evaluating the muscles of the hand, care must be taken to use graduated and appropriate resistance, especially following surgical intervention. Because of the small muscle mass of the hand muscles, the therapist should use one or two fingers to resist hand motions.

Clinical judgment is required when applying appropriate resistance in a safe fashion, especially in the postsurgical hand. In the postop hand, the therapist may only want to assure the presence of a muscle contraction, as certain movements may be prohibited by the surgeon. Similarly, the amount of motion allowed or encouraged should be monitored in conjunction with the surgeon. Too much force or too quickly applied force may be harmful to the surgical repair or reconstruction. The therapist should have a thorough understanding of the type of surgery and any contraindications to movement before muscle testing the postop hand. Considerable practice in testing normal hands and comparing injured hands with their normal contralateral sides should provide some of the necessary judgment with which to approach the surgically repaired hand.

It is difficult to differentiate between Grades 5 and 4 in many of the small muscles of the hand, and differentiating between Grades 5 and 4 may not be clinically relevant. Therefore, Grades 5 and 4 have been combined for some muscles. It takes experience and skill to discern weakness in the actively contracting hand muscle. This text remains true to the principles of testing in the ranges of grades 5, 4, and 3 with respect to gravity. It is admitted, however, that the influence of gravity on the fingers is inconsequential, so gravity and antigravity positions are not considered in valid muscle tests of the hand.

Two common groupings of the hand muscles are the intrinsics, innervated mostly by the median and ulnar nerve, and the extrinsics, innervated primarily by the radial and median nerves. The extrinsics originate in the forearm and the intrinsics originate distal to the wrist. In general, each finger has six muscles controlling its movements, three extrinsic muscles (two long flexors and one long extensor) and three intrinsic muscles (dorsal and palmar interosseous and lumbrical muscles). The little finger and index finger each have an additional extrinsic extensor.[54]

The hand section of this chapter is organized by extrinsics, intrinsics, and the thumb (combined extrinsic and intrinsics).

EXTRINSIC MUSCLES

The extrinsic muscles of the hand originate above the wrist on the forearm and are made up of flexors and extensors. The tendons of the extrinsics are held in place at the wrist by the palmar carpal ligament and flexor retinaculum. The extrinsics are innervated by the radial, ulnar, and median nerves.

(Flexor digitorum superficialis and Flexor digitorum profundus)

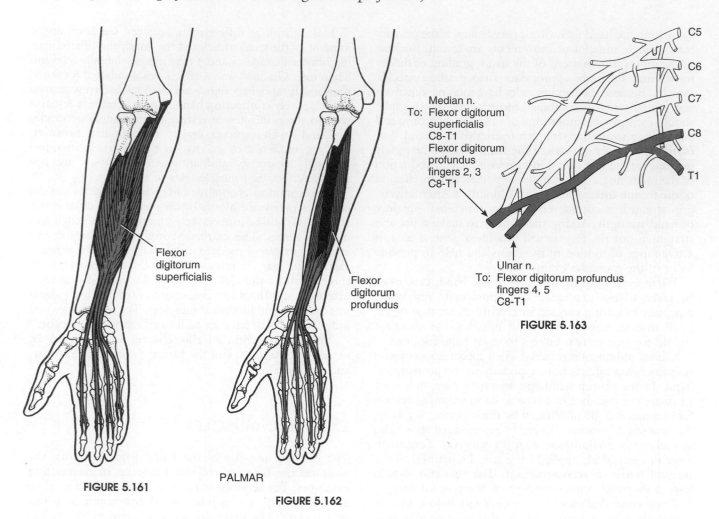

Flexor digitorum superficialis

FIGURE 5.161

Flexor digitorum profundus

PALMAR

FIGURE 5.162

Median n.
To: Flexor digitorum superficialis
C8-T1
Flexor digitorum profundus
fingers 2, 3
C8-T1

Ulnar n.
To: Flexor digitorum profundus
fingers 4, 5
C8-T1

C5
C6
C7
C8
T1

FIGURE 5.163

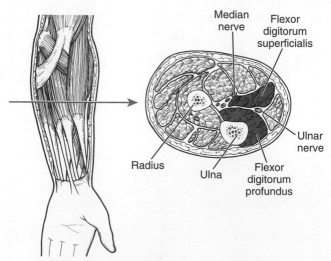

Median nerve

Flexor digitorum superficialis

Radius

Ulna

Flexor digitorum profundus

Ulnar nerve

FIGURE 5.164 Arrow indicates level of cross section.

(Flexor digitorum superficialis and Flexor digitorum profundus)

Range of Motion
PIP joints: 0°–100°
DIP joints: 0°–90°

Table 5.20 PIP AND DIP FINGER FLEXION

I.D.	Muscle	Origin	Insertion	Function
156	**Flexor digitorum superficialis (2 heads)**	Humeroulnar head: humerus (medial epicondyle via common flexor tendon)	Four tendons arranged in 2 pairs Superficial pair: middle and ring fingers (sides of middle phalanges)	Flexion of PIP joints of digits 2–5 Flexion of MCP joints of digits 2–5 (assist) Flexion of wrist (accessory, especially in forceful grasp)
		Ulna (medial collateral ligament of elbow joint); coronoid process (medial side) Intermuscular septum *Radial head*: radius (oblique line on anterior shaft)	Deep pair: index and little fingers (sides of middle phalanges)	
157	**Flexor digitorum profundus**	Ulna (proximal ¾ of anterior and medial shaft; medial coronoid process) Interosseous membrane (ulnar)	Four tendons to digits 2–5 (distal phalanges, at base of palmar surface)	Flexion of DIP joints of digits 2–5 Flexion of MCP and PIP joints of digits 2–5 (assist) Flexion of wrist (accessory)

MCP, Metacarpophalangeal; *PIP*, proximal phalanges.

FINGER PIP AND DIP FLEXION

(Flexor digitorum superficialis and Flexor digitorum profundus)

The flexor digitorum superficialis (FDS) is innervated by the median nerve while the flexor digitorum profundus (FDP) is innervated by the median and ulnar nerve. The FDP has two heads, flexing the middle and ring fingers together and the index and little fingers. If a tendon injury or nerve injury is the reason for testing, each digit should be tested separately. Otherwise, all digits can be tested together to assess the integrity and strength of the finger flexors.

COMBINED DIP AND PIP TESTS

Grade 5, Grade 4, and Grade 3

Position of Patient: Forearm supinated, wrist in neutral. Fingers are relaxed.

Instructions to Therapist: Sit in front of the patient, with patient's forearm and hand supported on a table with wrist fully supinated. Ask patient to touch the pads of the fingers to the distal palm while keeping the metacarpals extended (flat on the table) (Fig. 5.165).

If sufficient range is present, proceed to apply resistance. Stabilization is provided by the hand position. With a finger of the hand providing resistance in the patient's palm under the digits, pull up to try to straighten the digits (Fig. 5.166).

Grading

Grade 5 and Grade 4: Holds against strong resistance.

Grade 3: Completes range of motion without resistance.

Grade 2, Grade 1, and Grade 0: Refer to isolated proximal phalanges (PIP) and distal phalanges (DIP) tests.

FIGURE 5.165

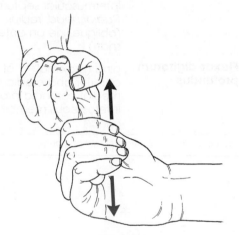

FIGURE 5.166

Grade 5, Grade 4, and Grade 3

Position of Patient: Forearm supinated, wrist in neutral. Finger to be tested is in slight flexion at the metacarpophalangeal (MCP) joint (Fig. 5.167).

Instructions to Therapist: Hold all fingers (except the one being tested) in extension at all joints (see Fig. 5.167) so as to block the action of the profundus action. Isolation of the index finger may not be complete. Ask the patient to bend the middle joint towards the proximal palm. If full range is present (Grade 3), apply appropriate resistance. Therapist resists the distal end of the middle phalanx of the test finger in the direction of extension (Fig. 5.168).

Test: Patient flexes the PIP joint without flexing the DIP joint. Do not allow motion of any joints of the other fingers. Repeat for other fingers, if indicated. Alternatively, you can test all fingers together (see Fig. 5.166, combined test above).

Flick the terminal end of the finger being tested with the thumb to make certain that the flexor digitorum profundus is not active; that is, the DIP joint goes into extension. The distal phalanx should be relatively floppy.

Instructions to Patient: "Bend your index [then long, ring, and little] finger at the middle joint; hold it. Don't let me straighten it. Keep your other fingers relaxed."

Grading

Grade 5 and Grade 4: Holds against strong finger resistance.

Grade 3: Completes range of motion without resistance (see Fig. 5.167).

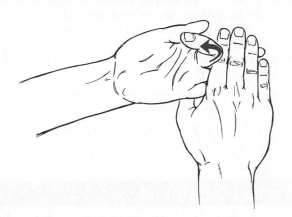

FIGURE 5.167

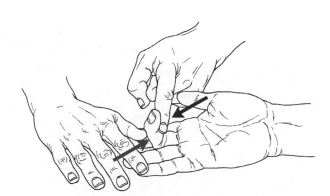

FIGURE 5.168

(Flexor digitorum superficialis)

Grade 2, Grade 1, and Grade 0

Position of Patient: Forearm is in mid position to eliminate the influence of gravity on finger flexion.

Instructions to Therapist: Same as for Grades 5, 4, and 3.

Palpate the flexor digitorum superficialis on the palmar surface of the wrist between the palmaris longus and the flexor carpi ulnaris (Fig. 5.169).

Test: Patient flexes the PIP joint.

Instructions to Patient: "Bend your middle finger." (Select other fingers individually.)

Grading

Grade 2: Completes range of motion.

Grade 1: Palpable or visible contractile activity, which may or may not be accompanied by a flicker of motion.

Grade 0: No discernable palpable contractile activity.

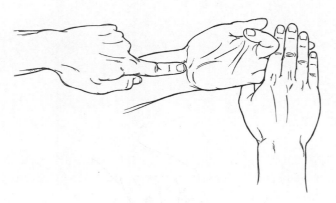

FIGURE 5.169

Substitutions

- The major substitution for this motion is offered by the flexor digitorum profundus, and this will occur if the DIP joint is allowed to flex.
- If the wrist is allowed to extend, tension increases in the long finger flexors, and may result in passive flexion of the IP joints. This is referred to as a "tenodesis" action.
- Relaxation of IP extension will result in passive IP flexion.

Helpful Hint

Many people cannot isolate the little finger. When this is the case, test the little and ring fingers at the same time.

(Flexor digitorum profundus)

Grade 5, Grade 4, and Grade 3

Position of Patient: Forearm in supination, wrist in neutral, and proximal PIP joint in extension.

Instructions to Therapist: Stabilize the middle phalanx in extension by grasping it on either side (Fig. 5.170). Ask the patient to bend the tip of the finger. If full range is present (Grade 3), apply appropriate resistance. Resistance is provided on the distal phalanx in the direction of extension (not illustrated).

Test: Test each finger individually if indicated. Patient flexes distal phalanx of each finger. Test all digits together by patient flexing all distal phalanxes together.

Instructions to Patient: "Bend the tip (or tips) of your finger. Hold it (them). Don't let me straighten it (them)."

Grading

Grade 5 and Grade 4: Able to hold flexed position against strong, finger resistance.

Grade 3: Completes active range without resistance (see Fig. 5.170).

Grade 2, Grade 1, and Grade 0

Testing grades 2, 1, and 0 is the same as that used with higher grades except that the position of the forearm is in neutral to eliminate the influence of gravity.

Grades are assigned as for the PIP tests.

The tendon of the flexor digitorum profundus can be palpated on the palmar surface of the middle phalanx of each finger.

Substitutions

- The wrist must be kept in a neutral position and must not be allowed to extend, to rule out the tenodesis effect of the wrist extensors.
- Don't be fooled if the patient extends the distal phalanges joint and then relaxes, which can give the impression of active finger flexion.
- In a power grip task, greater forces are applied on the distal phalanges of the long fingers compared with the middle and proximal ones, making the flexor digitorum profundus an important muscle to strengthen.[55]

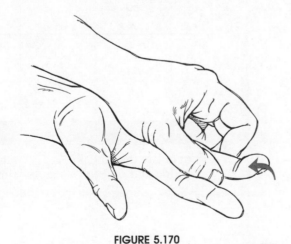

FIGURE 5.170

(Extensor digitorum, Extensor indicis, and Extensor digiti minimi)

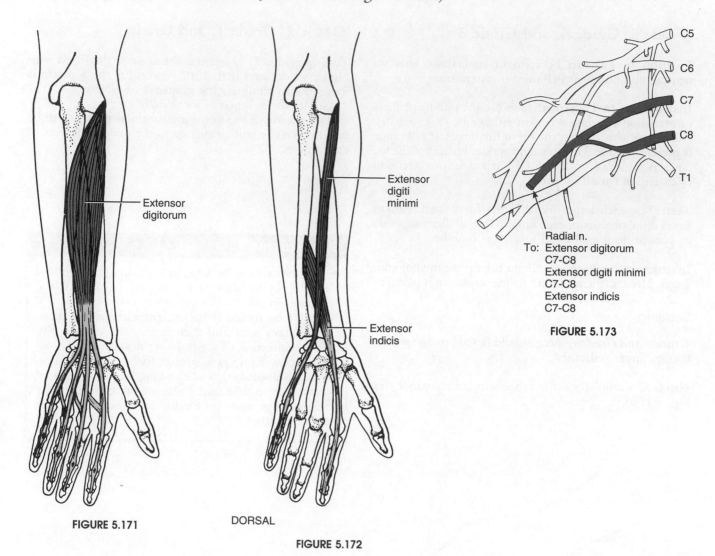

Extensor
digitorum

FIGURE 5.171

Extensor
digiti
minimi

Extensor
indicis

DORSAL

FIGURE 5.172

C5
C6
C7
C8
T1

Radial n.
To: Extensor digitorum
C7-C8
Extensor digiti minimi
C7-C8
Extensor indicis
C7-C8

FIGURE 5.173

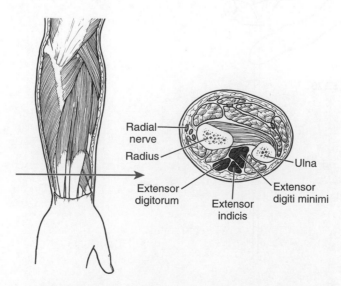

Radial
nerve
Radius

Extensor
digitorum

Extensor
indicis

Ulna

Extensor
digiti minimi

FIGURE 5.174 Arrow indicates level of cross section.

(Extensor digitorum, Extensor indicis, and Extensor digiti minimi)

Range of Motion
0°–45°

Table 5.21 MCP FINGER EXTENSION

I.D.	Muscle	Origin	Insertion	Function
154	**Extensor digitorum**	Humerus (lateral epicondyle via common extensor tendon) Intermuscular septum Antebrachial fascia	Via 4 tendons to digits 2–5 (via the extensor expansion, to dorsum of middle and distal phalanges; one tendon to each finger)	Extension of metacarpophalangeal (MCP) and proximal (PIP) and distal interphalangeal (DIP) joints, digits 2–5 Extensor digitorum can extend any and all joints over which it passes via the dorsal expansion Independent action of the extensor digitorum: Hyperextends MCP joint (proximal phalanges) by displacing dorsal expansion proximally Extends interphalangeal (IP) joints (middle and distal phalanges) when MCP joints are slightly flexed by intrinsics Wrist extension (accessory) Abduction of ring, index, and little fingers with extension but no such action on the middle finger
155	Extensor indicis	Ulna (posterior surface of shaft) Interosseous membrane	2nd digit (via tendon of extensor digitorum into extensor hood)	Extension of MCP joint of index finger Extension of IP joints (with intrinsics) Adduction of index finger (accessory) Wrist extension (accessory)
158	Extensor digiti minimi	Humerus (lateral epicondyle via common extensor tendon) Intermuscular septa	5th digit (extensor hood)	Extension of MCP, IP, and DIP joints of digit 5 (little finger) Wrist extension (accessory) Abduction of digit 5 (accessory)

FINGER MCP EXTENSION

(Extensor digitorum, Extensor indicis, and Extensor digiti minimi)

Grade 5, Grade 4, and Grade 3

Position of Patient: Forearm in pronation, wrist in neutral. MCP and IP joints are in relaxed flexion posture.

Instructions to Therapist: Sit at table or side of patient. Stabilize the wrist in neutral. Place the index finger of the resistance hand across the dorsum of all proximal phalanges just distal to the MCP joints to stabilize. Ask the patient to straighten the knuckles as far as possible. Demonstrate motion to patient and instruct to copy. If full range is present (Grade 3), apply appropriate resistance. Give resistance in the direction of flexion.

Test:

Extensor Digitorum: Patient extends MCP joints (all fingers simultaneously), allowing the IP joints to be in slight flexion (Fig. 5.175).

Extensor Indicis: Patient extends the MCP joint of the index finger.

Extensor Digiti Minimi: Patient extends the MCP joint of the 5th digit.

Instructions to Patient: "Straighten (lift) your knuckles as far as they will go."

Grading

Grade 5 and Grade 4: Able to hold position with appropriate level of resistance. (Extensor is not as strong as the flexor.)

Grade 3: Completes active range without resistance.

Grade 2, Grade 1, and Grade 0

Procedures: Test is the same as that for Grades 5, 4, and 3 except that the forearm is in the mid position.

The four tendons of the extensor digitorum, the tendon of the extensor indicis, and the tendon of the extensor digiti minimi are readily apparent on the dorsum of the hand as they course in the direction of each finger.

Grading

Grade 2: Completes range.

Grade 1: Visible tendon activity but no joint motion.

Grade 0: No discernable palpable contractile activity.

Substitution

Flexion of the wrist will produce interphalangeal extension through a tenodesis action.

Helpful Hints

- Metacarpophalangeal extension of the fingers is not a strong motion, and only slight resistance is required to "break" the end position.
- It is usual for the active range of motion to be considerably less than the available passive range. In this test, therefore, the "full available range" is not used, and the active range is accepted.
- Another way to check whether there is functional extensor strength in the fingers is to "flick" the proximal phalanx of each finger downward; if the finger rebounds, it is functional.

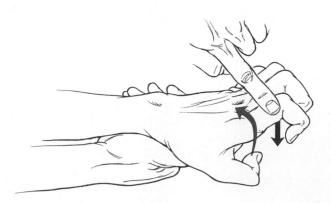

FIGURE 5.175

(Extensor digitorum, Extensor indicis, and Extensor digiti minimi)

INTRINSIC MUSCLES

The intrinsic muscles are traditionally divided into five groups: thenar, hypothenar, palmar interossei, dorsal interossei, and lumbricals (Table 5.22). The primary function of the interossei is MCP flexion/stabilization with extension of the IP joints. This motion is assisted by the lumbricals which can contract without adding flexion torque at the MCP joint.[54] Although efficient, the lumbricals are weak with the smallest physiological cross-sectional area of all the intrinsic hand muscles. Without the interossei, the fingers are unstable and will collapse into the "claw" (i.e., intrinsic minus) position of

hyperextension of the MCP joint and flexion of the IP joints when loaded.[54] The Mannerfelt sign is a sign of interosseous muscle weakness when the index PIP joint "collapses" resulting in hyperflexion, often greater than 90°. Another sign of weakness is the Thomas sign, when wrist flexion occurs to try to open the hand by means of increasing the pull on the extensor digitorum.[54]

The inability to adduct and abduct the fingers occurs with the loss of the interossei muscles. These actions are quite important to people who play musical instruments or operate keyboards, but for most people does not result in a severe deficit.[54]

Table 5.22 GROUPS OF INTRINSIC HAND MUSCLES

Groups	Function	Muscles
Thenar	Thumb is brought lateral to medial position across the palm in opposition to the 4 ulnar digits	Abductor pollicis brevis Flexor pollicis brevis Opponens pollicis
Hypothenar	Little finger is brought in opposition to the thumb	Opponens digiti minimi Adductor pollicis
Palmar interossei (3)	Adduct the 4 ulnar digits together toward the 3rd finger First palmar interossei: tip pinch	
Dorsal interossei	First dorsal interossei: key pinch[54] Flex the MCP joints and extend the IP joints; adduct the 4 ulnar digits toward the 3rd finger	4 interossei Abductor digiti minimi
Lumbricals	Extension of the IP joints in any position of the MCP joints	2 radial lumbricals 2 ulnar lumbricals

IP, Interphalangeal; *MCP,* metacarpophalangeal.

(Interossei and Lumbricals)

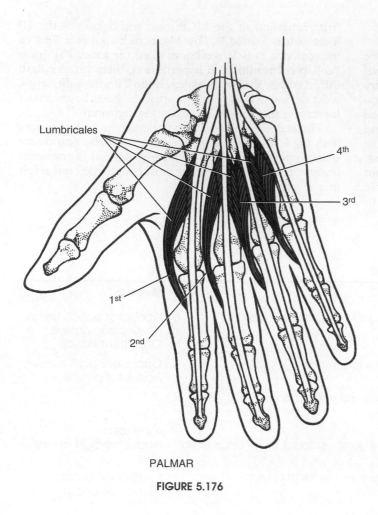

Lumbricales

4th

3rd

1st

2nd

PALMAR

FIGURE 5.176

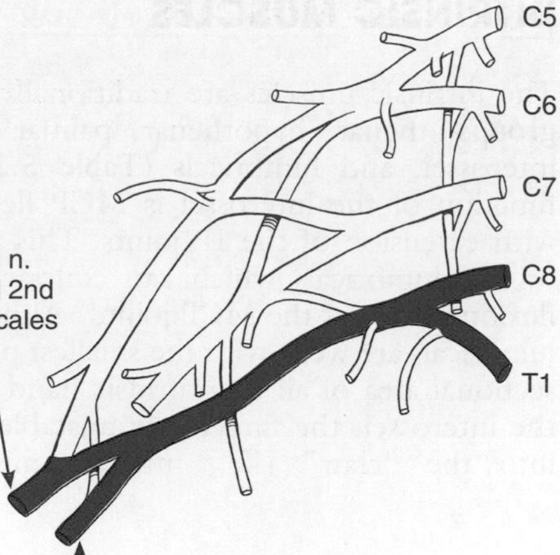

Median n.
To: 1st and 2nd
Lumbricales
C8-T1

Ulnar n.
To: 3rd and 4th Lumbricales
C8-T1
Interossei (dorsal and
palmar)
C8-T1

C5
C6
C7
C8
T1

FIGURE 5.177

Range of Motion
MCP joints: 0°–90°

Table 5.23 MCP FLEXION AND ABDUCTION AND ADDUCTION OF THE FINGERS

I.D.	Muscle	Origin	Insertion	Function
164	Dorsal interossei (four bipennate muscles) 1st dorsal interosseus (often named *Abductor indicis*)	Metacarpal bones (each muscle arises by two heads from adjacent sides of metacarpals between which each lies)	All: dorsal expansion Proximal phalanges (bases)	Abduction of fingers away from an axis drawn through the center of the long (middle) finger Flexion of fingers at MCP joints (assist) Extension of fingers at IP joints (assist) Thumb adduction (assist)
		1st dorsal: between thumb and index finger	1st dorsal: index finger (radial side)	Contributes 73% to the overall moment of MCP flexion[56]
		2nd dorsal: between index and long finger	2nd dorsal: long finger (radial side)	
		3rd dorsal: between long and ring fingers	3rd dorsal: long finger (ulnar side)	
		4th dorsal: between ring and little fingers	4th dorsal: ring finger (ulnar side)	
165	Palmar interossei three muscles (a 4th muscle often is described)	Metacarpal bones 2, 4, and 5 (muscles lie on palmar surfaces of metacarpals rather than between them) No palmar interosseous on long finger All muscles lie on aspect of metacarpal facing the long finger	All: Dorsal expansion Proximal phalanges	Adduction of fingers (index, ring, and little) toward an axis drawn through the center of the long finger Flexion of MCP joints (assist) Extension of IP joints (assist) Opposition of digit 5 (3rd interosseous)
		1st palmar: 2nd metacarpal (ulnar side)	1st palmar: index finger (ulnar side)	
		2nd palmar: 4th metacarpal (radial side)	2nd palmar: ring finger (radial side)	
		3rd palmar: 5th metacarpal (radial side)	3rd palmar: little finger (radial side)	
159	Abductor digiti minimi	Pisiform bone Tendon of flexor carpi ulnaris Pisohamate ligament	5th digit (base of proximal phalanx, ulnar side) Dorsal expansion of extensor digiti minimi	Abduction of 5th digit away from ring finger Flexion of proximal phalanx of 5th digit at the MCP joint Opposition of 5th digit (assist)
163	Lumbricals (4 in number)	Tendons of flexor digitorum profundus:	Extensor digitorum expansion Each muscle runs distally to the *radial* side of its corresponding digit, attaches to the dorsal digital expansion	Flexion of MCP joints (proximal phalanges) of digits 2–5 and simultaneous extension of the PIP and DIP joints
	1st lumbrical	Index finger (radial side, palmar surface)	1st lumbrical to index finger	
	2nd lumbrical	Middle finger (radial side, palmar surface)	2nd lumbrical to long finger	
	3rd lumbrical	Middle and ring fingers (double heads from adjacent sides of tendons)	3rd lumbrical to ring finger	

Continued

Table 5.23 MCP FLEXION AND ABDUCTION AND ADDUCTION OF THE FINGERS—cont'd

I.D.	Muscle	Origin	Insertion	Function
	4th lumbrical	Ring and little fingers (adjacent sides of tendons)	4th lumbrical to little finger	Opposition of digit 5 (4th lumbrical) Flexion of MCP joints (proximal phalanges) of digits 2–5 and simultaneous extension of the PIP and DIP joints
Others				
156	Flexor digitorum superficialis	See Table 5.20		
157	Flexor digitorum profundus	See Table 5.20		
160	Flexor digiti minimi brevis			
161	Opponens digiti minimi			
154	Extensor digitorum (no action on long finger)	See Table 5.21		
158	Extensor digiti minimi (little finger)	See Table 5.21		

DIP, Distal phalanges; *IP,* interphalangeal; *MCP,* metacarpophalangeal; *PIP,* proximal phalanges.

The lumbricals are the smallest muscles of all the intrinsic hand muscles and thus are weak as compared with the interossei muscles. It is impossible to separate the interossei from the lumbricals because of their synergistic action through the extensor hood mechanism.[54] The lumbricals have a rich composition of muscle spindles making them important for sensory input and in fast, alternating movements, for example, in typing and playing musical instruments.[54]

The test for the interossei and lumbricals is often called the lumbrical test, but it is the interossei that are being graded for their strength in stabilizing the MCP joints in flexion and therefore is more accurately referred to as the intrinsics-plus test (or roof-top)[53] (Fig. 5.178). This position demands the interosseous muscles (and to some extent the lumbricals) to move adjacent joints in opposite directions, creating a competition between movement at the MCP and IP joints.

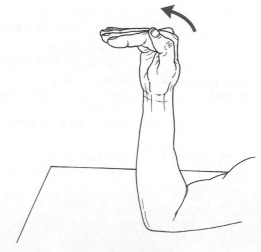

FIGURE 5.178

Grade 5, Grade 4, and Grade 3

Position of Patient: Short sitting or elbow flexed and resting on table with hand pointed up. Forearm in neutral. Hand relaxed.

Instructions to Therapist: Sit in front or to the side of the patient. Demonstrate the intrinsic plus position (see Fig. 5.178) to patient and insist on practice to get the motions performed correctly and simultaneously. While stabilizing the metacarpals (dorsum of hand on the table) to maintain flexion of the MCP joints, ask the patient to lift the fingers so that IP joints are straight. This action tests the lumbricals of each finger. If this position can be achieved (Grade 3), apply appropriate resistance over each digit, one finger at a time, distal to the PIP joint (pushing down) (Fig. 5.179).

To test the MCP flexion part of the lumbrical function, the patient should be in the intrinsic plus position in fully pronated position. Stabilize the metacarpals. Give resistance on the palmar PIP, in the direction of extension (Fig. 5.180).

Test: Patient simultaneously flexes the MCP joints and extends the IP joints (intrinsic plus position). Fingers may be tested separately if indicated (see Fig. 5.179). Do not allow fingers to curl; they must remain extended.

Instructions to Patient:

MCP joint portion: "Lift your fingers up. Hold them. Don't let me move your fingers."

IP portion: "Hold your fingers straight. Don't let me bend them."

Grading (Both Movements Are Graded Together)

Grade 5 and Grade 4: Patient holds position against strong resistance. Resistance can be given to fingers individually because of the variant strength of the different interossei and lumbricals and because the interossei and lumbricals have different innervations.

Grade 3: Patient completes both motions correctly and simultaneously without resistance.

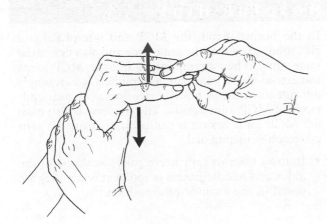

FIGURE 5.179

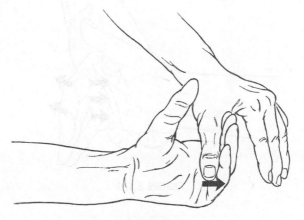

FIGURE 5.180

FINGER MCP FLEXION

(Interossei and Lumbricals)

Grade 2, Grade 1, and Grade 0

Position of Patient: Forearm and wrist in mid position to remove influence of gravity. MCP joints are fully extended; all IP joints are flexed.

Instructions to Therapist: Stabilize metacarpals.

Test: Patient attempts to flex MCP joints through full available range while extending IP joints (Fig. 5.181).

Instructions to Patient: "Try to straighten your fingers while keeping your knuckles bent." Demonstrate motion to patient and allow practice.

Grading

Grade 2: Completes full range of motion in gravity-minimized position.

Grade 1: Except in the hand that is markedly atrophied, the palmar interossei and lumbricals cannot be palpated. A grade of 1 is given for minimal motion.

Grade 0: A grade of 0 is given in the absence of any discernable palpable contraction.

Substitution

The long finger flexors may substitute for the lumbricals. To avoid this pattern, make sure that the patient's interphalangeal joints fully extend.

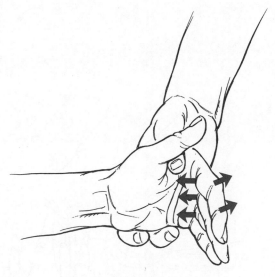

FIGURE 5.181

Helpful Hint

In the normal hand, the MCP and interphalangeal (IP) joints extend at the same time and also flex at the same time. When attempting to flex the MCP joints and extend the IP joints simultaneously, it is increasingly difficult to maintain full IP extension at or near end-range of MCP joint flexion. The converse is also true: full MCP joint flexion is not possible if full IP joint extension is maintained.

• In most cases of early nerve palsy, weakness of the index and middle fingers is apparent when they are tested in the intrinsic-plus position.[53]

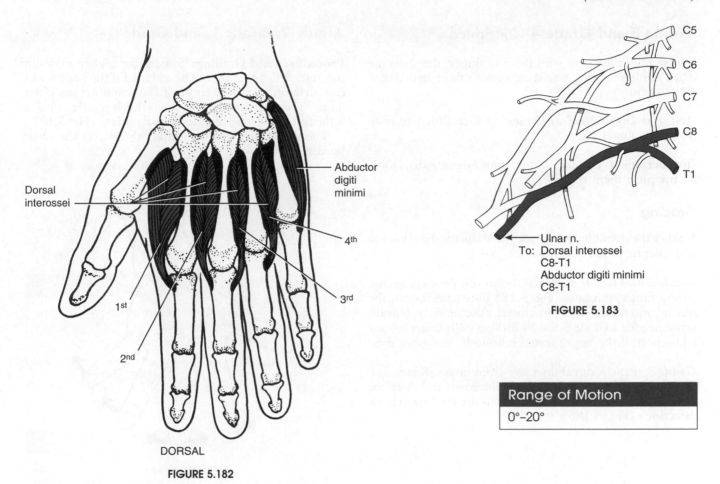

Dorsal interossei

Abductor digiti minimi

4th

1st

2nd

3rd

DORSAL

FIGURE 5.182

C5
C6
C7
C8
T1

Ulnar n.
To: Dorsal interossei
C8-T1
Abductor digiti minimi
C8-T1

FIGURE 5.183

Range of Motion
0°–20°

Grade 5 and Grade 4

Position of Patient: Forearm pronated, wrist in neutral. Fingers start in extension and adduction. MCP joints in neutral and avoid hyperextension.

Instructions to Therapist: Sit at table or side of patient. Support the wrist in neutral. Ask the patient to spread the fingers. If full range is present (Grade 3), apply appropriate resistance. The fingers of the other hand are used to give resistance on the distal phalanx, on the radial side of the finger, and the ulnar side of the adjacent finger (i.e., they are squeezed together). The direction of resistance will cause any pair of fingers to approximate (Fig. 5.184).

Test: Abduction of fingers (individual tests):

Dorsal Interossei:
Abduction of ring finger toward little finger
Abduction of middle finger toward ring finger
Abduction of middle finger toward index finger
Abduction of index finger toward thumb
    The long (middle) finger (digit 3, finger 2) will move one way when tested with the index finger and the opposite way when tested with the ring finger (see Fig. 5.182, which shows a dorsal interosseous on either side). When

FIGURE 5.184

FINGER ABDUCTION

(Dorsal interossei)

Grade 5 and Grade 4 Continued

testing the little finger with the ring finger, the abductor digiti minimi is being tested along with the fourth dorsal interosseous.

Abductor Digiti Minimi: Patient abducts fifth digit away from ring finger.

Instructions to Patient: "Hold your fingers apart. Don't let me push them together."

Grading

Neither the dorsal interossei nor the abductor digiti minimi will tolerate much resistance.

Grade 5 and Grade 4: Patient holds test position against strong finger resistance. Fig. 5.185 illustrates the test for second and fourth dorsal interossei. Alternatively, provide resistance for a Grade 5 test by flicking each finger toward adduction; if the finger tested rebounds, the grade is 5.

Grade 3: Patient can abduct any given finger. Remember that the long finger has two dorsal interossei and therefore must be tested as it moves away from the midline in both directions (Fig. 5.186).

Grade 2, Grade 1, and Grade 0

Procedures and Grading: Same as for higher grades in this test. A Grade 2 should be assigned if the patient can complete only a partial range of abduction for any given finger. The only dorsal interosseous that is readily palpable is the first at the base of the proximal phalanx (Fig. 5.187).

The abductor digiti minimi is palpable on the ulnar border of the hand.

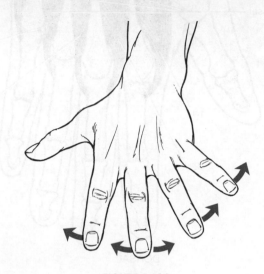

FIGURE 5.186

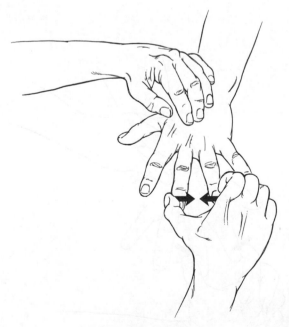

FIGURE 5.185

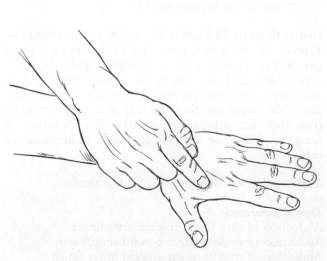

FIGURE 5.187

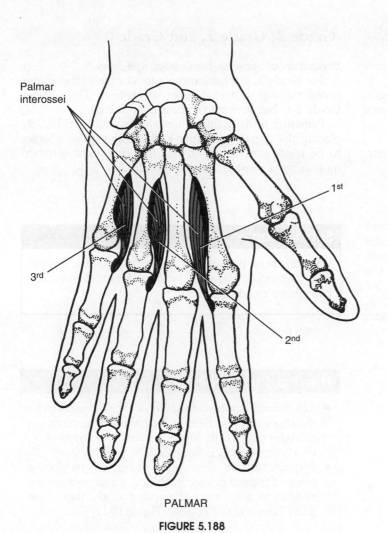

Palmar interossei

1st

2nd

3rd

PALMAR

FIGURE 5.188

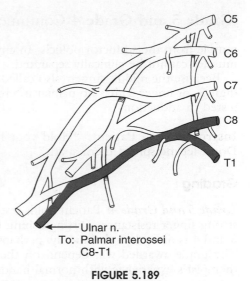

C5

C6

C7

C8

T1

Ulnar n.
To: Palmar interossei
C8-T1

FIGURE 5.189

Range of Motion
20°–0°

Grade 5 and Grade 4

Position of Patient: Forearm pronated (palm down), wrist in neutral, and fingers extended and adducted. MCP joints are neutral; avoid flexion.

Instructions to Therapist: Sit at table or to side of patient. Ask the patient to hold the fingers together. If the patient is able (Grade 3) and resistance is appropriate, grasp the middle phalanx on each of two adjoining fingers (Fig. 5.190) and try to pull the finger in the direction of abduction for each finger tested. The therapist is trying to "pull" the fingers apart. Each finger should be resisted separately.

Test: Adduction of fingers (individual tests):
Adduction of little finger toward ring finger
Adduction of ring finger toward long finger
Adduction of index finger toward long finger
Adduction of thumb toward index finger
    Occasionally there is a fourth palmar interosseous (not illustrated in Fig. 5.188) that some consider a separate

FIGURE 5.190

FINGER ADDUCTION

(Palmar interossei)

Grade 5 and Grade 4 Continued

muscle from the adductor pollicis. In any event, the two muscles cannot be clinically separated.

Because the middle finger (also called the long finger, digit 3, or finger 2) has no palmar interosseous, it is not tested in adduction.

Instructions to Patient: "Hold your fingers together. Don't let me spread them apart."

Grading

Grade 5 and Grade 4: Patient holds test position against strong finger resistance. Distinguishing between Grades 5 and 4 is difficult and clinically, perhaps not important. The grade awarded will depend on the amount of the therapist's experience with normal hands.

Grade 3: Patient can adduct fingers toward middle finger (Fig. 5.191).

Grade 2, Grade 1, and Grade 0

Procedures: Same as for Grades 5, 4, and 3.

For Grade 2, the patient can adduct each of the fingers tested through a partial range of motion. The test for Grade 2 is begun with the fingers abducted.

Palpation of the palmar interossei is rarely feasible. By placing the therapist's finger against the side of a finger to be tested, the therapist may detect a slight outward motion for a muscle less than Grade 2.

Substitution

Caution must be used to ensure that finger flexion does not occur because the long finger flexors can contribute to adduction.

Helpful Hints

- The fingers can be assessed quickly by grasping the distal phalanx and flicking the finger in the direction of abduction. If the finger rebounds or snaps back, that interosseous is functional.
- A quick test for ulnar nerve integrity is to place a piece of paper between each finger and instruct the patient to not let the therapist pull the paper out from between the fingers (Fig. 5.192).

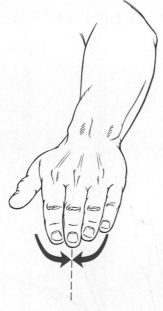

FIGURE 5.191

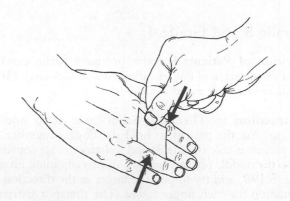

FIGURE 5.192

THUMB MUSCLES

The thumb muscles are made up of three extrinsics and four intrinsics. Three of these muscles, the abductor pollicis brevis (APB), opponens pollicis (OP), and flexor pollicis brevis (FPB), form the fleshy mass at the radial border of the thumb. There are eight motions of the thumb (Plate 5), which are possible because of the medial and lateral rotation at its carpometacarpal (CMC) joint.[57] To fully understand the muscles of the thumb, the complex motions of the thumb must be understood. The thumb musculature dynamically allows for precision pinching and power gripping. Thumb stability is actively maintained by muscles rather than articular constraints.

The thenar intrinsics that medially rotate and oppose the thumb (APB, OP, and FPB) can be quickly assessed by asking the patient to touch the tip of the thumb to each of the pads of the fingers, so that thumb nail is parallel to the finger tips. It is important to palpate the thenar muscles to note an active contraction.

It is difficult to differentiate between Grade 5 and 4 in many of the small muscles of the hand, and may not be clinically relevant. Therefore, Grades 5 and 4 have been combined for some muscles. It takes experience and skill to discern weakness in the actively contracting hand muscle.

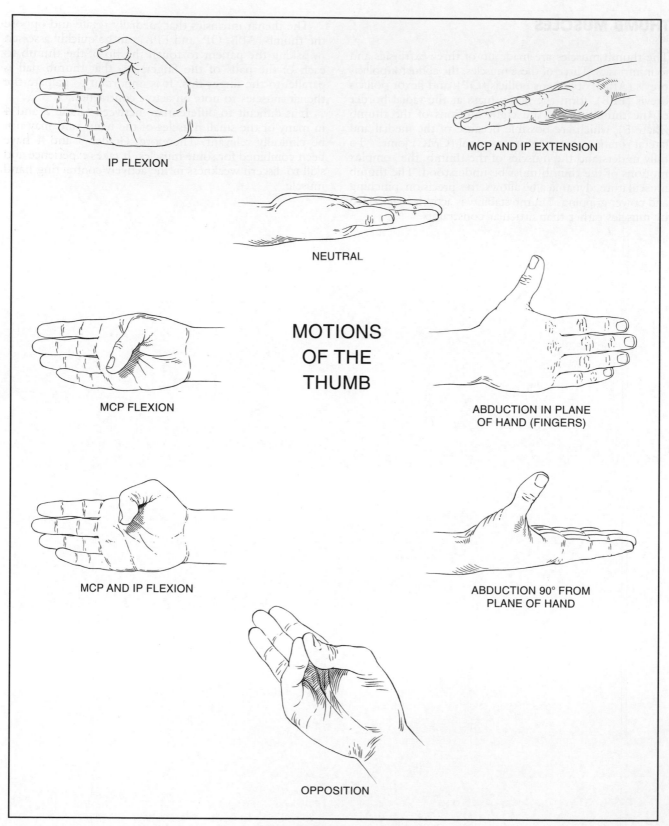

IP FLEXION

MCP AND IP EXTENSION

NEUTRAL

MCP FLEXION

MOTIONS
OF THE
THUMB

ABDUCTION IN PLANE
OF HAND (FINGERS)

MCP AND IP FLEXION

ABDUCTION 90° FROM
PLANE OF HAND

OPPOSITION

PLATE 5 Motions of the thumb.

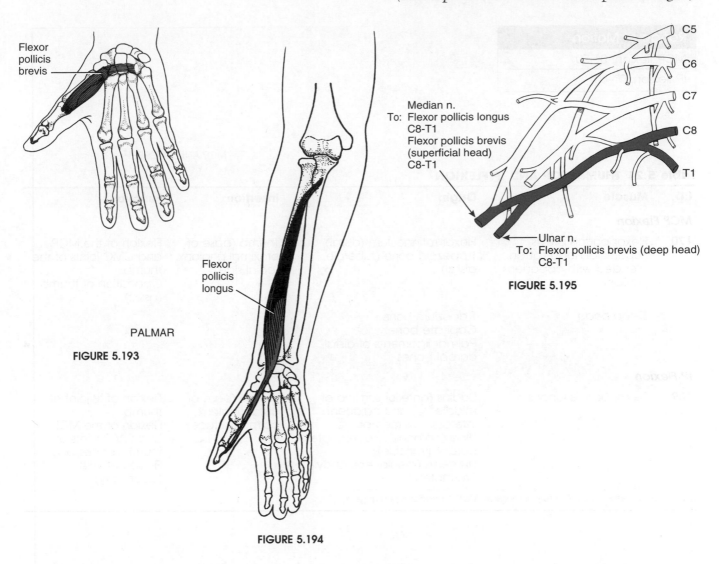

Flexor
pollicis
brevis

PALMAR

FIGURE 5.193

Flexor
pollicis
longus

FIGURE 5.194

Median n.
To: Flexor pollicis longus
C8-T1
Flexor pollicis brevis
(superficial head)
C8-T1

Ulnar n.
To: Flexor pollicis brevis (deep head)
C8-T1

C5
C6
C7
C8
T1

FIGURE 5.195

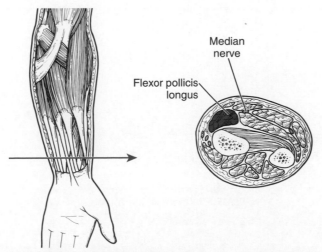

Flexor pollicis
longus

Median
nerve

FIGURE 5.196 Arrow indicates level of cross section.

THUMB MCP AND IP FLEXION

(Flexor pollicis brevis and Flexor pollicis longus)

Range of Motion
MCP flexion: 0°–50°
IP flexion: 0°–80°

Table 5.24 THUMB MCP AND IP FLEXION

I.D.	Muscle	Origin	Insertion	Function
MCP Flexion				
170	Flexor pollicis brevis Superficial head (often blended with opponens pollicis)	Flexor retinaculum (distal) Trapezoid bone (tubercle, distal)	Thumb (base of proximal phalanx, radial side)	Flexion of the MCP and CMC joints of the thumb Opposition of thumb (assist)
	Deep head	Trapezium bone Capitate bone Palmar ligaments of distal carpal bones		
IP Flexion				
169	Flexor pollicis longus	Radius (anterior surface of middle ½) and adjacent interosseous membrane Ulna (coronoid process, lateral border (variable)) Humerus (medial epicondyle (variable))	Thumb (base of distal phalanx, palmar surface)	Flexion of IP joint of thumb Flexion of the MCP and CMC joints of thumb (accessory) Flexion of wrist (accessory)

CMC, Carpometacarpal; *IP*, interphalangeal; *MCP*, metacarpophalangeal.

The FPB is an intrinsic muscle of the thumb. The innervation of the two heads can be variable, innervated by the median nerve, the ulnar nerve, or both.[58] The FPB and longus are implicated in texting motions.

Grade 5 to Grade 0

Position of Patient: Forearm in supination, wrist in neutral. Carpometacarpal (CMC) joint is at 0°; IP joint is at 0°. Thumb in adduction, lying relaxed and adjacent to the second metacarpal.

Instructions to Therapist: Sit at table or to side of patient. Demonstrate thumb flexion and have patient practice the motion. Stabilize the first metacarpal firmly to avoid any wrist or CMC motion. Ask the patient to bend the thumb toward the palm, keeping the IP straight. If the motion can be accomplished (Grade 3), apply appropriate resistance with one-finger resistance to MCP flexion on the proximal phalanx in the direction of extension (Fig. 5.197).

Test: Patient flexes the MCP joint of the thumb, keeping the IP joints straight (see Fig. 5.197).

Instructions to Patient: "Don't bend the tip of the finger. Hold it. Don't let me pull it back."

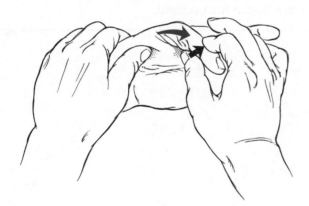

FIGURE 5.197

Grading

Grade 5 and Grade 4: Can hold position against strong thumb resistance. Distinguishing between Grades 5 and 4 is difficult and clinically, perhaps not important. The grade awarded will depend on the amount of the therapist's experience with normal hands.

Grade 3: Completes full range of motion.

Grade 2: Cannot complete full range of motion.

Grade 1: Palpate the muscle by initially locating the tendon of the flexor pollicis longus in the thenar eminence (Fig. 5.198). Then palpate the muscle belly of the FPB on the ulnar side of the longus tendon in the thenar eminence.

Grade 0: No discernable palpable activity.

Substitution by Flexor Pollicis Longus

- The long thumb flexor can substitute but only after flexion of the IP joint begins. To avoid this substitution, do not allow flexion of the distal joint of the thumb.
- Work-related thumb pain in physiotherapists is related to decreased stability and strength of the thumb.[59] This instability may result in the inability to maintain thumb extension during mobilization techniques, a frequent complaint of therapists.[60]

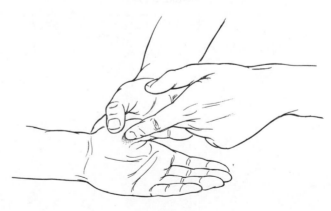

FIGURE 5.198

(Flexor pollicis longus)

Grade 5 to Grade 0

Position of Patient: Forearm supinated with wrist in neutral and MCP joint of thumb in extension.

Instructions to Therapist: Sit at table or side of patient. Stabilize the MCP joint of the thumb firmly in extension by grasping the patient's thumb across that joint. Ask the patient to bend the tip of the thumb. If sufficient range is present (Grade 3), apply resistance with the tip of your finger against the palmar surface of the distal phalanx of the thumb in the direction of extension (Fig. 5.199).

Test: Patient flexes the IP joint of the thumb.

Instructions to Patient: "Bend the end of your thumb. Hold it. Don't let me straighten it."

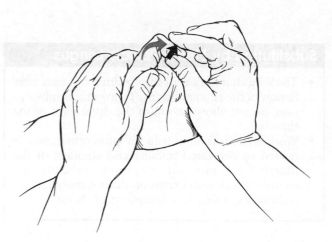

FIGURE 5.199

Grading

Grade 5 and Grade 4: Patient tolerates maximal finger resistance from therapist for Grade 5. This muscle is very strong, and a Grade 4 muscle will also tolerate strong resistance.

Grade 3: Completes a full range of motion with minimal resistance because gravity is minimized.

Grade 2: Holds test position.

Grade 1 and Grade 0: Palpate the tendon of the flexor pollicis longus on the palmar surface of the proximal phalanx of the thumb. Palpable activity is graded 1; no discernable palpable activity is graded 0.

Substitution

Do not allow the distal phalanx of the thumb to extend at the beginning of the test. If the distal phalanx is extended and then relaxes, the therapist may think active flexion has occurred.

(Extensor pollicis brevis and Extensor pollicis longus)

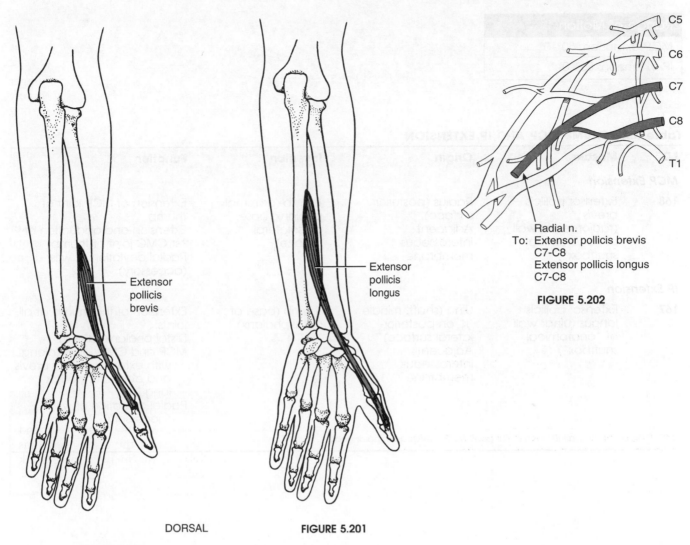

Extensor pollicis brevis

Extensor pollicis longus

C5
C6
C7
C8
T1

Radial n.
To: Extensor pollicis brevis
C7-C8
Extensor pollicis longus
C7-C8

FIGURE 5.202

DORSAL

FIGURE 5.201

FIGURE 5.200

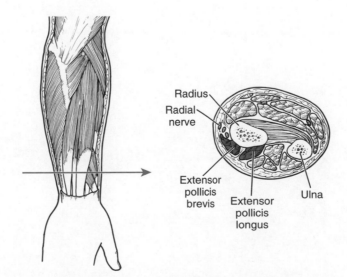

Radius
Radial nerve

Extensor pollicis brevis
Extensor pollicis longus
Ulna

FIGURE 5.203 Arrow indicates level of cross section.

THUMB MCP AND IP EXTENSION

(Extensor pollicis brevis and Extensor pollicis longus)

Range of Motion
MCP extension: 50°–0°
IP extension: 80°–0°

Table 5.25 THUMB MCP AND IP EXTENSION

I.D.	Muscle	Origin	Insertion	Function
MCP Extension				
168	Extensor pollicis brevis (radiomedial wall of "anatomical snuffbox")	Radius (posterior surface) Adjacent interosseous membrane	Thumb (proximal phalanx, base, dorsolateral surface)	Extension of MCP joint of thumb Extension and abduction of 1st CMC joint of thumb Radial deviation of wrist (accessory)
IP Extension				
167	Extensor pollicis longus (ulnar wall of "anatomical snuffbox")	Ulna (shaft, middle ⅓ on posterior-lateral surface) Adjacent interosseous membrane	Thumb (base of distal phalanx)	Extension of the thumb at all joints: Distal phalanx (alone) MCP and CMC joints (along with extensor pollicis brevis and abductor pollicis longus) Radial deviation of wrist (accessory)

CMC, Carpometacarpal; *IP*, interphalangeal; *MCP*, metacarpophalangeal.

The extensor pollicis brevis (EPB) is a muscle with common variations that often blends with the extensor pollicis longus (EPL); therefore it is not possible to separate the brevis from the longus by clinical tests, and the test for the longus prevails. The EPL and EPB with the abductor pollicis longus form the borders of the anatomical snuff box. The snuff box is most visible with thumb extension.

Grade 5, Grade 4, and Grade 3

Position of Patient: Forearm in mid position, wrist in neutral with ulnar side of hand resting on the table. Thumb relaxed in a flexion posture.

Instructions to Therapist: Sit or stand near the patient. Use the table to support the hand. Ask patient to lift just the thumb. If full range is present (Grade 3), apply the appropriate resistance over the dorsal surface of the distal phalanx of the thumb in the direction of flexion (Fig. 5.204).

Test: Patient lifts the thumb from the table, extending the IP joint of the thumb.

Instructions to Patient: "Hold it. Don't let me push it down."

Grading

Grade 5 and Grade 4: This is not a strong muscle, so resistance must be applied accordingly. The distinction between Grades 5 and 4 is based on comparison with the contralateral normal hand and, barring that, extensive experience in testing the hand.

Grade 3: Completes full range of motion without resistance.

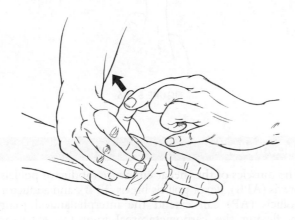

FIGURE 5.204

THUMB MCP AND IP EXTENSION

(Extensor pollicis brevis and Extensor pollicis longus)

Grade 2, Grade 1, and Grade 0

Position of Patient: Forearm in pronation with wrist in neutral and thumb in relaxed flexion posture to start.

Instructions to Therapist: Stabilize the wrist over its dorsal surface. Stabilize the fingers by gently placing the other hand across the fingers just below the MCP joints (Fig. 5.205).

Test: Patient extends distal joint of the thumb (see Fig. 5.205).

Instructions to Patient: "Straighten the end of your thumb."

Grading

Grade 2: Thumb completes range of motion.

Grade 1: Palpate the tendon of the extensor pollicis longus on the ulnar side of the "anatomical snuffbox" or, alternatively, on the dorsal surface of the proximal phalanx (Fig. 5.206).

Grade 0: No discernable palpable contractile activity.

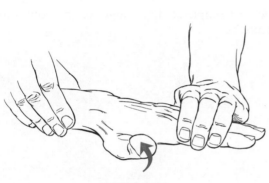

FIGURE 5.205

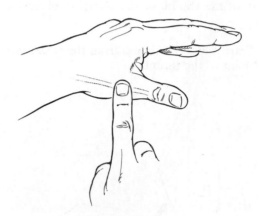

FIGURE 5.206

Substitution

The muscles of the thenar eminence (abductor pollicis brevis (APB), flexor pollicis brevis (FPB), and adductor pollicis (AP) can extend the interphalangeal joint by flexing the carpometacarpal joint (an extensor tenodesis).

Helpful Hints

- A quick way to assess the functional status of the long thumb extensor is to flick the distal phalanx into flexion; if the finger rebounds or snaps back, it is a useful muscle.
- The trapeziometacarpal (TMC) joint is the most common site of symptomatic osteoarthritis in the hand, with radiographic prevalence of 7% for men and 15% for women over age,[30,61] reaching 90% in both men and women at 80 years of age.[62]
- TMC arthritis leads to a loss of abduction-adduction in the TMC joint and at the MCP joint and often reduces pronation-supination.[63]

- TMC pain affects the ability to open jars (grasp) and turn keys (pinch).
- Resisted thumb extension that reproduced the patients' pain had a sensitivity of 0.94 and specificity of 0.95 for trapeziocarpal (TMC) arthritis. A positive test of either adduction or extension movements yielded a sensitivity of 1.00 and specificity of 0.91 for TMC arthritis.[62]
- The dorsal radial ligament is the prime opposer of TMC translation, and is also mechanically robust, anatomically thick, and well innervated.[64]

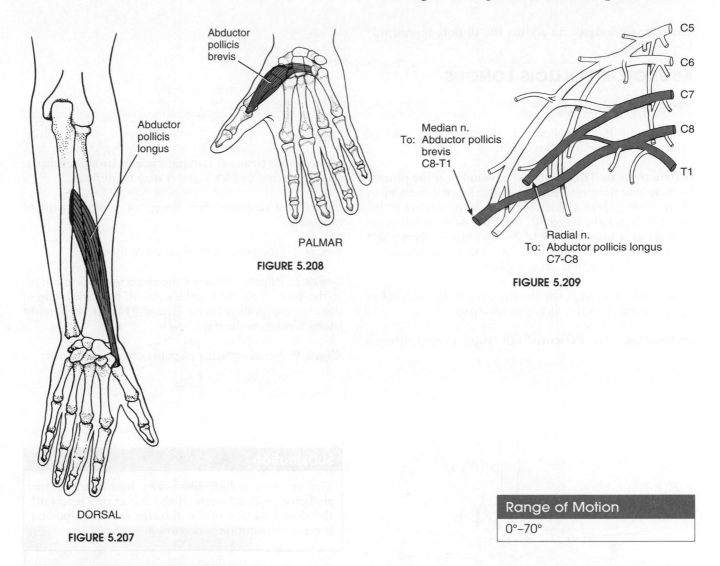

Abductor pollicis longus

Abductor pollicis brevis

PALMAR

FIGURE 5.208

DORSAL

FIGURE 5.207

Median n.
To: Abductor pollicis brevis
C8–T1

Radial n.
To: Abductor pollicis longus
C7–C8

FIGURE 5.209

C5
C6
C7
C8
T1

Range of Motion
0°–70°

Table 5.26 THUMB ABDUCTION

I.D.	Muscle	Origin	Insertion	Function
166	Abductor pollicis longus (radiolateral wall of "anatomical snuffbox")	Ulna (posterior surface laterally) Radius (shaft, middle ⅓ of posterior aspect) Interosseous membrane	Thumb: 1st metacarpal (radial side of base) Trapezium bone	Abduction of thumb at carpometacarpal (CMC) joint Extension of thumb at interphalangeal (IP) joint (in concert with thumb extensors) Radial deviation of wrist (assist)
171	Abductor pollicis brevis	Flexor retinaculum Scaphoid bone (tubercle) Trapezium bone (tubercle) Tendon of abductor pollicis longus	Medial fibers: Thumb (base of proximal phalanx, radial side) Lateral fibers: Extensor expansion of thumb	Abduction of thumb CMC and metacarpophalangeal (MCP) joints (in a plane 90° from the palm) Opposition of thumb (assist) Extension of IP joint (assist)
Others				
152	Palmaris longus (if present)			
168	Extensor pollicis brevis	See Table 5.25		

The palmaris longus can abduct the thumb, if present.[65]

ABDUCTOR POLLICIS LONGUS

Grade 5 to Grade 0

Position of Patient: Forearm supinated and wrist in neutral; thumb relaxed in adduction.

Instructions to Therapist: Sit or stand near the patient. Demonstrate the movement. Then stabilize the metacarpals of the four fingers and the wrist. Ask the patient to lift the thumb straight up to 90° from the palm. If full range of motion is present (Grade 3), then apply appropriate resistance on the **distal** end of the first metacarpal in the direction of adduction (Fig. 5.210).

Test: Patient abducts the thumb away from the hand in a plane parallel to the finger metacarpals.

Instructions to Patient: "Lift your thumb straight up."

Grading

Grade 5 and Grade 4: Can hold against strong resistance. Distinguishing Grades 5 and 4 may be difficult.

Grade 3: Completes full range of motion without resistance.

Grade 2: Completes partial range of motion.

Grade 1: Palpate tendon of the abductor pollicis longus at the base of the first metacarpal on the radial side of the extensor pollicis brevis (Fig. 5.211). It is the most lateral tendon at the wrist.

Grade 0: No discernable palpable contractile activity.

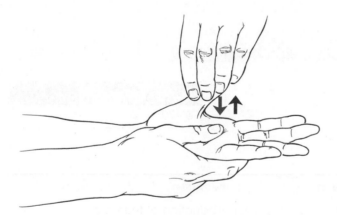

FIGURE 5.210

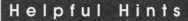

Substitution

The extensor pollicis brevis can substitute for the abductor pollicis longus. If the line of pull is toward the dorsal surface of the forearm (extensor pollicis brevis), substitution is occurring.

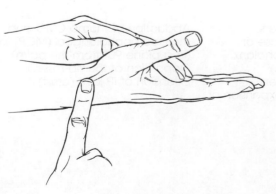

FIGURE 5.211

Helpful Hints

- If the abductor pollicis longus is stronger than the brevis, the thumb will deviate toward the radial side of the hand.
- If the abductor pollicis brevis is stronger, deviation will be toward the ulnar side.
- De Quervain's tenosynovitis, affecting the abductor pollicis longus and extensor pollicis brevis tendons, is indicated by the Finkelstein Test. To perform this test, ask the patient to close the fingers around the thumb so the thumb is tucked into the palm. Then ask the patient to ulnarly deviate the wrist. If pain is on the thumb side of the wrist, the test is positive. The condition has been linked to texting more than 50 messages/day.[66,67] Can also be referred to as "Gamer's thumb."

ABDUCTOR POLLICIS BREVIS

Grade 5, Grade 4, and Grade 3

Position of Patient: Dorsum of hand is on table with forearm in supination, wrist in neutral, and thumb relaxed in adduction.

Instructions to Therapist: Sit or stand near the patient. Demonstrate the movement. Ask the patient to lift the thumb to point towards the ceiling. If full range is present (Grade 3), apply appropriate resistance with index finger to the lateral aspect of the proximal phalanx of the thumb in the direction of adduction (Fig. 5.212).

Test: Patient abducts the thumb in a plane perpendicular to the palm. Observe wrinkling of the skin over the thenar eminence.

Instructions to Patient: "Lift your thumb vertically until it points to the ceiling." Demonstrate motion to the patient.

Grading

Grade 5: Holds motion with maximal finger resistance.

Grade 4: Tolerates moderate resistance.

Grade 3: Completes full range of motion without resistance.

Grade 2, Grade 1, and Grade 0

Position of Patient: Forearm in mid position, wrist in neutral, and thumb relaxed in adduction.

Instructions to Therapist: Stabilize wrist in neutral.

Test: Patient abducts thumb in a plane perpendicular to the palm.

Instructions to Patient: "Try to lift your thumb so it points at the ceiling."

Grading

Grade 2: Completes partial range of motion.

Grade 1: Palpate the belly of the APB in the center of the thenar eminence, medial to the OPP (Fig. 5.213).

Grade 0: No discernable palpable contractile activity.

Substitution

If the plane of motion is not perpendicular, but toward the radial side of the hand, the substitution may be by the abductor pollicis longus.

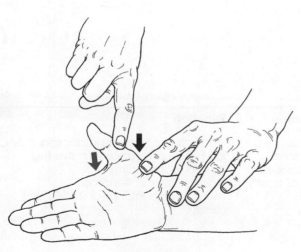

FIGURE 5.212

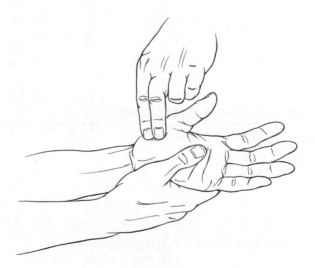

FIGURE 5.213

THUMB ADDUCTION

(Adductor pollicis)

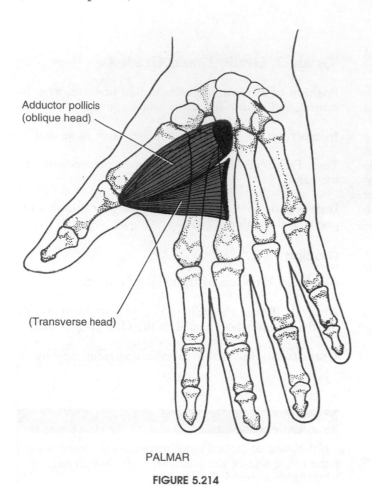

Adductor pollicis
(oblique head)

(Transverse head)

PALMAR

FIGURE 5.214

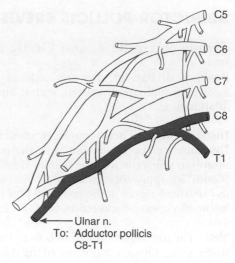

C5
C6
C7
C8
T1

Ulnar n.
To: Adductor pollicis
C8-T1

FIGURE 5.215

Range of Motion
70°–0°

Table 5.27 THUMB ADDUCTION

I.D.	Muscle	Origin	Insertion	Function
173	Adductor pollicis		Thumb (proximal phalanx, ulnar side of base)	Adduction of carpometacarpal (CMC) joint of thumb (approximates the thumb to the palm) Adduction and flexion of metacarpophalangeal (MCP) joint (assist)
	Oblique head	Capitate bone 2nd and 3rd metacarpals (bases) Palmar ligaments of carpal bones Sheath of tendon of flexor carpi radialis		
	Transverse head	3rd metacarpal bone (palmar surface of distal ⅔)		

Grade 5, Grade 4, and Grade 3

Position of Patient: Forearm in pronation, wrist in neutral, and thumb relaxed and hanging down in abduction.

Instructions to Therapist: Sit or stand near the patient. Demonstrate the movement. Stabilize the metacarpals of the four fingers by grasping the patient's hand around the ulnar side. If full range is present (Grade 3), apply appropriate resistance on the medial side of the proximal phalanx of the thumb in the direction of abduction (Fig. 5.216). Do not allow ulnar deviation. Alternatively, place a sheet of paper between the thumb and the index finger (adduction) and ask the patient to hold it while the therapist tries to pull the paper away. This is strong movement and the patient should be able to hold a paper without difficulty.

Test: Patient adducts the thumb by bringing the first metacarpal up to the second metacarpal.

Instructions to Patient: "Bring your thumb up to your index finger." OR "Hold the paper. Don't let me pull it out."

Grading

Grade 5 and Grade 4: Holds test position against strong resistance. Patient can resist rigidly (Grade 5), or the muscle yields (Grade 4).

Grade 3: Completes full range of motion without resistance.

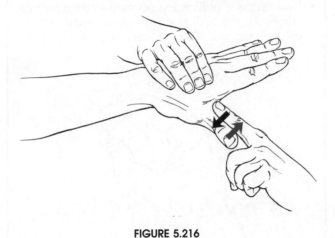

FIGURE 5.216

THUMB ADDUCTION

(Adductor pollicis)

Grade 2 and Grade 1

Position of Patient: Forearm in mid position, wrist in neutral resting on table, and thumb in abduction.

Instructions to Therapist: Stabilize wrist on the table, and use a hand to stabilize the finger metacarpals (Fig. 5.217).

Test: Patient moves thumb horizontally in adduction. The end position is shown in Fig. 5.217.

Instructions to Patient: "Return your thumb to its place next to your index finger." Demonstrate motion to patient.

Grading

Grade 2: Completes full range of motion.

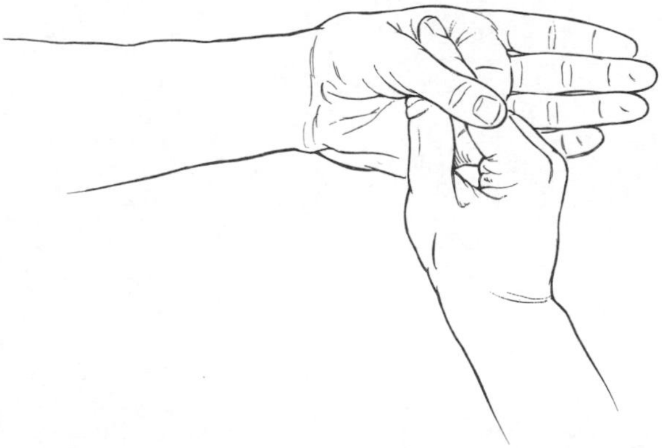

Grade 1: Palpate the adductor pollicis on the palmar side of the web space of the thumb by grasping the web between the index finger and thumb (Fig. 5.218). The adductor lies between the first dorsal interosseous and the first metacarpal bone. This muscle is difficult to palpate, and the therapist may have to ask the patient to perform a palmar pinch to assist in its location.

FIGURE 5.217

FIGURE 5.218

Substitutions

- A positive Froment's sign indicates the lack of strength of the adductor pollicis when the motor branch of the ulnar nerve is affected. The patient will use the flexor pollicis longus for pinch grip which will result in obvious bending of the interphalangeal joint of the thumb (Fig. 5.219).
- The extensor pollicis longus may attempt to substitute for the adductor pollicis, in which case the carpometacarpal joint will extend (not shown).

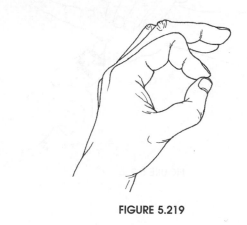

FIGURE 5.219

Helpful Hints

- Resisted thumb adduction that reproduces the patient's pain had a sensitivity of 0.94 and specificity of 0.93 for trapeziometacarpal (TMC) arthritis. A positive test of either thumb adduction or thumb extension yielded a sensitivity of 1.00 and specificity of 0.91 for TMC arthritis.[62]
- The tip pinch (index finger to thumb) is the functional task that is most compromised in people with MCP osteoarthritis.[68]

OPPOSITION (THUMB TO LITTLE FINGER)

(Opponens pollicis and Opponens digiti minimi)

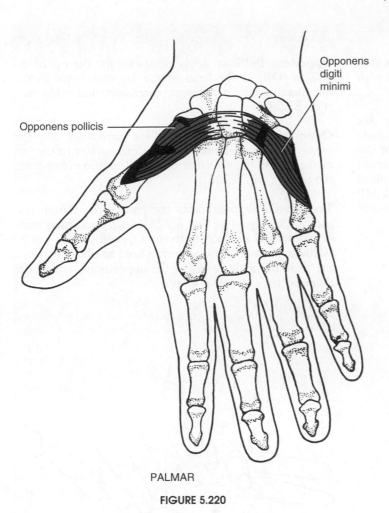

PALMAR

FIGURE 5.220

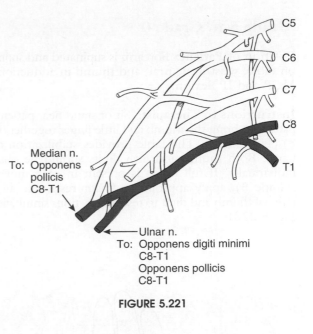

Median n.
To: Opponens pollicis
C8-T1

Ulnar n.
To: Opponens digiti minimi
C8-T1
Opponens pollicis
C8-T1

FIGURE 5.221

Range of Motion

Pad of thumb to pad of fifth digit

Table 5.28 OPPOSITION (THUMB TO LITTLE FINGER)

I.D.	Muscle	Origin	Insertion	Function
172	Opponens pollicis	Trapezium bone (tubercle) Flexor retinaculum	1st metacarpal (entire length of lateral border and adjoining lateral half of palmar surface)	Flexion of carpometacarpal (CMC) joint medially across the palm Medial rotation of CMC joint
161	Opponens digiti minimi	Hamate (hook) Flexor retinaculum	5th metacarpal (whole length of ulnar margin and adjacent palmar surface)	
Others				
171	Abductor pollicis brevis	See Table 5.26		
170	Flexor pollicis brevis	See Table 5.24		

This motion is a combination of abduction, flexion, and medial rotation of the thumb. The two muscles in thumb-to-fifth-digit opposition (opponens pollicis and opponens digiti minimi) should be graded separately.

OPPOSITION (THUMB TO LITTLE FINGER)

(Opponens pollicis and Opponens digiti minimi)

Grade 5 to Grade 0

Position of Patient: Forearm is supinated and supported on table, wrist in neutral, and thumb in adduction with MCP and IP flexion.

Instructions to Therapist: Sit or stand near patient. Ask patient to bring the thumb and little finger together (Grade 3) (Fig. 5.222). The table provides stabilization of the hand. Both thumb and fifth digits should be observed individually. If full range is present in each movement (Grade 3), apply appropriate finger resistance at CMP joint of thumb and digit to test both actions simultaneously Fig. 5.223).

Opponens Pollicis: Apply resistance for the opponens pollicis (OP) at the head of the 1st metacarpal in the direction of lateral rotation, extension, and adduction (Fig. 5.224).

Opponens Digiti Minimi: Give resistance for the opponens digiti minimi on the palmar surface of the 5th metacarpal in the direction of medial rotation (flattening the palm) (Fig. 5.225).

Test: Patient approximates the pad of the thumb and pad of fifth digit (see Fig. 5.222). Such apposition must be pad to pad and not tip to tip. Opposition also can be evaluated by asking the patient to hold an object between the thumb and little finger (in opposition), which the therapist tries to pull it away.

FIGURE 5.222

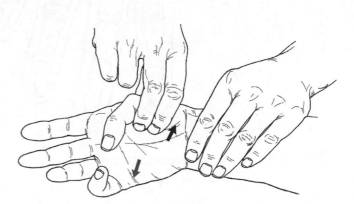

FIGURE 5.224

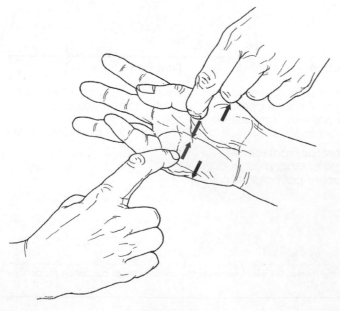

FIGURE 5.223

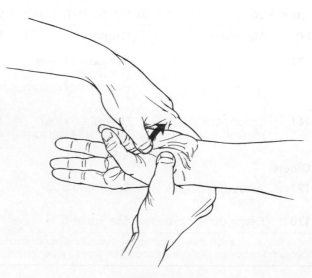

FIGURE 5.225

(Opponens pollicis and Opponens digiti minimi)

Grade 5 to Grade 0 Continued

Instructions to Patient: "Bring your thumb to your little finger and touch the two pads, forming the letter 'O' with your thumb and little finger." Demonstrate motion to the patient and require practice.

Grading

Grade 5: Holds against maximal thumb resistance.

Grade 4: Holds against moderate resistance.

Grade 3: Moves thumb and fifth digit through full range of opposition without resistance.

Grade 2: Moves through range of opposition. (The two opponens muscles are evaluated separately.)

Grade 1: Palpate the OP along the radial shaft of the 1st metacarpal (Fig. 5.226). It lies lateral to the APB. During Grades 5 and 4 contractions, the therapist will have difficulty in palpating the OP because of nearby muscles. In Grade 3 muscles and below, the weaker contractions do not obscure palpation.

Palpate the opponens digiti minimi on the hypothenar eminence on the radial side of the fifth metacarpal (Fig. 5.227). The therapist should be careful not to cover the muscle with the finger or thumb used for palpation lest any contractile activity be missed.

Grade 0: No discernable palpable contractile activity.

FIGURE 5.226

Substitutions

- The flexor pollicis longus and the flexor pollicis brevis can draw the thumb across the palm toward the little finger. If such motion occurs in the plane of the palm, it is not opposition; contact will be at the tips, not the pads, of the digits.
- The abductor pollicis brevis may substitute, but the rotation component of the motion will not be present.

Helpful Hints

The muscles involved in opening a 66-mm diameter jar lid are the flexor pollicis longus, flexor pollicis brevis, abductor pollicis brevis, adductor pollicis and opponens pollicis.[69]

Pinch strength, especially key pinch is less in patients with early thumb CMC arthritis.[70]

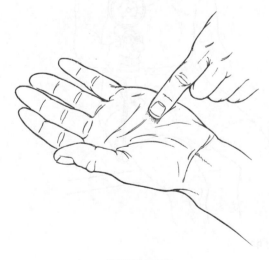

FIGURE 5.227

Grip strength is an efficient way to measure the composite strength of the hand and wrist, but grip strength is also related to general health and age. For example, grip strength peaks at 20 to 40 years and declines thereafter with advancing age.[71,72] In the older adult, grip strength has been shown to be a reliable predictor of mortality.[73] In many clinics, grip strength is used as a general indicator of total body strength.[74,75]

Position of Patient: Seated erect with shoulders level and neutrally rotated. The elbow is flexed to 90°, forearm in neutral and wrist between 0° and 30° of extension (Fig. 5.228A).[71]

Instructions to Therapist: Both hands are tested, one at a time. Record which hand is dominant as it will be most often stronger. Stand in front of the patient to be able to see the dial. Place the dynamometer in the patient's hand with the dial facing away from patient (see Fig. 5.228B). Adjust the position of the dynamometer handle so that the patient's fingers can comfortably grasp and squeeze it. Most often this is in the second position. Repeat three times. Alternate hands with each trial.

Instructions to Patient: "When I say go, squeeze as hard as you can, in a smooth manner. Do not jerk the tool while you are gripping. Stop immediately if you experience any unusual pain or discomfort." See Fig. 5.228.

Scoring

Three trials are recorded for each hand, averaging the three for the final score. Scores are compared with the appropriate age and sex categories for accurate interpretation (see Tables 5.28 and 5.29).[74]

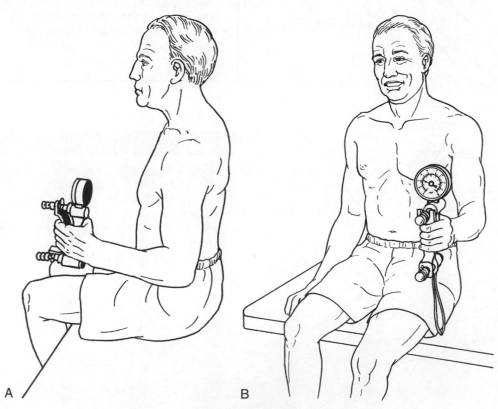

FIGURE 5.228A and B

Helpful Hints

- Grip strength of 9 kg (20 pounds) is commonly considered functional and is necessary to perform most daily activities.[72] A maximal grip strength of 5 kg (11 pounds) was found to be associated with a high risk of death in elderly women admitted to geriatric wards after acute illness.[73,74]
- A possible explanation for the relationship between weak grip strength and mortality is the fact that grip strength seems to be an indicator of nutritional status.[75] Protein deficiency may result in generalized muscle weakness and decreased cell-mediated immunity. Thus, severe weakness of grip may identify older patients at risk for dying as a result of protein malnutrition.[75]

- Grip strength is correlated significantly with upper limb function in older adults and in people with certain disorders, but not in young, healthy patients.[76,77]
- Grip strength is affected by certain disorders that impair results, such as carpal tunnel syndrome, lateral epicondylitis, dementia, arthritis, and stroke.
- The interossei can be tested by hand grip using a hand-grip dynamometer. Use the smallest distance between handle positions because the intrinsics are most active in this position.[78]
- The average decrease in grip strength after an ulnar nerve block is 38%.[79]

Table 5.29 MEAN NORMATIVE HAND GRIP STRENGTH (KG)[80]

Age	MEN			WOMEN		
	Right	Left	BMI	Right	Left	BMI
20–29	47 (9.5)	45 (8.8)	26.4 (5.1)	30 (7)	28 (6.1)	25.1 (5.8)
30–39	47 (9.7)	47 (9.8)	28.3 (5.2)	31 (6.4)	29 (6)	27.3 (6.8)
40–49	47 (9.5)	45 (9.3)	28.4 (4.6)	29 (5.7)	28 (5.7)	27.7 (7.7)
50–59	45 (8.4)	43 (8.3)	28.7 (4.3)	28 (6.3)	26 (5.7)	29.1 (6.4)
60–69	40 (8.3)	38 (8)	28.6 (4.4)	24 (5.3)	23 (5)	28.1 (5.1)
70+	33 (7.8)	32 (7.5)	27.2 (3.9)	20 (5.8)	19 (5.5)	27 (4.7)

Date collected using the position described in Fig. 5.224A and B.

BMI, Body mass index.

GRIP STRENGTH

Table 5.30 GRIP STRENGTH VALUES FOR AGES 4–14 IN kg[81]

AGE	BOYS			GIRLS		
	Dominant	Non-dominant	BMI	Dominant	Non-dominant	BMI
4	5.7 (2)	5.3 (2)	15.42	5.1 (2)	4.7 (2)	15.42
6	10.2 (3)	9.4 (3)	16	9.0 (3)	8.3 (3)	16
8	15.9 (4)	14.6 (3)	16.5	14.4 (3)	13.1 (3)	17.75
10	19.6 (2)	18.1 (3)	17.6	19.1 (4)	17.2 (4)	18.5
12	24.7 (5)	22.9 (5)	19	24.2 (5)	22.3 (4)	18.75
14	36.0 (7)	33.5 (7)	19.6	29.1 (5)	26.6 (5)	19.3

BMI, Body mass index.

1. Standring S, ed. *Gray's Anatomy the Anatomical Basis for Clinical Practice*. 41st ed. New York: Elsevier; 2016.
2. Basmajian JV, Travill J. Electromyography of the pronator muscles in the forearm. *Anat Rec.* 1961;139:45–49.
3. Inman VT, Saunders JB, Abbott LC. Observations on the function of the shoulder joint. *J Bone Joint Surg.* 1944;26:1–30.
4. Scibek JS, Carcia CR. Assessment of scapulohumeral rhythm for scapular plane shoulder elevation using a modified digital inclinometer. *World J Orthop.* 2012;3(6):87–94.
5. Sagano M, Magee D, Katayose M. The effect of glenohumeral rotation on scapular upward rotation in different positions of scapular-plane elevation. *J Sport Rehab.* 2006;15:144–155.
6. Ekstrom RA, Donatelli RA, Soderberg GL. Surface electromyographic analysis of exercises for the trapezius and serratus anterior muscles. *J Orthop Sports Phys Ther.* 2003;33:247–258.
7. Escamilla RF, Yamashiro K, Paulos L, et al. Shoulder muscle activity and function in common shoulder rehabilitation exercises. *Sports Med.* 2009;39(8):663–685.
8. Cricchio M, Frazer C. Scapulothoracic and scapulohumeral exercises: a narrative review of electromyographic studies. *J Hand Ther.* 2011;24(4):322–333.
9. Schory A, Bidinger E, Wolf J, et al. A systematic review of the exercises that produce optimal muscle rations of the scapular stabilizers in normal shoulders. *Int J Sports Phys Ther.* 2016;11(3):321–336.
10. Smith J, Padgett DJ, Kaufman KR, et al. Rhomboid muscle electromyography activity during 3 different manual muscle tests. *Arch Phys Med Rehabil.* 2004;85:987–992.
11. Perry J. Muscle control of the shoulder. In: Rowe CR, ed. *The Shoulder*. New York: Churchill-Livingstone; 1988:17–34.
12. Arlotta M, LoVasco G, McLean L. Selective recruitment of the lower fibers of the trapezius muscle. *J Electromyogr Kinesiol.* 2011;21(3):403–410.
13. Kendall FP, McCreary EK, Provance PG, et al. *Muscles: Testing and Function with Posture and Pain*. 5th ed. Baltimore, MD: Lippincott, Williams & Wilkins; 2005:297–305.
14. De Freias V, Vitti M, Furlani J. Electromyographic study of levator scapulae and rhomboideus major muscles in movements of the shoulder and arm. *Electromyogr Clin Neurophysiol.* 1980;20:205–216.
15. Signorile JF, Zink AJ, Szwed SP. A comparative electromyographical investigation of muscle utilization patterns using various hand positions during the lat pull-down. *J Strength Cond Res.* 2002;16(4):539–546.
16. Lehman GJ, Buchan DD, Lundy A, et al. Variations in muscle activation levels during traditional latissimus dorsi weight training exercises: an experimental study. *Dyn Med.* 2004;3(1):4.
17. Park SY, Yoo WG. Comparison of exercises inducing maximum voluntary isometric contraction for the latissimus dorsi using surface electromyography. *J Electromyogr Kinesiol.* 2013;23(5):1106–1110.
18. Travell JG, Simons DG. *Myofascial Pain and Dysfunction. The Trigger Point Manual*. Baltimore MD: Williams & Wilkins; 1983:433.
19. Ackland DC, Pak P, Richardson M, et al. Moment arms of the muscles crossing the anatomical shoulder. *J Anat.* 2008;213(4):383–390.
20. Wickham J, Pizzari T, Stansfeld K, et al. Quantifying 'normal' shoulder muscle activity during abduction. *J Electromyogr Kinesiol.* 2010;20:212–222.
21. Freeman S, Karpowicz A, Gray J, et al. Quantifying muscle patterns and spine load during various forms of the push-up. *Med Sci Sports Exerc.* 2006;38(3):570–577.
22. Lauver JD, Cayot TE, Scheuermann BW. Influence of bench angle on upper extremity muscular activation during bench press exercise. *Eur J Sport Sci.* 2016;16(3):309–316.
23. Trebs AA, Brandenburg JP, Pitney WA. An electromyography analysis of 3 muscles surrounding the shoulder joint during the performance of a chest press exercise at several angles. *J Strength Cond Res.* 2010;24(7):1925–1930.
24. Boettcher CE, Ginn KA, Cathers I. Standard maximum isometric voluntary contraction tests for normalizing shoulder muscle. *J Orthop Res.* 2008;26(12):1591–1597.
25. Reinold MM, Wilk KE, Fleisig GS, et al. Electromyographic analysis of the rotator cuff and deltoid musculature during common shoulder external rotation exercises. *J Orthop Sports Phys Ther.* 2004;34:385–394.
26. Ferreira MI, Büll ML, Vitti M. Electromyographic validation of basic exercises for physical conditioning programmes. I. Analysis of the deltoid muscle (anterior portion) and pectoralis major muscle (clavicular portion) in rowing exercises with middle grip. *Electromyogr Clin Neurophysiol.* 1995;35(4):239–245.
27. Hereter Gregori J, Bureau NJ, Billuart F, et al. Coaptation/elevation role of the middle deltoid muscle fibers: a static biomechanical pilot study using shoulder MRI. *Surg Radiol Anat.* 2014;36(10):1001–1007.
28. Hegedus EJ, Goode A, Campbell S, et al. Physical examination tests of the shoulder: a systematic review with meta-analysis of individual tests. *Br J Sports Med.* 2008;42:80–92.
29. Holtby R, Razmjou H. Validity of the supraspinatus test as a single clinical test in diagnosing patients with rotator cuff pathology. *J Orthop Sports Phys Ther.* 2004;34:194–200.
30. Kelly BT, Kadrmas WR, Speer KP. The manual muscle examination for rotator cuff strength. An electromyographic investigation. *Am J Sports Med.* 1996;24(5):581.
31. Wilk KE, Arrigo CA, Andrews JR. Current concepts: the stabilizing structures of the glenohumeral joint. *J Orthop Sports Phys Ther.* 1997;25:364–379.
32. Hughes RE, An KN. Force analysis of rotator cuff muscles. *Clin Orthop Relat Res.* 1996;330:75–83.
33. Marcolin G, Petrone N, Moro T, et al. Selective activation of shoulder, trunk, and arm muscles: a comparative analysis of different push-up variants. *J Athl Train.* 2015;50(11):1126–1132.
34. Decker MJ, Tokish JM, Ellis HB, et al. Subscapularis muscle activity during selected rehabilitation exercises. *Am J Sports Med.* 2003;31(1):126–134.
35. Hughes PC, Green RA, Taylor NF. Isolation of infraspinatus in clinical test positions. *J Sci Med Sport.* 2014;17(3):256–260.
36. McKay MJ, Baldwin JN, Ferreira P, et al; 1000 Norms Project Consortium. Normative reference values for strength and flexibility of 1,000 children and adults. *Neurology.* 2017;88(1):36–43.
37. Gerber C, Krushell RJ. Isolated rupture of the tendon of the subscapularis muscle. Clinical features in 16 cases. *J Bone Joint Surg Br.* 1991;73:389–394.
38. Tokish JM, Decker MJ, Ellis HB, et al. The belly-press test for the physical examination of the subscapularis muscle: electromyographic validation in comparison to the lift-off test. *J Shoulder Elbow Surg.* 2003;12:427–430.
39. Kadaba MP, Cole A, Wooten ME, et al. Intramuscular wire electromyography of the subscapularis. *J Orthop Res.* 1992;10(3):394–397.
40. Kleiber T, Kunz L, Disselhorst-Klug C. Muscular coordination of biceps brachii and brachioradialis in elbow flexion

REFERENCES

with respect to hand position. *Front Physiol.* 2015;6: 215.

41. Klein CS, Marsh GD, Petrella RJ, et al. Muscle fiber number in the biceps brachii muscle of young and old men. *Muscle Nerve.* 2003;28(1):62–68.

42. Oliveira LF, Matta TT, Alves DS, et al. Effect of the shoulder position on the biceps brachii. in different dumbbell curls. *J Sports Sci Med.* 2009;8(1):24–29.

43. Snarr RL, Esco MR. Electromyographic comparison of traditional and suspension push-ups. *J Hum Kinet.* 2013;39:75–83.

44. Youdas JW, Budach BD, Ellerbusch JV, et al. Comparison of muscle-activation patterns during the conventional push-up and perfect· pushup™ exercises. *J Strength Cond Res.* 2010;24(12):3352–3362.

45. Gordon KD, Pardo RD, Johnson JA, et al. Electromyographic activity and strength during maximum isometric pronation and supination efforts in healthy adults. *J Orthop Res.* 2004;22(1):208–213.

46. Matsuoka J, Berger R, Berglund LJ, et al. An analysis of symmetry of torque strength of the forearm under resisted forearm rotation in normal subjects. *J Hand Surg.* 2006;31:801–805.

47. O'Sullivan LW, Gallwey TJ. Upper-limb surface electromyography at maximum supination and pronation torques: the effect of elbow and forearm angle. *J Electromyogr Kinesiol.* 2002;12:275–285.

48. Wong CK, Moskovitz N. New assessment of forearm strength: reliability and validity. *Am J Occup Ther.* 2010;64:809–813.

49. Narita A, Sagae M, Suzuki K, et al. Strict actions of the human wrist flexors: A study with an electrical neuromuscular stimulation method. *J Electromyogr Kinesiol.* 2015;25(4): 689–696.

50. O'Driscoll SW, Horii E, Ness R, et al. The relationship between wrist position, grasp size, and grip strength. *J Hand Surg Am.* 1992;17(1):169–177.

51. Kerver AL, Carati L, Eilers PH, et al. An anatomical study of the ECRL and ECRB: feasibility of developing a preoperative test for evaluating the strength of the individual wrist extensors. *J Plast Reconstr Aesthet Surg.* 2013;66(4): 543–550.

52. Richards RR, Gordon R, Beaton D. Measurement of wrist, metacarpophalangeal joint, and thumb extension strength in a normal population. *J Hand Surg Am.* 1993;18(2): 253–261.

53. Brandsma JW, Schreuders TA. Sensible manual muscle strength testing to evaluate and monitor strength of the intrinsic muscles of the hand: a commentary. *J Hand Ther.* 2001;14(4):273–278.

54. Schreuders TA, Brandsma JW, Stam HJ. The intrinsic muscles of the hand. Function, assessment and principles for therapeutic intervention. *Phys Med Rehab Kuror.* 2007;17:20–27. Accessed at: http://www.handexpertise.com/artikelen/intrinsicPhysMed06.pdf. May 31, 2017.

55. Goislard de Monsabert B, Rossi J, Berton E, et al. Quantification of hand and forearm muscle forces during a maximal power grip task. *Med Sci Sports Exerc.* 2012;44(10):1906–1916.

56. Ketchum LD, Thompson D, Pocock G, et al. A clinical study of forces generated by the intrinsic muscles of the index finger and the extrinsic flexor and extensor muscles of the hand. *J Hand Surg Am.* 1978;3(6):571–578.

57. Basmajian JV. *Muscles Alive.* 4th ed. Baltimore: Williams & Wilkins Company; 1978.

58. Gupta S, Michelsen-Jost H. Anatomy and function of the thenar muscles. *Hand Clin.* 2012;28:1–7.

59. Snodgrass SJ, Rivett DA, Chiarelli P, et al. Factors related to thumb pain in physiotherapists. *Aust J Physiother.* 2003;49(4):243–250.

60. Wajon A, Ada L, Refshauge K. Work-related thumb pain in physiotherapists is associated with thumb alignment during performance of PA pressures. *Man Ther.* 2007;12(1): 12–16.

61. Haara MM, Heliövaara M, Kröger H, et al. Osteoarthritis in the carpometacarpal joint of the thumb. Prevalence and associations with disability and mortality. *J Bone Joint Surg Am.* 2004;86-A(7):1452–1457.

62. Gelberman RH, Boone S, Osei DA, et al. Trapeziometacarpal arthritis: a prospective clinical evaluation of the thumb adduction and extension provocative tests. *J Hand Surg Am.* 2015;40(7):1285–1291.

63. Hamann N, Heidemann J, Heinrich K, et al. Effect of carpometacarpal joint osteoarthritis, sex, and handedness on thumb in vivo kinematics. *J Hand Surg Am.* 2014;39(11):2161–2167.

64. Lin JD, Karl JW, Strauch RJ. Trapeziometacarpal joint stability: the evolving importance of the dorsal ligaments. *Clin Orthop Relat Res.* 2014;472(4):1138–1145.

65. Gangata H, Ndou R, Louw G. The contribution of the palmaris longus muscle to the strength of thumb abduction. *Clin Anat.* 2010;23(4):431–436.

66. Ashurst JV, Turco DA, Lieb BE. Tenosynovitis caused by texting: an emerging disease. *J Am Osteopath Assoc.* 2010;110(5):294–296.

67. Ali M, Asim M, Danish SH, et al. Frequency of De Quervain's tenosynovitis and its association with SMS texting. *Muscles Ligaments Tendons J.* 2014;4(1):74–78.

68. Cantero-Téllez R, Martín-Valero R, Cuesta-Vargas A. Effect of muscle strength and pain on hand function in patients with trapeziometacarpal osteoarthritis. A cross-sectional study. *Reumatol Clin.* 2015;11(6):340–344.

69. Kuo LC, Chang JH, Lin CF, et al. Jar-opening challenges. Part 2: estimating the force-generating capacity of thumb muscles in healthy young adults during jar-opening tasks. *Proc Inst Mech Eng H.* 2009;223(5):577–588.

70. McQuillan TJ, Kenney D, Crisco JJ, et al. Weaker functional pinch strength is associated with early thumb carpometacarpal osteoarthritis. *Clin Orthop Relat Res.* 2016;474(2):557–561.

71. Fess EE. *Grip Strength.* 2nd ed. Chicago: American Society of Hand Therapists; 1992.

72. Bohannon RW, Bear-Lehman J, Desrosiers J, et al. Average grip strength: a meta-analysis of data obtained with a Jamar dynamometer from individuals 75 years or more of age. *J Geriatr Phys Ther.* 2007;30:28–30.

73. Shechtman O, Mann WC, Justiss MD, et al. Grip strength in the frail elderly. *Am J Phys Med Rehabil.* 2004;83: 819–826.

74. Desrosiers J, Bravo G, Hebert R, et al. Normative data for grip strength of elderly men and women. *Am J Occup Ther.* 1995;49:637–644.

75. Phillips P. Grip strength, mental performance and nutritional status as indicators of mortality risk among female geriatric patients. *Age Ageing.* 1986;15:53–56.

76. Kallman DA, Plato CC, Tobin JD. The role of muscle loss in the age-related decline of grip strength: cross-sectional and longitudinal perspectives. *J Gerontol.* 1990;45:M82–M88.

77. Hinson M, Gench BE. The curvilinear relationship of grip strength to age. *Occup Ther J Res.* 1989;9:53–60.

78. Janda DH, Geiringer SR, Hankin FM, et al. Objective evaluation of grip strength. *J Occup Med.* 1987;29(7): 569–571.

79. Kozin SH, Porter S, Clark P, et al. The contribution of the intrinsic muscles to grip and pinch strength. *J Hand Surg Am*. 1999;24(1):64–72.

80. Massy-Westropp NM, Gill TK, Taylor AW, et al. Hand grip strength: age and gender stratified normative data in a population-based study. *BMC Res Notes*. 2011;4:127.

81. Ploegmakers JJ, Hepping AM, Geetzen JH, et al. Grip strength is strongly associated with height, weight and gender in childhood a cross sectional of 2241 children and adolescents providing reference values. *J Physiotherapy*. 2013;59(4):255–261.

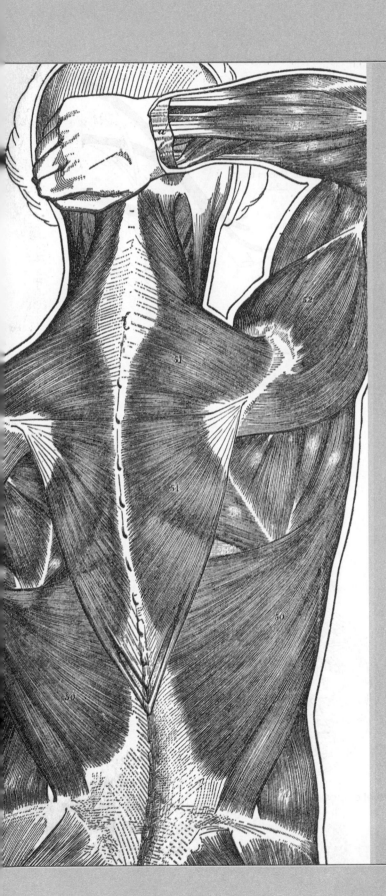

Testing the Muscles of the Lower Extremity

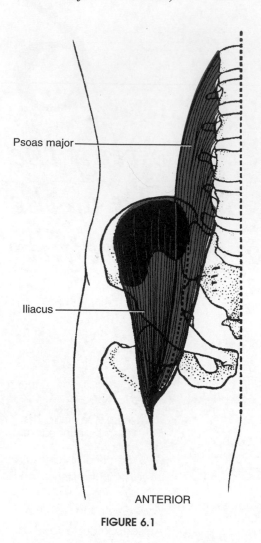

Psoas major

Iliacus

ANTERIOR

FIGURE 6.1

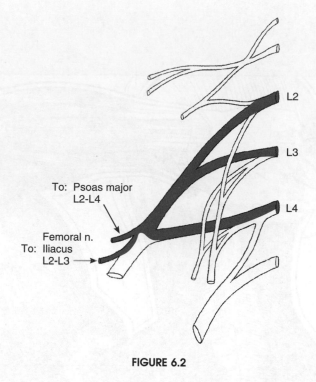

L2

L3

L4

To: Psoas major
L2-L4

Femoral n.
To: Iliacus
L2-L3

FIGURE 6.2

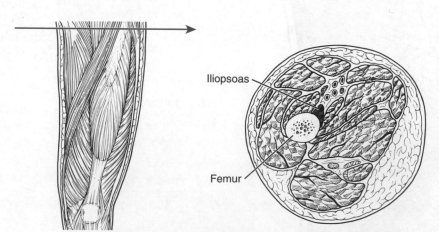

Iliopsoas

Femur

FIGURE 6.3 Arrow indicates level of cross section.

(Psoas Major and Iliacus)

Range of Motion
0°–120°

Table 6.1 HIP FLEXION

I.D.	Muscle	Origin	Insertion	Function
176	**Iliacus**	Ilium (superior ⅓ of Iliac fossa Iliac crest (inner lip) Anterior sacroiliac and iliolumbar ligaments Sacrum (upper lateral surface)	Femur (lesser trochanter via insertion on tendon of the psoas major) Femoral shaft below lesser trochanter	Hip flexion up to 110°[1] Internal rotation[1] Abduct femur in external rotation[1] Flexes pelvis on femur
174	**Psoas major**	L1-L5 vertebrae (transverse processes) T12-L5 vertebral bodies (sides) and their intervertebral discs	Femur (lesser trochanter)	Hip flexion with origin fixed Trunk flexion (sit-up) with insertion fixed (These two functions occur in conjunction with the iliacus) Hip external (lateral) rotation Flexion of lumbar spine (muscles on both sides) Lateral bending of lumbar spine to same side (muscle on one side)
Others				
196	Rectus femoris			Hip flexion
195	Sartorius			Hip flexion (combined with ER and abduction)
185	Tensor fasciae latae			Hip flexion Hip abduction
177	Pectineus			Accessory in hip flexion
183	Gluteus medius (anterior)			Accessory (if femur is moving from extension toward flexion)

The iliopsoas muscle is a compound muscle consisting of the iliacus and the psoas major, which join in a common tendon of insertion on the lesser trochanter of the femur. The iliopsoas contributes to hip compressive forces in walking and running, but relatively little to the gait cycle. Although the iliopsoas and rectus femoris are necessary for initiation of leg swing, they only contribute approximately 10% of the net metabolic cost of walking.[2] Hip flexion strength was found not to be a significant predictor of maximum walking speed.[3] The function of the iliopsoas may be more important in transfer activities and stair climbing as well as in uphill running.[4]

HIP FLEXION

(Psoas Major and Iliacus)

Grade 5, Grade 4, and Grade 3

Position of Patient: Short sitting with thighs fully supported on table and legs hanging over the edge. Patient may use arms to provide trunk stability by grasping table edge or with hands on table at each side (Fig. 6.4).

Instructions to Therapist: Stand next to limb to be tested. Ask the patient to lift the thigh off the table. If adequate range is present (thigh clears the table), proceed to apply maximum resistance at midrange (Grade 5) over distal thigh just proximal to the knee joint, being careful not to grasp the thigh (see Fig. 6.4).

Test: Patient flexes hip to end of range, clearing the table and maintaining neutral rotation. The patient then brings the hip to midrange and holds that position against the therapist's resistance, which is given in a downward direction toward the floor.

Instructions to Patient: "Sit tall and hold your thigh up. Don't let me push it down."

Grading

Grade 5: Patient holds test position against maximal resistance.

Grade 4: Patient holds test position against strong to moderate resistance. There may be some "give" with maximum resistance, making the grade a 4.

Grade 3: Patient completes test range and holds the position without resistance (Fig. 6.5).

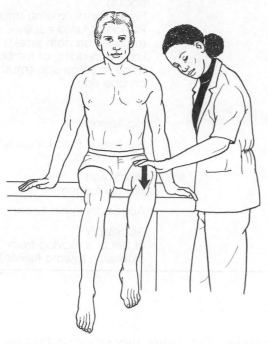

FIGURE 6.4

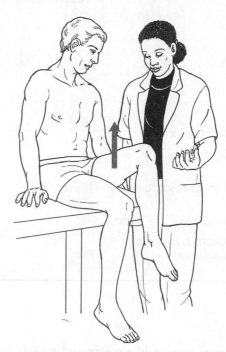

FIGURE 6.5

Helpful Hint

The position of the pelvis influences the action of the hip flexors. An anterior or posterior pelvic tilt influences the length tension of the hip flexors, thereby making them appear stronger or weaker. To eliminate the influence of the pelvis, the pelvis and spine should be in neutral as in Fig. 6.4.

Grade 2

Position of Patient: Side-lying with limb to be tested uppermost and supported by therapist (Fig. 6.6). Trunk in neutral alignment. Lowermost limb may be flexed for stability. A powder board under the upper limb may also be used to decrease friction.

Instructions to Therapist: Stand behind patient. Cradle test limb in one arm with hand support under the slightly flexed knee. Opposite hand maintains trunk alignment at hip (see Fig. 6.6).

Test: Patient flexes hip with supported limb. Knee is permitted to flex to prevent hamstring tension.

Instructions to Patient: "Bring your knee up toward your chest."

Grading

Grade 2: Patient completes the range of motion in side-lying position.

Grade 1 and Grade 0

Position of Patient: Supine.

Instructions to Therapist: Stand at side of limb to be tested. Test limb is supported under calf with hand behind knee. Free hand palpates the muscle just distal to the inguinal ligament on the medial side of the sartorius (Fig. 6.7).

Test: Patient attempts to flex hip.

Instructions to Patient: "Try to bring your knee up to your nose."

Grading

Grade 1: Palpable contraction but no visible movement.

Grade 0: No discernable palpable contraction of muscle.

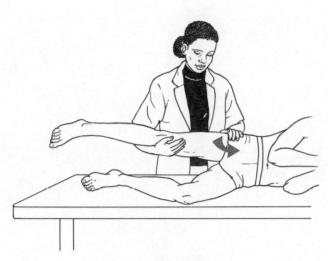

FIGURE 6.6

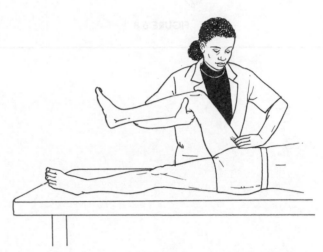

FIGURE 6.7

HIP FLEXION

(Psoas Major and Iliacus)

Substitutions

- Use of the sartorius will result in external rotation and abduction of the hip. The sartorius, because it is superficial, will be seen and can be palpated along its entire length (Fig. 6.8).
- If the tensor fasciae latae substitutes for the hip flexors, internal rotation and abduction of the hip will result. The tensor may be seen· and palpated at its origin on the anterior superior iliac spine.
- Patient may try to flex trunk as effort is made to flex hip or lean back to enhance length tension or the hip flexors.

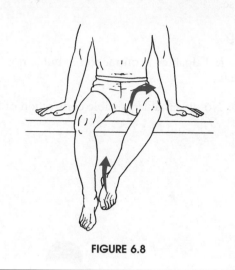

FIGURE 6.8

Helpful Hint

The hip flexors are rather small muscles (see Fig. 6.3) and therefore do not provide a lot of force, especially as compared with the quadriceps or gluteus maximus. Therefore a negative break test is rarely achieved if using a straight arm technique. Consequently, Fig. 6.4 shows the therapist with a bent arm while providing resistance. Experience is necessary to appreciate what constitutes a normal level of resistance.

Suggested Exercises for Iliopsoas

- Straight leg raise
- Marching (High Knees)
- Standing straight leg raise (SLR)
- V-situp

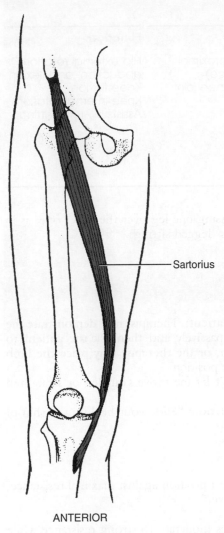

Sartorius

ANTERIOR

FIGURE 6.9

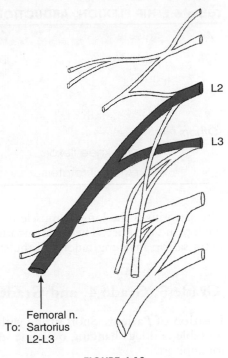

L2

L3

Femoral n.
To: Sartorius
L2-L3

FIGURE 6.10

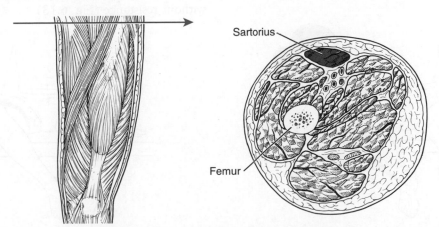

Sartorius

Femur

FIGURE 6.11 Arrow indicates level of cross section.

HIP FLEXION, ABDUCTION, AND EXTERNAL ROTATION WITH KNEE FLEXION

(Sartorius)

Table 6.2 HIP FLEXION, ABDUCTION, AND EXTERNAL ROTATION

I.D.	Muscle	Origin	Insertion	Function
195	**Sartorius**	Ilium (anterior superior iliac spine (ASIS)) Iliac notch below ASIS	Tibia (shaft, proximal medial surface) Capsule of knee joint (via slip) Aponeurosis	Hip external rotation, abduction, and flexion Knee flexion Knee internal rotation Assists in "tailor sitting"
	Others			
	Hip and knee flexors			
	Hip external rotators			

The sartorius is the longest muscle in the body crossing the hip and the knee. The word sartorius comes from the Latin sartor, meaning tailor and the sartorius allows the movement of crossing one leg over the other one, as in a "tailor sit" (cross-legged sitting).

Grade 5, Grade 4, and Grade 3

Position of Patient: Short sitting with thighs supported on table and legs hanging over side. Arms may be used for support.

Instructions to Therapist: Stand lateral to the leg to be tested. Ask the patient to flex, abduct, and externally rotate the hip, with the knee flexed. If adequate range is present, place one hand on the lateral side of the knee, the other hand over the medial-anterior surface of the distal leg (Fig. 6.12). Apply appropriate resistance with both hands, resisting hip flexion and abduction (in a down and inward direction) with the proximal hand and hip external rotation and knee flexion (up and outward) with the hand at the distal leg.

Test: Patient flexes, abducts, and externally rotates the hip while maintaining knee flexion (see Fig. 6.12).

Instructions to Patient: Therapist may demonstrate the required motion passively and then ask the patient to repeat the motion, or the therapist may place the limb in the desired test position.

"Hold it! Don't let me move your leg or straighten your knee."

Alternate instruction: "Slide your heel up the shin of your other leg."

Grading

Grade 5: Holds test position against maximal resistance, limb does not "give."

Grade 4: Tolerates moderate to strong resistance while maintaining position.

Grade 3: Completes movement and holds test position without resistance (Fig. 6.13).

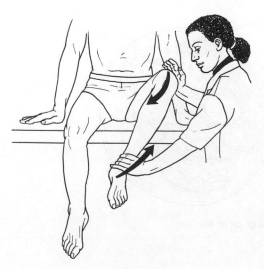

FIGURE 6.12

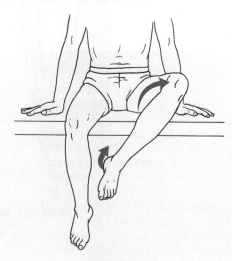

FIGURE 6.13

HIP FLEXION, ABDUCTION, AND EXTERNAL ROTATION WITH KNEE FLEXION

(Sartorius)

Grade 2

Position of Patient: Supine. Heel of limb to be tested is placed on contralateral shin (Fig. 6.14).

Instructions to Therapist: Stand at side of limb to be tested. Support limb as necessary to maintain alignment.

Test: Patient slides test heel upward along shin to knee.

Instructions to Patient: "Slide your heel up to your knee."

Grading

Grade 2: Completes desired movement.

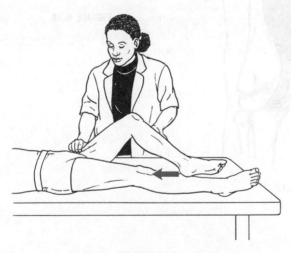

FIGURE 6.14

Grade 1 and Grade 0

Position of Patient: Supine.

Instructions to Therapist: Stand on side to be tested. Cradle test limb under calf with hand supporting limb behind knee. Opposite hand palpates sartorius on medial side of thigh where the muscle crosses the femur (Fig. 6.15). Therapist may prefer to palpate near the muscle origin just below the anterior superior iliac spine (ASIS).

Test: Patient attempts to slide heel up shin toward knee.

Instructions to Patient: "Try to slide your heel up to your knee."

Grading

Grade 1: Therapist can detect slight contraction of muscle; no visible movement.

Grade 0: No discernable palpable contraction.

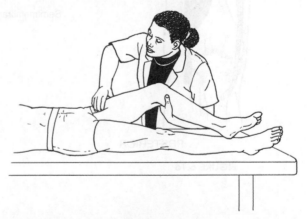

FIGURE 6.15

Substitution

Substitution by the iliopsoas or the rectus femoris results in pure hip flexion without abduction and external rotation.

Helpful Hints

- The therapist is reminded that failure of the patient to complete the full range of motion in the Grade 3 test is not an automatic Grade 2. The patient should be tested in the supine position to ascertain whether the correct grade is 2 or less.
- The abdominal muscles must generate a posterior pelvic tilt of sufficient force to neutralize the strong anterior pelvic tilt potential of the hip flexors.[5]
- In the presence of weakness, patients will attempt to substitute using the knee flexors, external rotators, and tensor fascia lata but the movement would deviate out of the expected plane.

Suggested Exercises for the Sartorius Muscle

- Multidirectional lunge (forward, side, lateral)
- High box step ups
- Closed stance squats
- Leg lifts with hip externally rotated

HIP EXTENSION

(Gluteus maximus and hamstrings)

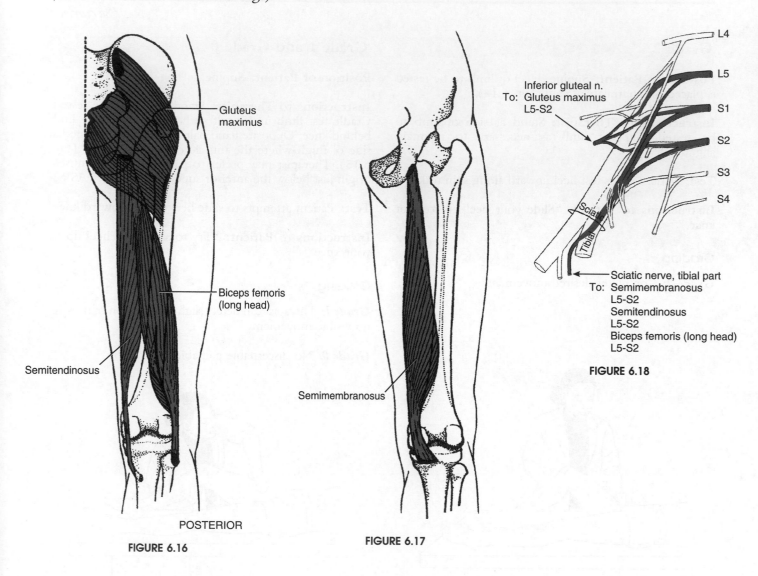

Gluteus
maximus

Biceps femoris
(long head)

Semitendinosus

POSTERIOR

FIGURE 6.16

Semimembranosus

FIGURE 6.17

Inferior gluteal n.
To: Gluteus maximus
L5-S2

L4
L5
S1
S2
S3
S4

Sciatic nerve, tibial part
To: Semimembranosus
L5-S2
Semitendinosus
L5-S2
Biceps femoris (long head)
L5-S2

FIGURE 6.18

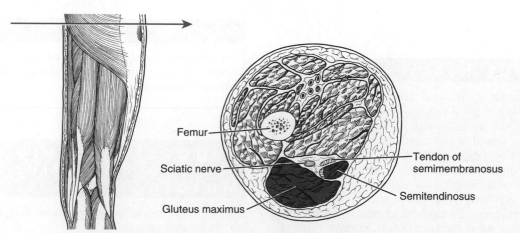

Femur

Sciatic nerve

Gluteus maximus

Tendon of
semimembranosus

Semitendinosus

FIGURE 6.19 Arrow indicates level of cross section.

Range of Motion
0°–20°
Some authors say as low as 0°–5°.

Table 6.3 HIP EXTENSION

I.D.	Muscle	Origin	Insertion	Function
182	**Gluteus maximus**	Ilium (posterior gluteal line) Iliac crest (posterior medial)	Femur (gluteal tuberosity)	Hip extension (powerful) Hip external (lateral) rotation Hip abduction (upper fibers) Hip adduction (lower fibers) Through its insertion into the iliotibial band it stabilizes the knee
		Sacrum (dorsal surface of lower part) Coccyx (side) Sacrotuberous ligament Aponeurosis over gluteus medius	Iliotibial tract of fascia lata	
193	Semitendinosus	Ischial tuberosity (upper area, inferomedial impression via tendon shared with biceps femoris) Aponeurosis (between the two muscles)	Tibia (proximal medial shaft) Pes anserinus	Knee flexion Hip extension Hip internal rotation (accessory)
194	Semimembranosus	Ischial tuberosity (superolateral impression)	Tibia (medial condyle, posterior aspect) Oblique popliteal ligament of knee joint Aponeurosis over distal muscle (variable)	Knee flexion Hip extension Hip internal rotation (accessory)
192	Biceps femoris (long head)	Ischial tuberosity (inferomedial impression via tendon shared with semitendinosus) Sacrotuberous ligament	Fibula (head) Tibia (lateral condyle) Aponeurosis	Hip extension and (weak) external rotation
Others				
181	Adductor magnus (inferior)			When the femur is flexed this muscle can be a powerful extensor. In earlier anatomy texts this muscle was classified as a fourth hamstring
183	Gluteus medius (posterior)			

The gluteus maximus is the largest muscle in the body, accounting for 16% of the total cross-sectional area of the lower extremity.[6] Eighty percent of the gluteus maximus inserts into the iliotibial band. It has at least six regions within the muscle that respond to different movements. The gluteus maximus is most effective in near full extension. Its pennate structure and long muscle length suggest it produces both high levels of force at low speeds through small ranges of motion and low levels of force at high speeds through large ranges of motion. It is a mix of slow and fast twitch fibers. It is often used to accelerate the body upward and forward from a position of hip flexion ranging from 40° to 60° (as in sprinting, squatting, and climbing a steep hill).[7]

HIP EXTENSION

(Gluteus maximus and hamstrings)

Grade 5, Grade 4, and Grade 3 (Aggregate of All Hip Extensor Muscles)

Position of Patient: Prone. Arms may be at the side of the body or abducted to hold sides of table. (Note: If there is a hip flexion contracture, immediately go to the test described for hip extension modified for hip flexion tightness [see page 240].)

Instructions to Therapist: Stand at level of pelvis on side of limb to be tested. (Note: Fig. 6.20 shows therapist on opposite side to avoid obscuring activity.) Ask the patient to lift the leg off the table as high as possible, while keeping the knee straight. If sufficient range is achieved, place the hand providing resistance on the posterior leg just above the ankle. The opposite hand may be used to stabilize or maintain pelvis alignment in the area of the posterior superior spine of the ilium (see Fig. 6.20). This is a demanding test because of the size of the muscle and the length of the lever arm.

Alternate Position: The hand that gives resistance is placed on the posterior thigh just above the knee (Fig. 6.21). This alternate position is a less demanding test. Optimal resistance cannot be applied because of the shorter lever arm and thus, the highest grade a patient can attain is a Grade 4. This test is not recommended unless absolutely necessary (e.g., unstable, painful knee, above-knee amputee).

Test: Patient extends hip through entire available range of motion. Resistance is given straight downward toward the floor.

Instructions to Patient: "Lift your leg off the table as high as you can without bending your knee. Hold it" (see Fig. 6.20).

Grading

Grade 5: Patient holds test position against maximal resistance.

Grade 4: Patient holds test position against strong to moderate resistance.

Grade 3: Completes range and holds the position without resistance (Fig. 6.22).

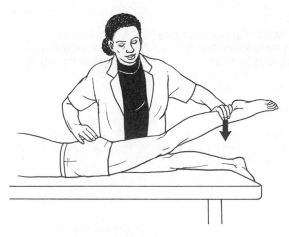

FIGURE 6.20

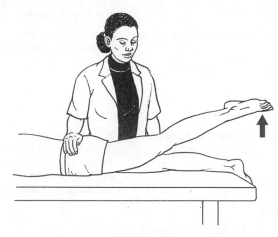

FIGURE 6.22

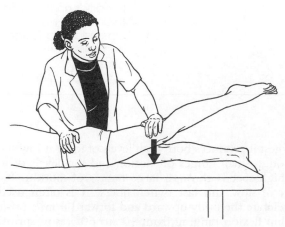

FIGURE 6.21

Helpful Hint

Knowledge of the ranges of hip motion is imperative before manual tests of hip strength are conducted. If the therapist does not have a clear idea of hip joint ranges, especially tightness in the hip flexor muscles, test results will be inaccurate. For example, in the presence of a hip flexion contracture, the patient must be standing and leaning over the edge of the table to test hip extension strength. This position (described on page 240) will decrease the influence of the flexion contracture and will allow the patient to move against gravity through the available range. The supine hip extensor test can also be used (see page 242).

Grade 2

Position of Patient: Side-lying with test limb uppermost. Knee straight and supported by therapist. Lowermost limb is flexed for stability.

Instructions to Therapist: Stand behind patient at thigh level. Therapist supports test limb just below the knee, cradling the leg (Fig. 6.23). Opposite hand is placed over the pelvic crest to maintain pelvic and hip alignment.

Test: Patient extends hip through full range of motion.

Instructions to Patient: "Bring your leg back toward me. Keep your knee straight."

Grading

Grade 2: Completes available range of motion in side-lying position.

FIGURE 6.23

Grade 1 and Grade 0

Position of Patient: Prone.

Instructions to Therapist: Stand at level of pelvis on side to be tested. Palpate hamstrings (deep into tissue with fingers) at the ischial tuberosity (Fig. 6.24). Palpate the gluteus maximus with deep finger pressure over the center of the buttocks including the upper and lower fibers.

Test: Patient attempts to extend hip in prone position or tries to squeeze buttocks together.

Instructions to Patient: "Try to lift your leg from the table." OR "Squeeze your buttocks together."

Grading

Grade 1: Palpable contraction of gluteus maximus but no visible joint movement. Contraction of gluteus maximus will result in narrowing of the gluteal crease.

Grade 0: No discernable palpable contraction.

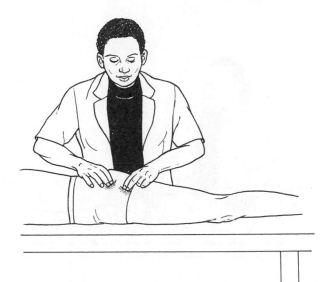

FIGURE 6.24

Helpful Hints

- Because of the strength of the gluteus maximus, it is imperative that the therapist achieve an optimal position for himself or herself, such as using a straight arm technique to apply as much force as the muscle can bear. Shorter therapists may need to step up on a stool or lower the plinth if it is adjustable to apply adequate resistance. See hip extensor test to isolate the gluteus maximus on page 242.
- The therapist should be aware that the hip extensors are among the most powerful muscles in the body, and most therapists will not be able to "break" a Grade 5 hip extension. Care should be taken not to overestimate a Grade 4 muscle.

Substitutions

Rotation of pelvis. Having the patient turn his or her head to the opposite side will help prevent trunk rotation.

Flexion of the knee to substitute hamstrings for gluteus maximus. The gluteus maximus (page 238) and hamstrings (page 266) isolation tests may be a better indicator of specific muscle action.

HIP EXTENSION

(Gluteus maximus and hamstrings)

HIP EXTENSION TEST TO ISOLATE GLUTEUS MAXIMUS

Grade 5, Grade 4, and Grade 3

Position of Patient: Prone with knee flexed to 90°, hip abducted and externally rotated. The abducted and externally rotated hip positions are difficult to visualize in Figs. 6.25 and 6.26. (Note: In the presence of a hip flexion contracture, do not use this test but refer to the test for hip extension modified for hip flexion tightness [see page 240].)

Instructions to Therapist: Stand at the level of the pelvis on the side to be tested. (Note: The therapist in the illustration is shown on the wrong side to avoid obscuring test positions.) Ask the patient to lift the thigh off the plinth as high as possible, while bending the knee. If sufficient range is achieved, place the hand for resistance over the posterior thigh just above the knee. The opposite hand may stabilize or maintain the alignment of the pelvis (see Fig. 6.25).

For the Grade 3 test, the knee may be supported in flexion (by cradling at the ankle) if needed because of hamstring weakness.

Test: Patient extends abducted and externally rotated hip through available extension range, maintaining knee flexion. Resistance is given in a straight downward direction (toward floor).

Instructions to Patient: "Lift your foot to the ceiling." OR "Lift your leg, keeping your knee bent."

Grading

Grade 5: Holds test position against maximal resistance.

Grade 4: Holds test position against strong to moderate resistance.

Grade 3: Completes available range of motion and holds test position but without resistance (see Fig. 6.26).

FIGURE 6.25

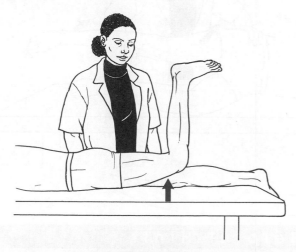

FIGURE 6.26

Grade 2

Position of Patient: Side-lying with test limb uppermost. Knee is flexed and supported by therapist. Lowermost hip and knee should be flexed for stability (Fig. 6.27). Therapist provides stabilization and alignment through the uppermost hip by assuring that the pelvis and hip are in line with the shoulder.

Instructions to Therapist: Stand at the level of the pelvis behind the patient. Therapist cradles uppermost leg with forearm. Other hand stabilizes pelvis in neutral alignment at the iliac crest.

Test: Patient extends hip with supported knee flexed.

Instructions to Patient: "Move your leg back toward me."

Grading

Grade 2: Completes available range of motion in side-lying position.

Grade 1 and Grade 0

This test is identical to the Grades 1 and 0 tests for aggregate hip extension (see Fig. 6.24). The patient is prone and attempts to extend the hip or squeeze the buttocks together while the therapist palpates the gluteus maximus.

Helpful Hints

- Hip extension range is less when the knee is flexed because of tension in the rectus femoris. A diminished hip extension range may be observed, therefore, in tests that isolate the gluteus maximus.
- Often, cramping of the hamstrings will occur when the patient performs this test. The authors have found that decreasing knee flexion to 70° or applying resistance in the middle of the muscle belly during the test will decrease the likelihood of a cramp.
- Hip extension torque increases with hip flexion (increase of 41% with 15° hip flexion and 112% with 45° hip flexion [average of 1.9 Nm per degree of flexion]).[8]

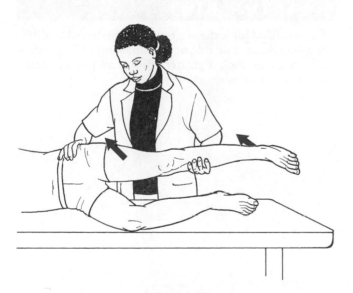

FIGURE 6.27

HIP EXTENSION

(Gluteus maximus and hamstrings)

HIP EXTENSION TESTS MODIFIED FOR HIP FLEXION TIGHTNESS

Grade 5, Grade 4, and Grade 3

Position of Patient: Patient leans over the table with hips flexed so that the ASIS is "hooked" on the end of table (Fig. 6.28). The arms are used to "hug" the table for support. The knee of the non-test limb should be flexed to allow the test limb to rest on the floor at the start of the test.

Instructions to Therapist: Stand at side of limb to be tested. (Note: Fig. 6.28 shows the therapist on the opposite side to avoid obscuring test positions.) Ask the patient to lift his leg toward the ceiling. If sufficient range is achieved, place the hand used to provide resistance over the posterior thigh just above the knee. The opposite hand stabilizes the pelvis laterally to maintain hip and pelvis posture (see Fig. 6.28). The therapist's stabilizing hand may need to be placed over the hip to prevent the pelvis from rising (not shown).

Test: Patient extends hip through available range, but hip extension range is less when the knee is flexed. Keeping the knee in extension will test all hip extensor muscles; with the knee flexed, the gluteus maximus will be evaluated in isolation.

Resistance is applied downward (toward floor).

Instructions to Patient: "Lift your foot off the floor as high as you can."

Grading

Grade 5: Holds test position against maximal resistance.

Grade 4: Holds test position against strong to moderate resistance.

Grade 3: Completes available range and holds test position without resistance.

Grade 2, Grade 1, and Grade 0

Do not test the patient with hip flexion contractures who has less than Grade 3 hip extensors in the standing position. Position the patient side-lying on the table. Conduct the test as described for the aggregate of extensor muscles (see page 239) or for the isolated gluteus maximus (see page 238).

Helpful Hint

The modified hip extensor test is the preferred test for people who are not able or are unwilling to lie prone. This test may elicit a greater effort than the alternate supine hip extensor test.

FIGURE 6.28

CROSS SECTIONS OF THE THIGH

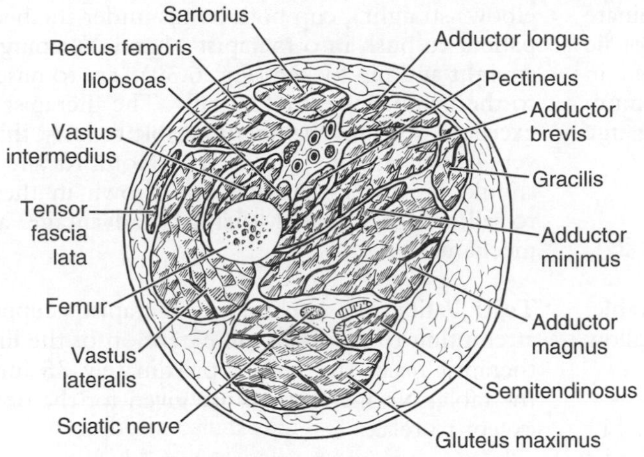

Sartorius
Rectus femoris
Iliopsoas
Vastus intermedius
Tensor fascia lata
Femur
Vastus lateralis
Sciatic nerve

Adductor longus
Pectineus
Adductor brevis
Gracilis
Adductor minimus
Adductor magnus
Semitendinosus
Gluteus maximus

HIGH
JUST BELOW LESSER TROCHANTER

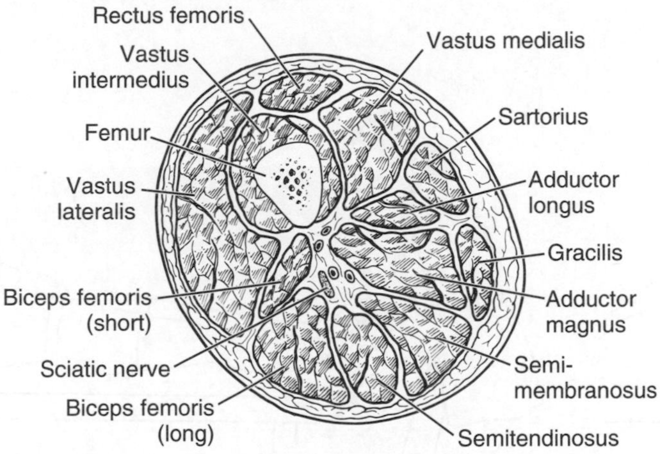

Rectus femoris
Vastus intermedius
Femur
Vastus lateralis
Biceps femoris (short)
Sciatic nerve
Biceps femoris (long)

Vastus medialis
Sartorius
Adductor longus
Gracilis
Adductor magnus
Semi-membranosus
Semitendinosus

MID
JUST ABOVE START OF TENDON OF RECTUS FEMORIS (ABOUT 7-8" ABOVE CENTER OF KNEE)

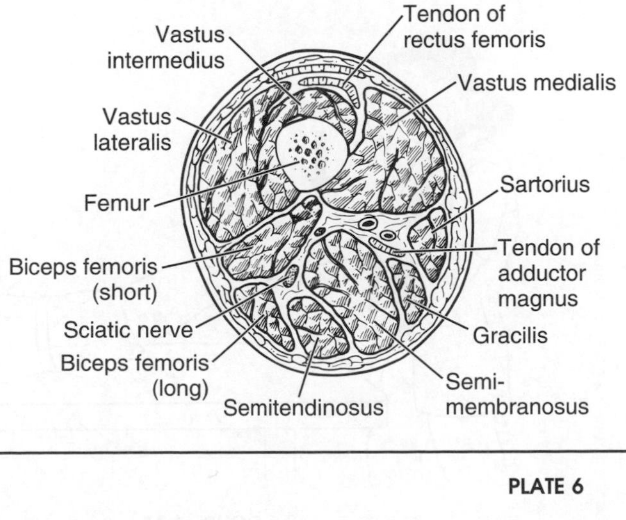

Vastus intermedius
Vastus lateralis
Femur
Biceps femoris (short)
Sciatic nerve
Biceps femoris (long)
Semitendinosus

Tendon of rectus femoris
Vastus medialis
Sartorius
Tendon of adductor magnus
Gracilis
Semi-membranosus

LOW
THROUGH TENDON OF RECTUS FEMORIS (ABOUT 4" ABOVE CENTER OF KNEE)

PLATE 6

Chapter 6 | Testing the Muscles of the Lower Extremity **241**

HIP EXTENSION

(Gluteus maximus and hamstrings)

SUPINE HIP EXTENSION TEST

An alternate hip extensor test is the supine hip extension test. This supine test may be substituted to eliminate change of patient position or for those who cannot lie prone. Grades 5, 4, 3, and 2 have been validated in this position ($n = 44$ subjects) by measuring maximum hip extension torques recorded via a strain gauge dynamometer.[9]

Grade 5, Grade 4, Grade 3, and Grade 2

Position of Patient: Supine with heels off end of table. Arms folded across chest or abdomen. (Do not allow patient to push into table with upper extremities.)

Instructions to Therapist: Stand at end of table. Lift patient's leg to at least 65° of flexion. Determine patient's hip range by measuring from the heel to the table (Fig. 6.29). Approximately 35 inches from heel to table (approximately 65° of flexion) is necessary to perform this test and is the distance the leg should be lifted during the test. In a squat position (knees and hips bent and elbows straight), cup both hands under the heel and ask patient to push into therapist's hands, keeping the knee straight and hip locked (Fig. 6.30). Try to raise the limb to the height measured initially. The therapist will need excellent body mechanics to be able to resist this typically very strong muscle (Fig. 6.31). (Note: Ideally, the table should be lower than the one shown in these figures to allow for optimal therapist advantage and body mechanics.)

Test: Patient presses heel into therapist's cupped hands, attempting to maintain full extension of the limb as the therapist raises the limb approximately 35 inches from the table. No instructions are given for the opposite leg except to relax.

Instructions to Patient: "Don't let me lift your leg from the table. Keep your hip locked tight (don't let it bend)."

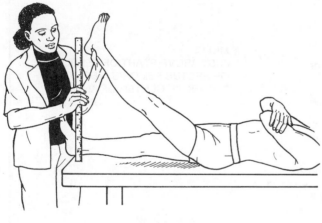

FIGURE 6.29

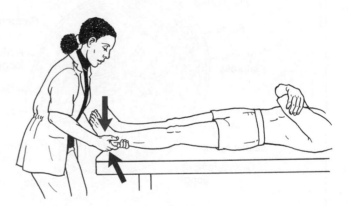

FIGURE 6.30

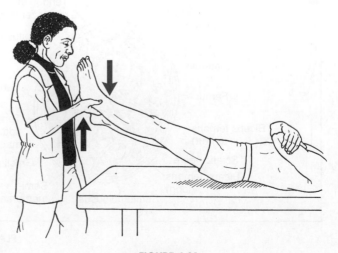

FIGURE 6.31

Grade 5, Grade 4, Grade 3, and Grade 2 Continued

Grading

Grade 5: Hip locks in neutral (full extension) throughout this test. Pelvis and back elevate as one locked unit as the therapist raises the limb (see Fig. 6.31). The opposite limb will rise involuntarily, illustrating a locked pelvis.

Grade 4: Hip flexes before pelvis and back elevate and lock as the limb is raised by the therapist. Hip flexion should not exceed 30° before locking occurs (Fig. 6.32). The other leg will rise involuntarily, but will have some hip flexion because the pelvis is not fully locked.

Grade 3: Full flexion of the hip to the end of the straight-leg raising range (65° of hip flexion) with little or no elevation of the pelvis, demonstrated by the other leg remaining on the table. Therapist feels strong resistance throughout the test (Fig. 6.33).

Grade 2: Hip flexes fully with only minimal resistance felt (therapist should check to ensure that the resistance felt exceeds the weight of the limb; see Fig. 6.33).

There is no Grade 1.

Grade 0: Hip flexes fully with no active resistance felt by the therapist as limb is raised. Therapist perceives that resistance is due to leg weight only.

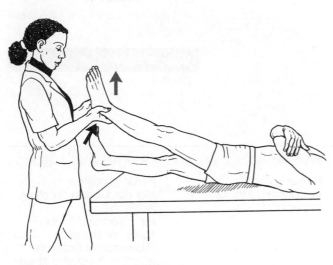

FIGURE 6.32

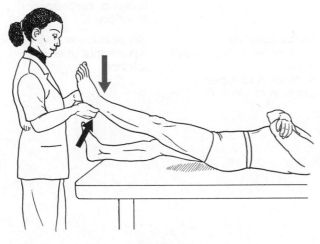

FIGURE 6.33

Helpful Hints

- To optimize the therapist's body mechanics and ability to generate sufficient force to resist this strong muscle, the therapist should start in a squat position to enable elbows to be straight, necessitating the patient to be positioned on a low table or mat table.
- The supine hip extensor test was found to have higher hamstring activation than the unilateral bridge test.[10]
- When the trunk is held relatively stationary, contraction of the hip extensors and abdominal muscles function as a force-couple to posteriorly tilt the pelvis.[5]

Suggested Exercises for the Gluteus Maximus

Exercises are over 40% MVIC in order of increasing MVIC.[7] Exercises producing the greatest gluteus maximus EMG amplitude will be those that place the gluteus maximus in a shortened position (pull-throughs, glute bridges, hip thrusts, horizontal back extensions).

- Sideways lunge
- Lateral step up
- Transverse lunge
- Quadruped with contralateral arm/leg lift
- Unilateral mini-squat
- Retro step up
- Wall squat
- Single-limb squat
- Single-limb deadlift
- Forward step up

EMG, Electromyography; *MVIC,* maximum voluntary isometric contraction.

HIP ABDUCTION

(Gluteus medius and gluteus minimus)

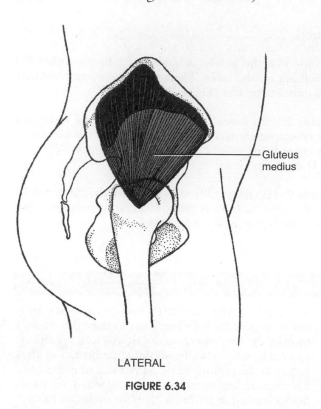

Gluteus medius

LATERAL

FIGURE 6.34

Superior gluteal n.
To: Gluteus medius
L4-S1
Gluteus minimus
L4-S1

L4

L5

S1

FIGURE 6.35

Range of Motion
0°–45°

Table 6.4 HIP ABDUCTION

I.D.	Muscle	Origin	Insertion	Function
183	**Gluteus medius**	Ilium (outer surface between crest and anterior and posterior gluteal lines) Fascia (over upper part)	Femur (greater trochanter, lateral aspect)	Pelvic stabilizer Hip abduction (in all positions) Hip internal rotation (anterior fibers) Hip external (lateral) rotation (posterior fibers) Hip flexion (anterior fibers) Hip extension (posterior fibers) as accessory functions
184	Gluteus minimus	Ilium (outer surface between anterior and inferior gluteal lines) Greater sciatic notch	Femur (greater trochanter, anterolateral ridge) Anterior and superior capsule of hip joint	Hip abduction Hip internal (medial) rotation
Others				
182	Gluteus maximus (upper fibers)			
185	Tensor fasciae latae			
187	Obturator internus (thigh flexed)			
189	Gemellus superior (thigh flexed)			
190	Gemellus inferior (thigh flexed)			
195	Sartorius			

The primary role of the gluteus medius is to stabilize the pelvis in the frontal plane and control femoral motion during dynamic limb motion. The greatest percentage of maximum voluntary contraction (MVC) in the gluteus medius was recorded during single limb stance when the subject was simultaneously abducting the opposite leg. This finding validates the gluteus medius as a pelvic stabilizer.[11,12] The gluteus medius is functionally divided into three parts: (1) anterior, (2) middle, and (3) posterior, each with separate branches from the superior gluteal nerve. Consequently, the three parts have different actions of rotation with abduction, dependent on the degree of hip flexion. The test below captures all three parts during hip abduction. Functionally, the gluteus medius generates an exceptional amount of force, given its size.[7]

Grade 5, Grade 4, and Grade 3

Position of Patient: Side-lying with test leg uppermost. Start test with the hip slightly extended beyond the midline and the pelvis rotated slightly forward (Fig. 6.36). Lowermost leg is flexed for stability.

Instructions to Therapist: Stand behind patient. Ask patient to lift the leg as high as possible, giving verbal and tactile clues as necessary to keep the pelvis from rotating and the hip from flexing. If sufficient range is achieved, place hand used to give resistance at the ankle (Fig. 6.37). Applying resistance at the ankle creates a longer lever arm, thus requiring more patient effort to resist the movement. If the patient cannot hold the limb against resistance at the ankle, then apply resistance at the lateral knee (Fig. 6.38). The therapist is reminded always to use the same lever in a given test sequence and in subsequent comparison tests.

Test: Patient abducts hip through the available range of motion without flexing the hip or rotating it in either direction. Resistance is given in a straight downward direction.

Instructions to Patient: "Lift your leg up and back. Hold it. Don't let me push it down."

FIGURE 6.36

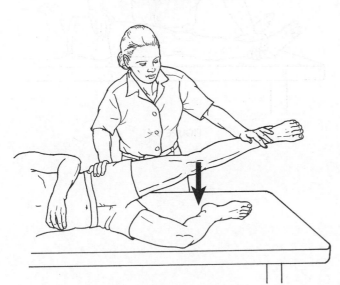

FIGURE 6.37

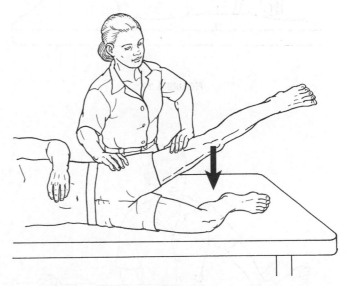

FIGURE 6.38

HIP ABDUCTION

(Gluteus medius and gluteus minimus)

Grade 5, Grade 4, and Grade 3 Continued

Grading

Grade 5: Holds test position against maximal resistance at the ankle.

Grade 4: Holds test position against strong to moderate resistance at the ankle (the limb cannot hold the position) or with maximum resistance given at the knee.

Grade 3: Completes range of motion and holds test position without resistance (Fig. 6.39). Hip should not flex into frontal plane or rotate.

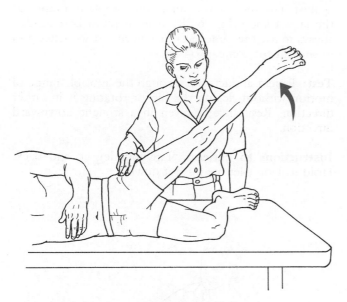

FIGURE 6.39

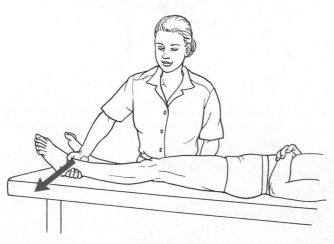

FIGURE 6.40

Grade 2

Position of Patient: Supine.

Instructions to Therapist: Stand on side of limb being tested. One hand supports and lifts the limb by holding it under the ankle to raise limb just enough to decrease friction. This hand offers no resistance, nor should it be used to offer assistance to the movement. On some smooth surfaces, such support may not be necessary (Fig. 6.40). (Note: Figs. 6.40 and 6.41 show therapist on opposite side of patient to avoid obscuring test positions.)

The other hand palpates the gluteus medius just proximal to the greater trochanter of the femur (see Fig. 6.41).

Test: Patient abducts hip through available range.

Instructions to Patient: "Bring your leg out to the side. Keep your kneecap pointing to the ceiling."

Grading

Grade 2: Completes range of motion supine with no resistance and minimal to zero friction.

FIGURE 6.41

Grade 1 and Grade 0

Position of Patient: Supine.

Instructions to Therapist: Stand at the side of the limb being tested at level of thigh. One hand supports the limb under the ankle just above the malleoli. The hand should provide neither resistance nor assistance to movement (see Fig. 6.40). Palpate the gluteus medius on the lateral aspect of the hip just above the greater trochanter. The weight of the opposite limb stabilizes the pelvis. It is not necessary therefore to use a hand to manually stabilize the contralateral limb.

Test: Patient attempts to abduct hip.

Instructions to Patient: "Try to bring your leg out to the side."

Grading

Grade 1: Palpable contraction of gluteus medius but no movement of the part.

Grade 0: No discernable contractile activity.

Substitutions

- Hip-hike substitution: If testing in the supine position, the patient may "hip hike" by approximating pelvis to thorax using the lateral trunk muscles, which moves the limb through partial abduction range (Fig. 6.42). This movement may be detected by observing the lateral trunk and hip (move clothing aside) and palpating the gluteus medius above the trochanter.

- External rotation and flexion (sartorius) substitution: The patient may try to externally rotate during the motion of abduction (Fig. 6.43). This could allow the oblique action of the hip flexors to substitute for the gluteus medius.
- Tensor fasciae latae substitution: If the test is allowed to begin with active hip flexion or with the hip positioned in flexion, there is an opportunity for the tensor fasciae latae to abduct the hip.

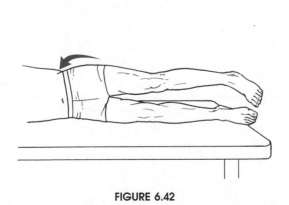

FIGURE 6.42

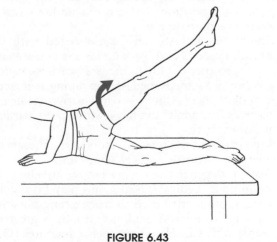

FIGURE 6.43

HIP ABDUCTION

(Gluteus medius and gluteus minimus)

Helpful Hints

- The therapist should not be able to "break" a Grade 5 muscle (resistance applied at the ankle) and most therapists will not be able to "break" a Grade 4 muscle. The force required to stabilize the body is about 2× the body weight, the majority produced by the hip abductors.[5] The therapist should be able to generate at least 100 pounds of push force for a valid test.
- A grade of 4 often indicates significant weakness because of the tremendous intrinsic strength of these muscles. Giving resistance at the ankle rather than at the knee is helpful in overcoming this problem. However, respect the long lever arm and apply resistance carefully, assessing whether the patient can adequately resist the movement through the long lever arm.
- A patient should be able to stand on one leg keeping the pelvis level with a muscle grade of 4 or 5. The inability to do so results in a gluteus medius limp, whereby the pelvis drops on the opposite side of the weakness. In gait, a pelvic drop would occur in every step. If weakness is bilateral, you will see the equivalent of a "waddling" gait where the pelvis drops on each side, with each step. This is a sign of marked gluteus medius weakness.
- When a hip flexion contracture of 30° or more is present, the gluteus medius is compromised as an abductor, as its anterior fibers are now in the plane of flexion instead of abduction.
- Hip abductor and lateral rotator weakness can lead to knee valgus, hip adduction, and hip internal rotation, a position that can put undue stress on lower extremity joints.
- Gluteus medius strength is associated with stair ascend/descend and 5-chair rise test performance. In the presence of gluteus medius weakness, patients will display a gluteus medius limp during stair ascent. A gluteus medius limp is particularly prevalent in inactive older adults and those with hip osteoarthritis or arthroplasties.
- Strengthening the hip abductors in the presence of knee osteoarthritis reduces symptoms.[13]
- Tears or degenerative changes of the attachment of the gluteus medius and minimus may be a source of pain, often attributed to trochanteric bursitis.[5]
- Gluteus medius and minimus atrophy is greater in people with fall-related hip/pelvic fractures (Odds ratio = 2.15).[14]
- The weight of the limb alone results in greater external peak torque during side-lying hip abduction than during other hip abductor exercises.[15]

Suggested Hip Abduction Exercises (>40% MVIC)[7,16]

Exercises are listed in order from least to greatest MVIC

- Lateral step up
- Quadruped with contralateral arm and leg lift
- Forward step up
- Unilateral bridge
- Transverse lunge
- Wall squat
- Side-bridge to neutral spine position
- Standing erect pelvic drop
- Single-limb deadlift
- Single-limb squat
- Side-bridge with hip abduction
- Side-lying hip abduction

MVIC, Maximum voluntary isometric contraction.

(Tensor fasciae latae)

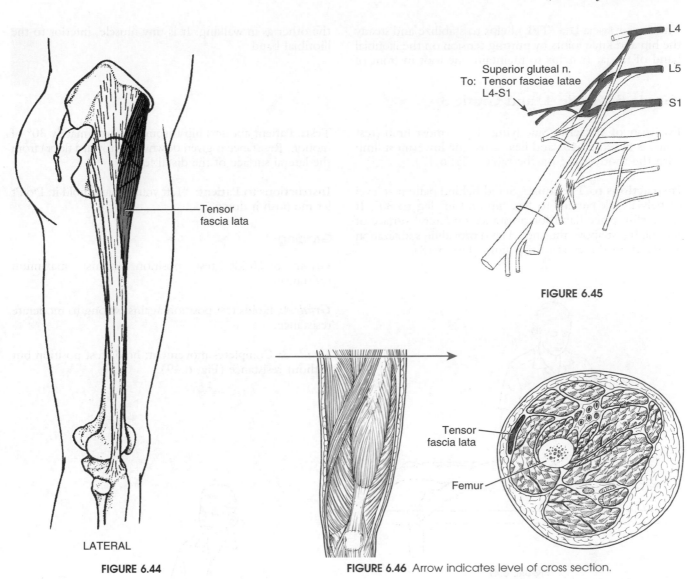

Superior gluteal n.
To: Tensor fasciae latae
L4-S1

L4
L5
S1

FIGURE 6.45

Tensor
fascia lata

LATERAL

FIGURE 6.44

Tensor
fascia lata

Femur

FIGURE 6.46 Arrow indicates level of cross section.

Range of Motion

Two-joint muscle. No specific range of motion can be assigned solely to the tensor.

Table 6.5 HIP ABDUCTION FROM FLEXION

I.D.	Muscle	Origin	Insertion	Function
185	**Tensor fasciae latae**	Iliac crest (outer lip) Fasciae latae (deep) Anterior superior iliac spine (lateral surface)	Iliotibial tract (between its two layers, ending $\frac{1}{3}$ of the way down)	Hip flexion Hip internal (medial) rotation
Others				
183	Gluteus medius			
184	Gluteus minimus			

HIP ABDUCTION FROM FLEXED POSITION

(Tensor fasciae latae)

The tensor fascia lata (TFL) helps to stabilize and steady the hip and knee joints by putting tension on the iliotibial band of fascia. It helps to maintain one foot in front of the other as in walking. It is tiny muscle, inferior to the iliotibial band.

Grade 5, Grade 4, and Grade 3

Position of Patient: Side-lying. Uppermost limb (test limb) is flexed to 45° and lies across the lowermost limb with the foot resting on the table (Fig. 6.47).

Instructions to Therapist: Stand behind patient at level of pelvis. Ask patient to flex hip and lift leg to 30°. If successful, place hand for resistance on lateral surface of the thigh just above the knee. Hand providing stabilization is placed on the crest of the ilium (Fig. 6.48).

Test: Patient abducts hip through approximately 30° of motion. Resistance is given downward (toward floor) from the lateral surface of the distal femur.

Instructions to Patient: "Lift your leg and hold it. Don't let me push it down."

Grading

Grade 5: Holds test position against maximum resistance.

Grade 4: Holds test position against strong to moderate resistance.

Grade 3: Completes movement; holds test position but without resistance (Fig. 6.49).

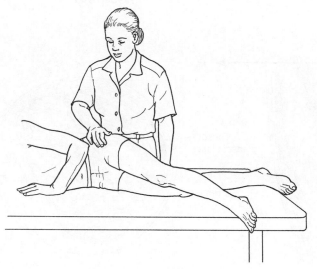

FIGURE 6.47

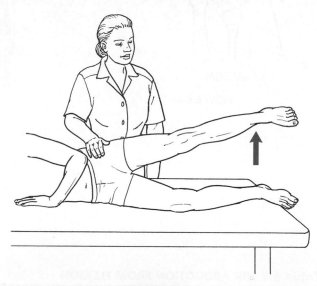

FIGURE 6.49

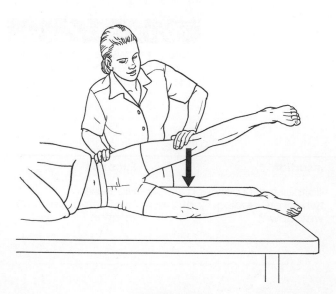

FIGURE 6.48

(Tensor fasciae latae)

Grade 2

Position of Patient: Patient is in long-sitting position, supporting trunk with hands placed behind body on table. Trunk may lean backward up to 45° from vertical (Fig. 6.50).

Instructions to Therapist: Stand at side of limb to be tested. (Note: Fig. 6.50 deliberately shows therapist on wrong side to avoid obscuring test positions.) One hand supports the limb under the ankle; this hand will be used to reduce friction with the surface as the patient moves but should neither resist nor assist motion. The other hand palpates the tensor fasciae latae on the proximal anterolateral thigh where it inserts into the iliotibial band.

Test: Patient abducts hip through 30° of range.

Instructions to Patient: "Bring your leg out to the side."

Grading

Grade 2 Completes hip abduction motion to 30°.

Grade 1 and Grade 0

Position of Patient: Long sitting.

Instructions to Therapist: One hand palpates the insertion of the tensor at the lateral aspect of the knee. The other hand palpates the tensor on the anterolateral thigh (Fig. 6.51).

Test: Patient attempts to abduct hip.

Instructions to Patient: "Try to move your leg out to the side."

Grading

Grade 1: Palpable contraction of tensor fibers but no limb movement.

Grade 0: No discernable palpable contractile activity.

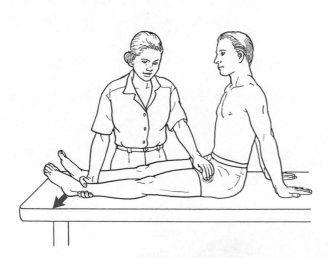

FIGURE 6.50

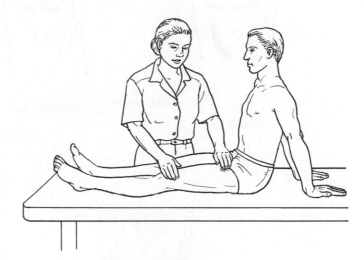

FIGURE 6.51

(Adductors magnus, brevis, and longus; Pectineus and Gracilis)

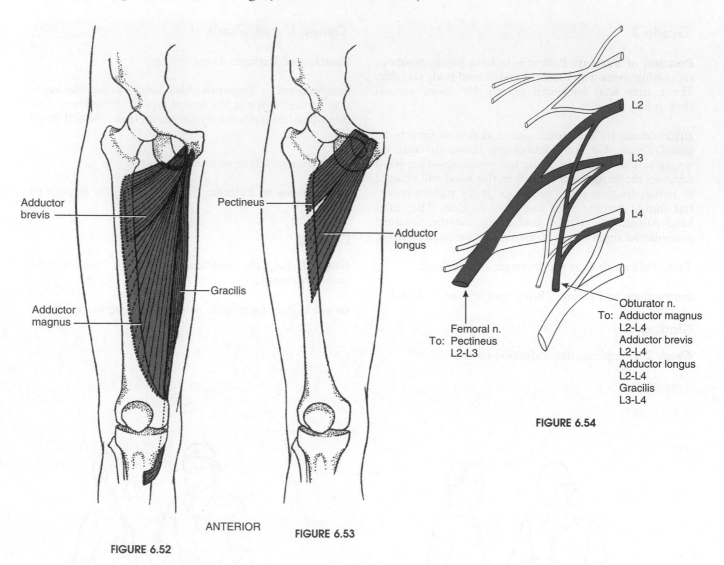

Adductor brevis

Adductor magnus

Gracilis

Pectineus

Adductor longus

ANTERIOR

FIGURE 6.52

FIGURE 6.53

L2

L3

L4

Femoral n.

To: Pectineus
L2-L3

Obturator n.
To: Adductor magnus
L2-L4
Adductor brevis
L2-L4
Adductor longus
L2-L4
Gracilis
L3-L4

FIGURE 6.54

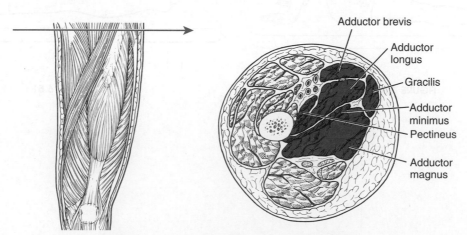

Adductor brevis

Adductor longus

Gracilis

Adductor minimus

Pectineus

Adductor magnus

FIGURE 6.55 Arrow indicates level of cross section.

	Range of Motion
	0°–15°–20°

Table 6.6 HIP ADDUCTION

I.D.	Muscle	Origin	Insertion	Function
181	**Adductor magnus**	Ischial tuberosity (inferolateral) Ischium (inferior ramus) Pubis (inferior ramus) Fibers from pubic ramus to femur (gluteal tuberosity), often named the *Adductor minimus*	Femur (linea aspera via aponeurosis, medial supracondylar line, and adductor tubercle on medial condyle)	Hip adduction Hip extension from a position of hip flexion toward extension (inferior fibers) Hip flexion (superior fibers; weak) if the hip is moving from extension toward flexion[5] The role of the adductor magnus in rotation of the hip is dependent on the position of the thigh[1]
180	Adductor brevis	Pubis (body and inferior ramus)	Femur (via aponeurosis to linea aspera)	Hip adduction Hip flexion
179	Adductor longus	Pubis (anterior aspect between crest and symphysis)	Femur (linea aspera via aponeurosis)	Hip adduction Hip flexion (accessory) Hip rotation (depends on position of thigh)
177	Pectineus	Pubic pectin Fascia of pectineus	Femur (on a line from lesser trochanter to linea aspera)	Hip adduction Hip flexion (accessory)
178	Gracilis	Pubis (body and inferior ramus) Ischial ramus	Tibia (medial shaft distal to condyle) Pes anserinus Deep fascia of leg	Hip adduction Knee flexion Internal (medial) rotation of knee (accessory)
Others				
188	Obturator externus			
182	Gluteus maximus (lower)			

The adductor magnus comprises 63% of the mass of adductor volume.[17] The hip adductors are required to work under both closed chain (e.g., in the stance leg, with the axial compression forces from gravity) and open chain (e.g., during kicking). The adductor longus may be more active during open chain activities than the adductor magnus. The adductor magnus is most active in weight-bearing tasks such as sit-to-stand and walking up stairs and during loading and initial contact phases of gait.[18]

HIP ADDUCTION

(Adductors magnus, brevis, and longus; Pectineus and Gracilis)

Grade 5, Grade 4, and Grade 3

Position of Patient: Side-lying with test limb (lowermost) resting on the table.

Instructions to Therapist: Stand behind patient at knee level. Support uppermost limb (non-test limb) in 25° of abduction with forearm, the hand supporting the limb on the medial surface of the knee (Fig. 6.56). Alternatively, the upper limb can be placed on a padded stool straddling the test limb and approximately 9 to 12 inches high (not shown). Ask the patient to lift the bottom leg to the uppermost one. If successful, place hand giving resistance on the medial surface of the distal femur of the lower limb, just proximal to the knee joint. Resistance is directed straight downward toward the table (Fig. 6.57).

Test: Patient adducts hip until the lower limb contacts the upper one.

Instructions to Patient: "Lift your bottom leg up to your top one. Hold it. Don't let me push it down."

For Grade 3: "Lift your bottom leg up to your top one. Don't let it drop!"

Grading

Grade 5: Holds test position against maximal resistance.

Grade 4: Holds test position against strong to moderate resistance.

Grade 3: Completes full range; holds test position but without resistance (Fig. 6.58).

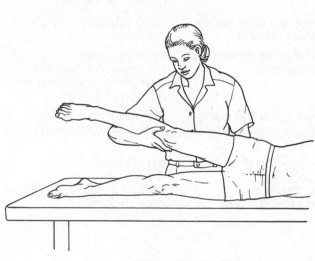

FIGURE 6.56

FIGURE 6.58

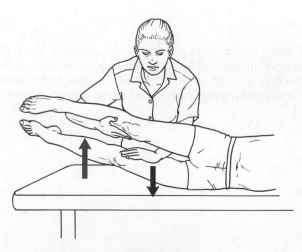

FIGURE 6.57

Grade 2

Position of Patient: Supine. The non-test limb is positioned in some abduction to prevent interference with motion of the test limb.

Instructions to Therapist: Stand at side of test limb at knee level. One hand supports the ankle and elevates it slightly from the table surface to decrease friction as the limb moves across the table (Fig. 6.59). The therapist uses this hand neither to assist nor to resist motion. The opposite hand palpates the adductor mass on the inner aspect of the proximal thigh. In the supine test position for Grades 2, 1, and 0, the weight of the opposite limb stabilizes the pelvis, so there is no need for manual stabilization of the non-test hip.

Test: Patient adducts hip without rotation. Toes stay pointed toward the ceiling.

Instructions to Patient: "Bring your leg in toward the other one."

Grading

Grade 2: Patient adducts limb through full range with gravity minimized.

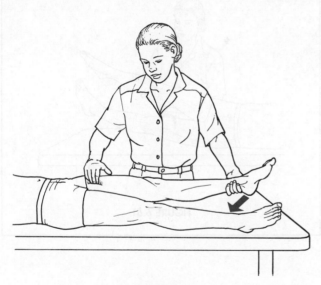

FIGURE 6.59

HIP ADDUCTION

(Adductors magnus, brevis, and longus; Pectineus and Gracilis)

Grade 1 and Grade 0

Position of Patient: Supine.

Instructions to Therapist: Stand on side of test limb. One hand supports the limb under the ankle. The other hand palpates the adductor mass on the proximal medial thigh (Fig. 6.60).

Test: Patient attempts to adduct hip.

Instructions to Patient: "Try to bring your leg in."

Grading

Grade 1: Palpable contraction, no limb movement.

Grade 0: No discernable palpable contraction.

Substitution

Hip flexor substitution: The patient may attempt to substitute the hip flexors for the adductors by internally rotating the hip (Fig. 6.61). The patient will appear to be trying to turn supine from side-lying. Maintenance of true side-lying is necessary for an accurate test.

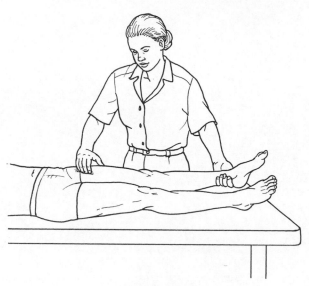

FIGURE 6.60

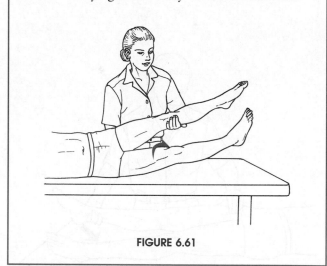

FIGURE 6.61

Helpful Hints

- Greater atrophy of the adductor magnus muscle occurs with bed rest, alluding to its function as a hip stabilizer.[18]
- The adductor muscles produce an extensor torque when the hip is markedly flexed, assisting the primary hip extensors. When the hip is flexed, the adductors augment the other extensor muscles.[5] As an example, when runners were permitted to use foot blocks in the Olympics during the 1930s (or dig a trough to permit a crouch position), times for the 100 m race were notably reduced as the adductors contributed explosive force to bring the femur from flexion toward extension.

Suggested Exercises for Hip Adductors

- Ball squeeze with hip in neutral (long lever)[19]
- Copenhagen exercise[20]
- Side-lying hip adduction

Suggested Exercise for Pectineus

- Supine hip flexion[21]

(Obturators internus and externus, Gemelli superior and inferior, Piriformis, Quadratus femoris, Gluteus maximus [posterior])

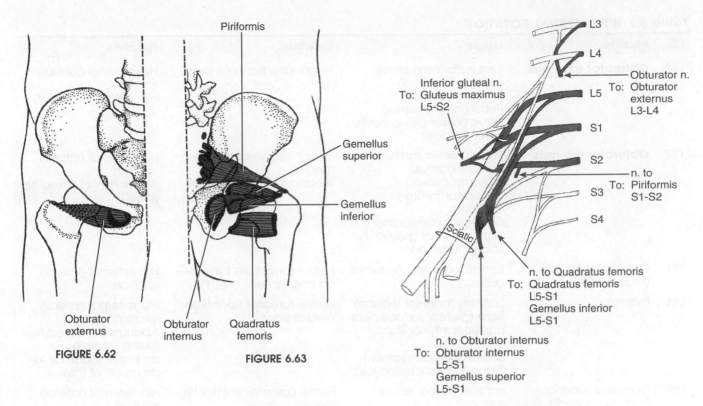

Piriformis

Gemellus superior

Gemellus inferior

Obturator externus

FIGURE 6.62

Obturator internus

Quadratus femoris

FIGURE 6.63

L3

L4

Inferior gluteal n.
To: Gluteus maximus
L5-S2

Obturator n.
To: Obturator externus
L3-L4

L5

S1

S2

n. to
To: Piriformis
S1-S2

S3

S4

Sciatic

n. to Quadratus femoris
To: Quadratus femoris
L5-S1
Gemellus inferior
L5-S1

n. to Obturator internus
To: Obturator internus
L5-S1
Gemellus superior
L5-S1

FIGURE 6.64

Range of Motion

0°–35°[22]

HIP EXTERNAL ROTATION

(Obturators internus and externus, Gemelli superior and inferior, Piriformis, Quadratus femoris, Gluteus maximus [posterior])

Table 6.7 HIP EXTERNAL ROTATION

I.D.	Muscle	Origin	Insertion	Function
188	**Obturator externus**	Obturator membrane (external surface) Ischium (ramus) Pubis (inferior ramus) Pelvis (lesser pelvic cavity, inner surface)	Femur (trochanteric fossa)	Hip external (lateral) rotation Hip adduction (assist)
187	**Obturator internus**	Pubis (inferior ramus) Ischium (ramus) Obturator fascia Obturator foramen (margin) Obturator membrane Upper brim of greater sciatic foramen	Femur (greater trochanter, medial) Tendon fuses with gemelli	Hip external (lateral) rotation Abduction of flexed hip (assist)
191	Quadratus femoris (may be absent)	Ischial tuberosity (external aspect)	Femur (quadrate tubercle on trochanteric crest)	Hip external (lateral) rotation
186	Piriformis	Sacrum (anterior surface) Ilium (gluteal surface near posterior inferior iliac spine) Sacrotuberous ligament Capsule of sacroiliac joint	Femur (greater trochanter, medial side)	Hip external (lateral) rotation Abducts the flexed hip (assist) (muscle probably too small to do much of this)
189	Gemellus superior (may be absent)	Ischium (spine, dorsal surface)	Femur (greater trochanter, medial surface) Blends with tendon of obturator internus	Hip external (lateral) rotation Hip abduction with hip flexed (accessory)
190	Gemellus inferior	Ischial tuberosity (upper part)	Femur (greater trochanter, medial surface) Blends with tendon of obturator internus	
182	Gluteus maximus Posterior fibers	Ilium (posterior gluteal line and crest) Sacrum (dorsal and lower aspects) Coccyx (side) Sacrotuberous ligament Aponeurosis over gluteus medius	Femur (gluteal tuberosity) Iliotibial tract of fascia lata	Hip external (lateral) rotation Hip abduction with hip flexed (weak assist)

Others

195	Sartorius
192	Biceps femoris (long head)
183	Gluteus medius (posterior)
174	Psoas major
181	Adductor magnus (position-dependent)
179	Adductor longus
202	Popliteus (tibia fixed)

The gluteus maximus is potentially the most powerful external rotator of the hip, depending on its line of force.[23]

(Obturators internus and externus, Gemelli superior and inferior, Piriformis, Quadratus femoris, Gluteus maximus [posterior])

Grade 5, Grade 4, Grade 3, and Grade 2

Position of Patient: Short sitting with thighs fully supported on table and legs hanging over the edge. (Trunk may be supported by placing hands flat or fisted at sides of chair or table [Fig. 6.65].)

Instructions to Therapist: Sit on a low stool or kneel beside limb to be tested. Ask the patient to turn the leg in. If sufficient range is present, position leg in mid position between internal and external rotation. Place the hand providing resistance on the medial aspect of the ankle just above the malleolus (Fig. 6.66). The other hand, which will offer counter-pressure, is contoured over the lateral aspect of the distal thigh just above the knee. Stabilization is provided in a medially directed force at the knee counteracting the resistance provided at the ankle. The two forces are applied in counter-directions for this rotary motion (see Fig. 6.66).

Test: Patient externally rotates the hip.

Instructions to Patient: "Don't let me turn your leg out."

Grading

Grade 5: Holds test position in midrange against maximal resistance.

Grade 4: Holds test position in midrange against strong to moderate resistance.

Grade 3: Able to complete full range of motion with mild to no resistance (this is a gravity-eliminated position, so if the patient is able to exert mild resistance, grade the effort a 3) (Fig. 6.67).

Grade 2: Completes full range of motion without resistance (this is a gravity-minimized position). Care needs to be taken to ensure that gravity is not the predominant force.

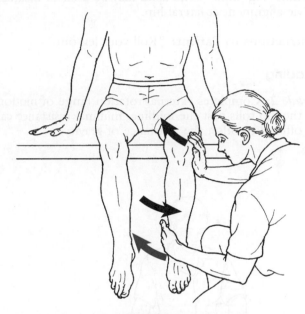

FIGURE 6.66

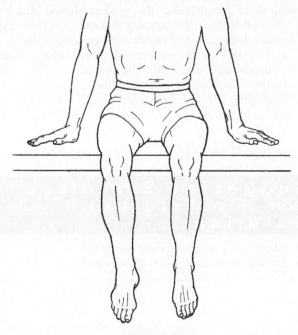

FIGURE 6.65

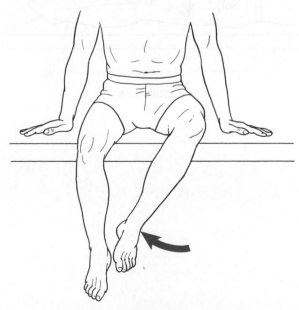

FIGURE 6.67

HIP EXTERNAL ROTATION

(Obturators internus and externus, Gemelli superior and inferior, Piriformis, Quadratus femoris, Gluteus maximus [posterior])

Grade 2 Alternate Test (if Patient Cannot Sit)

Position of Patient: Supine. Test limb is in internal rotation.

Instructions to Therapist: Stand at side of limb to be tested. The therapist may need to support the limb in internal rotation because gravity tends to pull the limb into external rotation.

Test: Patient externally rotates hip in available range of motion (Fig. 6.68). One hand may be used to maintain pelvic alignment at lateral hip.

Instructions to Patient: "Roll your leg out."

Grading

Grade 2: Completes external rotation range of motion. As the hip rolls past the midline, minimal resistance can be offered to offset the assistance of gravity.

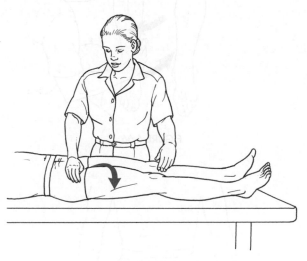

FIGURE 6.68

Grade 1 and Grade 0

Position of Patient: Supine with test limb placed in internal rotation.

Instructions to Therapist: Stand at side of limb to be tested.

Test: Patient attempts to externally rotate hip.

Instructions to Patient: "Try to roll your leg out."

Grading

Grade 1 and Grade 0: The external rotator muscles, except for the gluteus maximus, are not palpable. If there is any discernable movement (contractile activity), a grade of 1 should be given; otherwise, a grade of 0 is assigned on the principle that whenever uncertainty exists, the lesser grade should be awarded.

Helpful Hints

- There is wide variation in the amount of hip external rotation range that can be considered normal. It is imperative therefore that a patient's accurate range (in each test position) be known before manual muscle testing takes place. Muscles that are lengthened often test weak, which is why testing in the mid position between ER and IR is recommended.[24]
- There is greater range of rotation at the hip when the hip is flexed than when it is extended, probably secondary to laxity of hip joint structures.
- In short-sitting tests, the patient should *not* be allowed to use the following motions, lest they add visual distortion and confound the test results:
  a. Lift the contralateral buttock off the table or lean in any direction to lift the pelvis;
  b. Increase flexion of the test knee;
  c. Abduct the test hip.

Suggested Exercises for Hip External Rotation

- Clamshell exercise against resistance
- Seated external rotation against pulley

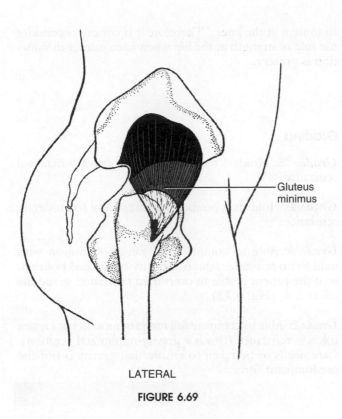

Gluteus minimus

LATERAL

FIGURE 6.69

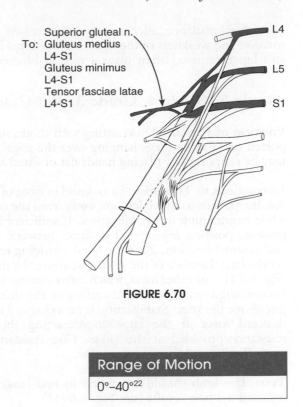

Superior gluteal n.

To: Gluteus medius
L4-S1
Gluteus minimus
L4-S1
Tensor fasciae latae
L4-S1

L4

L5

S1

FIGURE 6.70

Range of Motion
0°–40°[22]

Table 6.8 HIP INTERNAL ROTATION

I.D.	Muscle	Origin	Insertion	Function
184	**Gluteus minimus (anterior fibers)**	Ilium (outer surface between anterior and inferior gluteal lines) Greater sciatic notch	Femur (greater trochanter, anterior aspect) Fibrous capsule of hip joint	Hip abduction Hip internal (medial) rotation
185	Tensor fasciae latae	Iliac crest (outer lip) Fascia lata (deep) Anterior superior iliac spine (lateral surface)	Iliotibial tract (between its two layers ending ⅓ down femur)	Hip flexion Hip internal (medial) rotation
183	Gluteus medius (anterior fibers)	Ilium (outer surface between crest and posterior gluteal line) Gluteal fascia	Femur (greater trochanter, lateral surface)	Internal with hip flexion[23]
Others	Gluteus maximus (anterior fibers)			Internal rotator with hip flexed to 90°
193	Semitendinosus			
194	Semimembranosus			
181	Adductor magnus (position-dependent)			
179	Adductor longus (position-dependent)			

HIP INTERNAL ROTATION

(Glutei minimus and medius; Tensor fasciae latae)

Muscular imbalance, such as relative increased internal rotation and weakness of the abductors, external rotators, and hip extensors, often plays a role in biomechanical alignment at the knee.[5] Therefore it is critical to consider the role of strength at the hip when knee pain or dysfunction is present.

Grade 5, Grade 4, Grade 3, and Grade 2

Position of Patient: Short sitting with thighs fully supported on table and legs hanging over the edge. (Trunk may be supported by placing hands flat or fisted at sides.)

Instructions to Therapist: Sit or kneel in front of patient. Ask the patient to move leg out, away from the other leg while maintaining hip stabilization. If sufficient range is present, position leg in mid position between internal and external rotation. Place the hand providing resistance on the lateral surface of the ankle just above the malleolus (Fig. 6.71). The other hand, which offers counter-pressure, is contoured over the medial surface of the distal thigh just above the knee. Stabilization is provided in a medially directed force at the knee counteracting the lateral resistance provided at the ankle. Give resistance in a medially directed force at the ankle.

Test: The limb should be placed in mid-range of hip rotation for best results (see Fig. 6.69).[24]

Grading

Grade 5: Holds test position against maximal resistance.

Grade 4: Holds test position against strong to moderate resistance.

Grade 3: Able to complete full range of motion with mild to no resistance (this is a gravity-eliminated position, so if the patient is able to exert mild resistance, grade the effort a 3) (Fig. 6.72).

Grade 2: Able to complete full range of motion but cannot tolerate resistance (this is a gravity-minimized position). Care needs to be taken to ensure that gravity is not the predominant force.

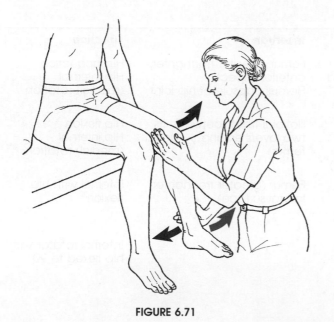

FIGURE 6.71

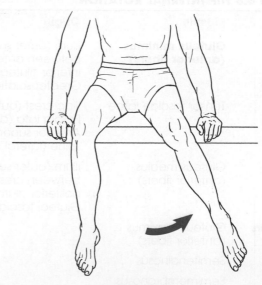

FIGURE 6.72

(Glutei minimus and medius; Tensor fasciae latae)

Alternate Grade 2 for the Patient Who Cannot Sit

Position of Patient: Supine. Test limb in partial external rotation.

Instructions to Therapist: Stand next to test leg. Palpate the gluteus medius proximal to the greater trochanter and the tensor fasciae latae (Fig. 6.73) over the antero-lateral hip below the ASIS.

Test: Patient internally rotates hip through available range.

Instructions to Patient: "Roll your leg in toward the other one."

Grading

Grade 2: Holds test position. As the hip rolls inward past the midline, minimal resistance can be offered to offset the assistance of gravity.

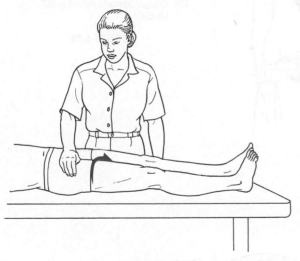

FIGURE 6.73

Grade 1 and Grade 0

Position of Patient: Patient supine with test limb placed in external rotation.

Instructions to Therapist: Stand next to test leg.

Test: Patient attempts to internally rotate hip. One hand is used to palpate the gluteus medius (over the postero-lateral surface of the hip above the greater trochanter). The other hand is used to palpate the tensor fasciae latae (on the anterolateral surface of the hip below the ASIS).

Instructions to Patient: "Try to roll your leg in."

Grading

Grade 1: Palpable contractile activity in either or both muscles.

Grade 0: No discernable contractile activity.

Helpful Hints

- The patient should neither be allowed to extend the knee nor adduct and extend the hip during performance of the test. These motions contaminate the test by offering visual distortion to the therapist.
- There is greater range of rotation at the hip when the hip is flexed than when it is extended, probably secondary to laxity of hip joint structures.
- In short-sitting tests, the patient should *not* be allowed to use the following motions, lest they add visual distortion and confound the test results:
  a. Lift the contralateral buttock off the table or lean in any direction to lift the pelvis;
  b. Increase flexion of the test knee;
  c. Adduct the test hip.

Suggested Exercises for Hip Internal Rotation[25]

- Prone isometric with knee in 90° of flexion (can use opposite leg for resistance)
- Reverse clams

(All hamstring muscles)

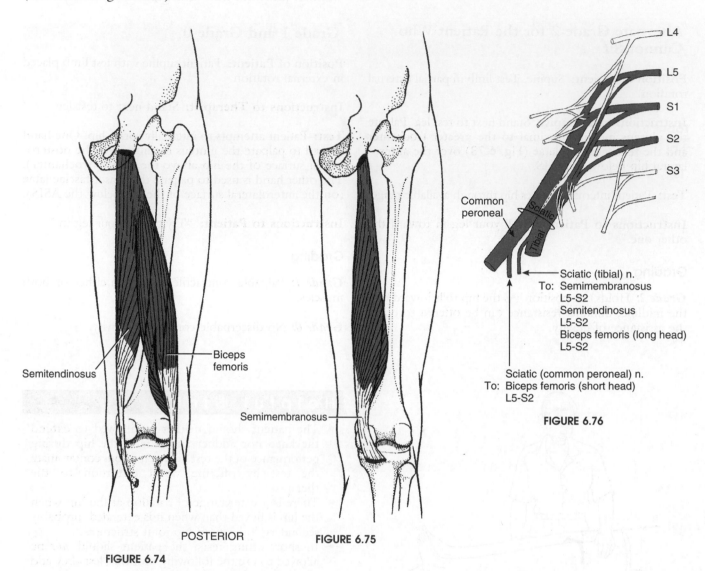

Semitendinosus

Biceps femoris

Semimembranosus

POSTERIOR

FIGURE 6.74

FIGURE 6.75

Common peroneal

Sciatic

Tibial

Sciatic (tibial) n.
To: Semimembranosus
    L5-S2
    Semitendinosus
    L5-S2
    Biceps femoris (long head)
    L5-S2

Sciatic (common peroneal) n.
To: Biceps femoris (short head)
    L5-S2

FIGURE 6.76

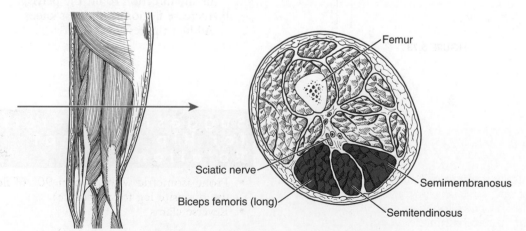

Femur

Sciatic nerve

Biceps femoris (long)

Semimembranosus

Semitendinosus

FIGURE 6.77 Arrow indicates level of cross section.

Range of Motion
0°–135°

Table 6.9 KNEE FLEXION

I.D.	Muscle	Origin	Insertion	Function
192	**Biceps femoris**			Knee flexor Hip extensor Knee external rotation
	Long head	Ischium (tuberosity) Sacrotuberous ligament	Aponeurosis (posterior) Fibula (head, lateral aspect) Fibular collateral ligament	Hip extension and external rotation (long head)
	Short head	Femur (linea aspera and lateral condyle) Lateral intermuscular septum	Tibia (lateral condyle)	Knee flexion
193	Semitendinosus	Ischial tuberosity (inferior medial aspect) Tendon via aponeurosis shared with biceps femoris (long)	Tibia (proximal shaft) Pes anserinus Deep fascia of leg	Knee flexion Knee internal rotation Hip extension Hip internal rotation (accessory)
194	Semimembranosus	Ischial tuberosity Sacrotuberous ligament	Distal aponeurosis Tibia (medial condyle) Oblique popliteal ligament of knee joint	Knee flexion Knee internal rotation Hip extension Hip internal rotation (accessory)
Others				
178	Gracilis			
185	Tensor fasciae latae (knee flexed more than 30°)			
195	Sartorius			
202	Popliteus			Knee flexion Knee internal rotation (proximal attachment fixed) Hip external rotation (tibia fixed)
205	Gastrocnemius			
207	Plantaris			

Hamstring muscle strain injuries have the highest prevalence in sport and especially in track and field. One of the proposed risk factors for acute hamstring injuries in track and field athletes is muscle weakness during concentric and/or eccentric contractions. The hamstring muscles act as hip extensors and knee flexors during both stance and swing phase of sprinting, the most common mechanism of injury in track and field athletes. They work eccentrically during the late stance phase of gait and during the late swing phase of overground running.[26]

KNEE FLEXION

(All hamstring muscles)

Grade 5, Grade 4, and Grade 3

There are three basic muscle tests for the hamstrings at Grades 5 and 4. The therapist should test first for the aggregate of the three hamstring muscles (with the foot in midline). Only if there is deviation (or asymmetry) in the movement or a question in the therapist's mind is there a need to test the medial and lateral hamstrings separately. The hamstrings are two joint muscles, and should be tested in mid-range.

HAMSTRING MUSCLES IN AGGREGATE

Position of Patient: Prone with legs straight and toes hanging over the edge of the table. A towel roll placed just above the knee may make this position more comfortable (not shown in Figue 6.78).

Instructions to Therapist: Stand next to limb to be tested. Ask the patient to flex the knee as far as possible. Observe possible tightness in the rectus femoris that may be indicated by limited knee flexion or the hip flexing. If sufficient range is present, place limb in about 45° of knee flexion (mid-range). Hand provides resistance on posterior surface of the leg just above the ankle (Fig. 6.78). The other hand provides stabilization over the hamstring tendons on the posterior thigh (optional). Firm pressure with the stabilizing hand may offset any cramping of the hamstring muscles. Resistance is applied in the direction of knee extension for Grades 5 and 4.

Test: Patient holds knee in 45° of knee flexion while maintaining leg in neutral rotation.

Instructions to Patient: "Hold it! Don't let me straighten it."

MEDIAL HAMSTRING TEST (SEMITENDINOSUS AND SEMIMEMBRANOSUS)

Position of Patient: Prone with knee flexed to 45°. Leg in internal rotation (toes pointing toward midline).

Instructions to Therapist: Therapist resists knee flexion at the ankle using a downward and outward force (Figure 6.79).

Test: Patient flexes knee, maintaining the leg in internal rotation (heel toward therapist, toes pointing toward midline).

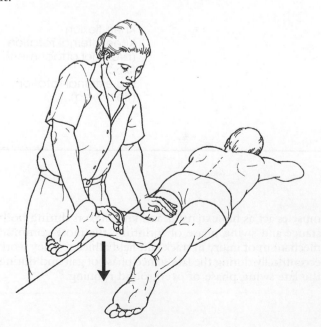

FIGURE 6.78

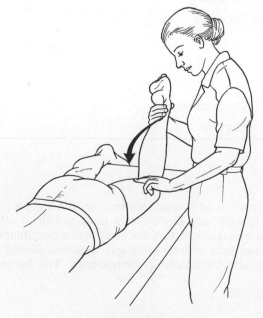

FIGURE 6.79

LATERAL HAMSTRING TEST (BICEPS FEMORIS)

Position of Patient: Prone with knee flexed to 45°. Leg is in external rotation (toes pointing laterally).

Instructions to Therapist: Therapist resists knee flexion at the ankle using a downward and inward force (Fig. 6.80).

Test: Patient flexes knee, maintaining leg in external rotation (heel away from therapist, toes pointing toward therapist) (see Fig. 6.78).

Grading the Hamstring Muscles (Grade 5, Grade 4, and Grade 3)

Grade 5 for All Three Tests: Patient holds test position against maximal resistance.

Grade 4 for All Three Tests: Holds test position against strong to moderate resistance.

Grade 3 for All Three Tests: Patient completes full range of motion without external resistance (Fig. 6.81).

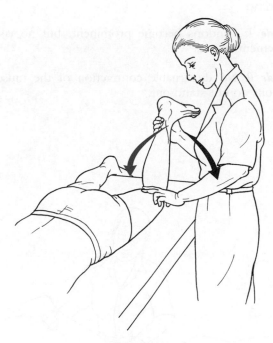

FIGURE 6.80

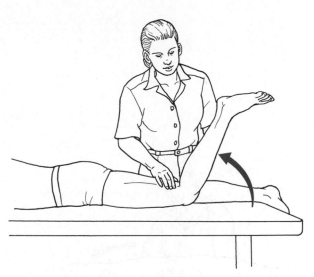

FIGURE 6.81

(All hamstring muscles)

Grade 2

Position of Patient: Side-lying with test limb (uppermost limb) supported by therapist or resting on suitable height stool. Lower limb flexed for stability.

Instructions to Therapist: Stand behind patient at knee level. One arm is used to cradle thigh, providing hand support at medial side of knee. Other hand supports the leg at the ankle just above the malleolus (Fig. 6.82).

Test: Patient flexes knee through available range of motion.

Instructions to Patient: "Bend your knee."

Grading

Grade 2: Completes available range of motion in side-lying position, with gravity minimized.

Grade 1 and Grade 0

Position of Patient: Prone. Limbs are straight with toes extending over end of table. Knee is partially flexed and supported at ankle by therapist.

Instructions to Therapist: Stand next to test limb at knee level. (Therapist shown on opposite side to avoid obscuring test position.) One hand supports the flexed limb at the ankle (Fig. 6.83). The opposite hand palpates both the medial and the lateral hamstring tendons just above the posterior knee.

Test: Patient attempts to flex knee.

Instructions to Patient: "Try to bend your knee."

Grading

Grade 1: Tendons become prominent, but no visible movement occurs.

Grade 0: No discernable contraction of the muscles; tendons do not stand out.

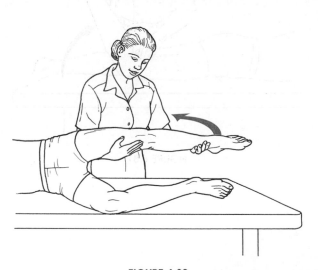

FIGURE 6.82

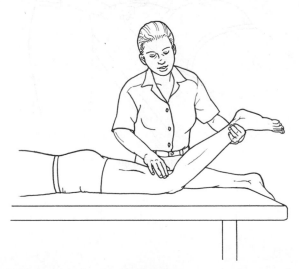

FIGURE 6.83

Substitutions

- Hip flexion substitution: The prone patient may flex the hip to start knee flexion. The buttock on the test side will rise as the hip flexes, and the patient may appear to roll slightly toward supine (Fig. 6.84).
- Gastrocnemius substitution: Do not permit the patient to strongly dorsiflex in an attempt to use the tenodesis effect of the gastrocnemius.

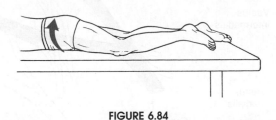

FIGURE 6.84

Helpful Hints

- If the biceps femoris is stronger than the medial hamstrings, the leg will externally rotate during knee flexion. Similarly, if the semitendinosus and semimembranosus are the stronger components, the leg will internally rotate during knee flexion. This is the situation that, when observed, indicates asymmetry and the need to test the medial and lateral hamstrings separately.
- If the hip flexes at the end of the knee flexion range of motion, check for a tight rectus femoris muscle because this tightness will limit the range of knee motion.
- The optimum quadriceps to hamstring strength ratio of 1:1 has been proposed as a rehabilitation goal in many types of knee injuries, especially the anterior cruciate ligament deficient and repaired knee.

Suggested Exercises for Hamstrings

- Single-leg deadlifts
- Slide leg curl[26]
- Good mornings with at least 25% body weight[27]
- Nordic hamstring exercise
- Eccentric leg curls

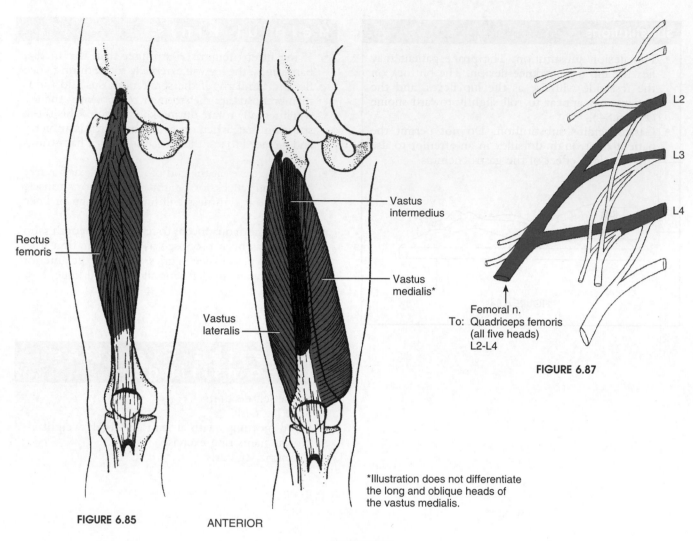

Rectus
femoris

Vastus
intermedius

Vastus
medialis*

Vastus
lateralis

Femoral n.
To: Quadriceps femoris
(all five heads)
L2-L4

L2

L3

L4

FIGURE 6.87

*Illustration does not differentiate
the long and oblique heads of
the vastus medialis.

FIGURE 6.85

ANTERIOR

FIGURE 6.86

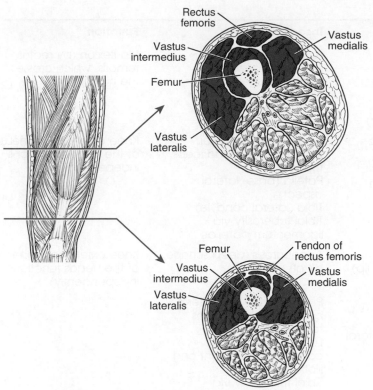

Rectus femoris

Vastus intermedius

Vastus medialis

Femur

Vastus lateralis

Femur

Tendon of rectus femoris

Vastus intermedius

Vastus medialis

Vastus lateralis

FIGURE 6.88 Arrows indicate level of cross section.

Range of Motion

135° to –2°[22]

KNEE EXTENSION

(Quadriceps femoris)

Table 6.10 KNEE EXTENSION

I.D.	Muscle	Origin	Insertion	Function
196	**Rectus femoris**	Ilium (anterior inferior iliac spine) Acetabulum (groove above) Capsule of hip joint Aponeurosis (anterior)	Aponeurosis (posterior) Patella (base via quadriceps tendon) Tibial tuberosity via ligamentum patellae	Hip flexion (by rectus femoris, which crosses the hip joint)
198	**Vastus intermedius**	Femur (shaft, upper ⅔ lateral and anterior surfaces) Intermuscular septum (lateral)	Aponeurosis (anterior forming deep quadriceps tendon) Patella (base, lateral aspect) Tibia (lateral condyle) Tibial tuberosity via ligamentum patellae	Knee extension (none of the heads functions independently)
197	**Vastus lateralis**	Femur Linea aspera (lateral lip) Greater trochanter (inferior) Intertrochanteric line (via aponeurosis) Gluteal tuberosity (lateral lip) Lateral intermuscular septum	Aponeurosis (deep surface, distal) Patella (base and lateral border via quadriceps tendon) Lateral expansion to capsule of knee joint and iliotibial tract Tibial tuberosity via ligamentum patellae	Knee extension (none of the heads functions independently)
199	**Vastus medialis longus (two parts)**	Femur (linea aspera, medial lip; intertrochanteric line) Origin of vastus medialis oblique Tendon of adductor magnus Intermuscular septum (medial)	Aponeurosis (deep) Patella (medial border) Tibial tuberosity via ligamentum patellae	Knee extension (none of the heads functions independently)
200	Vastus medialis oblique (considered part of the vastus medialis) (see Fig. 6.86)	Femur: linea aspera (distal); supracondylar line Tendon of adductor magnus Intermuscular septum	Aponeurosis to capsule of knee joint Patella (medial aspect) Quadriceps tendon (medial) Tibial tuberosity via ligamentum patellae	Knee extension (none of the heads functions independently)

The quadriceps femoris muscles are tested together as a functional group. None of the four muscle heads can be separated from any other by manual muscle testing. The rectus femoris may be partially isolated from the other quadriceps during a hip flexion test. At one time, the vastus medialis was thought to be activated during the terminal 15° of knee extension; however this has been conclusively disproven.[28-30]

Knowledge of the patient's knee flexion range of motion is useful before conducting tests for knee extension strength, because tight (shortened) hamstrings will limit knee extension. The shorter the hamstrings, the greater the backward trunk lean in short sitting.

A combined force of 1.1 N-m-kg^{-1} is the minimum strength threshold of the knee extensors required for walking.[3] Knee extensor strength contributes to maximum walking speed; however strength greater than a combined knee extensor force of 2.3 N-m-kg^{-1} is considered reserve and does not further increase maximum walking speed.

Grade 5, Grade 4, and Grade 3

Position of Patient: Short sitting. Place a towel roll under the patient's distal thigh for comfort. The patient's hands rest on the table on either side of the body for stability or may grasp the table edge. The patient should be allowed to lean backward slightly to relieve hamstring muscle tension. Do not allow the patient to hyperextend the knee because this may lock the knee into position, thus masking weakness.

Instructions to Therapist: Stand at side of limb to be tested. Ask the patient to straighten the knee. If sufficient range is present, position the knee in approximately 15° of knee flexion. Place the palm of the hand providing resistance over the anterior surface of the distal leg just above the ankle, using a straight arm technique because of the potential strength of these muscles. For Grades 5 and 4, resistance is applied in a downward direction toward the floor (Fig. 6.89).

Test: Patient extends knee through available range of motion but not beyond 0°.

Instructions to Patient: "Hold it! Don't let me bend it."

Helpful Hint

To prevent the patient's pelvis from rising (a common occurrence in a Grade 4 or 5 test), the patient may be secured to the testing surface by a belt or strap (not shown).

Grading

Grade 5: Holds test position against maximal resistance. The therapist should not be able to break the Grade 5 knee extensors.

Grade 4: Holds test position against strong to moderate resistance.

Grade 3: Completes available range, including the last 15° (Fig. 6.90).

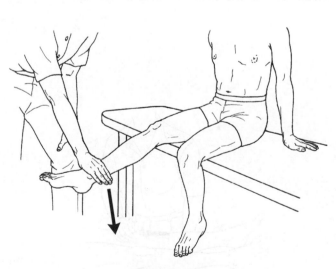

FIGURE 6.89

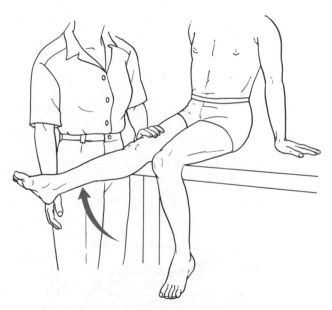

FIGURE 6.90

KNEE EXTENSION

(Quadriceps femoris)

Grade 2

Position of Patient: Side-lying with test limb uppermost. Lowermost limb may be flexed for stability. Limb to be tested is held in about 90° of knee flexion. The hip should be in full extension.

Instructions to Therapist: Stand behind patient at knee level. One arm cradles the test limb around the thigh with the hand supporting the underside of the knee (Fig. 6.91); alternatively, the test limb may be placed on a powder board. The other hand holds the leg just above the malleolus.

Test: Patient extends knee through the available range of motion. The therapist supporting the limb provides neither assistance nor resistance to the patient's voluntary movement.

Instructions to Patient: "Straighten your knee."

Grading

Grade 2: Completes available range of motion.

Grade 1 and Grade 0

Position of Patient: Supine.

Instructions to Therapist: Stand next to limb to be tested at knee level. Hand used for palpation should be on the quadriceps tendon just above the knee with the tendon "held" gently between the thumb and fingers. The therapist also may want to palpate the patellar tendon just below the knee (Fig. 6.92).

Test: Patient attempts to extend knee.

As an alternate test, the therapist may place one hand under the slightly flexed knee; palpate either the quadriceps or the patellar tendon while the patient tries to extend the knee.

Instructions to Patient: "Push the back of your knee down into the table." OR "Tighten your kneecap" (quadriceps setting).

For Alternate Test: "Push the back of your knee down into my hand."

Grading

Grade 1: Contractile activity can be palpated in muscle through the tendon. No joint movement occurs.

Grade 0: No discernable contractile activity.

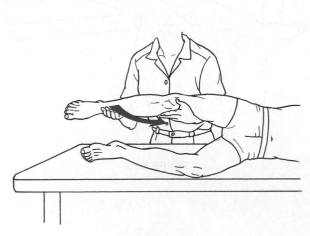

FIGURE 6.91

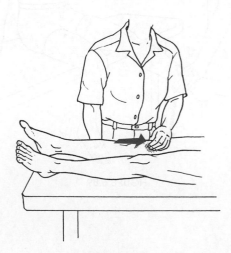

FIGURE 6.92

Substitution

When the patient is side-lying (as in the Grade 2 test), he or she may use the hip internal rotators to substitute for the quadriceps, thereby allowing the knee to fall into extension.

Suggested Exercises for Quadriceps

- Squats (knee angle and hip position will selectively recruit different quad muscles)
- Back squats
- Split squats
- Single-leg press
- Lunges

Helpful Hints

- To assess functional strength, the quadriceps can be tested by a chair stand test (see description in Chapter 8, page 334) where strength equal to half the body weight is needed to rise from a chair unassisted (no arm use).[31]
- In stair descent, the forces transmitted through the knee are equal to nearly 3×/body weight,[32,33] necessitating a greater magnitude of strength than can be detected in a manual muscle test.
- To avoid over-grading the quadriceps, quantitative methods can be used such as hand-held muscle dynamometry (Chapter 9) or a 1-repetition maximum leg press (see Chapter 7). These tests have age- and sex-appropriate norms.

(Gastrocnemius and Soleus)

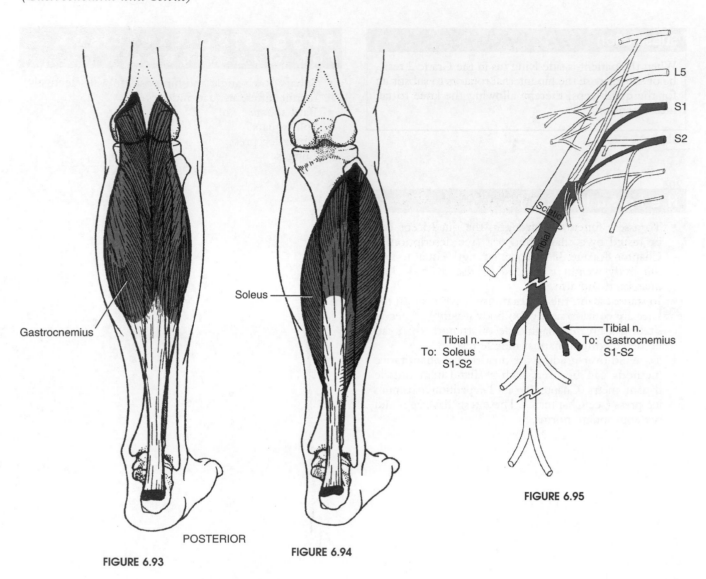

Gastrocnemius

Soleus

Tibial n.
To: Soleus
S1-S2

Tibial n.
To: Gastrocnemius
S1-S2

L5

S1

S2

Sciatic

Tibial

POSTERIOR

FIGURE 6.93

FIGURE 6.94

FIGURE 6.95

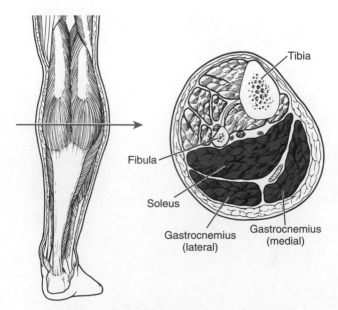

Tibia

Fibula

Soleus

Gastrocnemius
(lateral)

Gastrocnemius
(medial)

FIGURE 6.96 Arrow indicates level of cross section.

Range of Motion
0°–45°

Table 6.11 PLANTAR FLEXION

I.D.	Muscle	Origin	Insertion	Function
206	**Soleus**	Fibula (head, posterior aspect, and proximal ⅓ of shaft) Tibia (soleal line and middle ⅓ of medial shaft) Aponeurosis between tibia and fibula over popliteal vessels Aponeurosis (anterior)	Aponeurosis (posterior; tendinous raphe in midline of muscle) Tendo calcaneus when tendon of soleus joins tendon of gastrocnemius Calcaneus via tendo calcaneus	Ankle plantar flexion Foot inversion
205	Gastrocnemius			Ankle plantar flexion Knee flexion (accessory) Foot eversion
	Medial head	Femur (medial condyle, popliteal surface) Capsule of knee joint	Anterior aponeurosis Tendo calcaneus (tendon of Achilles) formed when tendon of gastrocnemius joins tendon of soleus	
	Lateral head	Femur (lateral condyle, lateral surface, and supracondylar line) Capsule of knee joint Aponeurosis (posterior)	Calcaneus (posterior)	
Others				
204	Tibialis posterior			
207	Plantaris			
208	Fibularis longus			
209	Fibularis brevis			
213	Flexor digitorum longus			
222	Flexor hallucis longus			

If the gastrocnemius-soleus complex is paralyzed, there is negligible capacity for the accessory muscles to substitute for the action of plantar flexion.

ANKLE PLANTAR FLEXION

(Gastrocnemius and Soleus)

The two ankle plantar flexors make up the triceps surae group. They differ in structure, anatomical position, function, and fiber-type characteristics. The medial gastrocnemius is the larger of the two heads. The gastrocnemius has 49% type 1 fibers compared to 80% in the soleus. This difference in fiber type makes the gastrocnemius more amenable to faster, more explosive movements while the soleus is more active during lower intensity and longer duration activities.[34] Because of the architecture and size of the soleus, the soleus generates 2.5 to 3× the force compared with the gastrocnemius. The soleus is isolated by flexing the knee during heel rise (Fig. 6.97).

GASTROCNEMIUS AND SOLEUS TEST

Grade 5, Grade 4, and Grade 3

Position of Patient: Patient stands on limb to be tested with knee extended, facing a wall. Patient is likely to need external support; thus, fingers can be placed on the wall, above shoulder height. Alternatively, no more than one or two fingers should be used on a table (or other horizontal surface) (Fig. 6.98).

Instructions to Therapist: Assess range of motion of the ankle to assure sufficient range is present. Demonstrate heel rise to patient. Then stand or sit with a lateral view of test limb to ascertain height of heel rise. Ask patient to lift heel while keeping knee straight. If patient can clear the floor by 2 inches, ask the patient to continue lifting the heel until the patient can no longer achieve 1 inch of rise. This is when the test is terminated. Patient should not bear weight through arms.

FIGURE 6.97

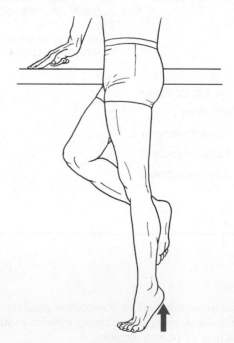

FIGURE 6.98

Grade 5, Grade 4, and Grade 3 Continued

Test: Patient raises heel from floor consecutively through maximum available range at a rate of one rise every 2 seconds until patient no longer achieves 50% of initial plantar range (Fig. 6.99).

Instructions to Patient: "Stand on one leg. Lift your heel. Now down. Repeat this as many times as possible, lifting your heel as high as you can." Repeat test for other limb, if both are tested.

Grading

Grade 5: Patient successfully completes 25 heel rises through full range of motion without a rest between rises.[35,36] Twenty-five heel rises elicit approximately 60% of the maximum electromyographic activity of the plantar flexors.[11] In the current standardized tests that have been in use for many years, 25 repetitions is the accepted norm. However, a more recent study suggests that the average number of repetitions in the sample studied is less than 25 repetitions (Table 6.12).[37] The therapist should be aware that strength deficits in the plantar flexors are common, particularly with advancing age, and strength deficits will affect the heel rise portion of the gait cycle and thus reduce gait speed.

Grade 4: A grade of 4 is conferred when the patient completes between 2 and 24 heel rises of at least 50% of initial heel raise height at a consistent rate of one rise every 2 seconds using correct form in all repetitions. The criterion for Grade 4 is not well defined.

Grade 3: Able to hold body weight once in a heel up position, but unable to raise body weight from neutral more than one time.

If the patient cannot complete at least one correct full-range heel rise in the standing position, the grade must be less than 3. Regardless of the force of resistance in a non-standing position for any reason, the patient must be given a grade of less than 3.[35]

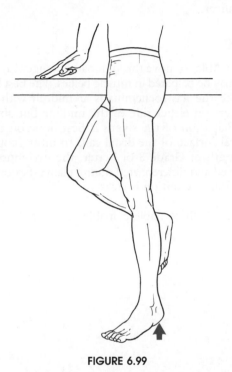

FIGURE 6.99

Table 6.12 AVERAGE VALUES OF UNTRAINED SUBJECTS

	MALES (BY AGE)				FEMALES (BY AGE)			
	Lunsford and Perry[36]	Jan et al.[37]	Jan et al.[37]	Jan et al.[37]	Lunsford and Perry[36]	Jan et al.[37]	Jan et al.[37]	Jan et al.[37]
Age (mean or range)	34.7 (8.5)	21–40	41–60	61–80	29.3 (5.0)	21–40	41–60	61–80
Mean repetitions	27.8 (11.5)	22.1 (9.8)	12.1 (6.6)	4.1 (1.9)	28.4 (9.8)	16.1 (6.7)	9.3 (3.6)	2.7 (1.5)
Range of repetitions	6–70	9–46	4–30	0–7	7–51	6–30	5–19	0–5
80th percentile		17	7	2		10	5	1

ANKLE PLANTAR FLEXION

(Gastrocnemius and Soleus)

Grade 2

Position of Patient: Prone with feet off end of table.

Instructions to Therapist: Stand at foot of patient. Ask patient to flex and extend ankle to assure sufficient range is present. Hand giving resistance is placed against the plantar surface at the level of the metatarsal heads with foot in 80° of dorsiflexion. These muscles are capable of tremendous force, which is why a more stable point of resistance is needed (Fig. 6.100).

Test: Patient plantar flexes ankle against manual resistance.

Grading

Grade 2: Holds test position against maximal manual resistance.[36] Because of the functional strength of these muscles, the therapist should not expect to break the contraction in a Grade 2 (prone) test.

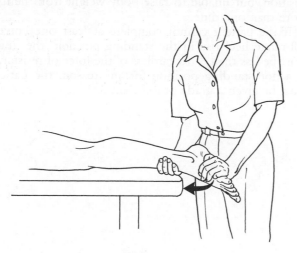

FIGURE 6.100

Grade 1 and Grade 0

Position of Patient: Prone with feet off end of table.

Instructions to Therapist: Stand at end of table in front of foot to be tested. One hand palpates gastrocnemius-soleus activity by monitoring tension in the Achilles tendon just above the calcaneus (Fig. 6.101). The muscle bellies of the two muscles also may be palpated (not illustrated).

Test: Patient attempts to plantar flex the ankle.

Instructions to Patient: "Point your toes down, like a ballet dancer."

Grading

Grade 1: Able to move through partial range. Contractile activity may be palpated in muscle bellies. The best location to palpate the gastrocnemius is at midcalf with thumb and fingers on either side of the midline but above the soleus. Palpation of the soleus is best done on the posterolateral surface of the distal calf. In most people with calf strength of Grade 3 or better, the two muscles can be observed and differentiated during plantar flexion testing because their definition is clear.

Grade 0: No discernable palpable contraction.

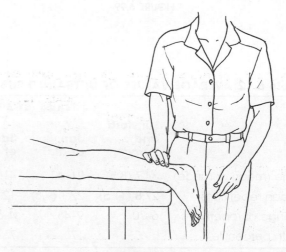

FIGURE 6.101

Helpful Hints

- Patient may try to flex knee and rock forward to ball of foot to raise heel from floor in standing test, which indicates weakness (Grade 2 or less).
- If for any reason the patient cannot lie prone for Grades 2, 1, or 0, an alternative for any of these tests is to use the supine position for non-weight–bearing testing. The highest grade awarded in this case is a Grade 2.
- During standing plantar flexion tests, the tibialis posterior and the fibularis longus and brevis muscles must be Grades 5 or 4 to stabilize the forefoot to attain and hold the tiptoe position.
- Because of the potential strength of the gastrocnemius soleus muscles, even if the patient is unable to raise the heel in a standing position, it may be advantageous to use a wall to support the therapist's weight while resisting plantar-flexion in the prone position. However, even with therapist stabilization, hand-held dynamometry of this muscle group in prone or supine is not reliable.
- Care must be taken to avoid transferring weight through the finger tips used for balance. Therefore it is recommended to place the patient's arms above the head on the wall in front of the patient. However, be sure that the patient maintains a fully erect posture. If the subject leans forward or flexes the knee, such posture can bring the heel off the ground, creating a testing artifact.
- Normative repetitions for children (5–12) are[38]:
  - Ages 5–6: 12.5 ± 5.4
  - Ages 7–8: 18.1 =/− 3.6
  - Ages 9–10: 22.3 =/− 8.0
  - Ages 11–12: 31.6 =/− 12.5
- Young women who wear shoes with a heel height of at least 5 cm high for 40 hours or more/week for 1 year demonstrated decreased strength and power in the soleus and reduced ankle range.[39]

Suggested Exercises for Gastrocnemius and Soleus

- Straight leg heel raises for gastrocnemius[34]
- Seated calf machine for soleus[34]
- Agility drills on toes

CROSS SECTIONS OF THE LEG

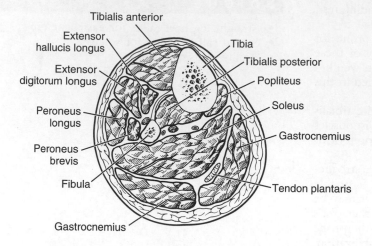

Tibialis anterior
Extensor hallucis longus
Extensor digitorum longus
Peroneus longus
Peroneus brevis
Fibula
Gastrocnemius
Tibia
Tibialis posterior
Popliteus
Soleus
Gastrocnemius
Tendon plantaris

MID LEG
AT UPPER PORTION OF
GASTROCNEMIUS AND
SOLEUS AT LARGEST
CIRCUMFERENCE OF CALF

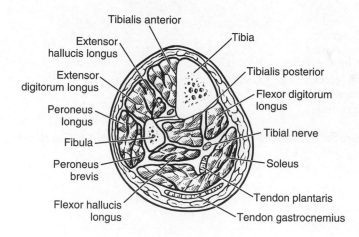

Tibialis anterior
Extensor hallucis longus
Extensor digitorum longus
Peroneus longus
Fibula
Peroneus brevis
Flexor hallucis longus
Tibia
Tibialis posterior
Flexor digitorum longus
Tibial nerve
Soleus
Tendon plantaris
Tendon gastrocnemius

LOWER LEG
NEAR END OF MUSCULAR
PORTIONS OF TRICEPS
SURAE. GASTROCNEMIUS
IS ALL TENDINOUS.

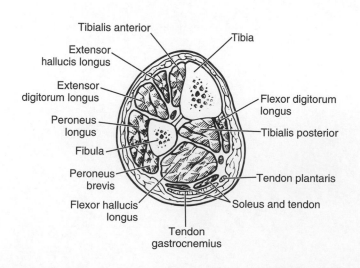

Tibialis anterior
Extensor hallucis longus
Extensor digitorum longus
Peroneus longus
Fibula
Peroneus brevis
Flexor hallucis longus
Tendon gastrocnemius
Tibia
Flexor digitorum longus
Tibialis posterior
Tendon plantaris
Soleus and tendon

HIGH ANKLE
LOWER LEG WHERE
GASTROCNEMIUS,
SOLEUS, AND PLANTARIS
ARE TENDINOUS

PLATE 7

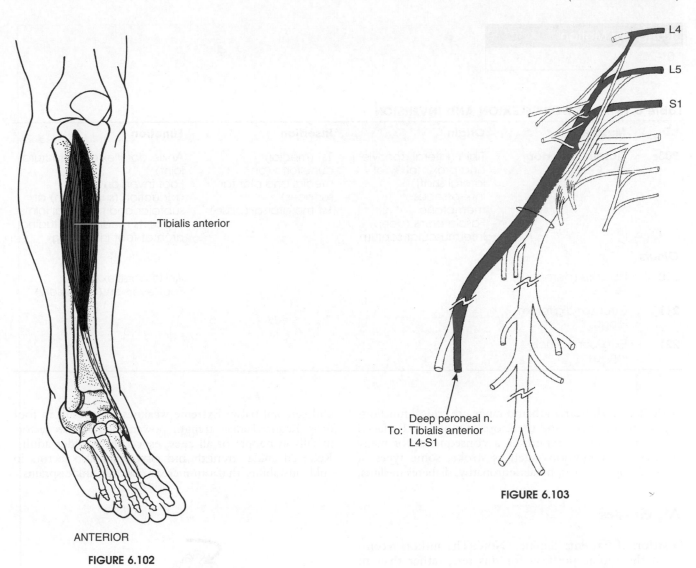

ANTERIOR

FIGURE 6.102

Tibialis anterior

L4

L5

S1

Deep peroneal n.
To: Tibialis anterior
L4-S1

FIGURE 6.103

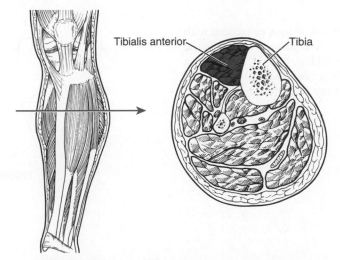

Tibialis anterior

Tibia

FIGURE 6.104 Arrow indicates level of cross section.

FOOT DORSIFLEXION AND INVERSION

(Tibialis anterior)

Range of Motion
0°–25°[22]

Table 6.13 FOOT DORSIFLEXION AND INVERSION

I.D.	Muscle	Origin	Insertion	Function
203	**Tibialis anterior**	Tibia (lateral condyle and proximal ⅔ of lateral shaft) Interosseous membrane Fascia cruris (deep) Intermuscular septum	1st (medial) cuneiform (on medial and plantar surfaces) 1st metatarsal (base)	Ankle dorsiflexion (talocrural joint) Foot inversion and adduction (supination) at subtalar and midtarsal joints Supports medial-longitudinal arch of foot in walking
Others				
210	Fibularis (peroneus) tertius			Ankle dorsiflexion Foot eversion (accessory)
211	Extensor digitorum longus			
221	Extensor hallucis longus			

Ankle dorsiflexion strength and range are critical functions of gait and balance[40] and therefore of mobility. Reduced ankle dorsiflexion strength is a consequence of many diseases and conditions such as stroke, some types of cancer, idiopathic peripheral neuropathy, diabetes mellitus, and cerebral palsy. Extreme weakness can result in foot drop. Reduced ankle strength, power, and range are factors in falls in people of all ages, especially in older adults. Reduced ankle strength and power are also factors in ankle instability that can increase risk for ankle sprains.

All Grades

Position of Patient: Supine. (Note: The authors recommend the supine position for this test, rather than an anti-gravity position, because of the mechanical advantage it affords the therapist when providing adequate resistance to this very strong muscle.)

Instructions to Therapist: Stand at foot of patient with patient's heel resting on table. Ask patient to bring the foot up and in, towards the body (Fig. 6.105). If sufficient range exists, place hand providing resistance on the medial aspect of the foot over the first ray. Resistance is provided

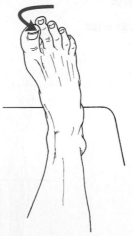

FIGURE 6.105

All Grades Continued

down and out (Fig. 6.106). This is a strong muscle, so applying resistance with the hand and flexed forearm can help provide enough resistance for a valid test. Additionally, this position is not against gravity, so this test should be graded stringently.

Test: Patient dorsiflexes ankle and inverts foot, keeping toes relaxed.

Instructions to Patient: "Bring your foot up and in. Hold it! Don't let me pull it down."

Grading

Grade 5: Holds test position against maximal resistance.

Grade 4: Holds test position against strong to moderate resistance.

Grade 3: Completes available range of motion without resistance (see Fig. 6.105).

Grade 2: Completes only a partial range of motion.

Grade 1: Therapist will be able to detect some contractile activity in the muscle, or the tendon will "stand out." There is no joint movement.

   Palpate the tendon of the tibialis anterior on the anteromedial aspect of the ankle at about the level of the malleoli (Fig. 6.107). Alternatively, palpate the muscle for contractile activity over its belly just lateral to the "shin" (not shown).

Grade 0: No discernable palpable contraction.

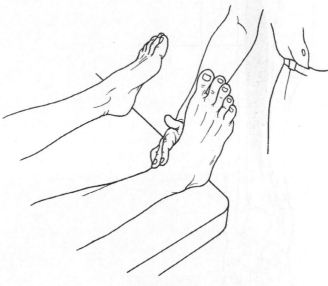

FIGURE 6.107

Substitution

Substitution by the extensor digitorum longus and the extensor hallucis longus muscles results in toe extension. Instruct the patient therefore to keep the toes relaxed so that they are not part of the test movement.

Helpful Hints

- In the sitting and supine positions, make sure the knee is flexed to put the gastrocnemius on slack. If the knee is extended and there is gastrocnemius tightness, the patient will not be able to achieve full dorsiflexion range.
- Because the supine position is not against gravity, the therapist should expect to give maximum resistance utilizing body weight of the therapist. A pull force will be more protective of the therapist's shoulder than a push force.

Suggested Exercises for Tibialis Anterior

- Resisted dorsiflexion using elastic resistance or pulling against a pedal or other object
- Foot taps
- Heel walking

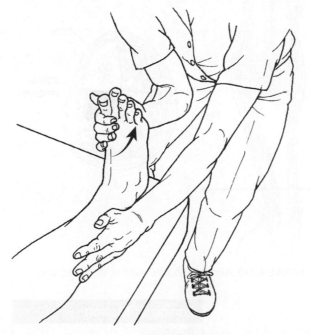

FIGURE 6.106

FOOT INVERSION

(Tibialis posterior)

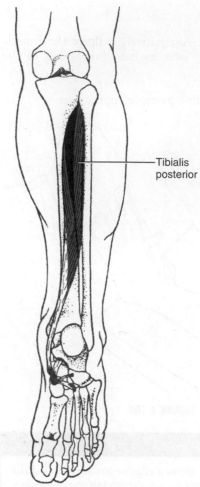

POSTERIOR VIEW OF LEG
PLANTAR VIEW OF FOOT

FIGURE 6.108

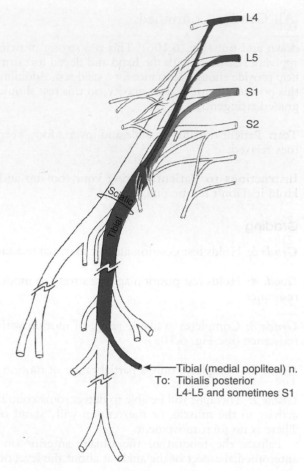

Tibial (medial popliteal) n.
To: Tibialis posterior
L4-L5 and sometimes S1

FIGURE 6.109

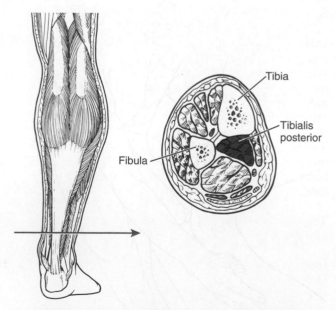

Tibia

Tibialis
posterior

Fibula

FIGURE 6.110 Arrow indicates level of cross section.

Range of Motion

0°–35°

Table 6.14 FOOT INVERSION

I.D.	Muscle	Origin	Insertion	Function
204	**Tibialis posterior**	Tibia (proximal ⅔ of posterior lateral shaft below soleal line) Interosseous membrane (posterior) Fibula (shaft, proximal posterior medial ⅔) Deep transverse fascia Intermuscular septa	Navicular bone (tuberosity) Cuneiform bones Sustentaculum tali (distal) Metatarsals 2–4 (via tendinous band)	Foot inversion (supination) Ankle plantar flexion (accessory)

Others

203	Tibialis anterior			
213	Flexor digitorum longus			
222	Flexor hallucis longus			
206	Soleus			
221	Extensor hallucis longus			

The tibialis posterior muscle provides function of the subtalar and midtarsal joints during the stance phase of gait, providing an inversion moment at the subtalar joint and stabilizing the medial longitudinal arch. Dysfunction of the tibialis posterior tendon, a relatively recently recognized degenerative and progressive condition, is a common cause of adult-acquired flat-footedness and tendon rupture.

Grade 5, Grade 4, Grade 3, and Grade 2

Position of Patient: Sitting with ankle in slight plantar flexion.

Instructions to Therapist: Sit on low stool in front of patient or on side of test limb (anti-gravity position). With patient's heel resting on therapist's thigh, ask the patient to move the foot down and in. Perform this movement passively if needed. If sufficient active range exists, place stabilizing hand on the posterior calf just above the malleoli (Fig. 6.111). The majority of resistance is toward forefoot abduction (up and out direction). Hand providing resistance is placed on the foot with the hand providing resistance over the medial side of the forefoot.

Test: Patient inverts foot through available range of motion.

Instructions to Patient: "Turn your foot down and in. Hold it. Don't let me move it."

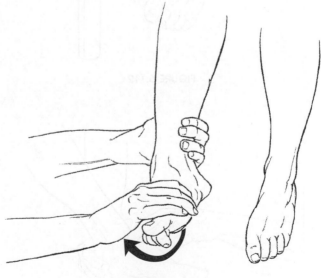

FIGURE 6.111

FOOT INVERSION

(Tibialis posterior)

Grade 5, Grade 4, Grade 3, and Grade 2
Continued

Grading

Grade 5: The patient holds the test position against maximal resistance.

Grade 4: The patient holds the test position against strong to moderate resistance.

Grade 3: The patient will be able to invert the foot through the full available range of motion (Fig. 6.112).

Grade 2: The patient will be able to complete only partial range of motion.

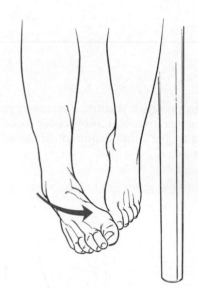

FIGURE 6.112

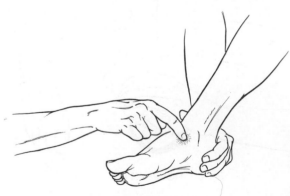

FIGURE 6.113

Grade 1 and Grade 0

Position of Patient: Sitting or supine.

Instructions to Therapist: Sit on low stool or stand in front of patient. Palpate tendon of the tibialis posterior between the medial malleolus and the navicular bone (Fig. 6.113). Alternatively, palpate tendon above the malleolus.

Test: Patient attempts to invert foot.

Instructions to Patient: "Try to turn your foot down and in."

Grading

Grade 1: The tibialis posterior tendon will stand out if there is contractile activity in the muscle. If palpable activity occurs in the absence of movement, the grade is 1.

Grade 0: No discernable palpable contraction.

Substitution

Flexors of the toes should remain relaxed to prevent substitution by the flexor digitorum longus and flexor hallucis longus.

Helpful Hints

The single-leg heel raise is painful or impossible in the presence of tibialis posterior dysfunction.

If heel inversion does not occur or is asymmetrical during the heel rise, this may indicate insufficiency in tibialis posterior.

The action of the tibialis posterior is to plantarflex and invert the ankle having the effect of placing the forefoot into adduction. To isolate the tibialis posterior, resisted forefoot adduction should be the primary force with less force toward dorsiflexion (producing the up and out movement).

Suggested Exercises for Tibialis Posterior

- Foot inversion exercise (pushing soles of feet together)
- Eccentric foot inversion exercise with elastic resistance
- Heel rise with inversion (heels together)

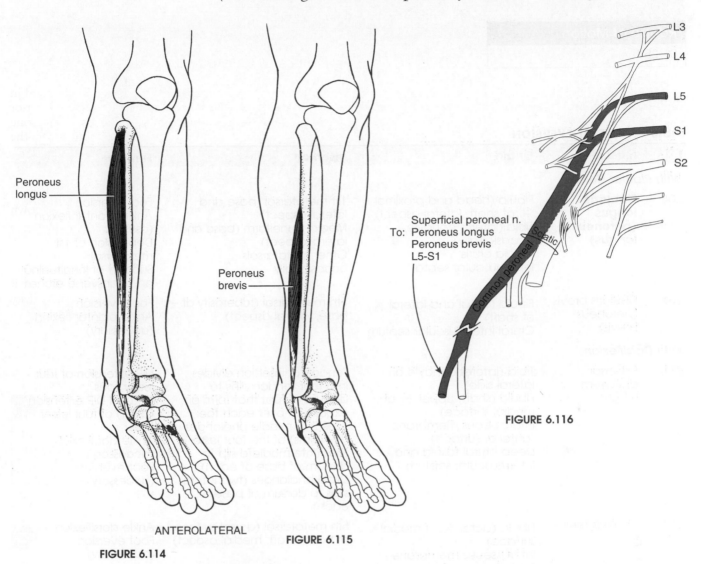

Peroneus longus

Peroneus brevis

Superficial peroneal n.
To: Peroneus longus
Peroneus brevis
L5-S1

L3
L4
L5
S1
S2

Common peroneal

Sciatic

FIGURE 6.116

ANTEROLATERAL

FIGURE 6.115

FIGURE 6.114

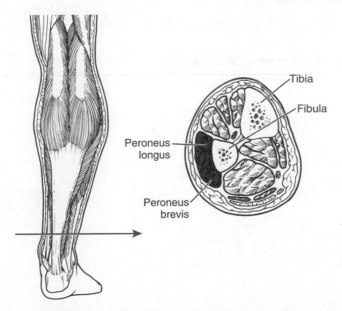

Tibia

Fibula

Peroneus longus

Peroneus brevis

FIGURE 6.117 Arrow indicates level of cross section.

FOOT EVERSION WITH PLANTAR FLEXION

(Fibularis longus and brevis—previously called Peroneus longus and brevis)

Range of Motion
0°–25°

Table 6.15 FOOT EVERSION

I.D.	Muscle	Origin	Insertion	Function
With Plantar Flexion				
208	**Fibularis longus (peroneus longus)**	Fibula (head and proximal ⅔ of shaft, lateral aspect) Tibia (lateral condyle, occasionally) Fascia cruris Intermuscular septa	1st metatarsal (base and lateral aspect) Medial cuneiform (base and lateral aspect) Other metatarsals occasionally	Foot eversion Ankle plantar flexion (assist) Depression of 1st metatarsal Support of longitudinal and transverse arches
209	Fibularis brevis (peroneus brevis)	Fibula (distal and lateral ⅔ of shaft) Crural intermuscular septum	5th metatarsal (tuberosity at base, lateral aspect)	Foot eversion Ankle plantar flexion (accessory)
With Dorsiflexion				
211	Extensor digitorum longus	Tibia (lateral condyle on lateral side) Fibula (shaft: upper ¾ of medial surface) Interosseous membrane (anterior surface) Deep crural fascia and intermuscular septum	Tendon of insertion divides into four tendon slips to dorsum of foot that form an expansion over each toe: Toes 2–5: middle phalanges (PIP joints) of the four lesser toes (intermediate slip to dorsum of base of each) Distal phalanges (two lateral slips to dorsum of base of each)	MP extension of four lesser toes PIP and DIP extension (assist) of four lesser toes Ankle dorsiflexion (accessory) Foot eversion (accessory)
210	Fibularis tertius	Fibula (distal ⅓ of medial surface) Interosseous membrane (anterior) Intermuscular septum	5th metatarsal (dorsal surface of base; shaft, medial aspect)	Ankle dorsiflexion Foot eversion (accessory)
Other				
205	Gastrocnemius			

DIP, Distal phalanges; *MP*, metatarsophalangeal; *PIP*, proximal phalanges.

Grade 5, Grade 4, Grade 3, and Grade 2

Position of Patient: Sitting with ankle in neutral position (midway between dorsiflexion and plantar flexion). Test also may be performed with patient supine.

Instructions to Therapist: Sit on low stool in front of patient or stand at end of table if patient is supine. Ask patient to turn foot down and out (eversion). If sufficient range is present, place stabilizing hand at the ankle just above the malleoli. Take care not to squeeze the distal tibia. Hand providing resistance is contoured around the dorsum and lateral border of the forefoot (Fig. 6.118). Resistance is directed toward inversion and slight dorsiflexion (up and in).

Test: Patient everts foot with depression of first metatarsal head and some plantar flexion.

Instructions to Patient: "Turn your foot down and out. Hold it! Don't let me move it in."

Grading

Grade 5: Patient holds test position against maximal resistance.

Grade 4: Patient holds test position against strong to moderate resistance.

Grade 3: Patient completes available range of eversion but without resistance (Fig. 6.119).

Grade 2: Patient will be able to complete only a partial range of eversion motion.

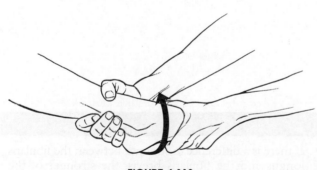

FIGURE 6.118

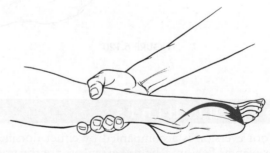

FIGURE 6.119

FOOT EVERSION WITH PLANTAR FLEXION

(Fibularis longus and brevis—previously called Peroneus longus and brevis)

Grade 1 and Grade 0

Position of Patient: Short sitting or supine.

Instructions to Therapist: Sit on low stool or stand at end of table. To palpate the fibularis longus, place fingers on the lateral leg over the upper one-third just below the head of the fibula. The tendon of the muscle can be felt posterior to the lateral malleolus but behind the tendon of the fibularis brevis.

To palpate the tendon of the fibularis brevis, place index finger over the tendon as it comes forward from behind the lateral malleolus, proximal to the base of the fifth metatarsal (Fig. 6.120). The belly of the fibularis brevis can be palpated on the lateral surface of the distal leg over the fibula.

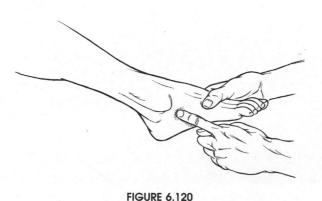

FIGURE 6.120

Grading

Grade 1: Palpation will reveal contractile activity in either or both muscles, which may cause the tendon to stand out. No motion occurs.

Grade 0: No discernable palpable contractile activity.

Isolation of Fibularis Longus

Give resistance against the plantar surface of the head of the first metatarsal in a direction toward inversion and dorsiflexion.

Foot Eversion With Dorsiflexion

If the fibularis tertius is present, it can be tested by asking the patient to evert and dorsiflex the foot. In this motion, however, the extensor digitorum longus participates.

The tendon of the fibularis tertius can be palpated on the lateral aspect of the dorsum of the foot, where it lies lateral to the tendon of the extensor digitorum longus slip to the little toe.

Helpful Hints

- Foot eversion is accompanied by either dorsiflexion or plantar flexion. The toe extensors are the primary dorsiflexors accompanying eversion because the fibularis tertius is not always present.
- The primary motion of eversion with plantar flexion is accomplished by the fibularis brevis because the fibularis longus is primarily a depressor of the first metatarsal head rather than an evertor.
- The fibularis brevis cannot be isolated if both longus and brevis are innervated and strong.

- If there is a difference in strength between the fibularis longus and the fibularis brevis, the stronger of the two can be ascertained by the relative amount of resistance taken in eversion versus the resistance taken at the first metatarsal head. If greater resistance is taken at the first metatarsal head, the fibularis longus is the stronger muscle.

Suggested Exercise for Foot Eversion

Lateral hop[41]

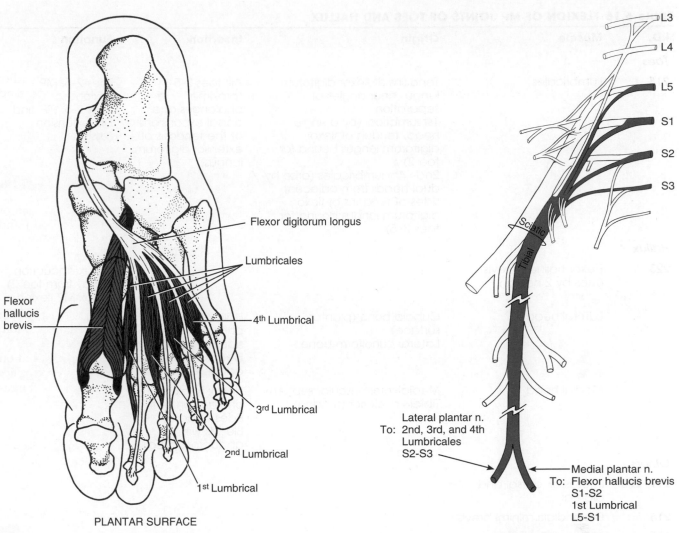

Flexor digitorum longus

Lumbricales

Flexor hallucis brevis

4th Lumbrical

3rd Lumbrical

2nd Lumbrical

1st Lumbrical

PLANTAR SURFACE

FIGURE 6.121

Sciatic

Tibial

Lateral plantar n.
To: 2nd, 3rd, and 4th Lumbricales
S2–S3

Medial plantar n.
To: Flexor hallucis brevis
S1–S2
1st Lumbrical
L5–S1

L3
L4
L5
S1
S2
S3

FIGURE 6.122

Range of Motion	
Great toe, 0°–45°	
Lateral four toes, 0°–40°	

HALLUX AND TOE MP FLEXION

(Lumbricales and Flexor hallucis brevis)

Table 6.16 FLEXION OF MP JOINTS OF TOES AND HALLUX

I.D.	Muscle	Origin	Insertion	Function
Toes				
218	Lumbricales	Tendons of flexor digitorum longus near angles of separation 1st lumbrical (by a single head, tendon of flexor digitorum longus bound for toe 2) 2nd--4th lumbricales (arise by dual heads from adjacent sides of tendons of flexor digitorum longus bound for toes 3-5)	All: toes 2-5 (proximal phalanges and dorsal expansions of the tendons of extensor digitorum longus)	Toes 2-5: MP flexion Toes 2-5: PIP and DIP extension (assist)
Hallux				
223	Flexor hallucis brevis (rises by 2 heads)			Hallux abduction (away from toe 2) Hallux MP flexion
	Lateral head	Cuboid bone (plantar surface) Lateral cuneiform bone	Hallux (proximal phalanx on both sides of base) Blends with adductor hallucis	
	Medial head	Medial intermuscular septum Tibialis posterior (tendon)	Hallux (proximal phalanx on both sides of base) Blends with abductor hallucis	
Others				
219, 220	Interossei, dorsal and plantar			
216	Flexor digiti minimi brevis			
213	Flexor digitorum longus			
214	Flexor digitorum brevis			
222	Flexor hallucis longus			
224	Abductor hallucis			
225	Adductor hallucis			

DIP, Distal interphalangeal; *MP*, metatarsophalangeal; *PIP*, proximal interphalangeal.

HALLUX MP FLEXION *(Flexor hallucis brevis)*

Grades 5 to 0

Position of Patient: Sitting (alternate position: supine) with legs hanging over edge of table. Ankle is in neutral position (midway between dorsiflexion and plantar flexion).

Instructions to Therapist: Sit on low stool in front of patient. Alternate position: stand at side of table near patient's foot.

Test foot rests on therapist's lap. Ask the patient to bend the big toe over finger. If sufficient range is present, place stabilizing hand over the dorsum of the foot just below the ankle (Fig. 6.123). The index finger of the other hand is placed beneath the proximal phalanx of the great toe. Alternatively, the tip of the finger (with very short fingernails) is placed up under the proximal phalanx.

Test: Patient flexes great toe.

Instructions to Patient: "Bend your big toe over my finger. Hold it. Don't let me straighten it."

Grading

Grade 5: Patient holds position against strong resistance.

Grade 4: Patient holds test position against moderate to mild resistance.

Grade 3: Patient completes available range of metatarsophalangeal (MP) flexion of the great toe without resistance.

Grade 2: Patient completes only partial range of motion.

Grade 1: Therapist may note contractile activity but no toe motion.

Grade 0: No discernable contractile activity.

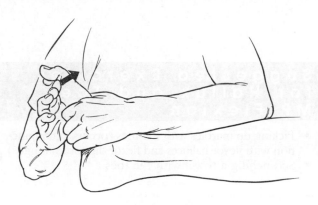

FIGURE 6.123

Helpful Hints

- The muscle and tendon of the flexor hallucis brevis cannot be palpated.
- When the flexor hallucis longus is not functional, the flexor hallucis brevis will flex the metatarsophalangeal joint but without flexion of the interphalangeal joint. In the opposite condition, when the flexor hallucis brevis is not functional, the IP joint flexes and the metatarsophalangeal joint may hyperextend. (When this condition is chronic, the posture is called hammer toe.)
- Loss of the flexor hallucis longus results in balance instability as it stabilizes the big toe against the ground during each step.

(Lumbricales, Interossei)

TOE MP FLEXION

Grades 5 to 0

Position of Patient: Sitting with foot on therapist's lap. Alternate position: supine. Ankle is in neutral (midway between dorsiflexion and plantar flexion).

Instructions to Therapist: Sit on low stool in front of patient. Alternate position: stand next to table beside test foot. Ask the patient to bend the toes over therapist's fingers. If sufficient range is present, place stabilizing hand over the dorsum of the foot (as in test for flexion of the hallux) (Fig. 6.124). The index finger of the other hand is placed under the MP joints of the four lateral toes to provide resistance to flexion.

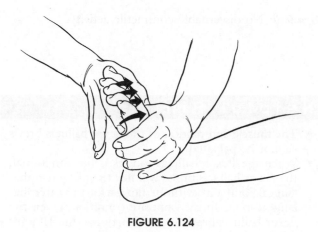

FIGURE 6.124

Test: Patient flexes lateral four toes at the MP joints, keeping the interphalangeal (IP) joints neutral.

Instructions to Patient: "Bend your toes over my finger. Hold it!"

Grading

Grading is the same as that used for the great toe.

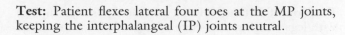

Helpful Hints

In actual practice, the great toe and the lateral toes are rarely tested independently. Many patients cannot separate hallux motion from motion of the lateral toes, nor can they separate metatarsophalangeal and interphalangeal motions.

The therapist could test each toe separately because the lumbricales are notoriously uneven in strength. This may not, however, be practicable.

Suggested Exercises for Hallux and Toe MP Flexion

- Picking up marbles with the toes (occurs in conjunction with flexor halluces and flexor digitorum longus)
- Scrunching a towel with the toes

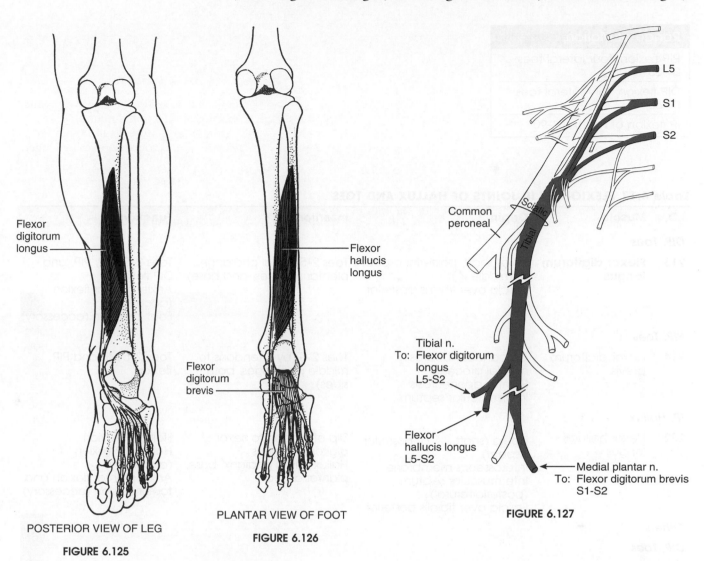

Flexor digitorum longus

Flexor hallucis longus

Flexor digitorum brevis

POSTERIOR VIEW OF LEG

FIGURE 6.125

PLANTAR VIEW OF FOOT

FIGURE 6.126

L5

S1

S2

Common peroneal

Sciatic

Tibial

Tibial n.
To: Flexor digitorum longus
L5-S2

Flexor hallucis longus
L5-S2

Medial plantar n.
To: Flexor digitorum brevis
S1-S2

FIGURE 6.127

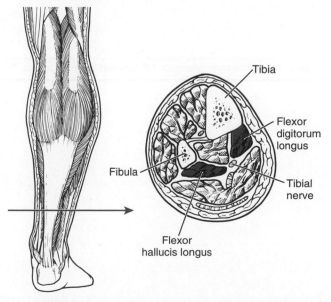

Tibia

Flexor digitorum longus

Fibula

Tibial nerve

Flexor hallucis longus

FIGURE 6.128 Arrow indicates level of cross section.

HALLUX AND TOE DIP AND PIP FLEXION

(Flexor digitorum longus, Flexor digitorum brevis, Flexor hallucis longus)

Range of Motion
PIP flexion, four lateral toes: 0°–35°
DIP flexion, four lateral toes: 0°–60°
IP flexion of hallux: 0°–90°

Table 6.17 FLEXION OF IP JOINTS OF HALLUX AND TOES

I.D.	Muscle	Origin	Insertion	Function
DIP, Toes				
213	**Flexor digitorum longus**	Tibia (shaft, posterior aspect of middle ⅔) Fascia over tibialis posterior	Toes 2–5 (distal phalanges, plantar surfaces, and base)	Toes 2–5: MP, PIP, and DIP flexion Ankle plantar flexion (accessory) Foot inversion (accessory)
PIP, Toes				
214	Flexor digitorum brevis	Calcaneus (tuberosity, medial process) Plantar aponeurosis Intermuscular septum	Toes 2–5 (by 4 tendons to middle phalanges, both sides)	Toes 2–5 MP and PIP flexion
IP, Hallux				
222	Flexor hallucis longus	Fibula (shaft, ⅔ of posterior aspect) Interosseous membrane Intermuscular septum (posterior crural) Fascia over tibialis posterior	Slip of tendon to flexor digitorum longus Hallux (distal phalanx, base, plantar aspect)	Hallux IP flexion Hallux MP flexion (accessory) Ankle plantar flexion and foot inversion (accessory)
Others				
DIP, Toes				
217	Quadratus plantae			
PIP, Toes				
213	Flexor digitorum longus			

DIP, Distal interphalangeal; *IP,* interphalangeal; *MP,* metatarsophalangeal; *PIP,* proximal interphalangeal.

(Flexor digitorum longus, Flexor digitorum brevis, Flexor hallucis longus)

Grades 5 to 0

Position of Patient: Sitting with foot on therapist's lap, or supine.

Instructions to Therapist: Sit on a short stool in front of the patient or stand at the side of the table near the patient's foot. Ask the patient to curl toes (or big toe). If sufficient range is present, place stabilizing hand over the anterior foot with the fingers placed across the dorsum of the foot and the thumb under the proximal phalanges (PIP) or distal phalanges (DIP) or under the IP of the hallux (Figs. 6.129, 6.130, and 6.131). The other hand applies resistance using the four fingers or the thumb under the middle phalanges (for the IP test) (see Fig. 6.129), under the distal phalanges for the DIP test (see Fig. 6.130), and with the index finger under the distal phalanx of the hallux (see Fig. 6.131). Resistance will be minimal.

Test: Patient flexes the toes or hallux.

Instructions to Patient: "Curl your toes; hold it. Curl your big toe and hold it."

Grading

Grade 5 and Grade 4: Patient holds test position of toes and then hallux; resistance in both tests may be minimal.

Grade 3 and Grade 2: Patient holds test position without resistance (Grade 3) or completes only a partial range (Grade 2).

Grade 1 and Grade 0: Minimal to no palpable contractile activity occurs. Tendon of the flexor hallucis longus may be palpated on the plantar surface of the proximal phalanx of the great toe.

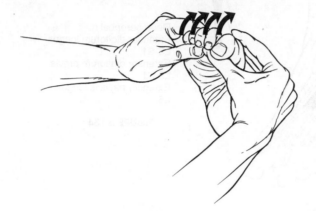

FIGURE 6.129

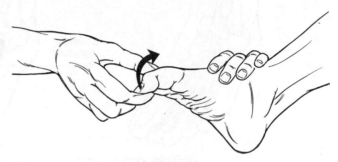

FIGURE 6.131

FIGURE 6.130

Helpful Hints

- As with all toe motions, the patient may not be able to move one toe separately from another or separate MP from IP activity among individual toes.
- Some people can separate hallux activity from toe motions, but fewer can separate MP from IP hallux activity.
- Many people can "pinch" with their great toe (adductor hallucis), but this is not a common clinical test.
- The abductor hallucis is not commonly tested because it is only rarely isolated. Its activity can be observed by resisting adduction of the forefoot, which will bring the great toe into abduction, but the lateral toes commonly extend at the same time.

(Extensor digitorum longus and brevis, Extensor hallucis longus)

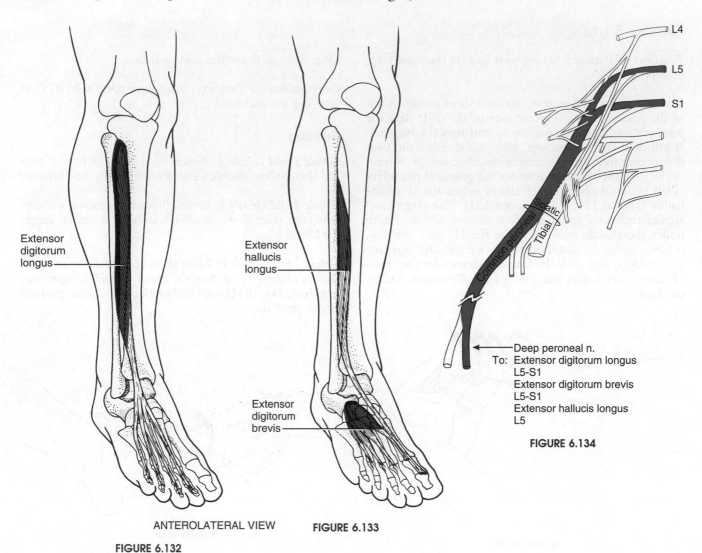

Extensor digitorum longus

Extensor hallucis longus

Extensor digitorum brevis

L4

L5

S1

Common peroneal

Tibial

Sciatic

Deep peroneal n.
To: Extensor digitorum longus
L5-S1
Extensor digitorum brevis
L5-S1
Extensor hallucis longus
L5

FIGURE 6.134

ANTEROLATERAL VIEW

FIGURE 6.133

FIGURE 6.132

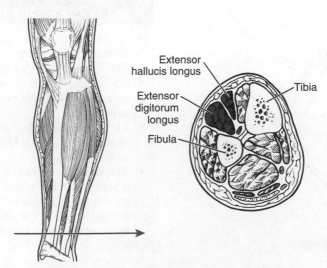

Extensor hallucis longus

Extensor digitorum longus

Tibia

Fibula

FIGURE 6.135 Arrow indicates level of cross section.

Range of Motion
Hallux: 0°–75°–80°
Digits 2–5: 0°–40°

Table 6.18 EXTENSION OF MP JOINTS OF TOES AND IP JOINT OF HALLUX

I.D.	Muscle	Origin	Insertion	Function
211	**Extensor digitorum longus**	Tibia (lateral condyle) Fibula (shaft, proximal ¾ of medial surface) Fascia cruris (deep) Interosseous membrane (anterior) Intermuscular septum	Toes 2–5 (to each middle and each distal phalanx, dorsal surface)	MP extension of four lesser toes PIP and DIP extension (assist) of four lesser toes Ankle dorsiflexion (accessory) Foot eversion (accessory)
212	Extensor digitorum brevis	Calcaneus (anterior superolateral surface) Lateral talocalcaneal ligament Extensor retinaculum (inferior)	Ends in four tendons: hallux (proximal phalanx, dorsal surface (may be named *extensor hallucis brevis*)) Toes 2–4: join tendons of extensor digitorum longus (lateral sides)	Hallux (great toe): MP extension Toes 2–4: MP extension Toes 2–4: IP extension (assist)
221	Extensor hallucis longus	Fibula (shaft, middle ½ of medial aspect) Interosseous membrane	Hallux (distal phalanx, dorsal aspect of base) Expansion to proximal phalanx	Hallux: MP and IP extension Ankle dorsiflexion (accessory) Foot inversion (accessory)

DIP, Distal interphalangeal; *IP,* interphalangeal; *MP,* metatarsophalangeal; *PIP,* proximal interphalangeal.

HALLUX AND TOE MP AND IP EXTENSION

(Extensor digitorum longus and brevis, Extensor hallucis longus)

Grades 5 to 0

Position of Patient: Sitting with foot on therapist's lap. Alternate position: supine. Ankle in neutral (midway between plantar flexion and dorsiflexion).

Instructions to Therapist: Sit on low stool in front of patient, or stand beside table near the patient's foot. Ask patient to straighten big toe or all the toes.

Lateral Toes: One hand stabilizes the metatarsals with the fingers on the plantar surface and the thumb on the dorsum of the foot (Fig. 6.136). The other hand is used to give resistance with the thumb placed over the dorsal surface of the proximal phalanges of the toes.

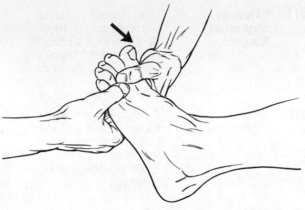

FIGURE 6.136

(Extensor digitorum longus and brevis, Extensor hallucis longus)

Grades 5 to 0 Continued

Hallux: Stabilize the metatarsal area by contouring the hand around the plantar surface of the foot with the thumb curving around to the base of the hallux (Fig. 6.137). The other hand stabilizes the foot at the heel. For resistance, place thumb over the MP joint (see Fig. 6.136) or over the IP joint (Fig. 6.138).

Test: Patient extends lateral four toes or extends hallux.

Instructions to Patient: "Straighten your big toe. Hold it." OR "Straighten your toes and hold it."

Grading

Grade 5 and Grade 4: Patient can extend the toes fully against variable resistance (which may be small).

Grade 3 and Grade 2: Patient can complete range of motion with no resistance (Grade 3) or can complete a partial range of motion (Grade 2).

Grade 1 and Grade 0: Tendons of the extensor digitorum longus can be palpated or observed over dorsum of metatarsals. Tendon of the extensor digitorum brevis often can be palpated on the lateral side of the dorsum of the foot just in front of the malleolus.

Palpable contractile activity is a Grade 1; no discernable palpable contractile activity is a Grade 0.

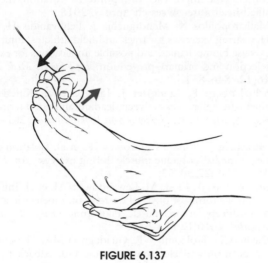

FIGURE 6.137

Helpful Hints

- Many (if not most) patients cannot separate great toe extension from extension of the four lateral toes. Nor can most separate MP from IP activity.
- The test is used not so much to ascertain strength as to determine whether the toe muscles are active.
- Normal strength in the ankle and foot muscles allows us to walk on uneven surfaces and supplies the major muscle forces needed for balance.

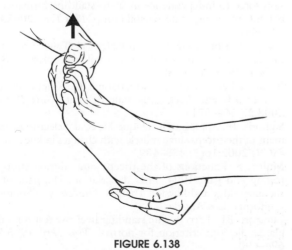

FIGURE 6.138

REFERENCES

1. Pressel T, Lengsfeld M. Functions of hip joint muscles. *Med Eng Phys*. 1998;20(1):50–56.

2. Gottschall JS, Kram R. Energy cost and muscular activity required for leg swing during walking. *J Appl Physio*. 2005;99:23–30.

3. Rantanen T, Guralnik JM, Izmirlian G, et al. Association of muscle strength with maximum walking speed in disabled older women. *Am J Phys Med Rehabil*. 1998;77(4):299–305.

4. Yokozawa T, Fujii N, Ae M. Muscle activities of the lower limb during level and uphill running. *J Biomech*. 2007;40:3467–3475.

5. Neumann DA. Kinesiology of the hip: A focus on muscular action. *J Orthop Sports Phys Ther*. 2010;40(2):82–94.

6. Winter D. *Biomechanics and Motor Control of Human Movement*. Hoboken, NJ: John Wiley & Sons.; 2005.

7. Reinman MP. A literature review of studies evaluating gluteus maximus and gluteus medius activation during rehabilitation exercises. *Physiother Theory Pract*. 2012;28(4):257–268.

8. Waters RL, Perry J, McDaniels JM, et al. The relative strength of the hamstrings during hip extension. *J Bone Joint Surg Am*. 1974;56:1592–1597.

9. Perry J, Weiss WB, Burnfield JM, et al. The supine hip extension manual muscle test: a reliability and validity study. *Arch Phys Med Rehabil*. 2004;85(8):1345–1350.

10. Youdas JW, Hartman JP, Murphy BA, et al. Electromyographic analysis of gluteus maximus and hamstring activity during the supine resisted hip extension exercise versus supine unilateral bridge to neutral. *Physiother Theory Pract*. 2017;33(2):124–130.

11. Bolgla LA, Uhl TL. Electromyographic analysis of hip rehabilitation exercises in a group of healthy subjects. *J Orthop Sports Phys Ther*. 2005;35:487–494.

12. Boudreau SN, Dwyer MK, Mattacola CG, et al. Hip-muscle activation during the lunge, single-leg squat, and step-up-and-over exercises. *J Sport Rehabil*. 2009;18:91–103.

13. Bennell KL, Hunt MA, Wrigley TV, et al. Hip strengthening reduces symptoms but not knee load in people with medial knee osteoarthritis and varus malalignment: a randomized controlled trial. *Osteoarthritis Cartilage*. 2010;18:621–628.

14. Chi AS, Long SS, Zoga AC, et al. Association of gluteus medius and minimus muscle atrophy and fall-related hip fracture in older individuals using computed tomography. *J Comput Assist Tomogr*. 2016;40(2):238–242.

15. Jacobs CA, Lewis M, Bolgla LA, et al. Electromyographic analysis of hip abductor exercises performed by a sample of total hip arthroplasty patients. *J Arthroplasty*. 2009;24(7):1130–1136.

16. Ekstrom RA, Donatelli RA, Carp KC. Electromyographic analysis of core trunk, hip, and thigh muscles during 9 rehabilitation exercises. *J Orthop Sports Phys Ther*. 2007;37(12):754–762.

17. Takizawa M, Suzuki D, Ito H, et al. Why adductor magnus muscle is large: the function based on muscle morphology in cadavers. *Scand J Med Sci Sports*. 2014;24(1):197–203.

18. Hides JA, Beall P, Franettovich Smith MM, et al. Activation of the hip adductor muscles varies during a simulated weight-bearing task. *Phys Ther Sport*. 2016;17:19–23.

19. Light N, Thorborg K. The precision and torque production of common hip adductor squeeze tests used in elite football. *J Sci Med Sport*. 2016;19(11):888–892.

20. Ishøi L, Sørensen CN, Kaae NM, et al. Large eccentric strength increase using the Copenhagen Adduction exercise in football: a randomized controlled trial. *Scand J Med Sci Sports*. 2016;26(11):1334–1342.

21. Giphart JE, Stull JD, Laprade RF, et al. Recruitment and activity of the pectineus and piriformis muscles during hip rehabilitation exercises: an electromyography study. *Am J Sports Med*. 2012;40(7):1654–1663.

22. McKay MJ, Baldwin JN, Ferreira P, et al. 1000 Norms Project Consortium. Normative reference values for strength and flexibility of 1,000 children and adults. *Neurology*. 2017;88(1):36–43.

23. Delp SL, Hess WE, Hungerford DS, et al. Variation of rotation moment arms with hip flexion. *J Biomech*. 1999;32:493–501.

24. Cibulka MT, Strube MJ, Meier D, et al. Symmetrical and asymmetrical hip rotation and its relationship to hip rotator muscle strength. *Clin Biomech (Bristol, Avon)*. 2010;25(1):56–62.

25. Multibriefs. 2018. http://exclusive.multibriefs.com/content/the-importance-of-hip-internal-rotation/medical-allied-healthcare. Accessed April 3, 2018.

26. Malliaropoulos N, Mendiguchia J, Pehlivanidis H, et al. Hamstring exercises for track and field athletes: injury and exercise biomechanics, and possible implications for exercise selection and primary prevention. *Br J Sports Med*. 2012;46(12):846–851.

27. Schellenberg F, Lindorfer J, List R, et al. Kinetic and kinematic differences between deadlifts and good mornings. *BMC Sports Science, Medicine and Rehabilitation*. 2013;5(1):27.

28. Mirzabeigi E, Jordan C, Gronley JK, et al. Isolation of the vastus medialis oblique muscle during exercise. *Am J Sports Med*. 1999;27:50–53.

29. Bronikowski A, Kloda M, Lewandowska M, et al. Influence of various forms of physical exercise on bioelectric activity of quadriceps femoris muscle. Pilot study. *Orthop Traumatol Rehabil*. 2010;12:534–541.

30. Davlin CD, Holcomb WR, Guadagnoli MA. The effect of hip position and electromyographic biofeedback training on the vastus medialis oblique: vastus lateralis ratio. *J Athl Train*. 1999;34:342–346.

31. Eriksrud O, Bohannon RW. Relationship of knee extension force to independence in sit-to-stand performance in patients receiving acute rehabilitation. *Phys Ther*. 2003;83:544–551.

32. Davy DT, Kotzar GM, Brown RH, et al. Telemetric force measurements across the hip after total arthroplasty. *J Bone Jt Surg*. 1988;70:45–50.

33. Beaulieu FG, Pelland L, Robertson DG. Kinetic analysis of forwards and backwards stair descent. *Gait Posture*. 2008;27:564–571.

34. Signorile JF, Applegate B, Duque M, et al. Selective recruitment of the triceps surae muscle with changes in knee angle. *JSCR*. 2002;16(3):433–439.

35. Mulroy S. Functions of the triceps surae during strength testing and gait; 1994. PhD dissertation, Department of Biokinesiology and Physical Therapy. University of Southern California: Los Angeles.

36. Lunsford BR, Perry J. The standing heel-rise test for ankle plantar flexion: criterion for normal. *Phys Ther*. 1995;75:694–698.

37. Jan MH, Chai HM, Lin YF, et al. Effects of age and sex on the results of an ankle plantar-flexor manual muscle test. *Phys Ther*. 2005;85:1078–1084.

38. Yocum A, McCoy SW, Bjornson KF, et al. Reliability and validity of the standing heel-rise test. *Phys Occup Ther Pediatr*. 2012;30(3):http://informahealthcare.com/potp.

39. Farrag A, Elsayed W. Habitual use of high-heeled shoes affects isokinetic soleus strength more than gastrocnemius in healthy young females. *Foot Ankle Int*. 2016;37(9): 1008–1016.

40. Fujimoto M, Hsu WL, Woollacott MH, et al. Ankle dorsiflexor strength relates to the ability to restore balance during a backward support surface translation. *Gait Posture*. 2013;38(4):812–817.

41. Yoshida M, Taniguchi K, Katayose M. Analysis of muscle activity and ankle joint movement during the side-hop test. *JSCR*. 2011;25(8):2255–2264.

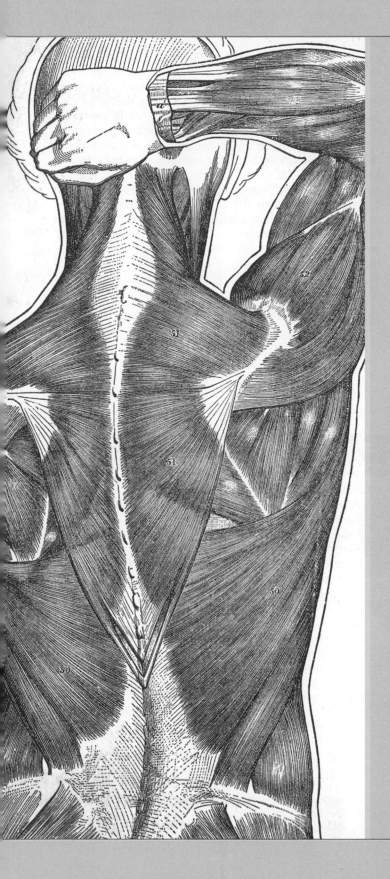

Alternatives to Manual Muscle Testing

CHAPTER 7

ALTERNATIVES TO MANUAL MUSCLE TESTING

INTRODUCTION

Manual muscle testing is a foundational measure of strength that is widely used across the health professions for both diagnosis and rehabilitation. Yet manual muscle testing has specific limitations, as discussed in Chapter 2. Consequently, alternative strength measures are needed in certain cases. Examples include: when strength exceeds a functional threshold, strength of the patient is greater than that of the therapist, subtle differences exist between sides or between the agonist and antagonist, or power or endurance need to be measured. Equipment-based tests are the most commonly used alternatives to manual muscle testing.

There are many options for equipment-based testing, and each has its advantages and disadvantages. Choosing the best option depends on clinic space constraints, available budget, the type of patient, the goals of treatment, and how comprehensive the evaluation needs to be. For example, in a small outpatient clinic where most patients have low back or neck pain, the approach to equipment-based testing will differ substantially from that required in most acute care settings. Strength-testing instruments that can be used effectively for children and older adults will differ from those used for a sports team. The equipment-based tests presented in this chapter represent the more popular approaches, are appropriate for adults regardless of age, and have demonstrated reliability and validity.

General Testing Considerations

It is presumed that any therapist conducting a strength-testing session, particularly one requiring maximal effort from a large muscle group, will perform a prescreening exam for red flag conditions. Maximal strength testing for the trunk flexors in a patient with severe osteoporosis or a recent compression fracture, for example, may not be appropriate. Likewise, patients with unstable blood pressure may have an adverse reaction while exerting maximum effort on a leg press, particularly if the patient—incorrectly—holds his or her breath. It is also presumed that muscular strength will be assessed after the patient has warmed up the muscle before testing. The typical warm-up includes completing three to five submaximal contractions at 40% to 50% of maximum using the muscle or muscle group that is being tested.[1] Active range of motion should be assessed to determine if adequate joint range and muscle length will allow maximum effort in the correct test position.

Tips for Achieving Optimal Results in Alternative Muscle Testing

Before starting any of the alternative muscle tests described in this chapter, have all the tools and data collection materials ready so recording proceeds smoothly. Efficiency in testing will grow with clinical experience.

1. Calibrate the device (if appropriate). Any device that records force or torque will drift away from accuracy over time. All testing devices should be routinely calibrated at least once a month, sometimes each session if deviations are suspected.
2. Provide a conducive test environment. The more diversions there are (such as radio noise or crowding), the more unlikely it is that an optimal effort will be made.
3. Once the patient is in the clinic, the first thing to do is educate the patient. Explain and demonstrate each test. Allow the patient to practice using light weights. This practice could be incorporated into the warm up (see below). Patient cooperation is critical for achieving accurate results.
4. Provide a warm-up of some sort. Some therapists will have their patients walk on a treadmill or pedal a stationary cycle for 5 min before muscles are tested. It is also feasible to warm up cold muscles by performing the test with three to five submaximal contractions

at 40% to 50% of maximum using the muscle or muscle group that is being tested, as described previously.
5. If there is suspected asymmetry in muscle performance, test the uninvolved side first. Side-to-side comparisons are critical, and testing the uninvolved side also permits the patient to "feel" what the test is going to entail on their weaker limb.
6. Stabilize the body part and patient. Depending on the test, each patient may need a seat belt, a stabilizing belt across the pelvis, or towels to position the arm or leg. After a part or extremity is stable, the test can be performed easily and accurately.
7. Standardize therapist commands to ensure that the test is performed the same way each time.
8. Allow patient to rest between efforts. No one can duplicate a maximum effort without at least 30 s of rest before the next repetition.
9. Provide feedback on the test. It is part of human nature to desire knowing if side-to-side differences exist, if test 1 is different from test 2, and so forth. Including the patient in the testing procedure optimizes their participation.

One-repetition Maximum Test

The one-repetition maximum (1-RM) test is regarded as the "gold standard" of standardized muscle strength testing. The 1-RM refers to the amount of load a patient can move 1 time (and 1 time only) through full range in a controlled manner with good form.[1] It is a safe technique, perhaps safer than a submaximum strength test, even though muscle soreness may occur and blood pressure may spike during a maximum exertion test.[2] 1-RM tests are highly reliable when specific procedures are followed, more so than any other type of strength assessment.[3] In addition, the fundamental method for establishing 1-RM is the same for each muscle group and thus the 1-RM test is more precise than most.

One-repetition maximum testing serves several functions. Obtaining a patient's maximum strength ability may serve to establish the amount of resistance needed for an exercise prescription; it may help to determine the progress of a progressive, resistive exercise program; or it may be used to compare a patient to established norms. Many normative values for men and women of all ages exist for movements such as bench press, latissimus dorsi pull-down, leg press, and knee extension and are included throughout this chapter.

Technique

There are several methods that can be used to determine a 1-RM. For patients with health conditions, especially known cardiovascular disease, or pulmonary or metabolic diseases, a conservative approach is recommended, such as a multiple RM, described later in this section. The technique described below is chosen because it works well in the clinic and is recommended by the American College of Sports Medicine (ACSM).[1] The basic steps for performing a 1-RM are as follows[1]:

1. Warm up by completing 3 to 5 submaximum repetitions. This warm-up also allows the patient to become familiar with the movement and the therapist to correct the form, if needed.
2. Select an initial weight that is within the patient's perceived capacity (~50%–70% of capacity).
3. Determine the 1-RM within four trials with rest periods of 3 to 5 minutes between tests.
4. Increments of weight should be increased by 5 to 10 lb until the patient cannot complete a repetition.

5. All repetitions should be performed at a constant and consistent rate of speed.
6. All repetitions should be performed through full range of motion (or the same range of motion if full range is not possible).

The final weight that the patient can move successfully 1 time only is recorded as the definitive 1-RM.

Selecting the Starting Weight

Selecting the amount of the starting weight is crucial because the fewer repetitions to reach 1-RM the better, to avoid muscular fatigue and to prevent an underestimation of the true 1-RM. It is helpful for the tester to have knowledge of norms. For example, standing from a chair requires quadriceps strength of nearly half a person's body weight, no matter what the age. Therefore, when performing a 1-RM using a leg press to test the quadriceps of a person who can successfully, but with difficulty stand from a chair without using one's arms, a starting weight might be 60% of patient's body weight. Alternatively, norms exist for the leg press based on age. These norms might present a starting point for establishing a 1-RM. Other variables that can be factored into the clinical decision of initial load are body size (muscular versus thin), fitness level, the presence of pain, and patient's self-perception of ability.

Other considerations that should be attended to during 1-RM testing include breathing, form, and pain. First and foremost, patients should *not* hold their breath during the test. Thus breath control should be practiced during the warm-ups. Second, the patient should maintain correct form throughout the test. For example, the patient should not be permitted to pitch the trunk forward during the knee extension test, to avoid muscle substitution or the use of momentum. Joint movements during the test should be executed smoothly and consistently throughout the entire concentric and eccentric phase, in a controlled manner without jerking the bar or weight. If the test causes pain, an alternative to the 1-RM test should be selected, such as a multiple repetition maximum test.

Multiple-repetition Maximum Test

A multiple-RM test is based on the principles of a 1-RM test. The multiple-RM test is the number of repetitions performed using good form and proper breath technique at the point of muscle failure. Although not as exact as a 1-RM, a multiple-RM test may be desirable for certain situations. For example, some untrained adults are not comfortable exerting the kind of effort necessary for a true 1-RM. A multiple-RM test may be a safer option when joint or soft tissues are compromised (e.g., connective tissue disease, rotator cuff tear, ligamentous injury, post surgery). For individuals without an exercise history and for patients who cannot tolerate high joint compression forces, such as those with osteoarthritis and rheumatoid arthritis, or with systemic weakness, the multiple-RM test, such as an 8- or 10-RM test is safer than the 1-RM test. Also, as mentioned above, a multiple-RM test is preferred if the patient has a health condition such as cardiovascular disease, or a pulmonary or metabolic condition.[1]

A 1-RM test can be estimated from a multiple-RM test (Table 7.1), although this estimation has been shown to be quite variable (Table 7.2).[4] The general principle is as the percentage of 1-RM increases, the number of repetitions decreases (Table 7.3). Large muscle group exercises allow the completion of more repetitions than small muscle groups at the same relative intensity.[5] Because the volume of work is greater with a 10-RM than a 1-RM, fatigue will be a factor. The 1-RM and multiple-RM tests can be performed using the same equipment.

The number of repetitions performed at a given percent of 1-RM is influenced by the amount of muscle mass available. For example, more repetitions can be performed during the back squat than either the bench press or arm curl.[5] The 4- to 6-RM is more accurate than the 10-RM. Variability in RM increases with decreased loads.[6]

The *kinetic chain* refers to all the muscles and joints that are involved in producing a given movement. For example, in gait, the kinetic chain consists of the trunk, hip, knee, and ankle. Most exercises and tasks involve more than one muscle group and joint, which work simultaneously to produce the movement. Exercises in the kinetic chain can be performed two ways, open and closed, referred to as open chain and closed chain.

Open chain exercises are performed such that the distal end of the kinetic chain is free to move. An example of an open chain activity is quadriceps knee extension sitting on a plinth where the leg moves from 90° of flexion to full extension.

Closed chain exercises are performed with the distal end of the kinetic chain fixed. An example of a closed chain exercise for the quadriceps is squatting. The knee is again moving through 90° of movement, but the leg is fixed in place and the thigh is moving over the fixed leg.

Table 7.1 ESTIMATING ONE-REPETITION MAXIMUM FROM A MULTIPLE-REPETITION MAXIMUM TEST

	GIVEN A 1-RM OF 100 POUNDS:									
	1-RM	2-RM	3-RM	4-RM	5-RM	6-RM	7-RM	8-RM	9-RM	10-RM
Multiple-RM loads are:	100	95	93	90	87	85	83	80	77	75

RM, Repetition maximum.

Table 7.2 NUMBER OF REPETITIONS PERFORMED AT 80% OF THE ONE-REPETITION MAXIMUM[4]

	TRAINED		UNTRAINED	
Exercise	Men	Women	Men	Women
Leg press	19	22	15	12
Lat pull-down	12	10	10	10
Bench press	12	14	10	10
Leg extension	12	10	9	8
Sit-up	12	12	8	7
Arm curl	11	7	8	6
Leg curl	7	5	6	6

Table 7.3 MAXIMUM WEIGHT THAT CAN BE LIFTED DECREASES WITH THE NUMBER OF REPETITIONS

Given:	1-RM	2-RM	3-RM	4-RM	5-RM	6-RM	7-RM	8-RM	9-RM	10-RM
The load would be (lb)	100	95	93	90	87	85	83	80	77	75
Number of repetitions	1	2	3	4	5	6	7	8	9	10

RM, Repetition maximum.

EQUIPMENT-BASED STRENGTH TESTING

Because practice patterns have changed extensively since the advent of manual muscle testing, methods to identify muscle weakness have also evolved. The days of polio-myelitis are behind us, and the need to identify deficiencies related to sports-related injuries, trauma, aging, and a host of other clinical conditions has resulted in the development of new and more specific testing techniques for the characterization of muscle weakness. This chapter segment will present an overview of some of the more popular approaches.

Equipment-based strength tests offer many advantages. The main advantage of using equipment (such as a strength-testing device) for repetition maximum testing is that the stability afforded by the device is far greater than in manual muscle testing and thus allows for highly controlled, single-plane movements and increased patient safety. In addition, normative data for many movements are available with equipment-based testing. The disadvantages of using equipment for testing are they take up space and may not be readily available, can test only one plane of movement, and can test only a finite number of muscle groups.

Interpretation of Equipment-Based Strength Testing Data

Equipment-based strength testing data are informative only if used in context with other clinical findings. For example, if the therapist identifies side-to-side strength differences for shoulder flexion in conjunction with difficulty lifting or the presence of pain on the weaker side, the therapist's clinical decision-making is enhanced and treatment can be confidently and competently applied. If gait speed is slow and there is evidence of gait deviation, equipment-based strength testing will help to inform the therapist about the reasons for the deviation and thus enhance treatment planning. Equipment-based strength testing, as with manual muscle testing, is only as good as the technique applied and is useful only in conjunction with other important functional findings. Clinical competence develops with practice, practice, and more practice, which includes all testing procedures, particularly those that provide information about strength deficits. Investing the time to learn correct testing procedures results in improved treatment planning, more targeted goal setting, better documentation of the patient's status and rate of improvement, and greater success in receiving reimbursements from health care providers.

Sitting Unilateral Knee Extension Test

Purpose: The sitting unilateral knee extension test is used primarily to determine quadriceps strength when the strength of the patient exceeds the strength of the therapist. If manual muscle testing reveals Grade 4 or better strength with the therapist's maximum resistance, the test cannot discriminate whether strength is greater than Grade 4 or Grade 5 and manual resistance is insufficient to elicit a maximum patient effort. Therefore the sitting unilateral knee extension test can be used to distinguish side-to-side differences in quadriceps force output and elicit a true maximum effort.

Position of Patient: Seated comfortably on a knee extension machine that has been adjusted for leg length. If necessary, padding may be placed beneath the thigh being tested, for patient's comfort.

The resistance pad should be positioned at distal third of tibia. A seat belt may be placed around the patient's pelvis, if needed, to provide stability (Fig. 7.1; seat belt not shown in figure).

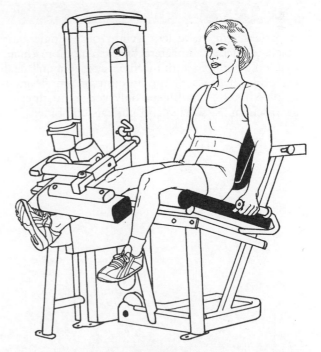

FIGURE 7.1

Sitting Unilateral Knee Extension Test
Continued

Instructions to Therapist: To achieve a 1-RM, select an initial weight from the weight stack, based on the screening exam. A good place to start is approximately 25% of body weight if the screening exam verifies the patient can stand unassisted. Note that the weight lifted will be less than on a leg press machine. Standing at the side of patient, with patient sitting and arms at sides, holding the handles, have patient completely extend the knee through full range of motion with the selected weight. If successful, after a minimum 60-second rest, another repetition with a higher weight is performed through full range of motion. After the load cannot be moved through full range or patient loses form, patient is asked to perform another repetition at that weight, after the appropriate rest period, to verify muscle failure and confirm that patient cannot complete another repetition.

Instructions to Patient: "Lift the weighted bar, completely straightening your knee."

Scoring

Record the highest weight the patient lifted 1 time to reach full knee extension for a 1-RM. The multiple RM is recorded as the weight lifted at last repetition and the number of repetitions the patient performed at that weight to achieve muscle failure. (Note: Knee extension through full range of motion, particularly the last 15° to 0°, must be achieved for a successful test.)

Helpful Hints

- A patient will move less weight on a single-joint machine, such as a unilateral knee extension machine, than on a multiple-joint machine, such as a unilateral leg press, because of the amount of muscle mass involved (e.g., quadriceps-only versus quadriceps, gastrocnemius/soleus, and gluteals combined).

Leg Press Test

The leg press machine is one of the most useful devices in a clinic as it is a closed chain activity, thus mimicking a common aspect of function such as standing, walking, and rising from a chair. The force output generated by a patient will tell the therapist whether a patient has enough strength to be functional in activities of daily living or with sport activities requiring a large amount of strength, such as soccer.

Purpose: The leg press assesses the force output of all extensor muscles in the lower extremities (hip and knee extensors and plantar-flexors).

Position of Patient: Seated comfortably on leg press machine, with head and spine in contact with seat back, both feet on the foot plate, approximately 12 in. apart, knees bent approximately 90° over the hips and in line with feet (avoid knees dropping toward each other in hip adduction), and hands on grab bars (Fig. 7.2). Feet on the footplate in either the low position (Fig. 7.3) or the high foot position (see Fig. 7.2).

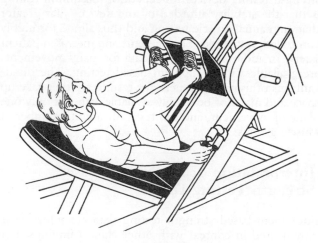

FIGURE 7.2

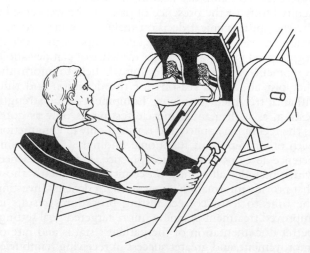

FIGURE 7.3

Leg Press Test Continued

Instructions to Therapist: Ensure the patient has painless and sufficient hip, knee, and ankle range to perform the test and is warmed up sufficiently. Select the initial weight that is 50% to 70% of capacity (see Table 7.4 for leg press norms), and ask the patient to fully extend the legs with feet against the footplate so that shins are parallel with the floor. The knees should be softly extended at the end of the push (avoid a "locked out" position). Note: Some leg press machines require therapist to place weights on either side of the footplate bar (e.g., two 25-lb weights) and lock the weights in place. Other machines will require the patient to sit upright. Obtain 1-RM.

Instructions to Patient: "Push the plate until your legs are straight. Don't hold your breath during the test or lock your knees out. Keep your knees in line with your feet."

Scoring

Record the highest weight patient can push 1 time (for 1-RM) or for a multiple RM, the weight achieved, and number of repetitions with the end weight that produced muscle failure.

Helpful Hints

- The leg press uses the closed chain approach (distal end of the kinetic chain is fixed).
- Foot position low on the plate (see Fig. 7.3) elicits greater muscle activity from the rectus femoris and gastrocnemius at 80% 1-RM than high foot position (see Fig. 7.2), suggesting that the feet should routinely be positioned low on the plate when using a 40% or 80% 1-RM.[7]
- The high foot position elicits gluteus maximus more than low foot position.[7]
- Not all patients can comfortably assume a low-foot position; in terms of importance, comfort should outweigh desired muscle activation.
- There are established norms for leg press for men and women ages 20 through early 60s, which is hardly comprehensive of all age groups. Nonetheless, it is important to understand what should be expected in terms of "normal" strength. Norms are expressed as a ratio of force output to body weight. Thus a typical ratio for a young woman in her twenties is 2.05, meaning that she should be able to generate force equivalent to twice her body weight. Normative data for the leg press compiled from hundreds of men and women that have been tested by the Cooper Institute are presented in Table 7.4.

Table 7.4 LEG PRESS NORMS FOR MEN AND WOMEN IN VARIOUS AGE GROUPS; VALUES REFLECT ONE-REPETITION MAXIMUM/BODY WEIGHT

Percentile	20-29 YEARS		30-39 YEARS		40-49 YEARS		50-59 YEARS		60+ YEARS	
	Men	Women	Men	Women	Men	Women	Men	Women	Men	Women
90th	2.27	2.05	2.07	1.73	1.92	1.63	1.80	1.51	1.73	1.40
80th	2.13	1.66	1.93	1.50	1.82	1.46	1.71	1.30	1.62	1.25
70th	2.05	1.42	1.85	1.47	1.74	1.35	1.64	1.24	1.56	1.18
60th	1.97	1.36	1.77	1.32	1.68	1.26	1.58	1.18	1.49	1.15
50th	1.91	1.32	1.71	1.26	1.62	1.19	1.52	1.09	1.43	1.08
40th	1.83	1.25	1.65	1.21	1.57	1.12	1.46	1.03	1.38	1.04
30th	1.74	1.23	1.59	1.16	1.51	1.03	1.39	0.95	1.30	0.98
20th	1.63	1.13	1.52	1.09	1.44	0.94	1.32	0.86	1.25	0.94
10th	1.51	1.02	1.43	0.94	1.35	0.76	1.22	0.75	1.16	0.84

Descriptors for percentile rankings: 90, well above average; 70, above average; 50, average; 30, below average; 10, well below average.

Data for men provided by The Cooper Institute for Aerobics Research, The Physical Fitness Specialist Manual. Dallas, TX, 2005; http://hk.humankinetics.com/AdvancedFitnessAssessmentandExercisePrescription/IG/269618.indd.pdf; and Data for women provided by the Women's Exercise Research Center, The George Washington University Medical Center, Washington, DC, 1998.

Latissimus Dorsi Pull-Down Test

The latissimus dorsi pull-down test (lat pull-down test) is a general measure of bilateral scapular adduction and scapular downward rotation. The lat pull-down machine is commonly available in clinics, wellness centers, and workout facilities. The test is one of the safest and easiest to perform of all upper extremity exercises. This test is feasible for most adults without shoulder or neck problems.

Purpose: To measure the collective force of the latissimus dorsi muscles, rhomboids, and middle and lower trapezius.

Position of Patient: Seated, facing the weight stack, feet flat on floor. Arms overhead with hands on bar in overhand grip (pronation) (Fig. 7.4). Head position should be over shoulders, with attention to avoiding a forward head position. Forearms in supination (underhand grip) is easier (not shown).

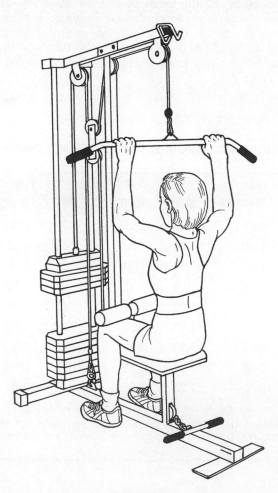

FIGURE 7.4

Instructions to Therapist: Ensure the patient has no shoulder pain and sufficient elbow range to perform the test. Bring the overhead bar to the patient. Hands placed on the bar should be in an overhand grip with hands slightly wider than shoulders. Select a weight based on the initial physical therapy screening that is relatively easy (e.g., can patient pull against manual resistance easily?), such as 20 lb for a woman and 40 lb for a man. Adjust the soft pad above the thighs so that it is comfortable and contributes to stability. The therapist then stands behind the patient to monitor the position of the scapulae. Correct form is when the bar is pulled down to shoulder height in front of the body with shoulders retracted (scapular adduction and downward rotation) and leaning slightly backwards. The position of pulling down in front of the head provides the greatest activation of the latissimus dorsi.[8] Depending on performance of the first repetition, increase or decrease weight as indicated to achieve a 1- or multiple RM.

Instructions to Patient: "In a smooth manner, pull the bar down in front of you level with your shoulders, while pulling your shoulder blades back and down. Don't hold your breath."

Scoring

Record the highest weight and number of repetitions the patient performs without losing form for a 1-RM or multiple RM. Norms for the latissimus pull-down activity are typically 66% of body weight for young men and 50% of body weight for young women.[9] Norms for men and women who are middle-aged and older have not been established.

Free Weights Testing

Free weights are the gold standard for reliability and validity of the 1-RM method because of their ease of application and specificity. They offer important advantages for muscle testing, such as permitting therapist to assess strength in both the concentric and eccentric modes. Free weights are readily available in any clinical setting and are readily accessible in the home, where household items can easily be substituted for weights. They can also be used through full range and through multiple planes.

Moreover, movements with free weights require greater motor coordination and better balance (if standing), resulting in greater muscle recruitment. They use important stabilizing muscles to complete a lift, compared with machines, which do not emphasize the stabilizing musculature because movements occur in only one plane of motion. And they allow the therapist the freedom to test different movement variations that can inform an exercise prescription.

However, several disadvantages of using free weights exist. Greater control is required through all planes of movement because of the stabilization required. Free weights can challenge the entire kinetic chain, thus stressing the "weakest link" rather than the targeted muscle or movement, unless proper stabilization is provided. Maximum muscle loading occurs only at the weakest point in the range, thus requiring an attentive therapist. Proper positioning is critical for safety and test reliability. Spotting is necessary because the weight can be unexpectedly dropped, potentially causing injury.

Examples of Free-Weights Testing

Biceps Curl

The biceps curl is an example of using free weights to determine a 1-RM or multiple RM. In this instance the biceps, brachialis, and brachioradialis are the muscles that will be challenged, particularly the biceps and brachialis. This test can easily discern side-to-side differences and whether strength is adequate for lifting during work.

Purpose: To determine maximum force capability of the biceps brachii and brachialis, as well as the brachioradialis and, to less extent, the pronator teres muscles.

Position of Patient: Either standing or seated comfortably in a standard chair with no arms. Provide seat belt if needed. Elbow should be straight, with arm at the side, forearm supinated. Standing requires stabilization of the trunk, which may be a more functional position although more difficult.

Instructions to Therapist: Based on prescreening, which may include questions such as "can you easily carry a bag of groceries" (approximately 10 lb) or "how much do you normally curl," and determination that full range of motion can be achieved painlessly, the therapist should

select a weight that is reasonably challenging, generally 50% more than what is routinely lifted. Standing next to the patient, place the weight in the patient's hand with the forearm supinated and ask the patient to flex the elbow through full range of motion in a supinated position (Fig. 7.5). After a rest of a minimum of 60 seconds, increase or decrease weight in appropriate intervals based on performance to achieve a 1-RM or multiple RM.

Instructions to Patient: "While holding the weight, bend your elbow until the weight touches your upper arm."

Scoring

Record 1-RM or multiple RM. Normative strength is approximately 25% of body weight for women and 33% of body weight for men.[6]

Note: The incremental increase in weight lifted is far less for the upper extremity compared with the lower extremity because of the difference in muscle mass.

A hammer curl is performed in the same manner but keeping the forearm in a neutral position with hand towards body.

Bench Press Test

The bench press is one of the most popular tests of upper extremity strength because it provides a composite value for many muscles, similar to the leg press.

Purpose: To achieve a repetition maximum while maximally challenging the larger anterior scapulohumeral muscles: pectoralis major, pectoralis minor, anterior deltoid, infraspinatus, serratus anterior, and upper and lower trapezius. In addition, the triceps brachii is critical to extend the elbow.

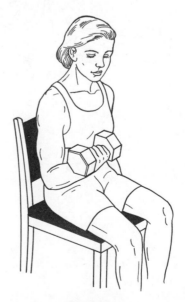

FIGURE 7.5

Examples of Free-Weights Testing Continued

Position of Patient: Supine on the testing bench, back flat against bench with feet flat on the floor. Nipple line is directly below the weight bar. Hand position is pronated (overhand grip) and slightly wider than shoulders (Fig. 7.6).

Instructions to Therapist: Prescreen the patient to ensure the presence of full, painless range. Observe the patient's muscle bulk, and ask prescreening questions such as "Do you chest press regularly?" Then select two equal weight plates and place them at each end of the bench press bar, locking the weights in place. Provide for a warm-up period. Once warmed up, adjust weight to approximately 40% of body weight for women and 50% body weight for men. Be sure to consider the weight of the bar itself, which often is 40 lb.

Stand at the patient's head to "spot" the patient throughout the movement (see Fig. 7.6). Have the patient grasp the bar with a pronated grip. At a signal from the patient, assist the patient in moving the bar off the supports and lowering the bar directly over the chest. Release the bar smoothly after you are confident the patient is in control of the bar. Ask the patient to lower the bar to the nipple level, keeping head flat against bench. Then ask the patient to push the bar overhead until the elbows are fully extended. The back should not extend (come off the bench). The weight is either decreased (if first attempt is not successful) or increased if the patient indicates multiple repetitions can be performed. Provide the patient a minimum of 60 seconds of rest between lifts. Test failure is observed when the patient is unable to complete full range of motion. At test failure, grasp the bar with alternating overhand and underhand grips (see Fig. 7.6), and place it on the rack supports.

Instructions to Patient: "Lower the weight slowly and smoothly, then push the bar straight up overhead until your elbows are completely straight. Do not hold your breath. Be sure to tell me if you need assistance with the bar."

Scoring

Record 1-RM or multiple RM . The norms for men and women are listed in Table 7.5.

FIGURE 7.6

Helpful Hints

- Many bench press bars weigh up to 40 lb, and this must be taken into consideration when determining ultimate load.
- It may be necessary for the therapist to take the weight bar away from the patient at test failure, so the therapist should be sure (in advance) that he or she is physically capable of handling the weight bar being lifted.
- If there is no weight bench and the patient is lying on a plinth, the therapist must place the fully loaded lifting bar into position above the patient, again approximately 6 in. above the chest at nipple level. Help may be needed if the therapist is unable to handle the loaded weight bar. "Spotting" the patient is even more important in this adaptation of the bench press.

Table 7.5 BENCH PRESS NORMS BY GENDER AND AGE VALUES REFLECT ONE-REPETITION MAXIMUM/BODY WEIGHT (IN POUNDS)

Percentile	20-29 YEARS Men	Women	30-39 YEARS Men	Women	40-49 YEARS Men	Women	50-59 YEARS Men	Women	60+ YEARS Men	Women	70+ YEARS Women
90th	1.48	0.54	1.24	0.49	1.10	0.46	0.97	0.40	0.89	0.41	0.44
80th	1.32	0.49	1.12	0.45	1.00	0.40	0.90	0.37	0.82	0.38	0.39
70th	1.22	0.42	1.04	0.42	0.93	0.38	0.84	0.35	0.77	0.36	0.33
60th	1.14	0.41	0.98	0.41	0.88	0.37	0.79	0.33	0.72	0.32	0.31
50th	1.06	0.40	0.93	0.38	0.84	0.34	0.75	0.31	0.68	0.30	0.27
40th	0.99	0.37	0.88	0.37	0.80	0.32	0.71	0.28	0.66	0.29	0.25
30th	0.93	0.35	0.83	0.34	0.76	0.30	0.68	0.26	0.63	0.28	0.24
20th	0.88	0.33	0.78	0.32	0.72	0.27	0.63	0.23	0.57	0.26	0.21
10th	0.80	0.30	0.71	0.27	0.65	0.23	0.57	0.19	0.53	0.25	0.20

Descriptors for percentile rankings: 90, well above average; 50, average; 30, below average; and 10, well below average.

Data for women are derived from the Women's Exercise Research Center, The George Washington University Medical Center, Washington, DC, 1998; and Data for men were provided by the Cooper Institute for Aerobics Research, The Physical Fitness Specialist Manual, Dallas, TX, 2005.

Isokinetic Testing

Isokinetic testing was developed in the 1960s and has gained popularity, especially for research, because of its objectivity. The advantages of isokinetic testing for evaluating muscle strength and contraction speed include testing through a spectrum of movement speeds (e.g., 0° to 400° per second), providing highly reliable data, and providing safety in testing by ensuring movement control. Most importantly, isokinetic machines (e.g., Cybex, Biodex, KinCom) allow maximal resistance throughout the entire range of motion, something that no other testing method can provide. Eccentric strength can also be objectively assessed.

The disadvantages of isokinetic testing include:
- The prohibitive cost and space requirements of the oversized testing equipment
- The time required to set up the tests
- The fact that only single planes of movement can be tested

- The fact that many sports-specific movements are faster than any isokinetic machine
- The fact that isokinetic contractions are nonphysiologic

An isokinetic machine allows the speed to remain constant but the force generated through the range is not consistent, which means that muscle demand (percentage of force required) is highly variable throughout the range of motion. To use the knee extensors as an example, under physiologic conditions, quadriceps strength demand is greatest at the end of the range, where length-tension and the patella lever-arm are poorest.

Although the setup for isokinetic testing is protocol driven, the actual test execution requires skill, computer interaction, and know-how that is beyond the scope of this book. For complete instruction in isokinetic testing, the reader is referred to the remarkable amount of material on the internet and the instruction booklets from the makers of isokinetic machines and instrumentation.[10]

Elastic Band Testing

Elastic band testing is a common form of strength testing that uses elastic resistance that is color coded according to level of resistance. Resistance of the band is based on the amount and kind of material used in the band. Thicker bands provide more resistance. Some bands use a polymerized synthetic rubber, whereas others use a natural rubber latex (TheraBand) that may provide better elasticity and lower susceptibility to rupture. The force of elastic resistance depends on its percentage of elongation, regardless of initial length. The elastic band should be the same length as the lever arm being tested to ensure elongation remains less than 200%.[11] For example, if the length of the patient's leg, from hip to heel, is 50 in., then a band of 50 in. should be used. Force elongation in pounds for 100% elongation of TheraBand elastic bands is listed in Table 7.6.

In addition to elastic band availability in nearly all clinics and ease of application for home use, there are several other advantages to elastic band testing. Elastic bands produce a curvilinear length-tension profile, which can be used to challenge the end range, potentially producing a higher peak force than might be achieved with a free weight or machine.[12] Elastic bands increase the agonist-antagonist cocontraction, challenging stability. Eccentric contractions are especially challenged with elastic bands. Patients receive immediate feedback about their progress because the color of band changes according to strength increases. The cost of bands is low compared with other methods of strength testing. Any movement can be tested, with a little creativity.

Disadvantages of elastic band testing include the need for stabilization and the patient's muscle activation is at the weakest link in the kinetic chain, as mentioned with free weights. Greater force is required with elongation of the band, which may prohibit correct performance. There is difficulty standardizing elements of band elongation and the patient and/or extremity positioning, and quantifying test interpretation is dependent on the manufacturer. For example, if you have two patients and one patient abducts the hip only 10° against a gray elastic band (high strength demand) whereas another abducts the hip 20° against a green elastic band (low strength demand), which patient has more strength? Strength indexes help to standardize this issue; however, they are widely known only for TheraBand elastic bands.[13] Different manufacturers use different color codes, and published strength indexes are not interchangeable.

For safety, test positions can be adapted. For example, testing of the elbow flexors can be done with the patient sitting or standing. See Fig. 7.7 for an illustration of elastic band testing used to test shoulder abduction strength.

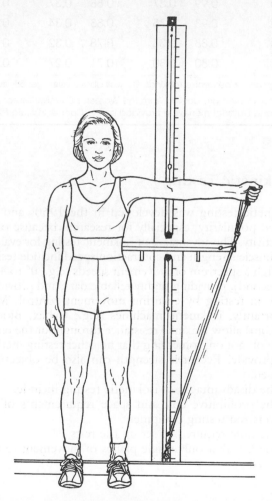

FIGURE 7.7

Table 7.6 FORCE ELONGATION FOR THERABAND ELASTIC BANDS AT 100% ELONGATION (VALUE = FORCE IN POUNDS)

Elongation (%)	Yellow	Red	Green	Blue	Black	Gray	Gold
100 (twice the length of the band)	3	4	5 -4	5.8	7.3	10.2	14.2

The percentage of elongation (change in length) is calculated with the following formula:

Percentage of elongation
= (final length) – (resting length)/(resting length) × 100.

http://www.thera-bandacademy.com/resource/x-showResource.aspx?id=5534.

Example of Elastic Band Testing

Testing the Shoulder Abductors

Purpose: To test the maximum strength of the shoulder abductors (deltoid and rotator cuff). Muscles also involved are the serratus anterior and upper/lower trapezius to upwardly rotate the scapula to support the humerus.

Position of Patient: Standing. If patient cannot stand, the test can be performed in sitting.

Instructions to Therapist: Before patient testing, shoulder abduction should be assessed for available range and the absence of pain. To assess strength, a color elastic band based on prescreening is selected for use. In general, a medium band is feasible for most trained patients who are without shoulder pain. Measure the band so that it is the same length as the length of the arm. Secure one end to an immovable object or knot the end and have the patient stand on the end of the band with knot on the inside of the foot. Stand to the side and slightly behind patient. Ask patient to hold the other end of band, with any slack in band removed. Ask the patient to lift the arm into 90° of abduction to height of shoulder, keeping the hand/forearm pronated and the elbow straight. At this position, the band should be elongated 2× (100%) its original length. Then ask the patient to slowly lower the arm (generally 3× slower than the lifting phase). Decrease the resistance color of the band if the patient is unable to complete full range or has discomfort, and increase resistance if the patient can perform multiple repetitions. Therapist should monitor form to include stabilization of the trunk, head and neck position, pronation of the forearm/hand, and scapular adduction and downward rotation.

Instructions to Patient: "Lift your arm out and away from the side of your body to the height of your shoulder. Keep your elbow straight and hand pointed down. Don't hold your breath during the test."

Scoring

Record the color of the band used to complete a full 90° of abduction and how many repetitions were performed to muscle failure, if more than one repetition was completed. Consult appropriate chart for force in pounds (depending on manufacturer of band). Force elongation for 100% elongation of TheraBand elastic bands as described by the manufacturer is listed in Table 7.6.

Helpful Hints

- Some companies sell handles to attach to the end of the band, thus making it more feasible for patients to use the band.
- With repeated use and age of the band, elastic bands lose their elasticity and/or become brittle and should be replaced. Bands should always be inspected for small tears or holes that may weaken the band and cause it to break during elongation. Periodic calibration will determine if it is time to discard the original band.
- If the therapist underestimated the strength of the patient, the patient's force may overcome the elastic properties of the band and cause it to break, creating a potentially unpleasant and unsafe condition.

Isometric Cable Tensiometry Testing

A cable tensiometer is an objective and precise device that can be used to measure isometric muscle contraction. The cable gauge (dynamometer) is attached to a static object and to the distal end of the limb. No limb movement is allowed. Advantages of cable tensiometry include the numerical data that are produced from the patient's efforts and reproducibility of repeat tests and the isometric nature of the test, which makes this type of instrumentation safer than most. Disadvantages of cable tensiometry are its lack of availability and only one muscle group in one plane can be tested. Consequently, only a limited number of muscle groups can be tested using this method.

Squat Test

Purpose: To assess maximum isometric strength of the quads, hip, and back extensors (primary movers)

Position of Patient: Stand facing the tensiometer with feet shoulder width apart. Knees should be bent approximately 110°. Arms should hang down naturally to grasp handle in an overhand grip (pronated). In this position the back should be bent slightly forward at the hips, the head should be held upright, and the patient should look straight ahead.

Instructions to Therapist: Attach tensiometer to the floor or to an immobile object that can be stabilized on the floor. Reset the dial to zero. With the patient standing with arms hanging down, adjust the chain so that the knees are bent at approximately 110° with no slack in the chain. Ask the patient to grab the bar in an overhand grip and to pull it as hard as possible in a smooth motion (Fig. 7.8). The pull should be held between 3 and 5 seconds. Reset the needle on the tensiometer dial back to zero, and repeat the test a second time.

Instructions to Patient: "Pull the bar up as hard as you can. Now pull a little harder."

Scoring

Average the two trials or record the highest value.

Summary

Except for the leg press, the procedures presented in this chapter are either isometric or concentric and patients are tested using the open chain approach. Day-to-day function requires performance of activities using a closed chain approach (e.g., sitting down or climbing stairs). Activities that include multiple joints are often multiplanar, require some degree of balance, and are speed dependent. There are few instrumented options available for specifically and accurately assessing strength using the closed chain functional approach, but change is likely on the horizon. Currently, power and functional tests are the best options for use in the clinical setting.

FIGURE 7.8

POWER TESTING

Power testing, also known as maximal anaerobic power testing, was initially developed to assess explosive strength in a sports setting. Maximal power is defined as force per unit of time, and thus a power measure includes not just muscular force production but the rate of force development. The specific formula for power is:

$$Power = work/seconds$$

Powerful athletes can accelerate rapidly with explosive force output (e.g., the Olympic 100-m dash). In addition, the rate of force development may be the critical determinant of a person's safety, especially in unexpected or emergency situations. For example, a patient must go from gas pedal to brake quickly enough to prevent a crash. Another important reason for rapid force development is to prevent a fall. Once a person loses balance, only the power of rapid limb movement can rescue the individual. Recently, power has been identified as a major determinant of functional impairment in the older adult and is now considered even more important than strength (e.g., in the chair rise).[14] Thus power is an important aspect of muscle performance.

Power testing is in its infancy. Although the concept of power determination has been around for half a century, actual tests for its measurement are limited. It is expected that more tests for power will be developed in the future or adaptations of existing tests will be made to include patients with muscular weakness and poor muscular endurance.

The power tests in the next section have been selected because they do not require special equipment or extensive preparation. In addition, these tests require maximum muscle power. Because maximal muscular activity is involved in performing power tests, they are anaerobic and are of short duration.

Margaria-Kalamen Stair Sprint Test[15]

Since the early 1960s, numerous adaptations of the original Margaria stair sprint test[15] have been made as the relevance and importance of power testing has become evident. Modified versions include running two stairs at a time and shortening the starting distance. Regardless, the test is of short duration (lasting less than 5 seconds). It is considered a standard test for determining peak power. A disadvantage of the test is that typically only the young and healthy can perform it.

Purpose: To measure maximal anaerobic strength and power of the lower extremities.

Test Instructions[16]: Ensure the patient can safely negotiate nine stairs, three steps at a time. Weigh patient in kilograms. Each stair should be 17.5 cm (~7 in.) tall. The therapist should stand at the bottom of the stairs to monitor the effort. A timer start switch mechanism is placed on the third step, and a stop switch mechanism placed on the ninth step. With the patient positioned 6 meters (20 ft) from the bottom stair, ask the patient to run towards stairs, taking three steps at a time at maximal speed. Repeat the test 2× with a 3-minute recovery period between each trial.

Scoring

The time from third- to ninth-step contact is determined to the nearest 0.01 seconds using the timing system. Power in watts is calculated according to the following formula:

$$\text{Power (in watts)} = \text{Weight (body weight in kg)} \times 9.807 \times \text{Vertical height of six stairs in meters (step 3–step 9)/Time (seconds)}$$

Example: Mark weighs 210 lb and scored a best attempt of 1.2 seconds when climbing six steps with a combined height of 49.5 inches.

$$210 \, lb = 95.25 \, kg$$

$$\text{Vertical height} = 17.5 \, cm \, stairs \times 6 = 1.05 \, meters$$

$$\text{Power} = (92.25 \times 9.807) \times 1.05)/1.2 = 831 \, watts$$

Normative data are described in Table 7.7.

Table 7.7 MARGARIA-KALAMEN STAIR SPRINT TEST NORMATIVE DATA (WATTS)

	AGE GROUPS (YEARS)									
	15-20		20-30		30-40		40-50		Over 50	
Classification	M	F	M	F	M	F	M	F	M	F
Excellent	Over 2197	Over 1785	Over 2059	Over 1648	Over 1648	Over 1226	Over 1226	Over 961	Over 961	Over 736
Good	1844-2197	1491-1785	1726-2059	1383-1648	1383-1648	1040-1226	1040-1226	814-961	814-961	608-736
Average	1471-1824	1187-1481	1373-1716	1098-1272	1098-1373	834-1030	834-1030	647-804	647-804	481-598
Fair	1108-1461	902-1177	1040-1363	834-1089	834-1088	637-824	637-824	490-637	490-637	373-471
Poor	Under 1108	Under 902	Under 1040	Under 834	Under 834	Under 637	Under 637	Under 490	Under 490	Under 373

Data from Hoffman, J. (2006). Norms for fitness, Performance, and Health. Champaign, Ill.: Human Kinetics. Adapted from Fox, E., Bowers, R., & Foss, M. (1993). The Physiological Basis for Exercise and Sport (5th ed.). Dubuque, Iowa: Wm C. Brown, 676, with permission of the McGraw-Hill Companies; based on data from Kalamen, J. (1968). Measurement of Maximum Muscular Power in Man, Doctoral Dissertation, The Ohio State University, and Margaria, R., Aghemo, I., & Rovelli, E. (1966). Measurement of muscular power (anaerobic) in man. Journal of Applied Physiology, 21, 1662-1664.

Medicine Ball Throw Test

Purpose: To determine the power of important scapulothoracic and glenohumeral muscles, particularly the pectoralis major and minor, anterior deltoid, supraspinatus, and infraspinatus.

Test Instructions: With the patient seated, assess the ability of the patient to throw a medicine ball from the chest.[16a] Weight of the ball usually ranges from 1.5 to 4 kg. Athletes perform this test seated on the floor with legs extended in front and back against the wall. If the patient can perform the task, place a 1.5 to 4-kg ball in patient's hands close to the chest (like a basketball) (Fig. 7.9A). Ask the patient to push the ball forward as rapidly as possible. An alternate method is depicted in Fig. 7.9B. In this instance, the patient throws the ball using an overhead technique. Either technique is acceptable.

Scoring

The test is repeated 3 times. Record the maximum or average distance from the front of the chair to where the medicine ball lands. No normative data exist and scores depend on the weight of the ball. However, the top score in the 2013 NHL Combine using a 4-kg ball was 6.25 meters (sitting on the floor).[16b] Older men and women (mean age 72.4 years) threw a 1.5 kg ball a range of 2 to 6 meters and a 3-kg ball a range of 2 to 4.5 meters.[16a]

Shot Put Test

Purpose: As with the medicine ball throw, the shot put test challenges the musculature of the glenohumeral and scapulothoracic muscles. However, the test is unilateral, which permits side-to-side comparisons. Because the test is done standing, it also challenges balance. The test can also been done sitting, similar to the two-handed medicine ball throw test.

Test Instructions: Assess the patient's ability to throw a shot put from overhead. If the patient can perform the test, select a "shot" that is appropriate for patient (1–7 kg). The therapist then places the shot put in the patient's hand. Ask the patient to bring the shot put to the shoulder, then rapidly thrust the shot put away from body as far as possible. The technique requires the patient momentarily balancing the shot put on the shoulder and chin (Fig. 7.10). The trial is repeated 3 times and the furthest distance recorded.

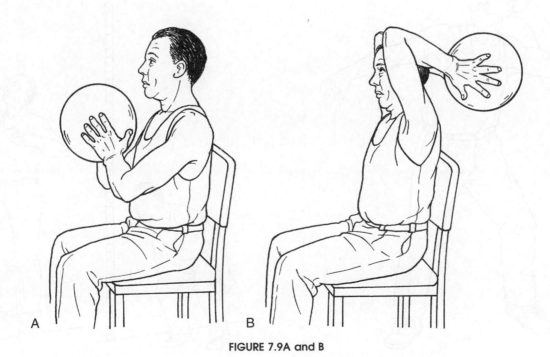

FIGURE 7.9A and B

Shot Put Test Continued

Scoring

The trial is repeated 3 times and the furthest distance recorded. No normative data exist; however, distances of more than 20 meters have been recorded for female and male athletes.

Alternative Shot Put Test: Standing and using two hands, the patient leans forward, brings the shot down between the legs, and throws the shot forward as far as possible. The throw is underhand instead of overhand and involves both arms instead of just one. This test is easier for the patient to perform. To score, record the distances of the effort.

Vertical Jump Test

Purpose: The vertical jump test assesses maximum muscle power and strength. It specifically challenges the extensors of the lower extremity, particularly the gluteus maximus and minimus, the hamstrings, quadriceps, gastrocnemius, and soleus. Only those with adequate balance can perform the test.

Test Instructions: Tape a yardstick or piece of paper with height markings onto the wall. The therapist chalks the patient's fingers on the dominant hand. Ask the patient to reach as high as possible with the dominant hand, touching the wall while keeping the feet flat. Note chalk mark that serves as starting position. Standing flat-footed without preparation, ask the patient to jump as high as possible, swinging arms backwards before reaching overhead, touching dominant, chalked hand to wall (Fig. 7.11). The patient may flex knees and hips with jump. Repeat test.

Scoring

The total distance jumped is recorded, which is the highest mark minus the initial mark. Score the best of the two trials. Normative data are listed in Table for athletes in various sports (Table 7.8).

FIGURE 7.10

FIGURE 7.11

Table 7.8 VERTICAL JUMP DESCRIPTIVE DATA FOR VARIOUS GROUPS

Group, Sport, or Position	Vertical Jump (in./cm)
NCAA Division I college football split ends, strong safeties, offensive and defensive backs	31.5/80
NCAA Division I college football wide receivers and outside linebackers	31/79
NCAA Division I football linebackers, tight ends, and safeties	29.5/75
NCAA Division I college football quarterbacks	28.5/72
NCAA Division I college basketball players (men)	28/71
High school football backs and receivers	24/61
College baseball players (men)	23/58
College tennis players (men)	23/58
17 year-old boys	20/51
NCAA Division I college basketball (girls)	17.5-19/44-48
18-34 year-old men	16/41
18-34 year-old sedentary women	8/20
17 year-old girls	13/33

NCAA, National Collegiate Athletic Association.

NSCA Essentials of Strength Training and Conditioning, ed 3, p. 278.

Hop and Standing Long Jump Tests

There are several variations on long jump power tests. As depicted in Fig. 7.12, the tests can be done on one leg, alternating from side to side or on both (Fig. 7.13). For a more challenging examination (done frequently in athletic training centers), the patient is required to clear an obstacle with each jump, with some obstacles being ≥18 in.

Purpose: To test the power of the lower extremity extensors and pelvic stabilizers, particularly the gluteals, quadriceps, and plantar flexors. Patients require adequate abdominals and balance control.

Test Instructions: For both tests, measure a 20-foot long area. Draw line on the floor as the starting position.

Single hop test: Ensure that the patient can balance easily on dominant leg. If able, ask the patient to stand on the line with feet just behind the line. Then ask the patient to leap upward and forward on dominant leg, completing three consecutive single leg hops (see Fig. 7.12). The total distance achieved in the three hops is measured and recorded.

Standing long jump: With both feet behind the starting line, ask the patient to jump 1 time, as far forward as possible (see Fig. 7.13). The patient must land on both feet for the jump to be scored. Measure from the starting line to the patient's heel. Repeat for two trials.

Scoring

Hop Jump: The cumulative total distance achieved in the three hops is recorded.

Standing Long Jump: Best of two trials is the score. Long jump scores for young athletes range from 1.88 m to 3.76 m. (1.2 to 2× body height for a 5- and 6-foot individual, respectively. For older adults, twice the length of patient's feet is considered "excellent."[17]

More difficult power tests are available, but it is rarely appropriate to use tests that are at the higher end of physical performance capacity in active rehabilitation. For more definitive work on this aspect of testing, the reader is referred to other sources.[18,19] Most power tests were developed for the young athlete. However, therapist judgment regarding the patient's abilities should be the key element, not age alone, in deciding whether a test is appropriate. Extreme care should be exercised in choosing a power test for those with significant weakness (Grade 3 or lower) or patients with painful conditions.

FIGURE 7.12

FIGURE 7.13

BODY-WEIGHT TESTING

Using body weight as resistance provides important information about the ability of patients to use the strength they possess to move their bodies in space. These tests are also effective exercises for strengthening the core as well as specific muscle groups. Several functional tests presented in Chapter 8 use body-weight resistance. Presented next are several other tests that use body mass as resistance. These tests are high demand and should not be used for patients with specific weakness.

Pull-ups (Chin-ups) Test

Purpose: The pull-up test uses patient's body weight to challenge the shoulder extensors (latissimus dorsi, teres major, triceps brachii, and posterior deltoid). The middle and lower trapezius, pectoralis minor, and rhomboids pull the scapula down. To pull the body up to the chin-up bar, the biceps brachii, brachialis and brachioradialis are contracting vigorously at the elbow. The wrist and finger flexors must also contract to hold the body on the bar.

Test Instructions: Assess the patient's ability to fully flex the shoulders and extend the elbows. If adequate range is present and no complaints of pain are presented, ask the patient to stand below an overhead bar that should be higher than the patient's outstretched arms. Have patient stand on a stool if unable to reach the bar. Ask the patient to grasp bar with an underhand (supinated) grip and hang from the bar with the elbows fully extended. Then, ask the patient to lift the entire body multiple times to muscle failure. For each repetition to count, the body must be raised so that the chin is brought above the bar. Subsequently, the body is lowered to the original starting position with each repetition.

Scoring

The number of pull-ups that can be performed successfully is recorded. Normative data for men and women are listed in Table 7.9.

> ### Helpful Hints
>
> - Norms for young boys and girls can be found at http://www.exrx.net/Testing/YouthNorms.html#anchor581034
> - Norms used by the Marine Corps can be found at http://www.military.com/military-fitness/marine-corps-fitness-requirements/usmc-physical-fitness-test

Table 7.9 NORMS FOR ADULTS FOR THE PULL-UP BY GENDER

Gender	Excellent	Above Average	Average	Below Average	Poor
Male	>13	9-13	6-8	3-5	<3
Female	>6	5-6	3-4	1-2	0

Adapted from Davis, B. et al: Physical education and the study of sport, 4th ed, London, 2000, Harcourt, p. 124.

Push-up Test

Purpose: A test of strength for the shoulder flexors, scapular stabilizers (especially serratus anterior), and triceps brachii. Push-ups are used not only as a test of strength but as a test of endurance, particularly in the US Armed Forces.

Test Instructions: Ensure that the patient does not have shoulder or any upper extremity pain and that adequate range of the shoulder, elbow, and wrist is present. Then, on the floor or other low surface, ask the patient to assume the starting position or "up" position with the hands shoulder width apart, back straight, head up, and using the toes as the pivotal point. The patient then lowers the body until the arms are parallel to the floor (Army standard) or until the chest touches the therapist's fist held vertically against the ground (ACSM standard). The Army uses the same position on toes for men and women. The ACSM allows women to perform push-ups on bent knees with ankles crossed. For both men and women, the back should be straight at all times and the patient must push up to a straight arm position.[1]

Scoring

The Army standard is as many repetitions as possible within a timed 2-minute period. The patient may only pause in the up position. For the ACSM standard, as many repetitions as possible are performed until failure. Norms for the ACSM and Army personnel are listed in Tables 7.10 and 7.11.[2,20]

Table 7.10 CONVERTING THE PUSH-UP SCORE (NUMBER) TO A HEALTH BENEFIT RATING

Age	Zone	Male	Female	Age	Zone	Male	Female
15-19	Excellent	≥39	≥33	40-49	Excellent	≥25	≥24
	Very Good	29-38	25-32		Very Good	17-24	15-23
	Good	23-28	18-24		Good	13-16	11-14
	Fair	18-22	12-17		Fair	10-12	5-10
	Poor	≤17	≤11		Poor	≤9	≤4
20-29	Excellent	≥36	≥30	50-59	Excellent	≥21	≥21
	Very Good	29-35	21-29		Very Good	13-20	11-20
	Good	22-28	15-20		Good	10-12	7-10
	Fair	17-21	10-14		Fair	7-9	2-6
	Poor	≤16	≤9		Poor	≤6	≤1
30-39	Excellent	≥30	≥27	60-69	Excellent	≥18	≥17
	Very Good	22-29	20-26		Very Good	11-17	12-16
	Good	17-21	13-19		Good	8-10	5-11
	Fair	12-16	8-12		Fair	5-7	2-4
	Poor	≤11	≤7		Poor	≤4	≤1

Table 7.11 PUSH-UP STANDARDS FOR U.S. ARMY PERSONNEL

Age Range	PUSH-UP STANDARDS FOR US ARMY PERSONNEL REPETITIONS IN 2 MINUTES																			
	M	F	M	F	M	F	M	F	M	F	M	F	M	F	M	F	M	F	M	F
17-21	6		13		20	2	28	8	35	13	42	19	49	25	57	31	64	36	71	42
22-26			5		14		23	2	31	11	40	17	49	24	58	32	66	39	75	46
27-31			1		11		20		30	10	39	17	49	25	58	34	68	42	77	50
32-36					7		17		26	9	36	15	46	23	56	30	65	38	75	45
37-41					5		15		24	7	34	13	44	20	54	27	63	33	73	40
42-46							12		21	6	30	12	39	18	48	25	57	31	66	37
47-51							8		17		25	10	34	16	42	22	51	28	59	34
52-56									11		20	9	29	15	38	20	47	26	56	31
57-61									9		18	8	27	13	36	18	44	23	53	28
62+									8		16	7	25	12	33	16	42	21	50	25
Points Awarded	10		20		30		40		50		60		70		80		90		100	

60 points is passing, 90 points is excellent.

Men and women start in up position on toes.

http://www.military.com/military-fitness/army-fitness-requirements/army-physical-fitness-test-score-chart.

CYRIAX METHOD OF TESTING CONTRACTILE LESIONS

A common reason for strength testing in orthopedics is to diagnose the tissues contributing to musculoskeletal pain lesions. Because manual muscle testing typically requires completion of full range of motion to assign a grade, an alternative system is needed. James Cyriax developed a system to differentiate between painful contractile and noncontractile (inert) soft tissues.[21] Contractile tissues are parts of the muscle (belly, tendon, and their bony insertions). Inert tissues are those without the capacity to contract or relax, such as joint capsule, ligaments, nerve roots, and the dura mater. The therapist selects passive movements to specifically test inert tissue and resisted movements to specifically stress contractile tissue. If passive movement is painful, it may be that inert tissues are at fault. If resisted movement is painful, the contractile tissue may be at fault. Active movement stresses both inert and contractile tissue. As an example, if a patient has a biceps tendonitis (long head), then resisted flexion (isometric, mid-range) will provoke pain. Passive movement through the flexion range of motion should not provoke pain because the biceps is relaxed. Theoretically, after the specific tissue is identified, the therapist can provide the appropriate treatment.

To test a muscle and its components (e.g., a contractile tissue), the therapist uses an isometric force to an immobilized limb segment so that the joint does not move. The joint is held in mid-range to keep from compromising the inert tissue. No joint movement should occur to direct the tension on the contractile tissue. If a contractile lesion is present, the resisted movement may provoke pain or demonstrate weakness, occasionally both. Normal contractions are strong and painless.

Because of the inherent strength of a normal muscle, the therapist should stand in a position of maximum advantage with proper hand placement to exert the strongest possible force as appropriate. In addition, the following rules, similar to manual muscle testing, should be followed:

- Muscles must be tested in such a way that the therapist's and patient's strength are evenly matched.
- The therapist uses one hand for resistance, the other hand for stabilization.
- Muscles other than those being tested must not be included. Proper hand placement should help to isolate the muscle(s) (e.g., preventing supination when isolating the brachialis muscle).
- The joint that the muscles control must not move and should be held at near mid-range.
- The patient must be encouraged to try as hard as possible.

Only one study was found that has examined the reliability of the Cyriax selective tissue tension method.[22] In this small study of otherwise healthy individuals between the ages of 20 and 40 years, with either unilateral shoulder or knee pain of undiagnosed origin, intrarater reliability for the knee ranged from 0.74 to 0.82 and interrater reliability ranged from 0.42 to 0.46. Both intrarater and interrater reliability were highest for knee flexion. For the shoulder, intrarater reliability ranged from 0.44 to 0.67 and interrater reliability ranged from 0.00 to 0.45, with the highest values for shoulder abduction.[22] Nearly all the disagreements between therapists came from whether a contraction was painful or not. The authors concluded that intrarater reliability for the knee was acceptable, but for the shoulder it was not. Interrater reliability was not acceptable for either joint.

REFERENCES

1. *ACSM's Guidelines for Exercise Testing and Prescription.* 8th ed. Baltimore, MD: Lippincott, Williams and Wilkins; 2010.
2. Lovell DI, Cuneo R, Gass GC. The blood pressure response of older men to maximum and submaximum strength testing. *J Sci Med Sport.* 2011;14:254–258.
3. LeBrasseur NK, Bhasin S, Miciek R, et al. Tests of muscle strength and physical function: reliability and discrimination of performance in younger and older men and older men with mobility limitations. *J Am Ger Soc.* 2008;56:2118–2123.
4. Hoger WW, Hopkins DR, Barette SL, et al. Relationship between repetitions and selected percentages of one repetition maximum: a comparison between untrained males and females. *J Strength Cond Res.* 1990;4:47–54.
5. Shimano T, Kraemer WJ, Spiering BA, et al. Relationship between the number of repetitions and selected percentages of one repetition maximum in free weight exercises in trained and untrained men. *J Strength Cond Res.* 2006;20:819–823.
6. Dohoney P, Chromiak JA, Lemire K, et al. Prediction of one repetition maximum (1-RM) strength from a 4-6 RM and a 7-10 RM submaximal strength test in healthy young adult males. *JEP online. J Exercise Physiol.* 2002;5(3):http://faculty.css.edu/tboone2/asep/Dohoney.pdf.
7. Da Silva EM, Brentano MA, Cadore AL, et al. Analysis of muscle activation during different leg press exercises at submaximum effort levels. *J Strength Cond Res.* 2008;22:1059–1065.
8. Signorile JF, Zink AJ, Szwed SP. A comparative electromyographical investigation of muscle utilization patterns using various hand positions during the lat pull-down. *J Strength Cond Res.* 2002;16:539–546.
9. Heyward VH. *Advanced Fitness Assessment & Exercise Prescription.* 2nd ed. Champaign, IL: Human Kinetics; 1991.
10. Brown L, ed. *Isokinetics in Human Performance.* Champaign, IL: Human Kinetics; 2000.
11. Arborelius UF, Ekholm J. Mechanics of shoulder locomotion system using exercises resisted by weight-and-pulley circuit. *Scand J Rehabil Med.* 1978;10:171–177.
12. Soria-Gila MA, Chirosa IJ, Bautista IJ, et al. Effects of variable resistance training on maximal strength: a meta-analysis. *J Strength Cond Res.* 2015;29(11):3260–3270.
13. Page P, Ellenbecker TS, eds. *The Scientific and Clinical Application of Elastic Resistance.* Champaign IL: Human Kinetics; 2003.
14. Bean JF, Kiely DK, LaRose S, et al. Are changes in leg power associated with clinically meaningful improvements in mobility in older adults? *J Am Soc Geriatr.* 2010;58:2363–2368.
15. Margaria R, Aghemo P, Rovelli E. Measurement of muscular power (anaerobic) in man. *J Appl Physiol.* 1966;5:1662–1664.
16. Haff GG, Triplett NT, eds. *Essential of Strength Training and Conditioning.* 4th ed. Champaign IL: Human Kinetics; 2016.
16a. Harris C, Wattles A, DeBeliso M, et al. The seated medicine ball throw as a test of upper body power in older adults. *J Strength Cond Res.* 2011;25(8):2344–2348.
16b. http://www.topendsports.com/sport/icehockey/nhl-combine-results-2013.htm.
17. http://mobile-pt.com/files/8._Fullerton_Advanced_Balance _Scale.pdf. Accessed February 8, 2018.
18. Wasserman B, Hansen J, Sue D, et al, eds. *Principles of Exercise Testing and Interpretation.* Philadelphia, PA: Lea and Febiger; 1987.
19. Hopkins WG, Schabort EJ, Hawley JA. Reliability of power in physical performance tests. *Sports Med.* 2001;31:211–234.
20. McArdle WD, Katch FI, Katch FL, et al. *Exercise Physiology.* 7th ed. Baltimore: Lippincott, Williams & Wilkins; 2010:518.
21. Cyriax J. *Textbook of Orthopedic Medicine.* Vol. 1. London: Bailliere Tindall; 1982.
22. Hayes KW, Petersen CM. Reliability of classifications derived from Cyriax's resisted testing in subjects with painful shoulders and knees. *J Orthop Sports Phys Ther.* 2003;33:235–246.

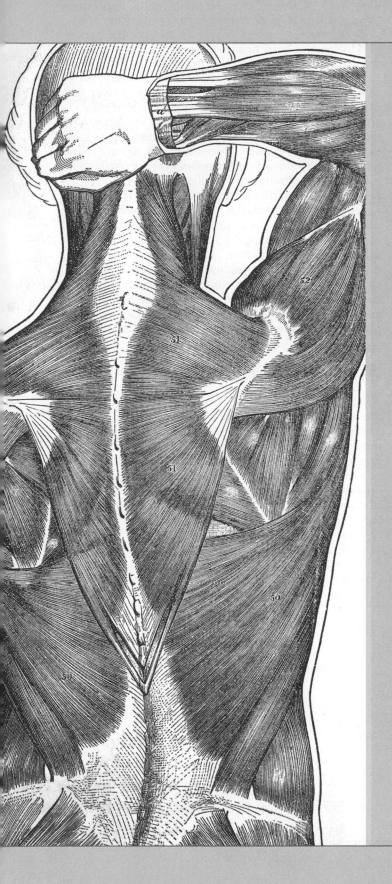

Testing Functional Performance

Current clinical practice presents a growing need to emphasize the relationship between strength and functional movement, especially in older adults. Each person has a threshold of strength that is minimal for the performance of activities of daily living (ADLs). The larger or taller the person is, for example, the more strength will be needed. Third-party payers require that therapists show a relationship between strength and function in their treatment plans, frequently denying payment if their assessments fail to show this relationship. It has always been important for therapists to show that patients have strength deficits, but it is now critical for them to show that strength deficits are tied to the patient's ability, or lack thereof, to independently complete ADLs, perform a job task (such as bricklaying), or play with their children or grandchildren. This chapter presents a series of functional tests, particularly relevant to older individuals, that require strength to be of a minimum threshold. Once a specific weakness is pinpointed, a strengthening program can be designed to help patients achieve their functional goals.

The functional assessment tests described in this chapter have been correlated to specific essential muscles. The list of muscles for each task is not comprehensive, but it provides a starting point for the beginning therapist to design a plan for muscle tests when a functional deficit is observed. Normative values are provided when available. Specific exercises for each muscle are listed after each muscle test in Chapters 5 and 6. In some cases, patients may be able to accomplish a task by compensating for a specific muscle weakness, so the therapist should be observant to accurately identify specific muscle weaknesses.

INTRODUCTION

Functional abilities represent a broad range of movements that require muscles to act in highly specific ways to achieve a desired purpose. These abilities include ADLs such as dressing, eating, bathing, transferring, and walking, as well as other tasks of mobility such as rising from a chair, climbing stairs, lifting, and rising from the floor. These functional activities are basic tasks of mobility that are required for all individuals to be independent in the home and community. Functional activity performance is especially important for older adults who may be at risk for institutionalization. An inability to independently perform specific functional tasks may lead to institutionalization. Many higher-level functional abilities such as those required for sports and work are discussed in Chapter 7, Alternatives to Manual Muscle Testing.

The Nagi Model of Disablement[1] and the newer International Classification of Functioning (ICF) disablement model[1] describe the impact of disease and pathology within the context of both function and societal roles and provide a conceptual model to guide clinical practice. In these models, diminished muscle strength is an impairment that affects a person's ability to perform functional tasks or to fulfill societal roles. Muscle strength testing takes place at the impairment level, whereas testing

functional task performance occurs at the function level. One goal of this chapter is to integrate impairment (strength deficit) and physical performance (function).

It is generally accepted that in the normal person, performance of basic functional tasks requires a relatively small amount of muscle strength in relation to the total amount of strength that existed before the injury, before a lifestyle of inactivity, or before the passage of years. The minimum amount of strength required is referred to as a "functional threshold." If patients have strength above the required threshold amount, they are unlikely to show deficits in performance. The relationship of strength to function up to a functional threshold is illustrated in Fig. 8.1. According to the principle illustrated in this graph, if the patient's strength sufficiently improves to the point at which the curve flattens out, the patient should be strong enough to perform the task. For example, about 45% of one's body weight is required to rise from a chair without using the arms.[2] If a person is unable to rise from a chair unassisted because of weakness in the lower extremities, strengthening will help to improve that function. Further strengthening will allow the person to rise more quickly and efficiently and will create a strength reserve to help preserve the ability to perform the task in the future.

Functional Testing

An analysis of any functional task shows that movements are multiplanar and asymmetrical, incorporate rotation, and are speed and balance dependent. Therefore, simply testing a muscle's maximum ability to generate force will not accurately represent its functional ability. Observation of the individual performing the functional task is the only way to accurately test functional ability. Such observation provides information about the quality of the performance, which in turn informs the therapist's clinical decision making. Inferring that a specific muscle has functional strength without direct observation of the functional task is incorrect and should be avoided as noted in Chapter 2. Table 8.1 shows the key muscles required for some basic functional tasks.

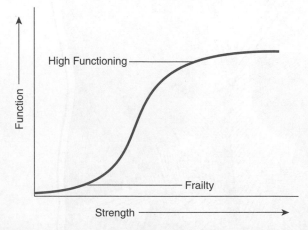

FIGURE 8.1 Conceptual diagram of curvilinear relationship between strength and function.

Table 8.1 KEY MUSCLES ESSENTIAL FOR FUNCTIONAL MOVEMENTS

Functional Movement	Key Muscles
Bed mobility	Abdominals, erector spinae, gluteus maximus
Transfers and squats	Gluteus maximus, medius, and obturator externus, piriformis, quadriceps
Ambulation and stair climbing	Abdominals, erector spinae, gluteus maximus and medius, obturator externus, piriformis, quadriceps, and anterior tibialis and gastrocsoleus
Floor transfers	Abdominals, erector spinae, gluteus maximus and medius, obturator externus, piriformis, quadriceps and gastrocsoleus
Fast gait and jumping	Gastrocsoleus, gluteus maximus and medius, quadriceps

Measurement

Functional task performance is measured in several ways. Ordinal scales showing hierarchical levels of performance are commonly used in both manual muscle testing and in some functional tests. In ordinal scales, numbers are sequentially and hierarchically assigned in accordance with the difficulty of the task. However, ordinal scales are limited by their susceptibility to subjectivity and their lack of responsiveness to small changes in performance. Therefore, using ratio scales, such as time, to measure individual patient performance, is the preferred method. Timing task performance provides a strong measure of reliability and responsiveness. However, when a functional task is timed, such as when a patient is instructed to rise from a chair as quickly as possible, it should be noted that power is a component in addition to strength. Ratio measures such as time and distance allow the therapist to compare an individual patient's performance against available normative data of similar individuals. This comparison aids in clinical decision making.

Purpose: The chair stand test is a test of mobility specifically targeting the force production of the leg muscles. There are two versions: the number of completed sit-to-stand motions (chair rises) completed in 30 seconds (30s STS) and the time required to complete five chair rises (5T-STS).

Essential Muscle Movements for Task Performance: Hip extension, hip abduction from a flexed position, hip external rotation, knee extension, ankle plantar flexion, ankle dorsiflexion and inversion,[3] and trunk extension and flexion.

Reliability: Test-retest reliability for all versions of the Chair Stand Test ($r = 0.89$).[4]

Validity: The 30s STS test correlates with measures of lower extremity strength, walking speed, stair-climbing ability, and balance[5,6] and correlates with one-repetition maximum (1-RM) leg press ($r = 0.78$ for men, 0.71 for women).[4] The 5T-STS is a valid measure of dynamic balance and functional mobility in older adults.[7] Inability to complete the 5T-STS in less than 13.7 seconds is highly predictive of future mobility disability.[8]

Equipment: A standard, armless chair, 17 in. (43 cm) high, and a stopwatch.

Testing Procedure: Both test versions are *always* done without the use of the patient's arms. Assess the ability of the patient to stand without the use of arms. If able, proceed to testing. If indicated, the therapist should demonstrate the sit-to-stand movement before testing.

30-Second Version: The patient rises from a sitting position and stands to a fully erect position as many times as possible in 30 seconds. The therapist starts timing when the patient begins to move (rather than on "Go!").

Timed Five-Repetition Version: The patient comes to a full standing position 5 times as quickly as possible.

The therapist begins timing on the command "Go!" The therapist times the effort from the command "Go!" until the patient returns to a seated position after five repetitions.

Position of Patient: Sitting with arms crossed over the chest. Feet are planted on the floor in the position chosen by the patient (Fig. 8.2).

Therapist Position: Stand to fully view the patient's quality of movement (Fig. 8.3).

Patient Position

30-Second Version: "When you're ready, stand up as many times as you can in 30 seconds without using your arms. I'll keep count. Make sure you stand all the way up."

Timed Five-Repetition Version: "When you are ready, stand up 5 times, as quickly as you can without using your arms. I will be timing you. Make sure you stand all the way up."

Scoring

30-Second Version: The number of repetitions is the patient's score. Count the repetition if the patient is more than halfway standing. If the patient cannot complete one repetition without the use of the arms, the score for the 30-second version is zero.

Timed Five-Repetition Version: The time taken to complete five repetitions is the score. If 60 seconds

FIGURE 8.2

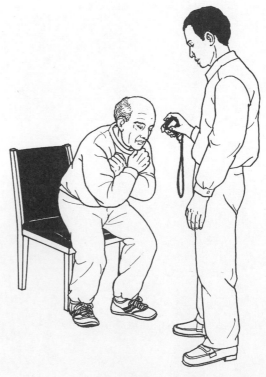

FIGURE 8.3

elapse before five repetitions are accomplished, the test is terminated and the score of 60 seconds is recorded with a notation. The odds of being disabled increases 1.4 times for every one-second increase in the 5T-STS test.

The minimal detectable change is 2.5 seconds.[7] Scores of greater than 10 s increase the risk of developing disability within 2 years.[9]

Helpful Hints

- Do not use a folding chair, a very soft chair, a deep chair, or a chair on wheels for the chair stand test. The chair should be placed against the wall for safety purposes.
- Chair heights from 80% to 90% of the patient's lower (tibia) leg length are optimal for the test.[10]
- Allow the patient to perform the sit-to-stand movement first, without coaching. If the patient has difficulty rising, then offer tips such as scooting to the edge of the chair, leaning forward, etc.
- It is useful to observe the position of the hips while the patient is attempting to stand and sit. If the hips are adducted and/or internally rotated, this may indicate weakness and specific muscle testing is indicated, especially of the gluteus medius (Fig. 8.4).
- Excessive bending forward of the trunk to stand may indicate that the patient has weak quadriceps (Fig. 8.5).
- Although it is preferable to have the patient cross the arms over the chest, some patients may need to extend their arms forward to help them stand. If this occurs, it could indicate that the patient's legs are weak or balance is impaired (Fig. 8.6).
- If you suspect the patient will not be able to complete five repetitions, the 30s STS version is the preferred test because the patient is required to only complete a minimum of one repetition for a successful test.

FIGURE 8.4

FIGURE 8.5

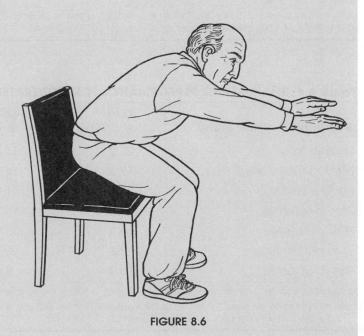

FIGURE 8.6

Tables 8.2 and 8.3 show normative ranges for physically active older men and women. Eight repetitions may be the threshold for physical disability.[4]

Table 8.4 shows 5T-STS test normative ranges for moderately disabled women—that is, those who have difficulty performing two or more ADL tasks. The Women's Health and Aging Study (of moderately to severely disabled women) found a mean time of 15.3 seconds for women ages 65 to 85 and older.[11] The more time required, the more likely it is that the individual is frail.[12]

Table 8.2 NORMAL RANGE OF CHAIR STANDS BY SEX AND AGE (MIDDLE 50% OF POPULATION)

Age	M	F
60–64	14–19	12–17
65–69	12–18	11–16
70–74	12–17	10–15
75–79	11–17	10–15
80–84	10–15	9–14
85–89	8–14	8–13
90–94	7–12	4–11

F, Female; M, male.

From Jones CJ, Rikli RE. Measuring functional fitness of older adults. *J Act Aging*. 2002;March–April:24–30.

Table 8.3 NORMATIVE DATA* FOR 30-SECOND CHAIR STAND TEST FROM 1000 AUSTRALIANS

Age	3–9 M	F	10–19 M	F	20–59 M	F	60+ M	F
Mean (SD)	23.1 (6.6)	23.4 (6.1)	25.5 (5.7)	24.2 (5.9)	24.2 (6.0)	22.6 (6.2)	18.3 (5.73)	15.9 (4.8)

*Each decade included 100 people (20 to 80+).

F, Female; M, male.

Data from McKay MJ, Baldwin JN, Ferreira P, Simic M, Vanicek N, Burns J. 1000 Norms Project Consortium. Normative reference values for strength and flexibility of 1,000 children and adults. *Neurology*. 2017;88(1):36–43.

Table 8.4 CHAIR STAND PERFORMANCE FOR MODERATELY DISABLED WOMEN

5-Repetition Chair Stand	Total N = 1002	65–74 Years N = 388	75–84 Years N = 311	85+ Years N = 303
Unable to do (%)	25.2	17.8	25.9	44.9
Mean Time to rise 5 × (s)	15.3	14.7	15.7	16.3
5th percentile	24.5	21.9	25.5	24.1
25th percentile	17.4	16.7	17.5	18.5
50th percentile	14.2	13.9	14.4	15.0
75th percentile	12.3	12.1	12.4	12.7
95th percentile	10.0	9.6	10.3	10.0

Moderately disabled women were those with difficulty in two or more activities of daily living tasks.

Data from Guralnik JM, Fried LP, Simonsick EM, Kasper JD, Lafferty ME, eds. *The Women's Health and Aging Study: Health and Social Characteristics of Older Women with Disability*. Darby PA: Diane Pub Co; 1995:44.

Purpose: Gait speed is a functional test of one's ability to walk at a comfortable (usual) speed. A fast-paced walk can demonstrate available reserve and the ability to accelerate rapidly, such as in the need to get across a street. Possible gait speed times range from the fastest sprinters to the slowest possible gait, often seen in individuals residing in nursing homes. Gait speed has been called the sixth vital sign because of its validity in predicting functional ability, frailty, nursing home placement, and the ability to walk in the community.[13] It can be measured in any person who can walk, even those using assistive devices.

Essential Muscle Movements for Task Performance: Core; hip extension, abduction, and adduction; quadriceps and hamstrings; ankle plantar flexion; and ankle dorsiflexion with inversion.[14,15] Hip flexion also contributes to walking velocity.[16] The reader is referred to the gait section of this chapter for a more specific list of muscles that are imperative for smooth and normal gait.

Reliability: $r = 0.78$[17]

Validity: Gait speed is related to age (Fig. 8.7) and muscle mass.[13,17] Gait speed at "usual pace" was found to be a consistent predictor of disability, cognitive impairment, institutionalization, falls, and/or mortality.[18] Fast gait speed is a robust predictor of disability when the annual decline exceeds -0.22 m/s.[19] A speed of less than 0.8 m/s is a predictor of 8-year mortality in predisabled women 75 years or older.[20] Women who had gait speeds of less than 0.60 m/s were 2.5 times more likely to die prematurely than those with faster gait speeds.[21] A speed of less than 1.2 m/s is highly predictive of future mobility disability.[8]

Equipment: A 4- to 8-m-long walkway and a stopwatch. It is helpful to have 1 to 2 m or so before and after the 4-m test course to allow for acceleration and deceleration, especially in people with stroke.[22] However, although this extra distance is desirable, it is not necessary to perform the test in people without pathology. However, each test administration should be performed the same way for

consistency of results and accuracy of interpretation. The length of the walkway does not influence the consistency of results.[23]

Testing Procedure: First, describe the test clearly to the individual. Assure the patient is safe to walk independently (without another person). Demonstrate the test if needed, taking care not to walk too fast. Then, have the patient perform two trials with adequate rest in between, scoring the faster one. Test both comfortable (usual) and fast gait speeds. Begin timing the individual when the first foot crosses the line at the beginning of the course (Fig. 8.8A) and stop timing when the first foot crosses the end line (Fig. 8.8B). Any part of the foot will do; it is just important to be consistent.

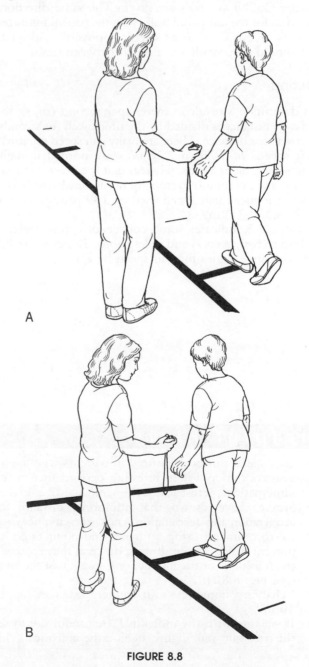

A

B

FIGURE 8.8

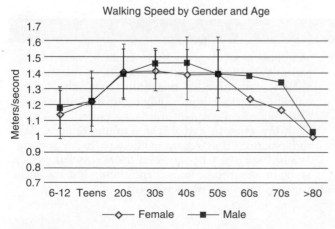

FIGURE 8.7 Self-selected walking speed categorized by gender and age.

Position of Patient: Standing, facing a marked-off walkway. Patient may use an assistive device if needed.

Therapist Instructions: Stand and hold the stopwatch perpendicular to the starting line. The therapist should walk with the patient to obtain an accurate view of when the first foot crosses the finish line without pacing the patient. The therapist begins timing when the patient's first foot (or part of the first foot) crosses the start line of the 4-m walkway (see Fig. 8.8A).

Patient Instructions: "Walk at your usual and comfortable speed from this line to (or past) the other line on the floor (indicate which line). I will be timing you. The first trial is for practice and then we'll time you. OK? Ready, Go!" Two trials are given. The same directions are given for the fast-paced walk, with the patient instructed to walk as quickly, but as safely, as possible. Adequate rest should be provided as needed between trials.

Scoring

To determine a result in meters per second (m/s), the walkway distance is divided by the time taken (in seconds) to cover that distance. There are many gait speed standards. Gait speeds of 1.75 to 2.25 m/s are normal in high-functioning older adults, whereas gait speeds slower than 0.5 m/s are common in nursing home residents. In one study, the mean gait speed used by 139 pedestrians was 1.32 (SD, 0.31) m/s.[24]

Table 8.5 indicates some conversions from meters/second to feet/second and miles/hour. Tables 8.6 to 8.9 list normative values for gait speed by age.

Table 8.5 CONVERSIONS FOR GAIT SPEED

Meters/ Second	Feet/ Second	Minutes/ Mile	Miles/ Hour
0.25	0.82	106.7	0.6
0.30	0.98	88.9	0.7
0.35	1.15	76.2	0.8
0.40	1.31	66.7	0.9
0.45	1.48	59.3	1.0
0.50	1.64	53.3	1.1
0.55	1.80	48.5	1.2
0.60	1.97	44.4	1.4
0.65	2.13	41.0	1.5
0.70	2.30	38.1	1.6
0.75	2.46	35.6	1.7
0.80	2.62	33.3	1.8
0.85	2.79	31.4	1.9
0.90	2.95	29.6	2.0
0.95	3.12	28.1	2.1
1.00	3.28	26.7	2.3
1.10	3.61	24.2	2.5
1.20	3.94	22.2	2.7
1.30	4.26	20.5	2.9
1.40	4.59	19.0	3.2
1.50	4.92	17.8	3.4
1.60	5.25	16.7	3.6
1.70	5.58	15.7	3.8
1.80	5.90	14.8	4.1
1.90	6.23	14.0	4.3
2.00	6.56	13.3	4.5

Helpful Hints

- Gait speed can be measured in patients who use an assistive device. When retesting performance in the same patient, retest using the same assistive device.
- Studies have shown that additional distance for acceleration and deceleration is not necessary; however, we recommend using a further end-point target to prevent patients from slowing down as they approach the finish line or the instructions, "walk past the line" (see Fig. 8.8B).
- Reliability improves with longer distances, up to 10 m.[17]
- If walking with the individual, be careful not to set the pace but walk slightly behind the individual. This will allow you to get a more realistic view of the patient's actual performance. While always maintaining a safe test situation, do not inhibit the individual by standing too close or providing too many instructions. Certainly, use a gait belt if it is warranted.
- Knowing when to start and stop timing requires skill and practice. It is recommended to use a specific "event," such as when the first foot crosses the line, as the moment to begin and end timing but any such event will do; just be consistent!

Table 8.6 MEAN FAST GAIT SPEED TIME FOR MEN AND WOMEN AGE 20 YEARS AND OLDER

Age	MAXIMUM GAIT SPEED (m/s) MEAN AND SD	
	Men	Women
20s	2.53 (0.29)	2.47 (0.25)
30s	2.46 (0.32)	2.34 (0.34)
40s	2.46 (0.36)	2.12 (0.28)
50s	2.07 (0.45)	2.01 (0.26)
60s	1.93 (0.36)	1.77 (0.25)
70s	2.08 (0.36)	1.75 (0.28)

Data from Bohannon RW. Comfortable and maximum walking speed of adults aged 20–79 years: reference values and determinants. *Age Ageing.* 1997;26(1):15–19.

Table 8.7 NORMATIVE RANGES OF USUAL GAIT SPEED FOR HEALTHY ADULTS AGES 20–99

Age	GAIT SPEED IN m/s	
	Men	Women
20–29	1.22–1.47	1.08–1.50
30–39	1.32–1.54	1.26–1.42
40–49	1.27–1.47	1.22–1.42
50–59	1.12–1.49	1.10–1.56
60–69	1.03–1.59	0.97–1.45
70–79	0.96–1.42	0.83–1.50
80–99	0.61–1.22	0.56–1.17

Data from Bohannon RW, Williams Andrews A. Normal walking speed: a descriptive meta-analysis. *Physiotherapy.* 2011;97(3):182–189.

Table 8.8 NORMS FOR USUAL GAIT SPEED TIME (M/S) FOR MODERATELY DISABLED WOMEN AGE 65 AND OLDER

	Total (n = 1002)	65–74	75–84	85+
Mean	0.6	0.7	0.6	0.4
5th percentile	0.2	0.3	0.2	0.1
25th percentile	0.4	0.5	0.4	0.3
50th percentile	0.6	0.6	0.6	0.6
75th percentile	0.7	0.7	0.8	0.6
95th percentile	1.1	1.1	1.1	0.8

m/s, Meters per second; *n,* number of subjects.

Moderately disabled women were those with difficulty in two or more activities of daily living tasks.

Subjects were asked to walk at their usual and customary pace for 4 m.

Modified from Ferrucci L, Guralnik JM, Bandeen-Roche KL, et al. Performance measures from the women's health and aging study. http://www.grc.nia.nih.gov/branches/ledb/whasbook/chap4/chap4.htm. Accessed 08.01.12.

Table 8.9 NORMS FOR FAST GAIT SPEED TIME (M/S) FOR MODERATELY DISABLED WOMEN AGE 65 AND OLDER

	Total (n = 1002)	65–74	75–84	85+
Mean	0.9	1	0.9	0.7
5th percentile	0.2	0.4	0.3	0.2
25th percentile	0.6	0.8	0.6	0.4
50th percentile	0.9	1	0.9	0.7
75th percentile	1.1	1.3	1.1	0.9
95th percentile	1.7	1.7	1.7	1.3

m/s, Meters per second; *n,* number of subjects.

Moderately disabled women were those with difficulty in two or more activities of daily living tasks.

Modified from Ferrucci L, Guralnik JM, Bandeen-Roche KL, et al. Performance measures from the women's health and aging study. http://www.grc.nia.nih.gov/branches/ledb/whasbook/chap4/chap4.htm. Accessed 08.01.12.

PHYSICAL PERFORMANCE TEST AND MODIFIED PHYSICAL PERFORMANCE TEST

Purpose: The physical performance test (PPT) measures aspects of physical function and ADLs in older adults using nine items that emphasize mobility tasks. There are two versions of the PPT test: one with seven items and one with nine; the nine-item version also includes stair-climbing tasks.

The Modified Physical Performance Test (M-PPT) includes most of the items of the PPT but substitutes three balance tests and a timed 5T-STS for the writing and eating task.

Essential Muscle Movements for Physical Performance Test Task Performance

Writing Task: (If the arm is supported, only hand and wrist muscles may be essential.) Wrist flexion and extension, finger metacarpophalangeal (MP), proximal phalanges (PIP), and distal phalanges (DIP) flexion.

Eating Task: Shoulder flexion, shoulder internal rotation, elbow flexion, forearm supination and pronation, wrist flexion and extension, and finger MP, PIP, and DIP flexion.

Essential Muscle Movements for Physical Performance Test and Modified Physical Performance Test Task Performance

Lifting a Book: Scapular protraction and upward rotation; shoulder flexion; shoulder external rotation; elbow flexion and extension; forearm supination and pronation; wrist flexion and extension; and finger MP, PIP, and DIP flexion.

Putting On and Taking Off a Garment (Depending on Technique): Scapular protraction and upward rotation; shoulder flexion; shoulder external rotation; elbow flexion and extension; forearm supination and pronation; wrist flexion and extension; and finger MP, PIP, and DIP flexion. Core stability (for sitting or standing). If the task is performed while standing: hip extension and abduction, knee extension, ankle plantar flexion, and ankle dorsiflexion with inversion.

Picking Up a Coin: Back extension; hip extension, knee extension; ankle plantar flexion; elbow flexion and extension; forearm supination and pronation; wrist flexion and extension; and finger MP, PIP, and DIP flexion.

360° Turn: Ankle dorsiflexion with inversion, plantar flexion, foot inversion, foot eversion with plantar flexion, knee extension, hip abduction and extension, and core stability.

Walking Task: Hip extension and abduction, knee extension, ankle plantar flexion, and ankle dorsiflexion with inversion.[14] Hip flexion also contributes to walking velocity.[15] The reader is referred to the gait section of this chapter for a more specific list of muscles that are imperative for smooth and normal gait.

Stair Climb Tasks: Ascent: hip flexion and extension, knee extension and flexion, ankle plantar flexion, ankle dorsiflexion, spine extension, and core stability. Descent: eccentric knee extension, hip flexion, and core muscles.[25] Balance is also a key component of successful stair ascent and descent.

Reliability: The intraclass correlation coefficient (ICC) for interrater reliability is 0.96 for the eight-item version (omitting the last item of four flights of stairs).[26] The ICC of test-retest reliability in the eight-item version is 0.88.[26] There is no reliability data for the M-PPT.

Validity: Predictive validity for classifying level of care as dependent or independent.[28] Construct validity based on self-reported ADL and instrumental ADL performance.[27] Predictive of major health outcomes such as death and nursing home placement.[29] Predictive of first time fall (within 12 months)[30] and recurrent falls.[31] The M-PPT can indicate whether an individual is frail.[32]

Equipment for Both Versions
Scoring form
Stopwatch
Table and chair (PPT)
Bowl (PPT)
Spoon (PPT)
Coffee can (PPT)
Five dry (uncooked) kidney beans (PPT)
5.5-lb book
Two adjustable shelves
Patient's jacket or front-button sweater or extra-large lab coat, hospital gown, or other front-opening garment
25-foot walkway
One flight of stairs (10 to 12 stairs)

Testing Procedure

Physical Performance Test and Modified Physical Performance Test: Both versions take about 10 minutes to complete. The test items can be done in any order; however, they will be described here in the order in which they appear on the scoring forms. Each task is timed, except for the 360° turn and climbing four flights of stairs. Two trials of each task are performed, except for the stair-climbing task.

An assistive device can be used for the walking and stair-climbing tasks, but not for the other tasks. All tasks are to be completed unassisted and without support. As in all tests, the patient's safety should be assured. Although assistance from the therapist is not permitted during performance of the test, the therapist should be vigilant for balance problems. A gait belt is always recommended during test performance.

The nine PPT tasks are:
1. Writing a sentence
2. Simulated eating
3. Lifting a book onto a shelf
4. Putting on and taking off a garment
5. Picking up a coin from the floor
6. 360° turn
7. 50-foot walk
8. Climbing one flight of stairs
9. Climbing four flights of stairs

The nine M-PPT tasks are:
1. Standing static balance
   a. Side-by-side stance
   b. Semi-tandem stance
   c. Full tandem stance
2. Chair stand (five repetitions)
3. Lifting a book onto a shelf
4. Putting on and taking off a garment
5. Picking up a coin from the floor
6. 360° turn
7. 50-foot walk
8. Climbing one flight of stairs
9. Climbing four flights of stairs

Physical Performance Test Tasks

1. Writing a Sentence

Testing Procedure: The patient writes a sentence. The sentence can be written on the back of the test form so there will be a record of the result. The therapist writes the sentence first: "Whales live in a blue ocean." A period is placed at the end of the sentence. Then, on the command of "Go!" the patient writes the same sentence. Timing begins on Go! and ends when the period is placed at the end of the sentence. The therapist records the time it takes the patient to write the sentence legibly (Fig. 8.9).

Instructions to Patient: "The first task is a writing task. I am going to write the sentence 'Whales live in a blue ocean.' Then I want you to write the same sentence while I time you. Are you ready? Go!"

2. Eating Task

Testing Procedure: The second task is a simulated eating task. Five kidney beans are placed in a bowl 5 in. from the edge of the table in front of the patient. An empty coffee can is placed on the table at the patient's nondominant side. A teaspoon is placed in the patient's dominant hand. The therapist may demonstrate the task. The patient is asked on the command "Go!" to pick up the beans, one at a time with the spoon, and place them in the coffee can (Fig. 8.10). Timing begins with the command "Go!" and ends when the last bean is heard hitting the bottom of the can. The patient can use the nondominant hand to steady the bowl, but not to move it in any way. The nondominant hand cannot help steady the can or complete the task except to help pick up a dropped bean. If the patient drops a bean, timing continues while the patient picks up the bean.

Instructions to Patient: "This next task is an eating task. When I say 'Go!' I want you to use your spoon to move one bean at a time from this can to the bowl. You cannot use your other hand except to steady the bowl. Are you ready? Go!"

PPT and M-PPT

FIGURE 8.9

FIGURE 8.10

Physical Performance Test Tasks Continued

3. Lifting a Book Onto a Shelf

Testing Procedure: This task is done with the patient sitting on a chair (or other surface) (Fig. 8.11), or standing (Fig. 8.12), depending on whether you want to assess the patient's standing or sitting balance while lifting. It is handy to use an open cabinet with multiple and/or two adjustable shelves, usually available in a clinic. Having multiple or two adjustable shelves helps accommodate the patient's height. The countertop can serve as the starting position for the book placement.

Adjust the higher shelf so that it is 12 in. above the patient's shoulders. A 5.5-lb book, similar to a *Physicians' Desk Reference,* is placed on the edge of the counter, with the book hanging slightly off the edge of the counter to make it easy for the patient to grab. The patient is asked to lift the book from the lower shelf to the upper shelf while the effort is timed. The therapist should demonstrate this task to ensure understanding.

Timing is stopped when the patient's hand is removed from the book after it is placed on the top shelf. In the original PPT test, the patient is seated during the task (see Fig. 8.11). However, the task can be performed standing if desired (see Fig. 8.12). The time is recorded on the scoring form.

Instructions to Patient: "For this task, I want you to lift this book to this shelf while I time you. Do you understand? Now, I'll demonstrate. OK, when I say 'Go!' you may begin."

4. Putting on and Taking Off a Garment

Testing Procedure: This task involves putting on and removing a garment in a standing position. An extra-large bathrobe, front-buttoned shirt, or hospital gown can be used and put on so that it opens in the front. If the patient has a jacket or sweater that opens in the front, use that. Make sure the garment is large enough to put on over any clothes the patient is wearing. To start, the garment is held so the label inside the garment is facing the patient (Fig. 8.13).

FIGURE 8.12

FIGURE 8.11

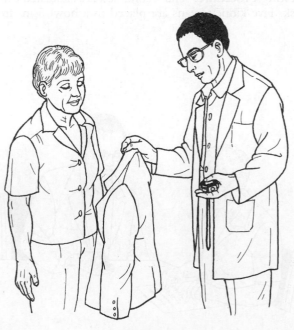

FIGURE 8.13

Physical Performance Test Tasks Continued

The patient is instructed to start with arms at sides and on "Go!" to take the garment, put it on (Fig. 8.14), square it on the shoulders, and then remove it completely, holding it out to the therapist. Timing begins on "Go!" and ends when the patient hands the jacket to the therapist.

Instructions to Patient: "This task involves putting on and taking off this jacket while I time you. When I say 'Go!' I want you to take the jacket from me, put it on so that it is square on your shoulders, and then take it off and hand it back to me. Now Go!"

5. Picking Up a Coin From the Floor

Testing Procedure: This is a timed task of the patient's ability to pick up a coin from the floor. A coin is placed approximately 12 in. from the patient's foot (usually the dominant side). On the command "Go!" the patient picks up the coin from the floor and returns to a fully upright position (Fig. 8.15). The timing will begin with the command "Go!" and end when the patient is standing erect with coin in hand.

Instructions to Patient: "I'm going to put a coin on the floor and on 'Go!' I want you to pick it up, completely stand up, and hand it to me. OK. Are you ready?"

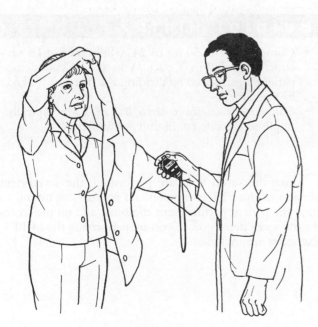

FIGURE 8.14

FIGURE 8.15

Physical Performance Test Tasks Continued

6. 360° Turn

Testing Procedure: The 360° turn task examines the patient's ability to turn in a complete circle in both directions (Fig. 8.16). This effort is not timed, but rather scored for the quality and safety of the effort.

Demonstrate the task. The demonstration speed of turning should not be so fast that it encourages the patient to mimic it, thus compromising his or her safety. Ask the patient to turn 360° at a comfortable pace (in either direction) beginning with the toes pointed forward and ending when the toes are pointed forward again. The performance is evaluated for continuity of movement and steadiness.

Instructions to Patient: "I want you to turn in a full circle so that your toes are back on this line. You can choose whichever direction you want to go toward first, since I will ask you to go in the other direction next. I will not be timing you." Upon completion, ask the patient to turn in the other direction, evaluating for continuity of movement and steadiness.

FIGURE 8.16

> ### Helpful Hint
>
> Both directions will be examined, so it does not matter which direction is performed first. Typically, the patient will choose his or her best direction to perform first.

7. Timed 50-Foot Walk

Testing Procedure: This is a timed 50-foot walk task designed to examine the speed and observe the quality of the patient's gait. The patient stands at the start of a 50-foot walk test course that consists of a walkway 25 ft out and 25 ft back. No acceleration or deceleration distance is needed because of the distance. Timing begins with the command "Go!" and ends when the starting line is crossed on the way back. The time is recorded on the scoring form. An assistive device may be used, and the type of device should be documented. Typically, demonstration is not needed on this task because walking is a familiar task.

Instructions to Patient: "I'd like you to walk out and back as quickly but as safely as you can. You will turn around at the end of the walkway and return to this spot. I will be timing you. Ready? Go!"

> ### Helpful Hints
>
> - Completing the 50 ft (15.24 m) distance in 15 s is equal to a 1.0 m/s pace. You can calculate the patient's gait speed by dividing the distance walked by the time.
> - Gait speeds of more than 0.8 m/s are typically required for safe community ambulation.

Once the seven tasks are performed, the seven-item version of the PPT is complete. If you do not intend to have the patient perform stair climbing, add up the scores for the seven items now. If you are performing the M-PPT, the stairs are included.

Physical Performance Test Tasks Continued

8. Climbing One Flight of Stairs*

Testing Procedure: Explain to the patient that he or she has the option of climbing up to four flights of stairs. Ask the patient if he or she feels comfortable and is willing to perform these tasks. Ask the patient to tell you of any symptom such as chest pain or shortness of breath, which should terminate the task. Vital signs should be monitored as indicated. Indications to monitor vital signs include evidence of more than ordinary effort expended in any previous task such as complaints of fatigue and the need to rest between tasks.

Ask the patient to climb one flight of stairs that has 9 to 12 steps. The timing starts with the command "Go!" and ends when the patient's first foot reaches the top of the top step. The patient may use a handrail and/or assistive device and this should be noted on the scoring form as well as the time taken to climb one flight of stairs.

Instructions to Patient: "This task involves climbing a flight of stairs as quickly but as safely as you can (Fig. 8.17). You may use the handrail if you need to. For this task, you are only required to go up to the landing. Stair climbing may require more than usual effort, so please let me know if you experience any tightness or pain in your chest or if you are short of breath and need to stop. OK? Go!"

FIGURE 8.17

If the patient is willing, he or she may continue the stairs to achieve up to four flights. This effort is not timed.

9. Climbing Four Flights of Stairs

Testing Procedure: The patient is asked to climb up to four flights of stairs. The scoring is based on how many flights, up and down, the patient completes. The patient descends the first flight of stairs, counted as one, and ascends the same flight up to four repetitions. This stair climbing and descent continues until the patient feels tired and wishes to stop, or until four flights, four ups and four downs total, have been completed.

Record the number of flights (maximum of four) climbed (up and down is one flight). A handrail and/or an assistive device may be used.

Instructions to Patient: "Now, the next task is to climb, up and down, as many times as you are comfortable, up to four times. You can determine how many flights you feel comfortable doing. Are you willing to try? How many flights do you think you can do?" Ready? Go!

Helpful Hints

- Typically, a demonstration is not needed and only one trial is given.
- Prior to beginning the stair tasks, it is helpful to ask the patient how many flights he or she thinks can be completed to give some idea of the anticipated level of performance.
- Patients should be gently encouraged, but not coerced or forced, to do more than they feel they can safely and comfortably do.
- Taking vital signs pre and post stair climbing or asking the patient to identify the level of exertion via the Borg Scale of Exertion may provide additional information to help inform the therapist's clinical decision making.

The stair tasks complete the nine-item PPT. See Fig. 8.18 for the PPT scoring form. To complete the M-PPT, ask the patient to perform the next two tasks.

---

*The stair climbing tasks (climbing one flight of stairs and climbing four flights of stairs) may be performed together, but they are scored separately. Generally, only one trial is given.

PHYSICAL PERFORMANCE TEST AND MODIFIED PHYSICAL PERFORMANCE TEST

Physical Performance Test Scoring Sheet

Physical Performance Test

		Time	Scoring	Score
1	Writing task: (Write the sentence "Whales live in a blue ocean.")	Sec*	≤10 sec = 4 10.5–15 sec = 3 15.5–20 sec = 2 >20 sec = 1 unable = 0	
2	Eating task (simulated eating)	Sec	≤10 sec = 4 10.5–15 sec = 3 15.5–20 sec = 2 >20 sec = 1 unable = 0	
3	Lift a book and put it on a shelf Book: approximately 5.5 lbs Bed height: 23 in Shelf height: 46 in	Sec	≤2 sec = 4 2.5–4 sec = 3 4.5–6 sec = 2 >6 sec = 1 unable 0	
4	Put on and remove a garment 1. Standing 2. Use of bathrobe, button-down shirt, or hospital gown	Sec	≤10 sec = 4 10.5–15 sec = 3 15.5–20 sec = 2 >20 sec = 1 unable = 0	
5	Pick up a coin from the floor	Sec	≤2 sec = 4 2.5–4 sec = 3 4.5–6 sec = 2 >6 sec = 1 unable = 0	
6	Turn 360°		Discontinuous steps = 0 Continuous steps = 2 Unsteady (grabs, staggers) = 0 Steady = 2	
7	50-foot walk test (15.24 meters) <15 sec = 3.33 feet/sec or 1.0 m/sec	Sec	≤15 sec = 4 15.5–20 sec = 3 20.5–25 sec = 2 >25 sec = 1 unable = 0	
8	Climb one flight of stairs	Sec	≤5 sec = 4 5.5–10 sec = 3 10.5–15 sec = 2 >15 sec = 1 unable = 0	
9	Climb four flights of stairs		Number of flights of stairs up and down (maximum of 4)	
	TOTAL SCORE (maxium 36 for nine-item; 28 for seven-item)			
	*For time measurements, round to nearest 0.5 seconds		Total score	

Data from: Reuben DB, Siu AL. An objective measure of physical function of elderly outpatients (the Physical Performance Test). *Journal of the American Geriatric Society* 1990; 38(10): 1105-1112.

FIGURE 8.18 Physical performance test (PPT) scoring form.

Modified Physical Performance Test

The modified physical performance test does not include the PPT tasks 1 (writing) and 2 (simulating eating). Instead, the following balance test is done first, followed by the chair stand test. Then tasks 3 to 9 from the physical performance test are performed.

1. Testing Procedures for Standing Static Balance Tasks

These balance tasks examine the patient's ability to stand in three positions: side-by-side, semi-tandem, and full tandem. The three positions should be tested in order because they increase in difficulty. The duration of the three balance positions is timed. If the patient cannot perform one position, then the next position is not performed but rather is scored as "unable." These positions are designed to maximally challenge balance, so the therapist should be alert for balance difficulties and maintain the patient's safety at all times.

Each balance position is timed for a maximum of 10 seconds. The semi-scoring tandem and tandem positions are tested with each foot forward. No out-toeing is permitted. Foot positioning should be strictly observed. If the patient cannot attain the proper position, the score is zero for that stance task. Only one trial is allowed for each position.

Each position is demonstrated before testing. If desired, ask the patient to practice the position. The patient may be assisted to assume the positions, but when timing starts, no support is given. Once the patient appears to be steady, the therapist begins timing, relinquishing support if it was initially needed to assume the correct position. The timing is continued until the patient moves a foot, uses a hand for support, or 10 seconds have elapsed. Record any time less than 10 seconds to the nearest hundredth of a second on the test form.

a. Feet Together Stance

Testing Procedure: The first balance task is feet together stance. In this position, the patient is asked to stand for 10 seconds with the feet together in a side-by-side stance position (Fig. 8.19).

Instructions to Patient: "These three balancing tasks require you to stand in three different positions for up to 10 seconds. First we'll start with the feet together stance position. You can use me to get into the position but then you have to stand by yourself. I will be timing you when you are ready.

"First, I want you to place your feet completely together, like this. Then hold the position as long as you can. Ready? Begin."

If the patient was able to hold the position for 10 seconds, proceed to the next balance position. If the position was held less than 10 seconds, record the seconds and proceed to the chair stand test.

b. Semi-tandem Stance

Testing Procedure: The second balance task is the semi-tandem stance position. Demonstrate the position. The patient stands with the heel of one foot placed to the side of and touching the big toe of the other foot. Either foot can be placed in the forward position. The position should be timed (Fig. 8.20). (Note: This task should be performed only in patients who were able to perform the previous feet together stance task for 10 seconds.) Score the worst performance.

Instructions to Patient: "Move one foot in front of the other so that the heel of the front foot is against the side of the big toe of the other foot, like this. Make sure you do not turn your foot out. You can choose whichever foot you like. Begin!"

If able to complete 10 seconds, proceed to the third balance test. If unable to hold the semi-tandem position for 10 seconds, record the time held and proceed to the chair stand test.

FIGURE 8.19   **FIGURE 8.20**

Modified Physical Performance Test Continued

c. Full Tandem Stance

Testing Procedure: The third and final position is the tandem stance position. Demonstrate the position. Ask the patient to place the heel of one foot directly in front of the toes of the other foot. Either foot can be placed in the forward position (Fig. 8.21). (Note: This task should be performed only in patients who were able to perform the semi-tandem stance for 10 seconds.)

Instructions to Patient: "Place the heel of one foot directly in front of the toes of the other foot, like this." "Either foot can be placed in the forward position. Are you ready? Begin."

Helpful Hint

- Allowing the patient to choose which foot to place forward in the semi-tandem or full tandem stance may indicate which foot the patient feels is stronger. Only one foot forward position is tested.
- The original instructions, stated here, were for research purposes. In the clinical situation, patients may not be able to assume the ideal position because of severe valgus, for example. Therefore, some latitude may be required.

FIGURE 8.21

2. Chair Stand (Five-Repetition)

Testing Procedure: The chair stand task is a test of leg strength and mobility. The patient is asked to stand from the chair with the arms folded across the chest while the therapist observes. If the patient is able to rise from the chair once, the patient is then asked to stand up and sit down five times as quickly as possible. Timing begins as soon as the command to stand is given and continues until the patient is fully upright at the end of the fifth stand.

Position of Patient: Seated, with arms crossed over the chest. Feet are planted on the floor in a comfortable position (Fig. 8.22).

Instructions to Patient: "Fold your arms across your chest and sit so that your feet are on the floor. Then, stand up, keeping your arms folded across your chest." (After it is observed that the patient can safely stand independently without the use of the arms, proceed to the timed five-repetition part of the chair stand task.) "Now stand up straight, as quickly as you can, five times, without stopping in between. Keep your arms folded across your chest. I'll be timing you with a stopwatch."

Helpful Hints

- Place the chair against a wall, to avoid any movement.
- Observe the quality of the movement such as the position of the hips, reflected in valgus.
- Refer to the chair stand test on page 334.

FIGURE 8.22

Modified Physical Performance Test
Continued

Scoring

Each task's performance is recorded on the PPT scoring form (see Fig. 8.18) or M-PPT scoring form (Fig. 8.23) using a scale of 0 to 4. Total possible scores for the seven-item version of the PPT is 28, whereas the nine-item version PPT is 36. The M-PPT total possible score is 36. Reuben and Siu established percentile norms for the PPT based on the performance of a 79-year-old male who is independent in all ADLs.[27]

25th percentile ... 21 (9-item), 15 (7-item)
75th percentile ... 29 (9-item), 22 (7-item)
90th percentile ... 31 (9-item), 24 (7-item)

See Table 8.10 for mean scores for men and women aged 60 to 101 for the PPT.[33] Reuben determined that the following scores indicated a degree of frailty.[27]

32 to 36 = not frail
25 to 32 = mild frailty
17 to 24 = moderate frailty
<17 = unlikely to be able to function in the community.

The minimal important difference in older adults is 2.4 points.[26]

Helpful Hint

- Timing a patient during task performance should be done with the utmost awareness of the influence of timing. Many patients may move faster than is safe, because of a competitive nature. In some cases, it may not be best practice to tell the patient the task is timed, especially in cases where balance is significantly impaired.
- It is recommended to use the lowest score because of the need to accurately record the patient's performance in the clinical setting. Although performance may improve with repeated trials, the most genuine real-life performance may be the lowest timed or poorest performance.

Table 8.10 7-ITEM PHYSICAL PERFORMANCE TEST SCORES*

Age	Male	Female
60–69	26	26.4 (0.9)
70–79	24.6 (1.7)	25.1 (0.9)
80–89	20.4 (4.8)	19.5 (3.8)
90–101	16.5 (6.4)	16.2 (6.0)

*Subjects were able to use an assistive device.

Data from Lusardi MM, Pellecchia GL, Schulman M. Functional performance in community living older adults. *J Geriatr Phys Ther.* 2003;26:14–22

Modified Physical Performance Test

1.	Standing Static Balance	Feet Together: _____sec	Semi-tandem: _____sec	Tandem: _____sec	Score
		❏ 10 sec	❏ 10 sec	❏ 10 sec	❏ 4
		❏ 10 sec	❏ 10 sec	❏ 3–9.9 sec	❏ 3
		❏ 10 sec	❏ 10 sec	❏ 0–2.9 sec	❏ 2
		❏ 10 sec	❏ 0–9 sec	Unable	❏ 1
		❏ 0–9 sec	Unable	Unable	❏ 0

		Time	**Scoring values**	Score
2.	Chair stand (5 × without arms)		≤11 sec = 4 11.1–14 sec = 3 14.1–17 sec = 2 >17 sec = 1 unable = 0	
3.	Lift a book and put it on a shelf		≤2 sec = 4 2.1–4 sec = 3 4.1–6 sec = 2 >6 sec = 1 unable = 0	
4.	Put on and remove a garment		≤10 sec = 4 10.1–15 sec = 3 15.1–20 sec = 2 >20 sec = 1 unable = 0	
5.	Pick up a coin from the floor		≤2 sec = 4 2.1–4 sec = 3 4.1–6 sec = 2 >6 sec = 1 unable = 0	
6.	Turn 360°	Discontinuous steps = 0 Continuous steps = 2		
		Unsteady (grabs, staggers) = 0 Steady = 2		
7.	50-foot walk		≤15 sec = 4 15.1–20 sec = 3 20.1–25 sec = 2 >25 sec = 1 unable = 0	
8.	Climb one flight of stairs		≤5 sec = 4 5.1–10 sec = 3 10.1–15 sec = 2 >15 sec = 1 unable = 0	
9.	Climb four flights of stairs	Number of flights of stairs up and down (maximum 4)		
TOTAL SCORE			9-item score	/36

FIGURE 8.23 Scoring form for modified physical performance test (M-PPT).

Purpose: The timed up and go test (TUG) is a test of general mobility that involves standing from a standard-height chair, walking, turning, and sitting down.[34] The test can be performed with an assistive device.[35] Typically, the use of an assistive device indicates slower performance.

The TUG takes only seconds to perform and can be used in all health-care settings because of the minimal equipment and space required. The test can be used to identify impairments related to mobility.

Essential Muscle Movements for Task Performance: Hip extension, hip abduction from a flexed position, hip external rotation, knee extension, ankle plantar flexion, ankle dorsiflexion and inversion,[3] and trunk extension and flexion. Hip flexion also contributes to walking velocity.[16] The reader is referred to the gait section of this chapter for a more specific list of muscles that are imperative for smooth and normal gait.

Reliability: ICC = 0.99; test-retest reliability, ICC = 0.99.[36] In individuals with Alzheimer disease, ICC = 0.97.[37]

Validity: Construct validity is for independence in mobility (the time taken is strongly correlated to the level of functional mobility). Similar to gait speed, it can predict global health and new ADL difficulty. Those who required more than 20 seconds to perform the TUG had a 50% chance of having difficulty performing household chores.[38] It has limited ability to predict falls in community-dwelling older adults and should not be used in isolation to identify individuals at risk for falls.[39]

Equipment: Standard 17-in.-high chair with arms, stopwatch, and 3 m measured on the floor.

Testing Procedure: A chair with arms is placed against a wall to prevent the chair from moving. Measure a distance of 3 m from the front legs of the chair. A line or other object should indicate the 3-m mark (Fig. 8.24). Demonstrate the task for the patient, using an assistive device if the patient will be using one. Ask the patient to walk at a usual and comfortable speed 3 m to a specified mark on the floor, turn around and walk back to the chair, sitting all the way back in the chair. Timing starts on "Go!" rather than when the patient starts to rise. Be clear so that the patient knows you are about to start the test. Stop timing when the patient is fully seated with his or her back against the chair. A practice trial is given before the two test trials are performed.

Position of Patient: Seated in a chair with arms, feet on the floor, and back against the back of the chair.

Position of Therapist: Stand to the side of the patient. The therapist may choose to walk with the patient if safety is a concern (Fig. 8.25).

Instructions to Patient: "On 'Go!' I want you to stand up and walk as quickly but as safely as you can to the mark on the floor, turn, and return to the chair, sitting down with your back against the back of the chair. I'll be timing you, OK? Go!"

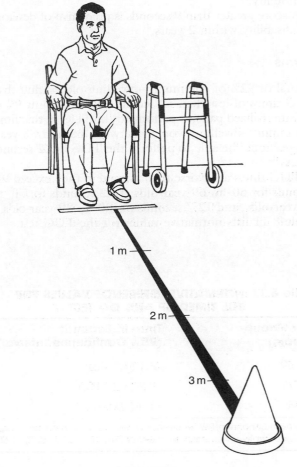

FIGURE 8.24

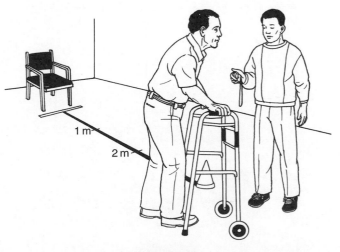

FIGURE 8.25

Scoring

The fastest trial time taken to perform the TUG is the score.

10 seconds or faster indicates the patient is freely mobile.

30 seconds or slower indicates the patient is dependent in mobility.[40]

A score greater than 9 seconds is predictive of developing disability within 2 years.[41]

Norms

A total of 92% of community-dwelling older adults had TUG times of less than 12 seconds, whereas only 9% of institutionalized patients performed the TUG in that time. Community-dwelling women between 65 and 85 years of age should be able to perform the TUG in 12 seconds or less.[42]

TUG times are worse than average if they exceed 9.0 seconds for 60- to 69-year-olds, 10.2 seconds for 70- to 79-year-olds, and 12.7 seconds for 80- to 89-year-olds.[43] Table 8.11 lists normative values for the TUG test.

Table 8.11 NORMATIVE REFERENCE VALUES FOR THE TIMED UP AND GO TEST

Age Group (Years)	Time in Seconds (95% Confidence Interval)
60–69	8.1 (7.1–9.0)
70–79	9.2 (8.2–10.2)
80–89	11.3 (10.0–12.7)

Data from Bohannon RW. Reference values for the timed up and go test: a descriptive meta-analysis. *J Geriatr Phys Ther.* 2006;29(2):64–68.

Helpful Hints

- Make sure the patient can hear you and waits for your "Go!"
- If using an object to mark the farthest point of the 3-m distance, make sure it is moved forward of the 3-m mark to avoid lengthening the course as the patient walks around the object (see Fig. 8.25).
- Always retest using the same assistive device as used in the original test.
- Avoid overcoaching. Valuable information that will inform clinical decision making can be obtained from observing how the patient chooses to perform the test.
- Using the general procedure for the TUG, a timed performance can be obtained from any surface, such as a couch or car seat, to assist in clinical decision making and objective documentation.
- Scoring may be either the fastest, the slowest, or an average of the trials. Each repeat test should reflect the same choice.

Purpose: The stair climb test assesses the ability to climb a flight of stairs. Qualitative and quantitative assessment can be made to determine the amount of assistance a patient needs, identify impairments that may contribute to stair climbing, and indicate how quickly and/or safely the patient can accomplish the task. The stair climb test is also used as a functional test of power.[44,45]

Essential Muscle Movements for Task Performance: Ascent: hip extension, knee flexion and extension, ankle plantar flexion, ankle dorsiflexion, spine extension, and core stability. Descent: eccentric knee extension, hip flexion, and core muscles. For a test that requires stability and balance, however, any lower extremity muscle or group will be used at some point during the task.

Reliability: ICC = 0.99[46]

Validity: Moderate validity as a functional measure with correlations to other functional measures such as TUG, gait speed, and sit-to-stand movement.[47] Also correlates with balance tests and lower extremity strength and power.

Equipment: Any flight of stairs with a railing can be used. The pediatric version (timed up and down stairs [TUDS]) requires 11 stairs to compare the score with normative data.

Testing Procedure: Timing starts when the patient's first foot is lifted from the floor and is stopped when both feet are on the top stair. Because descent is typically more difficult, the therapist should time ascent and descent separately. The therapist should document the use of handrails, assistive devices, gait belts, and the number of stairs.

Position of Therapist: Safety of the patient should be the therapist's primary concern. Therefore the therapist may need to closely guard the patient, ascending and descending the stairs with the patient (Fig. 8.26). If the therapist is confident of the safety of the patient, the therapist can choose to remain at the bottom of the flight of stairs during the test.

Instructions to Patient: "I want to see how safely and how quickly you can climb this flight of stairs. Do you feel safe to climb these stairs? You may hold onto the railing if you want to. Please stop at the top of the stairs before coming down so I can time how long it takes you to descend. Ready? Go!"

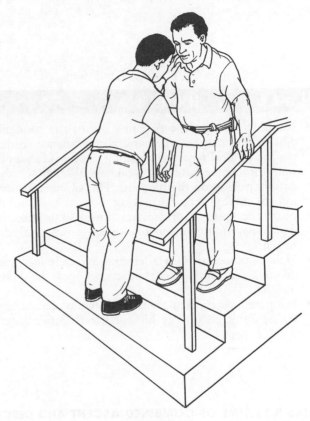

FIGURE 8.26

STAIR CLIMB

Scoring

Scoring the time it takes the patient to ascend and descend stairs must include the number of stairs. Time is calculated by dividing the number of stairs in the flight by the time taken to go up and down.

In nondisabled adult individuals, 0.5 second per stair (up and down) is typical (Table 8.12).[47] Stair ascent and descent (combined) decreases with age from 2.5 stairs per second in 20- to 39-year-olds to 1.2 stairs per second in 90+ year olds.[48] In children ages 8 to 14, 8.1 seconds for 14 steps (0.58 second per step) was determined to be normal for combined ascent and descent (Table 8.13).[49]

Table 8.12 GROUP DATA FOR STAIR CLIMB TIME FROM SYSTEMATIC REVIEW

Age	Ascent	Descent
18–49	0.48 ± 0.14	0.50 ± 0.14
50–65	0.46 ± 0.17	0.54 ± 0.29
>65	0.65 ± 0.41	1.4 ± 0.55
>65 with decreased mobility	0.95 ± 0.44	1.11 ± 0.47
Neurological	1.01 ± 0.57	0.9 ± 0.47
Medical	0.6 ± 0.15	0.81 ± 0.15
Musculoskeletal	0.82 ± 0.33	0.96 ± 0.41

Data from Nightengale EJ, Pourkazemi F, Hiller CE. Systemic review of timed stair tests. *J Rehabil Res Dev.* 2014;51(3):335–350.

Helpful Hints

- Carefully observe the patient's use of the handrail. The patient may use the handrail for balance or may use the handrail for weight bearing to off-load a painful joint or compensate for weakness. Watch for the patient pulling on the handrail. This observation can inform clinical decision making.
- Note the position of the feet during stair descent, which may indicate compensation for muscle weakness or pain.
- Stair climbing without a handrail typically increases ground reaction forces by seven times the body weight.[50,51]
- If a patient with eyeglasses has difficulty descending stairs, don't encourage him or her to move faster. Glasses sometimes cause the patient to see a step where it isn't and increased speed may result in a fall.
- It typically takes longer to ascend than descend stairs, in the healthy population. Stair ascent and descent time increase with age, with stair descent time increasing to a greater extent.[47]
- Single-leg squats can identify independent stair negotiation ability in older adults.[52]
- Standardization recommendations include a flight of at least 10 stairs timing ascent and descent times separately, and asking the patient to perform as quickly as possible with the handrail to be used for balance only.[47]

Table 8.13 TIME OF COMBINED ASCENT AND DESCENT ON FLIGHT OF 11 STAIRS (SEC/STAIR)

	3–9 Years M	F	10–19 Years M	F	20–59 Years M	F	60+ Years M	F
95th percentile	2.32	2.31	0.73	0.84	0.78	0.97	1.5	2.0

F, Female; M, male.

Data from McKay MJ, Baldwin JN, Ferreira P, Simic M, Vanicek N, Burns J. 1000 Norms Project Consortium. Normative reference values for strength and flexibility of 1,000 children and adults. *Neurology.* 2017;88(1):36–43.

Purpose: Floor rise ability is necessary for a patient's safety and confidence. Anyone who falls should be able to rescue themselves from the floor (unless they have become seriously injured). The floor rise test assesses the patient's ability to rise from the floor, thereby identifying impairments, functional ability, and informing clinical decision making.

Essential Muscle Movements for Task Performance: Knee extension, ankle plantar flexion, hip extension, core stability, and trunk rotation. If arms are needed to assist, scapular adduction and downward rotation, scapular depression and adduction, elbow extension, and shoulder horizontal adduction.

Reliability: Excellent reliability

Validity: An inability to rise from the floor is associated with older age, increased mortality, and lower functional abilities and risk for serious injury.[53]

Equipment: Stopwatch, chair with arms, and an unobstructed floor surface that allows the patient to lie flat.

Testing Procedure: The therapist should demonstrate the lowering of the body to the floor, lying supine, and rising again. During the test, the patient should lie supine so that 75% of the body is in contact with the floor. The patient may choose to place the head and trunk flat on the floor, bending the knees or lying flat with only the head and shoulders raised (Fig. 8.27). Either position is acceptable. A chair should be nearby to be used by the patient if needed. Timing begins on "Go!" and ends when the patient is fully standing again and steady. Document the type of assistance needed to rise, as appropriate.

Instructions to Patient: "I want you to get onto the floor, without assistance if possible, lying flat so that most of your body is flat on the floor, then get up again. You may get up in any way you choose and if you need to, you may use this chair. I can help you if you can't get up by yourself. I will demonstrate. I will be timing you and will stop timing when you are fully standing and steady. Are you ready? Good. Go!"

Scoring

The score is the time it takes to complete the floor transfer. There are no norms for this test, but in the author's experience, more than 10 seconds often involves the need for assistance with the transfer. The therapist may score only the time it takes to rise from the floor, rather than the combined floor descent and rise.

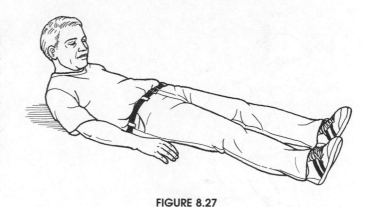

FIGURE 8.27

Helpful Hints

- When an individual has difficulty getting up from the floor, it often involves an inability to shift weight at the hips and roll onto the side as in side-sitting to the knees.
- The therapist should note the "cause" of any difficulty in rising—such as pain, weakness, or an inability to motor plan. These causes may form the basis of a treatment plan.
- Because there are several ways to rise from the floor, the method used by the patient should be noted in the documentation. The position requiring the most strength is rising without assistance (Fig. 8.28); using one knee to rise requires less strength (Fig. 8.29); and using assistance such as a chair requires the least amount of strength (Fig. 8.30).

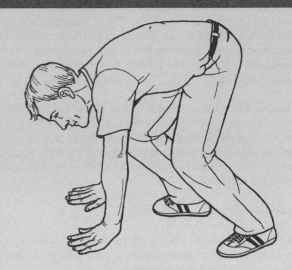

FIGURE 8.28

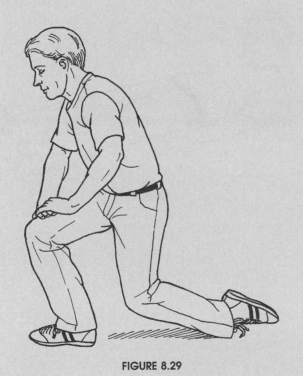

FIGURE 8.29

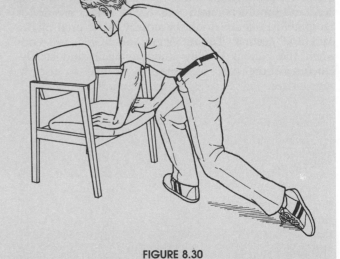

FIGURE 8.30

Human gait is a remarkable feat. Each step is a complex integration of muscular and neural events, all of which have to occur in proper sequence and magnitude to prevent loss of balance and maintain a smooth and integrated forward progression with the least expenditure of energy.[54,55] Loss of muscle strength has a devastating effect on gait, particularly velocity, safety, and energy cost.[56,57] An entire issue of the journal *Physical Therapy* was devoted to this and related topics in 2010.[58]

This chapter segment is focused only on five events in the gait cycle that occur smoothly and successfully if the muscles involved are sufficiently strong. Weakness in the gluteus medius, tibialis anterior, quadriceps, gluteus maximus, or gastroc-soleus will significantly blunt gait velocity and interrupt the integration of gait events and the limb segments involved.

Because locomotion is so important to humans, rehabilitation is often focused on its restoration. The key to successful rehabilitation, however, is the identification of the muscles or muscle groups that are weak. What follows are some common deviations in the gait cycle that are directly linked to specific muscle weakness. These deviations are easily observed, and once observed, the therapist can perform specific muscle testing for confirmation.

Gluteus Medius Weakness

During the loading phase of the gait cycle, as the stance limb is accepting the entire weight of the body (single limb support), the gluteus medius contracts vigorously to keep the pelvis from dropping to the opposite side. When electromyographic output during gait is measured and compared to the electromyographic output generated during a maximal isometric contraction, the demand on the gluteus medius appears to be approximately 25% of its maximum force capacity. Thus, in general, strength must be at least Grade 3 to prevent the pelvis from dropping.[59] If pelvic drop is observed, strength must be restored because gait velocity slows and the energy required to walk increases in the presence of gluteus medius weakness.[56]

Inman calculated the demand on the gluteus medius during single limb stance (most of the gait cycle) as 2.5 times the weight of the head, arms, and trunk.[60] Thus, for a 150-lb individual, the gluteus medius must generate approximately 100 lb of torque with each step. If the therapist is strength testing with a handheld dynamometer, a minimum of 100 lb should be the expected value in a 150-lb person.

Tibialis Anterior Weakness

Immediately following heel strike, the tibialis anterior (TA) decelerates the foot to the floor.[56,59] This eccentric contraction is a rapid event that places high demand on the muscle, estimated at between 45% and 75% of its maximum strength.[59,61] A demand this high requires a manual muscle grade of at least 4. Weakness of the TA immediately eliminates the foot-lowering portion of the normal gait cycle. With moderate weakness (approximately Grade 3) the therapist will observe a foot flat gait.[59] Stride length is shortened to permit the foot flat landing. A shorter stride results in slower gait velocity. Thus, if the therapist observes a patient who fails to execute heel strike and approaches each step with a foot flat approach, muscle test the TA to confirm its strength loss. If there is severe weakness, the therapist will observe (and hear) a foot slap gait.

Quadriceps Weakness

Another key event in the stance phase of gait is shock absorption at the knee shortly after heel strike.[59] During this instant in the gait cycle, the knee (in a normal person) rapidly goes from full extension to 15° of flexion and the quadriceps absorb a high amount of force, estimated to be 75% of maximum.[59] With shock absorption, the quadriceps permit a smooth transition to mid-stance. If the quadriceps are weak the entire shock absorption process disappears, which is another observable event. Instead of a brisk knee flexion following heel strike, the patient with weak quadriceps will shorten the stride and approach the entire first half of the stance phase with a nearly extended knee. No shock absorption takes place. Strength estimates vary, but the quadriceps must be at least a Grade 3 to absorb the shock of knee flexion immediately after heel strike.[59] If the therapist observes a failure of knee flexion during the initial phase of stance, quadriceps strength should be evaluated.

Gluteus Maximus Weakness

The highest strength demand on the gluteus maximus occurs during loading response and is complete by the mid-stance phase of gait.[62] Once total body weight is transferred onto the stance leg, the gluteus maximus must assume responsibility for the upright trunk (muscle acting on its origin). If muscle weakness is present, the patient will exhibit a forward trunk lean. Forward trunk lean may occur during the entire stance phase or occur suddenly, a "pitching forward," suggesting a sudden failure of the muscles to hold the trunk upright. Gluteus maximus strength should be sufficient to hold the weight of the head, arms, and trunk, or about 60% of body mass.[59] If suspected gluteus maximus weakness exists, as evidenced by a forward trunk lean during stance, with subsequent slowing of gait, further muscle testing is indicated for confirmation.

Gastrocnemius-Soleus Weakness

When the gastrocnemius and soleus act on their insertion, they produce plantar flexion and stabilize the ankle during roll-off.[61,63,64] The soleus is one of the most important muscles of the leg because it works not just to control

Gastrocnemius-Soleus Weakness Continued

the foot and ankle complex but has a critical role in stabilizing the knee.[65] Equally important is the role of the soleus to prevent forward translation of the tibia toward the end of the stance phase. If the soleus is functioning adequately, the ankle is stable and heel rise occurs.[59] The demand on the gastrocnemius and soleus is extremely high, measured at 75% of maximum for the gastrocnemius and at more than 80% for the soleus. When gastrocnemius-soleus muscle strength is at least Grade 4, the ankle will lock and heel rise will occur, which is another key event in the gait cycle that markedly influences velocity.[66] If heel rise is noticeably diminished or nonexistent, further muscle testing is indicated.

Each of the five gait events described has been identified as one of the "critical determinants of gait."[65-67] Without these five critical determinants, gait velocity is markedly

diminished, and as noted, if gait speed slows enough, community ambulation is no longer feasible and/or independence may be lost. Indeed, loss of gait function is a major reason for nursing home placement in a person's later years.[68]

Hicks and colleagues reported that the collective strength of 24% of normal is required to walk.[69] If strength is below 24% of normal, profound changes in gait speed have already occurred, and a person with this much weakness is on the threshold of frailty, loss of independence, and in need of an assistive device.[70] Physical therapists can recognize subtle but highly observable gait deviations long before strength losses become catastrophic. Muscle testing techniques as presented in this book permit identification of strength losses in the early phase of loss, when rehabilitation is more feasible and successful.

1. Jette AM. Toward a common language for function, disability and health. *Phys Ther*. 2006;86:726–734.

2. Eriksrud O, Bohannon RW. Relationship of knee extension force to independence in sit-to-stand performance in patients receiving acute rehabilitation. *Phys Ther*. 2003;83(6):544–551.

3. Gross MM, Stevenson PJ, Charette SL, et al. Effect of muscle strength and movement speed on the biomechanics of rising from a chair in healthy elderly and young women. *Gait Posture*. 1998;8(3):175–185.

4. Jones CJ, Rikli RE, Beam WC. A 30-s chair stand test as a measure of lower body strength in community-residing older adults. *Res Q Exerc Sport*. 1999;70(2):113–119.

5. Bohannon RW. Sit to stand test for measuring performance of lower extremity muscles. *Percept Mot Skills*. 1995;80:163–166.

6. Csuka M, McCarty DJ. A simple method for measurement of lower extremity muscle strength. *Am J Med*. 1985;78:77–81.

7. Goldberg A, Chavis M, Watkins J, et al. The five-times-sit-to-stand test: validity, reliability and detectable change in older females. *Aging Clin Exp Res*. 2012;24(4):339–344.

8. Deshpande N, Metter EJ, Guralnik J, et al. Predicting 3-year incident mobility disability in middle-aged and older adults using physical performance tests. *Arch Phys Med Rehabil*. 2013;94(5):994–997.

9. Makizako H, Shimada H, Doi T, et al. Predictive cutoff values of the Five Times Sit-to-Stand Test and the Timed "Up & Go" Test for disability incidence in older people dwelling in the community. *Phys Ther*. 2017;97:417–424.

10. Kuo YL. The influence of chair seat height on the performance of community-dwelling older adults' 30-second chair stand test. *Aging Clin Exp Res*. 2013;25(3):305–309.

11. Guralnik Jack M, Fried Linda P, Simonsick Eleanor M, et al, eds. *The Women's Health and Aging Study: Health and Social Characteristics of Older Women With Disability*. Darby PA: Diane Pub Co; 1995:44.

12. Brown M. Quick tests to aid in the diagnosis of physical frailty. *GeriNotes*. 1998;15(4):15.

13. Fritz S, Lusardi M. White paper: "Walking speed: The sixth vital sign.". *J Geriatr Phys Ther*. 2009;32(2):2–5.

14. Neptune RR, Sasaki K, Kautz SA. The effect of walking speed on muscle function and mechanical energetics. *Gait Posture*. 2008;28:135–143.

15. John CT, Seth A, Schwartz MH, et al. Contributions of muscles to mediolateral ground reaction force over a range of walking speeds. *J Biomech*. 2012;45(14):2438–2443.

16. Chang RW, Dunlop D, Gibbs J, et al. The determinants of walking velocity in the elderly. An evaluation using regression trees. *Arthritis Rheum*. 1995;38(3):343–350.

17. Kim HJ, Park I, Lee HJ, et al. The reliability and validity of gait speed with different walking pace and distances against general health, physical function, and chronic disease in aged adults. *J Exerc Nutrition Biochem*. 2016;20(3):46–50.

18. Abellan van Kan G, Rolland Y, Andrieu S, et al. Gait speed at usual pace as a predictor of adverse outcomes in community-dwelling older people: an International Academy on Nutrition and Aging (IANA) task force. *J Nutr Health Aging*. 2009;13(10):881–889.

19. Artaud F, Singh-Manoux A, Dugravot A, et al. Decline in fast gait speed as a predictor of disability in older adults. *J Am Geriatr Soc*. 2015;63(6):1129–1136.

20. Blain H, Carriere I, Sourial N, et al. Balance and walking speed predict subsequent 8-year mortality independently of current and intermediate events in well-functioning women aged 75 years and older. *J Nutr Health Aging*. 2010;14(7):595–600.

21. Ostir GV, Berges IM, Ottenbacher KJ, et al. Gait speed and dismobility in older adults. *Arch Phys Med Rehabil*. 2015;96(9):1641–1645.

22. Ng SS, Au KK, Chan EL, et al. Effect of acceleration and deceleration distance on the walking speed of people with chronic stroke. *J Rehabil Med*. 2016;48(8):666–670.

23. Ng SS, Ng PC, Lee CY, et al. Assessing the walking speed of older adults: the influence of walkway length. *Am J Phys Med Rehabil*. 2013;92(9):776–780.

24. Andrews AW, Chinworth SA, Bourassa M, et al. Update on distance and velocity requirements for community ambulation. *J Geriatr Phys Ther*. 2010;33(3):128–134.

25. McFadyen BJ, Winter DA. An integrated biomechanical analysis of normal stair ascent and descent. *J Biomech*. 1988;21(9):733–744.

26. King MB, Judge JO, et al. Reliability and responsiveness of two physical performance measures examined in the context of a functional training intervention. *Phys Ther*. 2000;80(1):8–16.

27. Reuben DB, Siu Al. An objective measure of physical function of elderly outpatients: the Physical Performance Test. *J Am Geriatr Soc*. 1990;38(10):1105–1112.

28. Beissner KL, Collins JE, Holmes H. Muscle force and range of motion as predictors of function in older adults. *Phys Ther*. 2000;80:556–563.

29. Reuben DB, Siu Al, Kimpau S. The predictive validity of self-report and performance-based measures of function and health. *J Gerontol*. 1992;47:M106–M110.

30. Delbaere K, Van den Noortgate N, et al. The Physical Performance Test as a predictor of frequent fallers: a prospective community-based cohort study. *Clin Rehabil*. 2006;20(1):83–90.

31. VanSwearingen JM, Paschal KA, Bonino P, et al. Assessing recurrent fall risk of community-dwelling, frail older veterans using specific tests of mobility and the physical performance test of function. *J Gerontol A Biol Sci Med Sci*. 1998;53A:M457–M464.

32. Brown M, Sinacore DR, Binder EF, et al. Physical and performance measures for the identification of mild to moderate frailty. *J Gerontol A Biol Sci Med Sci*. 2000;55A(6):M350–M355.

33. Lusardi MM, Pellecchia GL, et al. Functional performance in community living older adults. *J Geriatr Phys Ther*. 2003;26:14–22.

34. Herman T, Giladi N, Hausdorff JM. Properties of the 'timed up and go' test: more than meets the eye. *Gerontology*. 2010;57(3):203–210.

35. Mathias S, Nayak US, Isaacs B. Balance in elderly patients: the "get-up and go" test. *Arch Phys Med Rehabil*. 1986;67(6):387–389.

36. Podsiadlo D, Richardson S. The timed "up and go": a test of basic functional mobility for frail elderly persons. *J Am Geriatr Soc*. 1991;39:142–148.

37. Ries JD, Echternach JL, Nof L, et al. Test-retest reliability and minimal detectable change scores for the timed "up & go" test, the six-minute walk test, and gait speed in people with Alzheimer disease. *Phys Ther*. 2009;89(6):569–579.

38. Donoghue OA, Savva GM, Cronin H, et al. Using timed up and go and usual gait speed to predict incident disability in daily activities among community-dwelling adults aged 65 and older. *Arch Phys Med Rehabil*. 2014;95(10):1954–1961.

39. Barry E, Galvin R, Keogh C, et al. Is the Timed Up and Go test a useful predictor of risk of falls in community dwelling older adults: a systematic review and meta-analysis. *BMC Geriatr*. 2014;14:14.

REFERENCES

40. Steffen T, Seney M. Test-retest reliability and minimal detectable change on balance and ambulation tests, the 36-item short-form health survey, and the unified Parkinson disease rating scale in people with parkinsonism. *Phys Ther.* 2008;88(6):733–746.

41. Makizako H, Shimada H, Doi T, et al. Predictive cutoff values of the FiveTimes Sit-to-Stand Test and the Timed "Up & Go" Test for disability incidence in older people dwelling in the community. *Phys Ther.* 2017;97:417–424.

42. Bischoff HA, Stahelin HB, Monsch AU, et al. Identifying a cut-off point for normal mobility: a comparison of the timed "up and go" test in community-dwelling and institutionalised elderly women. *Age Ageing.* 2003;32(3):315–320.

43. Bohannon RW. Reference values for the timed up and go test: a descriptive meta-analysis. *J Geriatr Phys Ther.* 2006;29(2):64–68.

44. Zech A, Steib S, Sportwiss D, et al. Functional muscle power testing in young, middle-aged, and community-dwelling nonfrail and prefrail older adults. *Arch Phys Med Rehabil.* 2011;92(6):967–971.

45. Roig M, Eng JJ, MacIntyre DL, et al. Associations of the stair climb power test with muscle strength and functional performance in people with chronic obstructive pulmonary disease: a cross-sectional study. *Phys Ther.* 2010;90(12): 1774–1782.

46. LeBrasseur NK, Bhasin S, Miciek R, et al. Tests of muscle strength and physical function: reliability and discrimination of performance in younger and older men and older men with mobility limitations. *JAGS.* 2008;56:2118–2123.

47. Nightingale EJ. Systemic review of timed stair tests. *JRRD.* 2014;51(3):335–350.

48. Butler AA, Menant JC, Tiedemann AC, et al. Age and gender differences in seven tests of functional mobility. *J Neuroeng Rehabil.* 2009;6:31.

49. Zaino CA, Marchese VG, Westcott SL. Timed up and down stairs test: preliminary reliability and validity of a new measure of functional mobility. *Pediatr Phys Ther.* 2004;16(2):90–98.

50. Teh KC, Aziz AR. Heart rate, oxygen uptake, and energy cost of ascending and descending the stairs. *Med Sci Sports Exerc.* 2002;34:695–699.

51. Stolk J, Verdonschot N, Huiskes R. Stair climbing is more detrimental to the cement in hip replacement than walking. *Clin Orthop Relat Res.* 2002;405:294–305, Nightengale, 2014.

52. Hockings RL, Schmidt DD, Cheung CW. Single-leg squats identify independent stair negotiation ability in older adults referred for a physiotherapy mobility assessment at a rural hospital. *J Am Geriatr Soc.* 2013;61(7):1146–1151.

53. Bergland A, Laake K. Concurrent and predictive validity of "getting up from lying on the floor." *Aging Clin Exp Res.* 2005;17(3):181–185.

54. Kuo AD, Donelan JM. Dynamic principles of gait and their clinical implications. *Phys Ther.* 2010;90:157–176.

55. Borghese NA, Bianchi L, Lacquaniti F. Kinematic determinants of human locomotion. *J Physiol.* 1996;494:863–879.

56. Waters RL. The energy expenditure of normal and pathological gait. *Gait Posture.* 1999;9:207–231.

57. Bianchi L, Angelini D, Orani GP, et al. Kinematic coordination in human gait: relation to mechanical energy cost. *J Neurophysiol.* 1998;79:2155–2170.

58. Jacquelin Perry. Special issue: stepping forward with gait rehabilitation. *Phys Ther.* 2010;90(2):142–305.

59. Perry J, Burnfield JM. *Gait Analysis: Normal and Pathological Function.* 2nd ed. Thorofare NJ: Slack Inc; 2010:3–260.

60. Inman V. Functional aspects of the abductor muscles of the hip. *J Bone Joint Surg.* 1947;29:607–619.

61. Dubo HIC, Peat M, Winter DA, et al. Electromyographic temporal analysis of gait: normal human locomotion. *Arch Phys Med Rehabil.* 1976;57:415–420.

62. Lyons K, Perry J, Gronley JK, et al. Timing and relative intensity of hip extensor and abductor muscle action during levels and stair ambulation. *Phys Ther.* 1983;63:1597–1605.

63. Sutherland DH, Cooper L, Daniel D. The role of the ankle plantar flexors in normal walking. *J Bone Joint Surg.* 1980;62A:354–363.

64. Simon SR, Mann RA, Hagy JL, et al. Role of the posterior calf muscles in normal gait. *J Bone Joint Surg.* 1978;60A: 465–475.

65. Kerrigan DC, Della Croce U, Marciello M, et al. A refined view of the determinants of gait: significance of heel rise. *Arch Phys Med Rehabil.* 2000;81:1077–1080.

66. Saunders JB, Inman VT, Eberhardt HD. The major determinants in normal and pathological gait. *J Bone Joint Surg.* 1953;35A:543–548.

67. Pandy MG, Berme N. Quantitative assessment of gait determinants during single stance via a three-dimensional model-part 1. Normal gait. *J Biomech.* 1989;22:717–724.

68. Studenski S, Perera S, Patel K, et al. Gait speed and survival in older adults. *JAMA.* 2011;305:70–78.

69. Hicks GE, Shardell M, Alley DE, et al. Absolute strength and loss of strength as predictors of mobility decline in older adults: the InCHIANTI study. *J Gerontol A Biol Sci Med Sci.* 2012;67(1):66–73.

70. Bassey EJ, Fiatarone MA, O'Neill EF, et al. Leg extension power and functional performance in very old men and women. *Clin Sci.* 1992;52:321–327.

Handheld Muscle Dynamometry

HANDHELD MUSCLE DYNAMOMETRY

INTRODUCTION

Handheld dynamometry (HHD), also referred to as handheld myometry, is a manual muscle testing procedure by which a dynamometer is held in the hand of an examiner to quantitatively measure the strength of specific muscle actions of the limbs or trunk. Essentially, it is an extension of the human hand. The handheld dynamometer comes with different pads to be used for different body segments. HHD measures force on a continuous scale in Newtons (N), pounds (lb), or kilograms (kg) from 3.6 N up to 1320 N (0.2 to 300 lb), depending on the device. HHD should not be confused with grip strength dynamometry (see page 218) in which an instrument held in the hand of a patient is used to measure that patient's hand-grip strength.

Research published over the past 100 years describes the use of at least a dozen different handheld dynamometers.[1] Although handheld dynamometers are commonly used in research, they are less commonly used in the clinic, perhaps because the HHD technique is not routinely taught in entry-level programs. However, HHD has been used in a variety of settings that reflect the scope of physical therapist practice such as acute care,[2] inpatient rehabilitation,[3,4] home care,[5] and outpatient.[6]

Handheld dynamometers are accurate, easy to use, portable, and afford an objectivity that is lacking in manual muscle testing (MMT). The continuous scale used in HHD allows the identification of subtle differences in side-to-side comparisons and avoids the ceiling effect of MMT. HHD is also more responsive, making it possible to discern changes in strength within Grades 4 and 5. However, many of the issues and limitations of MMT discussed in Chapters 1 and 2 are relevant to the application of HHD. The reader is referred to these chapters to review the limitations of MMT and to extend the recommendations for enhancing the reliability of MMT to HHD, recognizing that the same procedures apply to HHD. The reader is reminded that HHD values are influenced by the tester's strength, position, ability to stabilize the body segment and the technique used. Large muscle forces (over 250 N) may not be accurate due to stabilization and tester strength issues.[7] The inability of some handheld dynamometers to record the high forces generated by strong muscles (e.g., quadriceps and plantar flexors), lack of clear meaning of the scores, and the lack of standardization of positions are additional limitations of HHD.

Clinimetric Properties

The clinimetric properties of strength measures obtained by HHD have been researched extensively over the past few decades. Research on HHD reveals conflicting results for both test-retest and intertester reliability, in part because of the methodological quality of studies and lack of standardization of method (e.g., lack of stabilization, patient position, rate of force applied, use of make or break tests).[8,9] Reliability tends to be lower when stronger actions, such as knee extension or plantar flexion, stronger patients, or weaker testers are involved.[10-13]

A systematic review of the intraexaminer reliability of HHD measurements obtained from the upper extremity demonstrated acceptable intra-rater and inter-rater reliability (ICC > 0.90) for only elbow flexion and extension;[8] however, subsequent studies show similar intra-rater and inter-rater reliability (ICC > 0.90) for shoulder internal and external rotation tested in the 0 degrees and 90–90 shoulder-elbow position in sitting, prone and supine.[14,15] Strength measurements are internally consistent when performed by a tester with adequate strength.[16] Intersession reliability is better than intrasession reliability.[8,17] Unfortunately, standardization of position and method is lacking in HHD; therefore the reliability demonstrated in these studies may not necessarily be applied to the positions described in this chapter.

The validity of HHD is supported by considerable research. Specifically, correlations between measurements obtained by HHD and measurements obtained by isokinetic dynamometry support the criterion validity of HHD.[9] Convergent validity is supported by correlations between lower limb strength measured by HHD and performance of activities such as dressing, toileting and transferring,[18] bed mobility,[19] sit-to-stand,[3,20] level ground ambulation,[21,22] and stair negotiation.[23] Known groups validity is upheld by differences in the dynamometrically measured strength of normal adults and adults with pathologies and problems as diverse as renal failure,[21] stroke,[24] osteoporosis,[25] diabetes,[26] osteoarthritis,[27] dementia,[18] and fear of falling.[27,28]

The responsiveness of HHD has been described mostly through reporting of minimal detectable change.[16,29] Responsiveness is variable and is affected by HHD methods. Generally, a change of greater than 22 N in the upper extremity must be attained for confidence in a true difference.[15,30] Minimal clinically important differences in force measured using HHD are lacking.

Normative reference values have been published for dynamometrically obtained measures of upper and lower limb strength.[7,31-37] These norms are limited by the positions and type of dynamometer used and the use of make or break tests. Nevertheless, they provide some indication of what might be expected from healthy adults.

General Procedures

The tests described in this chapter use the same manual muscle testing positions described elsewhere in this book, and thus the same testing procedures are followed. First, the position of the patient is described. Then the patient is asked to perform the test action to assess the quality and quantity of the action and to determine if application of resistance is appropriate (e.g., in the presence of pain or inflammation). Although HHD may be used on a muscle action that does not produce full range, it is important to discern what limitations prevent full range such as weakness, joint restrictions, or pain. If weakness is below a Grade 3 (i.e., the patient cannot tolerate any resistance other than gravity), HHD may not be practical. Next, appropriate stabilization is applied and is a critical element in HHD testing. The assistance of another person may be needed if the therapist suspects the patient's muscle action could overcome the therapist's strength or adequate stabilization cannot be achieved without extra help. Once adequate stabilization is achieved, place the HHD on the body segment and ask the patient to push or pull against the HHD with maximum effort. This effort should occur within 2 to 5 seconds adhering to the procedures outlined on page 309. The use of a break test elicits a slightly stronger and eccentric contraction[37] than a make test and thus is used in this text, similar to the recommended procedure for MMT. However, there may be times when a make test is more appropriate (e.g., in the presence of joint instability, patient cooperation, pain). To enhance reliability, a monotone command such as "push, push, push" is provided. At the completion of the effort, peak force is read from the dynamometer. Although a single effort may suffice in the experienced clinician,[38] a second or third trial should be conducted for the inexperienced therapist and patient. If multiple efforts are attained, the tester can choose whether to average the results, using the highest or lowest value. Allow a rest of at least 30 seconds between efforts. Scoring is recorded in Newtons, rather than as muscle grades.

Testing Specific Actions

Various methods of testing over 25 different actions of the limbs and trunk using HHD have been described in the literature. Procedures vary, revealing a lack of standardization. Therefore, we have chosen the standard muscle testing positions described in this book, which are known to be valid testing positions. Consistent positions may encourage adoption and broader use, especially as validity studies on these positions are published. The therapist should review the helpful hints for each muscle action described in previous chapters (Box 9.1).

Reference Scores

The lack of standardization of HHD makes the interpretation of normative scores difficult. In this chapter, we have used normative data from studies using positions similar to the standard MMT positions. These positions often require some dynamic stabilization that may influence the muscle force generated. The reader is cautioned to analyze any differences in scores achieved with normative scores achieved in different positions. We have used normative scores for the dominant upper limb. The reader should be aware that in normal adults without pain or muscle disease, the stronger side does not exceed the weaker one by more than 22%.[7] When normative scores do not exist for the MMT positions, we have used studies of large samples. Results from break tests are included whenever available. Because of the variability of normative scores across studies, we have opted to use mean scores and standard deviations using decade data. If more precise scores are desired, the reader is encouraged to read the referenced study. The mean score should give the beginner user an idea of approximate values for specific muscle actions. Scores are always recorded in Newtons. When normative scores were recorded in Kg, they were converted to Newtons, by multiplying Kg × 9.8. The reader is also cautioned about placing undue emphasis on values and results exceeding 250 N, because 250 N most likely exceeds the force necessary for the performance of most functional tasks[7] and may have reduced reliability as compared to lower values. Additionally, most therapists will not be able to effectively stabilize or resist muscle forces exceeding 250 N. Examples are the knee extensors and plantar flexors.

Box 9.1 Muscle Actions

Shoulder flexion	Hip flexion
Shoulder extension	Hip extension
Shoulder abduction	Hip flexion
Shoulder external rotation	Hip external rotation
Shoulder internal rotation	Hip internal rotation
Elbow flexion	Knee extension
Elbow extension	Knee flexion
Wrist extension	Foot dorsiflexion and inversion
Hip abduction	

SHOULDER FLEXION

(Anterior deltoid, Rotator cuff, Clavicular portion of pectoralis major, and Coracobrachialis)

Position of Patient: Short sitting with arms at sides, elbow slightly flexed, forearm pronated.

Instructions to Therapist: Stand at the test side. Ask the patient to raise the arm forward to shoulder height (see Fig. 5.50 on page 120). If application of resistance is appropriate, proceed to test. Position the patient's arm in 90° of flexion with the forearm in neutral rotation and the arm in the sagittal plane. Ask the patient to hold the position. Place the hand with the handheld dynamometer over the distal humerus just above the elbow. The other hand stabilizes the shoulder (Fig. 9.1). Resistance is given in a downward direction.

Test: The patient holds the shoulder in 90° of flexion without rotation or horizontal movement (see Fig. 9.1 and Fig. 5.50 on page 120). The scapula should be allowed to abduct and upwardly rotate.

Instructions to Patient: "Hold your arm. Don't let me push it down. Hold ... hold ... hold."

Reference Scores

Normative scores with standard deviations below are for a break test in sitting[35]:

Mean for 20- to 59-year-old men = 203.4 (43.1)
Mean for 20- to 59-year-old women = 102.6 (35.6)

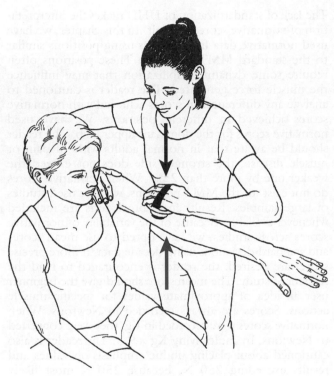

FIGURE 9.1

(Posterior deltoid, Latissimus dorsi, Teres major, Long head of triceps)

Position of Patient: Prone with arms at sides and shoulder internally rotated (palm up). Head turned toward the side being tested (see Fig. 5.56 on page 124).

Instructions to Therapist: Stand at the test side. Ask the patient to lift the arm as high as possible. If application of resistance is appropriate, proceed to test. Position the arm in full extension. Ask the patient to hold the position. Place the hand with the handheld dynamometer over the posterior arm just above the elbow. Stabilization is provided by the prone position. Resistance is applied in a downward direction (Fig. 9.2).

Test: Patient holds the arm off the table, with the elbow straight (see Fig. 5.58 on page 124).

Instructions to Patient: "Hold your arm. Don't let me push it down. Hold … hold … hold."

Reference Scores

Normative scores with standard deviations below are for a break test in the sitting position[35]:
Mean for 20- to 59-year-old men = 162.9 (41.7)
Mean for 20- to 59-year-old women = 80.9 (31.3)

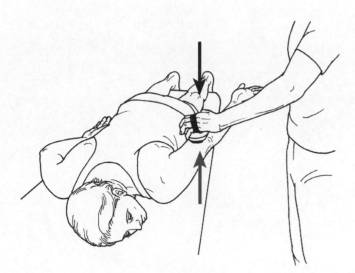

FIGURE 9.2

SHOULDER ABDUCTION

(Middle deltoid and Supraspinatus)

Position of Patient: Short sitting with arm at side and elbow slightly flexed.

Instructions to Therapist: Stand behind the patient. Ask the patient to lift the arm out to the side to shoulder level with the forearm in neutral, thumb pointed up. If application of resistance is appropriate, proceed to test. Position the patient's arm in 90° of abduction in the frontal plane. Ask the patient to hold the position. Place the hand with the handheld dynamometer over the arm, just above the elbow. Resistance is given in a downward direction. Stabilize at the top of the shoulder, if needed (Fig. 9.3).

Test: Patient abducts the arm to 90°, with the elbow straight and forearm pronated (see Fig. 5.65 on page 128).

Instructions to Patient: "Hold your arm. Keep your elbow straight. Don't let me push it down. Hold ... hold ... hold."

Reference Scores

Normative scores with standard deviations below are for a break test in sitting[35]:
Mean for 20- to 59-year-old men = 167.0 (47.2)
Mean for 20- to 59-year-old women = 84.4 (31.8)

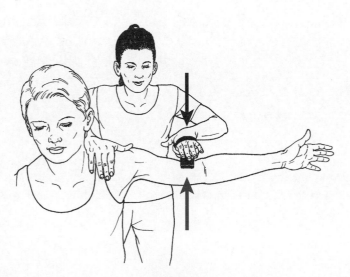

FIGURE 9.3

Position of the Patient: Short sitting, with elbow flexed to 90° and forearm in neutral.

Instructions to Therapist: Stand in front of or sit beside the patient. Ask the patient to move the forearm away from the trunk (see Fig. 5.86 on page 141). If application of resistance is appropriate, proceed to test. Position the patient's arm in neutral shoulder rotation with the elbow flexed to 90°. Ask the patient to hold the position. Place the hand with the handheld dynamometer over the dorsal (extensor) surface of the forearm, just proximal to the wrist. The other hand stabilizes the medial aspect of the elbow. Resistance is given with a medially directed force on the outside of the forearm. Because this is not an antigravity position, maximal resistance should be used, if appropriate (Fig. 9.4).

Test: Patient holds the shoulder and forearm in neutral position against a medially directed force.

Instructions to Patient: "Push your forearm against my hand. Hold it. Don't let me move it. Hold … hold … hold."

Reference Scores

Normative scores with standard deviations below are for a break test in sitting[35]:
Mean for 20- to 59-year-old men = 107.4 (31.5)
Mean for 20- to 59-year-old women = 59.2 (22.9)

Normative scores for a make test in sitting[31]
Mean for 20- to 59-year-old men = 134.7 (39.6)
Mean for 20- to 59-year-old women = 82.2 (20.9)
Mean for 60- to 80+-year-old men and older = 96.7 (25.3)
Mean for 60- to 80+-year-old women and older = 63.3 (19.2)

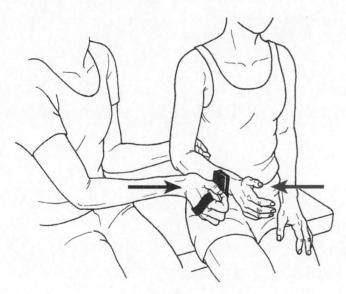

FIGURE 9.4

SHOULDER INTERNAL ROTATION

(Subscapularis)

Position of Patient: Short sitting with elbow flexed to 90° and forearm in neutral.

Instructions to Therapist: Stand in front of or sit beside the patient and ask the patient to move the forearm toward the trunk (see Fig. 5.94 on page 146). If application of resistance is appropriate, proceed to test. Position the shoulder in neutral rotation with the elbow flexed to 90°. Ask the patient to hold the position. Place the hand with the handheld dynamometer over the volar (flexor) surface of the forearm, just proximal to the wrist. The other hand stabilizes the lateral aspect of the elbow with one hand. Resistance is given in a lateral direction away from the trunk (Fig. 9.5). Because this is not an antigravity position, maximal resistance should be used, if appropriate.

Test: Patient holds the shoulder and forearm in neutral against a laterally directed force.

Instructions to Patient: "Pull your forearm in toward your stomach. Hold it. Don't let me move it. Hold ... hold ... hold."

Reference Scores

Normative scores with standard deviations below are for a break test in sitting[35]:
Mean for 20- to 59-year-old men = 112.7 (44.0)
Mean for 20- to 59-year-old women = 52.4 (22.1)

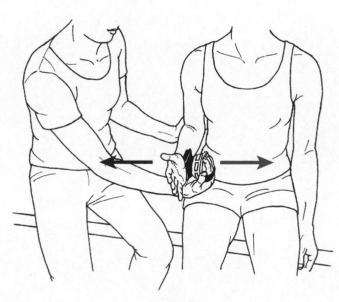

FIGURE 9.5

Position of Patient: Short sitting with arms at sides. Elbow flexed with forearm supinated.

Instructions to Therapist: Stand in front of the patient toward the test side. Ask the patient to bend the elbow. If testing is appropriate, proceed to test. Position the patient's elbow in 120° of flexion with the shoulder in the sagittal plane and forearm in supination (Fig. 9.6). Ask the patient to hold the position. Place the hand holding the handheld dynamometer over the volar (flexor) surface of the forearm proximal to the wrist in the direction of extension (Fig. 9.7). The other hand provides stabilization on the anterior surface of the shoulder. Resistance is given in a downward direction toward elbow extension.

Test: Patient holds the elbow position.

Instructions to Patient: "Hold your elbow. Don't let me move it. Hold … hold … hold."

Reference Scores

Normative scores with standard deviations below are for a break test in sitting[35]:

Mean for 20- to 59-year-old men = 287.5 (83.8)

Mean for 20- to 59-year-old women = 163.3 (49.6)

Normative scores for a make test in supine[31]:

Mean for 60- to 80+-year-old men and older = 209.4 (48.4)

Mean for 60- to 80+-year-old women and older = 129.7 (33.9)

FIGURE 9.6

FIGURE 9.7

ELBOW EXTENSION

(Triceps brachii)

Position of Patient: Prone on the table with the patient's head facing toward the test side. The patient starts the test with the shoulder in 90° of abduction and the elbow flexed to 90° and in neutral rotation with the thumb down. The forearm hangs over the side of the table (see Fig. 5.113 on page 157).

Instructions to Therapist: Stand to the side of the patient. Ask the patient to straighten the elbow. If the application of resistance is appropriate, proceed to test. Position the elbow in 160° (not full extension to avoid hyperextension or "locking"). Ask the patient to hold the position. Place the hand with the handheld dynamometer on the distal surface of the extended forearm just proximal to the wrist. Provide support of the arm just above the elbow with one hand. No stabilization is needed in this position. Resistance is applied in a downward direction (Fig. 9.8).

Test: Patient holds the position of elbow extension.

Instructions to Patient: "Hold it. Don't let me bend your elbow. Hold … hold … hold."

Reference Scores

Normative scores with standard deviations below are for a break test in sitting[35]:

Mean for 20- to 59-year-old men = 184.2 (46.7)

Mean for 20- to 59-year-old women = 120.0 (34.3)

Normative scores below are for a make test in supine[31]

Mean for 60- to 80+-year-old men and older = 162.1 (36.8)

Mean for 60- to 80+-year-old women and older = 102.8 (25.3)

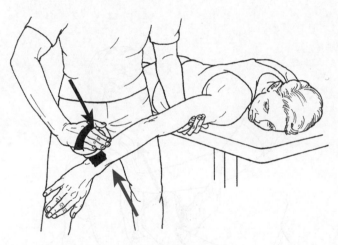

FIGURE 9.8

(Extensor carpi radialis longus, Extensor carpi radialis brevis, and Extensor carpi ulnaris)

Position of Patient: Short sitting with elbow flexed and forearm supported on a table. The forearm is fully pronated.

Instructions to Therapist: Sit or stand at a diagonal in front of the patient. Ask the patient to lift the hand. If resistance is appropriate, proceed to test. Position the wrist in full extension with forearm fully pronated. Ask the patient to hold the position (Fig. 9.9). Place the hand holding the handheld dynamometer over the dorsal (extensor) surface of the hand. Stabilization is provided by the resting position of the forearm on the table. Resistance is given in a downward direction (Fig. 9.10)

Test: For the combined test of the three wrist extensor muscles, the patient holds full wrist extension. Do not permit extension of the fingers.

Instructions to Patient: "Hold your wrist. Don't let me push it down. Hold … hold … hold."

Reference Scores

Normative scores with standard deviations below are for a break test in sitting[35]:

Mean for 20- to 59-year-old men = 186.1 (48.8)

Mean for 20- to 59-year-old women = 107.9 (41.2)

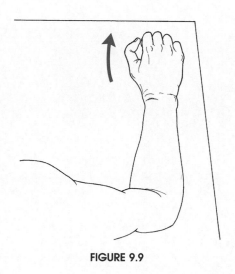

FIGURE 9.9

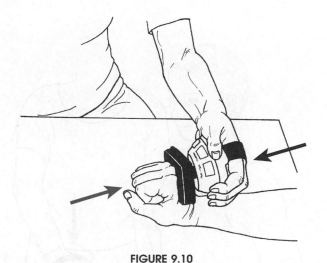

FIGURE 9.10

HIP FLEXION

(Psoas Major and Iliacus)

Position of Patient: Short sitting with thighs fully supported on the table and legs hanging over the edge. The patient may use the arms to provide trunk stability by grasping the table edge or with hands on the table at each side.

Instructions to Therapist: Stand next to the limb being tested. Ask the patient to lift the thigh off the table (see Fig. 6.5 on page 228). If the application of resistance is appropriate, proceed to test. Position the hip in maximum hip flexion. Ask the patient to hold the position. Place the hand holding the handheld dynamometer over the distal thigh just proximal to the knee joint. Stabilization is provided by the patient's arms. Resistance is given in a downward direction (Fig. 9.11).

Test: Patient holds the hip at the end range, clearing the table and maintaining neutral rotation.

Instructions to Patient: "Sit tall and hold your thigh up. Don't let me push it down. Hold ... hold ... hold."

Reference Scores

Normative scores with standard deviations below are for a make test in supine[31]:
Mean for 20- to 59-year-old men = 247.0 (17.0)
Mean for 20- to 59-year-old women = 80.0 (22.0)

Normative scores below are for a break test in supine position[34]:
Mean for 60- to 69-year-old men = 247.0 (17.0)
Mean for 60- to 69-year-old women = 167.0 (20.0)

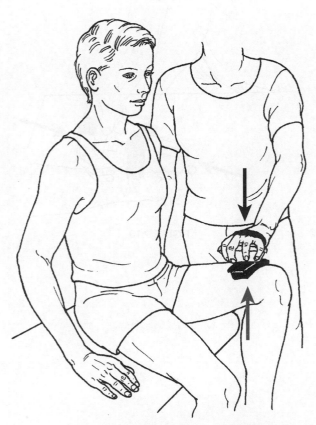

FIGURE 9.11

Test is for the aggregate of all hip extensor muscles

Position of Patient: Prone. Arms may be at the side of the body or abducted to hold the sides of the table. (Note: If there is a hip flexion contracture, immediately go to the test described for hip extension modified for hip flexion tightness [see Fig. 9.13].)

Instructions to Therapist: Stand at the level of the pelvis on the side of the limb to be tested. (Note: The figure shows the therapist on the opposite side to avoid obscuring activity.) Ask the patient to lift the leg off the table as high as possible, while keeping the knee straight and the pelvis stabilized against the table. Stabilization can be applied over the gluteus maximus to keep the pelvis from rising, if needed. If the application of resistance is appropriate, proceed to test. Position the leg in full extension with no pelvic rotation. Ask the patient to hold the position. Place the hand holding the handheld dynamometer on the posterior thigh just above the knee. Resistance is applied in a downward direction (Fig. 9.12).

Test: Patient holds the thigh up off table in the maximum available range.

Instructions to Patient: "Lift your leg off the table as high as you can. Don't bend your knee. Hold it. Don't let me push it down. Hold … hold … hold."

Reference Scores

Not available.

HIP EXTENSION TESTS MODIFIED FOR HIP FLEXION TIGHTNESS

Position of Patient: Patient stands with hips flexed and leans over the table so that the anterior superior iliac spine (ASIS) is "hooked" on the end of the table. The arms are used to "hug" the table for support. The knee of the nontest limb should be flexed to allow the test limb to rest on the floor at the start of the test.

Instructions to Therapist: Stand at the side of the limb to be tested. (Note: The figure shows the therapist on the opposite side to avoid obscuring the test position.) Ask the patient to lift the leg toward the ceiling. If the application of resistance is appropriate, proceed to test. Place the hand holding the handheld dynamometer over the posterior thigh just above the knee. The opposite hand stabilizes the pelvis laterally to maintain hip and pelvis posture Resistance is applied downward, toward the floor (Fig. 9.13),

Test: Patient holds the hip in full extension.

Instructions to Patient: "Lift your leg off the floor as high as you can. Keep your knee straight. Don't let me push it down. Hold … hold … hold."

Reference Scores

Not available

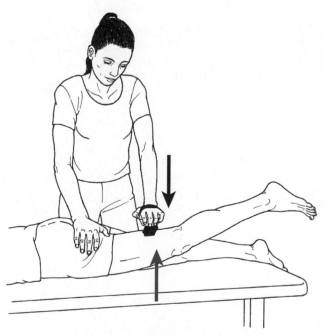

FIGURE 9.12

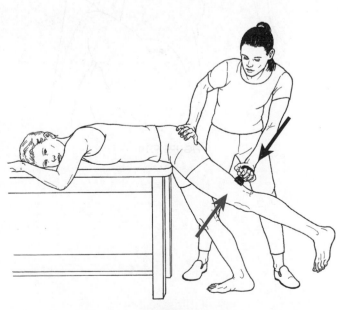

FIGURE 9.13

HIP ABDUCTION

(Gluteus medius and gluteus minimus)

Position of Patient: Side-lying with test leg uppermost. The patient's hip is slightly extended beyond the midline and the pelvis rotated slightly forward (see Fig. 6.36 on page 245). Lowermost leg is flexed for stability.

Instructions to Therapist: Stand behind the patient. Ask the patient to lift the leg as high as possible with verbal cues as needed to prevent the leg from rotating and the hip from flexing. The raised ankle should be in line with the pelvis. Stabilization on the hip may be needed. If the application of resistance is appropriate, proceed to test. Position the leg into full abduction with the ankle in line with the iliac crest. Place the hand holding the handheld dynamometer just proximal to the knee. Resistance is applied in a downward direction (Fig. 9.14).

Test: Patient holds the abducted hip at the end of the available range of motion without flexing the hip or rotating it in either direction.

Instructions to Patient: "Hold your leg. Don't let me push it down. Hold … hold … hold."

Reference Scores

Side-lying hip abduction using a strap to fix the handheld dynamometer to the distal thigh (not shown) has a high reliability (ICC = 0.95)[23] and may improve scores and reliability. Widler[39] found a 30% higher force value in the side-lying position, using a fixed dynamometer as compared to supine using a fixed dynamometer. However, normative scores do not exist for the side-lying position in large sample sizes.

Normative scores with standard deviations below are for a make test in the supine position.[31]
Mean for 20- to 59-year-old men = 170.7 (43.9)
Mean for 20- to 59-year-old women = 113.1 (32.4)
Mean for 60-year-old men and older = 124.8 (32.8)
Mean for 60-year-old women and older = 83.8 (23.5)

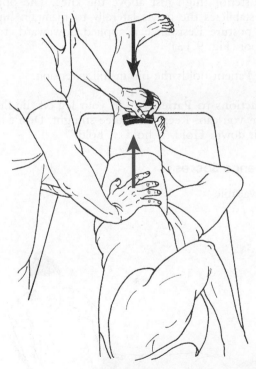

FIGURE 9.14

(Obturators internus and externus, Gemelli superior and inferior, Piriformis, Quadratus femoris, Gluteus maximus [posterior])

Position of Patient: Short sitting with thighs fully supported on the table and legs hanging over the edge. (Trunk may be supported by placing hands flat or fisted at the patient's side on the table).

Instructions to Therapist: Sit on a low stool or kneel beside limb to be tested. Ask the patient to turn the leg in toward the other leg without moving the thigh (see Fig. 6.67 on page 259).

If the application of resistance is appropriate, proceed to test. Position the leg into neutral rotation. Place the hand with the handheld dynamometer on the medial aspect of the ankle just above the malleolus. Extra padding may be needed under the dynamometer for the patient's comfort (not shown). The other hand, which will offer counterpressure, is contoured over the lateral aspect of the distal thigh just above the knee. Resistance is applied as a laterally directed force at the ankle. Stabilization is provided in a medially directed force at the knee counteracting the resistance provided at the ankle. The two forces are applied in counter-directions for this rotary motion (Fig. 9.15).

Test: Patient attempts to externally rotate the hip against maximum resistance.

Instructions to Patient: "Hold your leg. Don't let me turn your leg out. Hold … hold … hold."

Reference Scores

Normative scores with standard deviations below are for a make test in sitting[31]:

Mean for 20- to 59-year-old men = 169.4 (45.8)

Mean for 20- to 59-year-old women = 100.7 (29.1)

Mean for 60- to 80+-year-old men and older = 125.5 (33.9)

Mean for 60- to 80+-year-old women and older = 76.3 (23.7)

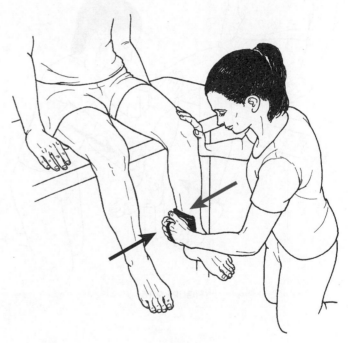

FIGURE 9.15

HIP INTERNAL ROTATION

(Glutei minimus and medius; Tensor fasciae latae)

Position of Patient: Short sitting with thighs fully supported on the table and legs hanging over the edge. (Trunk may be supported by placing hands flat or fisted at the patient's sides on the table.)

Instructions to Therapist: Sit or kneel in front of the patient. Ask the patient to move the lower leg out, away from the other leg without letting the thigh move (see Fig. 6.72 on page 262). If application of resistance is appropriate, proceed to test. Position the leg in mid position between internal and external rotation. Place the hand with the handheld dynamometer on the lateral surface of the ankle just above the malleolus. The other hand, which offers counterpressure, is contoured over the medial surface of the distal thigh just above the knee. Resistance is given in a medially directed force at the knee as a counterforce (Fig. 9.16).

Test: The patient holds the mid-range of hip rotation against resistance.

Reference Scores

Normative scores with standard deviations below are for a make test in sitting[31]:

Mean for 20- to 59-year-old men = 217.0 (62.4)

Mean for 20- to 59-year-old women = 136.1 (44.0)

Mean for 60- to 80+-year-old men and older = 169.7 (55.0)

Mean for 60- to 80+-year-old women and older = 108.4 (33.8)

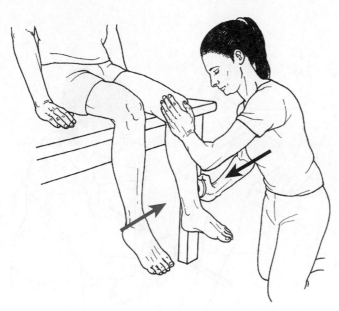

FIGURE 9.16

Position of Patient: Prone with legs straight and toes hanging over the edge of the table. A towel roll placed just above the knee may make this position more comfortable.

Instructions to Therapist: Stand next to the limb to be tested. Ask the patient to flex the knee as far as possible (see Fig. 6.81 on page 267). If the application of resistance is appropriate, proceed to test. Position the knee in about 45° of knee flexion (mid-range). Ask the patient to hold the position. Place the hand holding the handheld dynamometer on the posterior surface of the leg just above the ankle. Extra padding under the handheld dynamometer may be needed. The other hand provides stabilization over the hamstring tendons on the posterior thigh (optional). Firm pressure with this hand may offset any cramping of the hamstring muscles. Resistance is applied downward in the direction of knee extension (Fig. 9.17).

Test: Patient holds the knee in 45° of knee flexion.

Instructions to Patient: "Hold your leg. Don't let me straighten your knee. Hold ... hold ... hold."

References Scores

Normative scores not available.

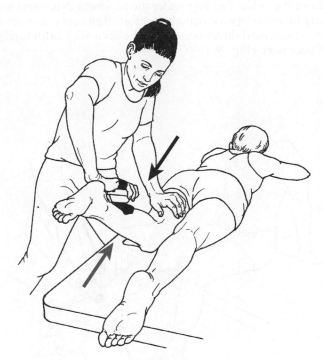

FIGURE 9.17

KNEE EXTENSION

(Quadriceps femoris)

Patient Position: Short sitting. Place either a wedge or a hand under the patient's distal thigh to cushion the thigh from the surface. The patient's hands rest on the table on either side of the body for stability or may grasp the table edge. The patient should be allowed to lean backward slightly to relieve hamstring muscle tension. Do not allow the patient to hyperextend the knee.

Instructions to Therapist: Stand at the side of the limb to be tested. Ask the patient to straighten the knee. If the application of resistance is appropriate, proceed to test. Position the knee in approximately 10° to 15° of knee flexion (avoiding hyperextension or the ability of the patient to "lock" the knee). Ask the patient to hold the position. Place the hand holding the handheld dynamometer over the anterior surface of the distal leg just above the ankle. Padding under the handheld dynamometer may be necessary for patient comfort. Resistance is applied in a downward direction toward the floor with both hands if necessary (Fig. 9.18).

Very often the patient's strength can overpower the therapist's strength during this muscle action. To prevent the patient's pelvis from rising (a common occurrence in a maximum effort test), the patient may be secured to the testing surface by a belt or strap.

Test: Patient holds the knee in 10° to 15° of knee flexion.

Instructions to Patient: "Hold your leg. Don't let me bend it. Hold ... hold ... hold."

Reference Scores

Normative scores with standard deviations below are for a make test in sitting[36]:

Mean for 20- to 59-year-old men = 551.2 (86.1) (20 subjects surpassed 650 N)

Mean for 20- to 59-year-old women = 398.7 (94.48) (1 subject surpassed 650 N)

Mean for 60- to 79-year-old men = 386.9 (94.2)

Mean for 60- to 79-year-old women = 241.9 (81.6)

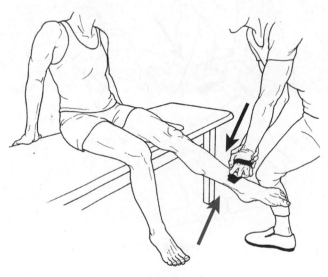

FIGURE 9.18

Position of Patient: Supine with the foot at the end of the table.*

Instructions to Therapist: Stand at the foot of the table with the patient's heel resting on the table. Ask the patient to bring the foot up and in, toward the body. If the application of resistance is appropriate, proceed to test. Position the foot in maximum dorsiflexion. Ask the patient to hold the position. Place the hand holding the handheld dynamometer over the dorsum of the foot just proximal to the toes. No stabilization is needed in this position. Resistance is given by pulling down and out (Fig. 9.19). You may need to use both hands to appropriately resist this potentially strong muscle action.

Test: Patient holds the position of full ankle dorsiflexion and inversion, keeping toes relaxed.

Instructions to Patient: "Bring your foot up and in. Hold it. Don't let me pull it down. Hold … hold … hold."

Reference Scores

Normative scores with standard deviations below are for a make test in long sitting[31]:
Mean for 20- to 59-year-old men = 224.6 (48.2)
Mean for 20- to 59-year-old women = 166.5 (41.6)
Mean for 60- to 80-year-old men and older = 173.3 (44.0)
Mean for 60- to 80-year-old women and older = 131.5 (38.9)

Normative scores with standard deviations below are for a break test in supine[34]:
Mean for 20- to 59-year-old men = 279.3 (23.0)
Mean for 20- to 59-year-old women = 240.3 (26.0)
Mean for 60- to 69-year-old men = 266.0 (30.0)
Mean for 60- to 69-year-old women = 216.0 (31.0)

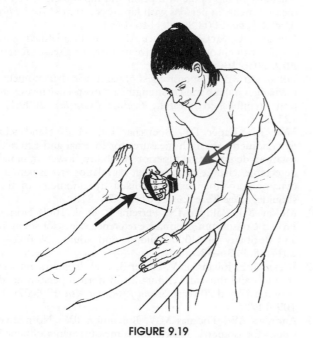

FIGURE 9.19

---

*We recommend the supine position, rather than an antigravity position, because of the mechanical advantage afforded the therapist in providing adequate resistance to this very strong muscle.

REFERENCES

1. Bohannon RW. Hand-held dynamometry: adoption 1900-2005. *Percept Mot Skills*. 2006;103:3–4.
2. Vanpee G, Sagers J, Van Mechelen H, et al. The interobserver agreement of handheld dynamometry for muscle strength assessment in critically ill patients. *Crit Care Med*. 2011;39:1929–1934.
3. Eriksrud O, Bohannon RW. Relationship of knee extension force to independence in sit-to-stand performance in patients receiving acute rehabilitation. *Phys Ther*. 2003;83:544–551.
4. Buckinx F, Croisier JL, Reginster JY, et al. Reliability of muscle strength measures obtained with a hand-held dynamometer in an elderly population. *Clin Physiol Funct Imaging*. 2017;37(3):332–340.
5. Bohannon RW. Alternatives for measuring knee extension strength of the elderly at home. *Clin Rehabil*. 1993;12:434–440.
6. Visser J, Mans E, de Visser M, et al. Comparison of maximal voluntary isometric contraction and hand-held dynamometry in measuring muscle strength of patients with progressive lower motor neuron syndrome. *Neuromuscul Disord*. 2003;13:744–750.
7. van der Ploeg RJO, Dosterhuis H, Reuvekamp J. Measuring muscle strength. *J Neurol*. 1984;231:200–203.
8. Schrama PP, Stenneberg MS, Lucas C, et al. Intraexaminer reliability of hand-held dynamometry in the upper extremity: a systematic review. *Arch Phys Med Rehabil*. 2014;95(12):2444–2469.
9. Stark T, Walker B, Phillips JK, et al. Hand-held dynamometry correlation with the gold standard isokinetic dynamometry: a systematic review. *PMR*. 2011;3(5):472–479.
10. Stone CA, Nolan B, Lawlor PG, et al. Hand-held dynamometry: tester strength is paramount, even in frail populations. *J Rehabil Med*. 2011;43(9):808–811.
11. Bohannon RW, Bubela DJ, Magasi SR, et al. Sit-to-stand test: Performance and determinants across the age-span. *Isokinet Exerc Sci*. 2010;18(4):235–240.
12. Wikholm JB, Bohannon RW. Hand-held dynamometer measurements: tester strength makes a difference. *J Orthop Sports Phys Ther*. 1991;13:191–198.
13. Wadsworth CT, Nielsen DH, Corcoran DS, et al. Interrater reliability of hand-held dynamometry: effects of rater gender, body weight, and grip strength. *J Orthop Sports Phys Ther*. 1992;16:74–81.
14. Awatani T, Morikita I, Shinohara J, et al. Intra- and inter-rater reliability of isometric shoulder extensor and internal rotator strength measurements performed using a hand-held dynamometer. *J Phys Ther Sci*. 2016;28(11):3054–3059.
15. Cools AM, De Wilde L, Van Tongel A, et al. Measuring shoulder external and internal rotation strength and range of motion:comprehensive intra-rater and inter-rater reliability study of several testing protocols. *J Shoulder Elbow Surg*. 2014;23(10):1454–1461.
16. Bohannon RW. Hand-held dynamometry: a practicable alternative for obtaining objective measures of muscle strength. *Isokinet Exerc Sci*. 2012;20:301–315.
17. Bohannon RW. Testing isometric limb muscle strength with dynamometers. *Crit Rev Phys Rehabil Med*. 1990;2:75–86.
18. Suzuki M, Kirimoto H, Inamura A, et al. The relationship between knee extension strength and lower extremity functions in nursing home residents with dementia. *Disabil Rehabil*. 2012;34(3):202–209.
19. Bohannon RW. Rolling to the nonplegic side: influence of teaching and limb strength in hemiplegic stroke patients. 1988;(3):215–218.
20. Schurr K, Sherrington C, Wallbank G, et al. The minimum sit-to-stand height test: reliability, responsiveness and relationship to leg muscle strength. *Clin Rehabil*. 2012;26(7):656–663.
21. Bohannon RW, Smith J, Hull D, et al. Deficits in lower extremity muscle and gait performance among renal transplant candidates. *Arch Phys Med Rehabil*. 1995;76:547–551.
22. Bohannon RW. Selected determinants of ambulatory capacity in patients with hemiplegia. *Clin Rehabil*. 1989;3:47–53.
23. Alnahdi AH, Zeni JA, Snyder-Mackler L. Hip abductor strength reliability and association with physical function after unilateral total knee arthroplasty: a cross-sectional study. *Phys Ther*. 2014;94(8):1154–1162.
24. Andrews AW, Bohannon RW. Short-term recovery of limb muscle strength after acute stroke. *Arch Phys Med Rehabil*. 2003;84:125–130.
25. McGrath RP, Kraemer WJ, Vincent BM, et al. Muscle strength is protective against osteoporosis in an ethni-cally diverse sample of adults. *J Strength Cond Res*. 2017.
26. McGrath R, Vincent BM, Al Snih S, et al. The association between muscle weakness and incident diabetes in older Mexican Americans. *J Am Med Dir Assoc*. 2017;18(5):452.e7–452.e12.
27. Pua YH, Wrigley TV, Cowan SM, et al. Intrarater test-retest reliability of hip range of motion and hip muscle strength measurements in persons with hip osteoarthritis. *Arch Phys Med Rehabil*. 2008;89(6):1146–1154.
28. Oliveira CC, McGinley J, Lee AL, et al. Fear of falling in people with chronic obstructive pulmonary disease. *Respir Med*. 2015;109:483–489.
29. Bohannon RW. Responsiveness of hand-held dynamometry to changes in limb muscle strength: a retrospective investiga-tion of published research. *Isokinet Exerc Sci*. 2009;17:221–225.
30. Holt KL, Raper DP, Boettcher CE, et al. Hand-held dynamometry strength measures for internal and external rotation demonstrate superior reliability, lower minimal detectable change and higher correlation to isokinetic dynamometry than externally-fixed dynamometry of the shoulder. *Phys Ther Sport*. 2016;21:75–81.
31. McKay MJ, Baldwin JN, Ferreira P, et al. 1000 Norms Project Consortium. Normative reference values for strength and flexibility of 1,000 children and adults. *Neurology*. 2017;88(1):36–43.
32. Bäckman E, Johansson V, Häger B, et al. Isometric muscle strength and muscular endurance in normal persons aged between 17 and 70 years. *Scand J Rehabil Med*. 1995;27(2):109–117.
33. Andrews AW, Thomas MW, Bohannon RW. Normative values for isometric muscle force measurements obtained with hand-held dynamometers. *Phys Ther*. 1996;76:248–259.
34. Phillips BA, Lo SK, Mastaglia FL. Muscle force measured using ''break'' testing with a hand-held myometer in normal subjects aged 20 to 69 years. *Arch Phys Med Rehabil*. 2000;81:653–661.
35. Van Harlinger W, Blalock L, Merritt JL. Upper limb strength: study providing normative data for a clinical handheld dynamometer. *PMR*. 2015;7(2):135–140.
36. Bohannon RW. Reference values for extremity muscle strength obtained by hand-held dynamometry from adults aged 20 to 79 years. *Arch Phys Med Rehabil*. 1997;78(1):26–32.

37. van der Ploeg RJ, Oosterhuis HJ. The "make/break test" as a diagnostic tool in functional weakness. *J Neurol Neurosurg Psychiatry*. 1991;54(3):248–251.

38. Bohannon RW, Chu J, Portz M. Measurement of hip extension strength with a portable device: description, reliability and validity of a procedure. *Isokinet Exerc Sci*. 2015;23:271–274.

39. Widler KS, Glatthorn JF, Bizzini M, et al. Assessment of hip abductor muscle strength. A validity and reliability study. *J Bone Joint Surg Am*. 2009;91(11):2666–2672.

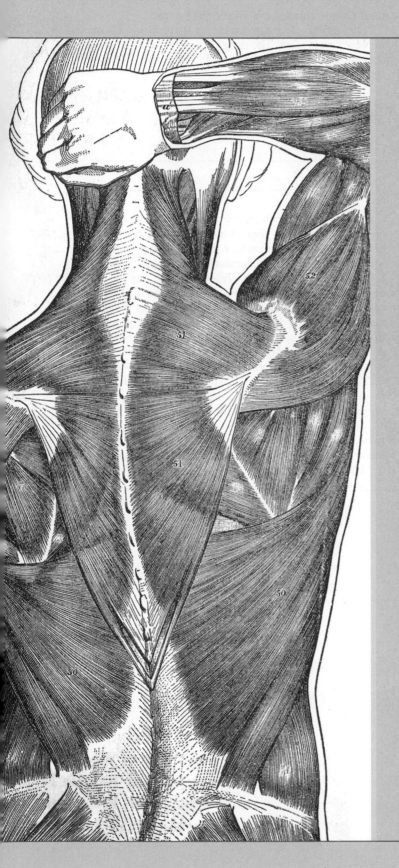

Case Studies

Introduction

Case 1. Shoulder Pain

Case 2. Compromised Gait and Function Secondary to Muscle Weakness

Case 3. Fatigue Secondary to Muscle Weakness

Case 4. Muscle Weakness Following Nerve Injury

Case 5. Muscle Weakness Following Hip Surgery

Case 6. Muscle Weakness Following Childbirth

CASE STUDIES

INTRODUCTION

This chapter serves as a brief summary of the muscle-testing performance concepts presented throughout this book. Concepts are amplified using a series of case studies that illustrate the need for various forms of muscle testing. Each case features a real patient with a need for specific data to verify clinical findings and understand functional deficits. An overview of the problem-solving approach used by the therapist is presented for each.

The variety of tests available to therapists is illustrated in these case studies. The diagnoses presented are common, and each case is intended to highlight the rationale for specific muscle test selection.

 ### Case 1. Shoulder Pain

The patient was a 56-year-old male investment banker who developed right shoulder pain after a weekend of working with his arms extended over his head while painting the ceilings in his home. Initial observation reveals forward shoulders and abducted scapulae. Because of his forward shoulder posture, weakness of scapular stabilizers was suspected. Testing of the scapular upward rotators revealed Grade 3 strength. Muscle testing of the glenohumeral muscles revealed Grade 3 of the right external rotators (teres minor and infraspinatus) and Grade 4 strength of the shoulder abductor (middle deltoid), with pain that limited full effort. Shoulder internal rotation, flexion, and extension strength were all Grade 5 and non-painful and considered non-contributing. Given his response of pain to shoulder abduction and weakness of the scapular upward rotators, faulty scapular-thoracic and glenohumeral mechanics were suspected as contributing to pain at the shoulder.

Attention to scapular function was part of the evaluation because glenohumeral joint movement is only possible if the scapula also moves simultaneously. It was thought that focusing on the glenohumeral joint would not resolve this patient's problem because of weakness of the scapulohumeral muscles, specifically the serratus anterior and lower trapezius. Strengthening of the scapular stabilizers repositions the scapula. When the scapula is repositioned through strength and muscle re-education, the humerus will be reseated properly in the glenoid fossa, thus opening the sub-acromial space and allowing more freedom for the supraspinatus to slide beneath the acromion process. This is likely to improve the joint mechanics, relieve pain, and possibly prevent a recurrence.

This case example reflects a typical patient who is referred to physical therapy. The original symptom was pain, but the patient's discomfort was the consequence of mechanical dysfunction related to muscle weakness. Knowledge of anatomy, kinesiology, and manual muscle testing enabled the therapist to isolate the root causes of the patient's painful condition.

Case 2. Compromised Gait and Function Secondary to Muscle Weakness

The patient is a 68-year-old retired man. One weekend he went to the movies with his wife and, after 2 hours of sitting, found he could not get up from the chair without a great amount of effort. This embarrassing incident prompted him to seek help, and he referred himself to an older-adult wellness clinic.

Evaluation revealed a pleasant-appearing gentleman with flexed hips (~20°) and knees (~15°) when standing upright. With therapist cueing, his lower extremity positioning could be corrected to a more erect posture, but only momentarily. He was of average height (68 in.) but was overweight, stating that he weighed approximately 240 lb at the time of initial evaluation (body mass index = 36, which is obese).

Observation revealed clear difficulty rising from the standard 17-in chair in the waiting room, as evidenced by using his arms and rocking back and forth several times before he could stand up. A physical activity history showed low activity, sitting being the predominant activity, and difficulty walking three blocks. Clinical impression was sarcopenia secondary to physical inactivity and age. Functional testing was conducted first, to focus the muscle strength exam. The gait evaluation revealed the following: slow usual gait speed (2 mph or 0.9 m/s), forward trunk lean during the entire gait cycle, pelvic drop bilaterally during the stance phase (exhibited by a "waddling" gait), failure to flex the knee at loading, and an absence of heel rise at the end of the stance phase as exhibited by a flat foot and shortened stride. These observations suggested possible weakness of the following muscle groups: core, hip extensors, hip abductors, knee extensors, and plantar flexors. Thus additional muscle testing was done.

Because this man was large, it became immediately apparent to the therapist that manual muscle testing was not feasible given the therapist's size in relation to the patient's. Therefore alternative testing using the leg press and the one-repetition maximum (1-RM) method was chosen. The patient was also tested using the standard 25× heel rise test for plantar flexors (described on page 278).

Total Lower Extremity Strength Testing

The leg press provides a composite value for total lower extremity extension (ankle plantar flexion, knee extension, and hip extension). The leg press is ideal because norms are available for men and women of all ages (see Table 7.4, page 313). Initial resistance was based on the norms for a 68-year-old man that were 1.4 times his body weight. However, because of this patient's difficulty in rising from a chair, a functional task that requires a minimum of 50% of the body's weight (120 pounds), RM testing was started at 120 pounds (50% of body weight). However, he could not move the weight stack, informing the therapist why he had difficulty rising from a chair unassisted. Further adjustments downward over two trials achieved a 3-RM at 90 pounds (~40% body weight).

Hip Extension

A prone hip extension test was performed bilaterally and the patient was able to lift one thigh from the table, but not complete full range. He was unable to lift the other leg from the table (Grade 2 bilaterally). To establish the appropriate amount of resistance for effective strengthening, RM testing was chosen next. Cuff weights were attached to his ankle (one side at a time) to provide resistance. In a standing position, the patient was able to extend his hip with 7 pounds for six repetitions on the right side, and 5 pounds for six repetitions on the left while using arm support for balance and stability.

Knee Extension

A RM using the leg extension machine (open chain approach) was used to isolate the knee extensors. The patient was seated on the leg extension machine, and initially 50 pounds was selected from the weight stack to test one leg at a time. Fifty pounds was chosen because it is slightly less than half of the bilateral leg press 1-RM. The patient was not able to complete the full range, so the weight was decreased by 10 pounds. He was then able to complete full range with utmost effort. To confirm the RM, the patient was asked to perform as many repetitions as possible. He was unable to do another repetition with full range; therefore his 1-RM for the first leg was 40 pounds. The test was then repeated on the other side and achieved a 4-RM at 30 pounds. (Note: Open chain movements generally produce less force than what is achieved on the leg press because of the isolation of the knee extensors.)

Hip Abduction

Manual muscle testing in a side-lying position revealed an inability to lift either leg against gravity, Grade 2, that was confirmed with the ability to abduct each leg in supine through full range. To provide a RM to inform the exercise prescription, the only feasible option for accurate testing given the patient's size was a cable tensiometer affixed to an immovable object such as the wall. The patient stood with his back against the wall using the back of a chair for balance and stability, with a cuff attached to the cable tensiometer around his ankle. He was asked to abduct his leg with as much force as possible while keeping his opposite heel against the wall. The tensiometer cable was set so that the contraction elicited was isometric in the nearly hip neutral position, which is consistent with the strength demand in gait. Three repetitions were requested and the top value of 67 pounds was recorded. The weight of this patient's head, arms, and trunk (i.e., the demand on his hip abductors) would be approximately 160 pounds. Thus a 67-pound force output is not sufficient to keep his pelvis in the midline during gait. Additionally, this lack of strength would increase the work of walking and increase his fatigue. Although not reported, the other hip was also tested and values were comparable.

Continued

Case 2. Compromised Gait and Function Secondary to Muscle Weakness—cont'd

Plantar Flexion

The patient's plantar flexors were tested using a standing plantar flexion test because of its ease and functionality. Given a lack of heel rise during gait, it was expected the patient would be in the lower part of the range of normal. Testing of each leg revealed an ability to accomplish five repetitions on the right and four on the left, which corresponds to a Grade 4. The traditional plantar flexion test (see page 278) requires 25 repetitions of at least 2-inch clearance.[1] Norms for a male of 60+ years require completing from 4 to 27 heel raises of at least 2-inch clearance.[2]

Core testing

Core testing was conducted using a modified plank test as the patient was unable to assume a full plank secondary to inflexible feet. Core testing was conducted because of the patient's flexed posture and fatigue when walking three blocks. The RM was 4 seconds. A "normal" plank is 60 seconds in a full plank (legs extended and weight on toes). His result is

consistent with individuals who exhibit a forward-leaning posture such as when using a walker. These individuals who cannot walk upright independently can exhibit trunk weakness of 85% or more.

In summary, this patient's knee extension strength was Grade 4 with a 4-RM of 30 pounds and 40 pounds, hip extensors were Grade 2 with 6 and 5 pounds at 6-RM, hip abductors were Grade 2 with RM of 67 pounds, and plantar flexors were Grade 4 with a 4- and 5-RM. Modified plank for core strength equaled 4 seconds. These grades indicate muscle weakness of a magnitude that compromises physical activity, alters the normal gait pattern, and explains his inability to rise from a chair without using the arms. The instrumented tests provided specific numbers that could be used in context with the body weight demands of daily activities and help establish the appropriate amount of resistance for an effective exercise program. It should be noted that this individual walked into the clinic unassisted and yet demonstrated profound muscle weakness when isolated testing was performed. This scenario is quite common.

 ### Case 3. Fatigue Secondary to Muscle Weakness

The patient was a physical therapy student participating in the muscle testing laboratory. During testing it was noticed that he could not walk on his toes symmetrically, and on questioning he admitted that he had calf muscle fatigue after walking across campus which seemed to affect his ability to walk quickly. On further questioning, he reported a history of multiple ankle sprains on the left side, with the most recent being 6 months earlier while he was playing volleyball. Initially he treated the sprain with ice and compression and had limited his weight-bearing until the swelling decreased. He never sought the consultation of a physician or physical therapist after any of his sprains. It took several months for the ankle stiffness to resolve, and he reported there was some swelling after activity such as walking across campus. He was playing volleyball once again but did not feel he had regained his ability to jump, cut side to side, or go for a ball with confidence.

There was no ankle pain at examination, but there was limited range of motion at the end range of dorsiflexion, eversion, and inversion. Strength was evaluated using manual muscle testing. Manual muscle testing was chosen for the following reasons: the therapist can compare strength values side to side, the forces produced by the evertors and invertors are small enough to resist manually, and body-weight resistance is used to challenge the plantar flexors.

The standing plantar flexion test revealed his ability to rise 25 times on the unaffected ankle clearing at least 2 inches

with each repetition (Grade 5). On the sprained side, he completed seven repetitions with difficulty before muscle fatigue occurred as evidenced by the inability to lift his heel the required 2 inches (Grade 4).

Inversion and eversion were then tested using manual resistance.

The unaffected side was tested first and was evaluated as Grade 5 in both movements secondary to a negative break test against maximum resistance. Strength on the affected side was Grade 5 for inversion but Grade 3 for eversion. It took minimal resistance before the fibularis longus and brevis (i.e., peroneal muscles) failed to hold against resistance. There was no pain with muscle resistance.

This case reflects a common finding: residual muscle strength deficits following what appears to be a simple injury. His involved plantar flexors were Grade 4, and his evertors were Grade 3. Given his commonplace injury, he expected a complete return of strength and range and did not seek the services of a clinician. He could have gone through life unable to fully participate in sports at his level of inherent skill and strength. It was the serendipity of being a student in a clinical program that resulted in evaluation and subsequent treatment. How many other men and women are "getting by" with diminished strength following a simple injury?

Case 4. Muscle Weakness Following Nerve Injury

The patient is a 34-year-old male who was referred to the clinic because of weakness in his forearm, wrist, and hand. History taking revealed the patient was caught in the 2010 earthquake in Haiti and suffered a crush injury of the arm when a portion of a wall collapsed on it. He had open reduction internal fixation surgery to repair the crush damage to the radius and ulna, and his arm and forearm were in a cast for 3 months (due to a lack of orthopedic physicians). After cast removal, he was placed in a cast brace that permitted some movement at the elbow, wrist, and fingers. The patient wore the cast brace for approximately 4 more months again because of the inconsistency of medical personnel providing follow-up care. He had his first physical therapy visit 2 months after removal of the cast brace. At that time his fractures were healed and he was cleared for all resistance activities for the upper extremity including wrist and hand.

The patient complained of an inability to hold onto objects including a water glass. The patient's fingers were swollen and stiff but movement was observable toward finger closure, finger opening, and spreading the fingers a small distance (abduction). Thumb movement was minimal in all directions. Gross sensory testing revealed diminished sensation along the forearm over the muscle bellies of the wrist extensors and over the dorsum of the thumb. Sensation was also diminished on the thumb pad and over the skin of the thumb web.

The initial findings were severe muscle weakness following almost 1 year of reduced mobility; generalized hand/finger stiffness; reduced range of motion throughout the forearm, wrist, and hand; and diminished sensation at multiple sites. The therapist suspected a nerve injury and chose to do a manual muscle test to rule out or confirm nerve injury.

Establishing a strength and muscle involvement baseline was needed in this case. Muscle tests performed:

Elbow flexion and extension: To confirm that nerve damage is below the elbow.

Elbow flexion: Grade 5
Elbow extension: Grade 5

Radial nerve: Wrist extension (flexor carpi radialis, ulnaris, metatarsophalangeal (MP) extension, thumb MP, and inter-phalangeal (IP) extension).

Results

Wrist extension: Grade 4
Finger extension: Grade 2
Thumb (DIP and IP) extension: Grade 2
Thumb MP: Grade 2
Thumb IP extension: Grade 2

Median nerve: pronation, wrist flexion, MP flexion, proximal phalanges (PIP) flexion (flexor digitorum superficialis), distal phalanges (DIP) flexion (flexor digitorum profundus), thumb MP and IP flexion, thumb abduction (abductor longus and brevis tests) and thumb opposition.

Results

Wrist flexion: Grade 3
PIP flexion: Grade 2
DIP flexion: Grade 2
MP flexion: Grade 2
Thumb opposition: Grade 2
Thumb PIP flexion: Grade 2
Thumb adduction: Grade 2
Thumb IP flexion: Grade 2
Ulnar nerve: Finger abduction and adduction, thumb adduction.

Results

Finger abduction: Grade 2
Thumb abduction: Grade 2

Grip strength was 4 pounds as measured with a handheld dynamometer, barely enough to hold a glass of water.

It is not uncommon for physical therapists to diagnose unsuspected findings, and in this instance, it was incomplete radial and median nerve damage. The patient reported signs of recovery beginning to occur.

Manual muscle testing was ideal in this instance because there were small muscles involved where the therapist could apply appropriate resistances and easily position the limbs and segments. In addition, specific knowledge was needed to define muscle loss. Grip strength testing could not have provided the important insights gained through individualized muscle testing necessary to diagnose the nerve injury.

CASE STUDIES

 ### Case 5. Muscle Weakness Following Hip Surgery

The patient is a 78-year-old woman weighing 170 lb (BMI = 26.6) who broke her right hip after a fall from her bicycle. She had an open reduction, internal fixation of the hip 7 months ago and had physical therapy for 5 weeks immediately following the surgery in a long-term care setting. Now the patient is reluctant to return to road cycling for fear of falling, so elected to regain her fitness level by training on a stationary cycle. Immediately after beginning her stationary cycling, she found her right leg (affected side) would not perform as well as her left. Her complaint was "lack of push power" on the right and that her leg "wore out" in seconds rather than minutes. Her goal was to cycle vigorously for 30 minutes daily and take a brisk walk every other day.

A posterior approach that bisects the gluteus maximus and medius was performed for the fracture repair, affecting strength. Following surgery she was non–weight bearing for nearly 3 months and used a walker to ambulate. At month 4 she was permitted toe-touch ambulation and over the next few months progressed to walking with a single-point cane. Gait observation indicated a shorter stride length on the right and a gluteus medius limp that was masked by the cane. As soon as the patient placed the cane on her arm and attempted to walk unaided, her gluteus medius limp became evident and the short stride on the right became even shorter.

Given the age and sex of the patient and the likely muscles involved, a manual muscle test was selected for use. In addition, a single-limb leg press was used bilaterally to provide side-to-side comparisons. Two functional tests were utilized: the 30-second chair rise test, and the timed stair climb for one flight and the total number of consecutive flights. Manual muscle testing for the gluteus medius was performed side lying. The patient was unable to lift her involved side against gravity (Grade 2). Her uninvolved side was Grade 4. Manual

muscle testing of the hip adductors, extensors, and internal and external rotators was performed, beginning with active range against resistance and then applying resistance, if successful, or changing the position to a Grade 2 if unsuccessful. Also tested were the muscles above and below the affected site, the knee flexors and extensors, and the core (abdominals, back extensors) because it is rare that weakness is present at one segment only. The modified plank position was used for the core muscles as the patient could not attain a full plank or perform a lateral plank.

Results

Core: Grade 3
Hip extensors: Grade 4 left, Grade 2 right
Hip abductors: Grade 4 left, Grade 2 right
Hip adductors: Grade 4 left, Grade 3 right
Internal rotation: Grade 4 left, Grade 4 right
External rotation: Grade 4 left, Grade 3 right
Knee flexion: Grade 4 left, Grade 4 right
Unilateral leg press: 140 pounds left, 45 pounds right
Chair rises: Without using the chair arms, the patient was able to do one chair rise and this one repetition required multiple attempts.
Stair climb: The patient ascended one flight of nine stairs up and down in 39 seconds.

This case illustrates the fairly classic scenario of patient discharge long before rehabilitation is complete. Fortunately, the patient had a long exercise history and her current state of weakness and reduced function were unacceptable to her. Thus she was a prime candidate for a home program of strengthening and endurance work and a continuing community exercise program.

 ### Case 6. Muscle Weakness Following Childbirth

The patient gave birth to her second child 2 years ago. Postpartum exercises were never initiated, and she had no history of engaging in any routine physical activity other than childcare. Now she is having difficulty with urine leakage when laughing, coughing, and lifting her toddler. The stress incontinence prompted her to seek help.

Muscles of the pelvic floor and abdomen elongate enormously to accommodate pregnancy and childbirth. In many women the stretched musculature fails to return to its prepartum strength and length. This pelvic floor/abdominal weakness scenario is especially likely in women who have had multiple births, particularly if they did not perform postpartum exercises.

For this woman, manual muscle testing of the abdominals and pelvic floor was chosen because these muscles are often

found to be weak following childbirth. Muscle testing revealed the following.

Abdominal curl: seven repetitions with difficulty
Prone plank: 3 seconds
Pelvic floor (manual test): Grade 3

In summary, childbirth weakened the pelvic floor and abdominal musculature. Even though this weakness is present in nearly all women after delivery, too few are counseled to perform pelvic floor exercises or strengthen abdominals. If the condition persists, urinary incontinence is likely. Standard muscle testing techniques were used to identify weakness.

1. Lunsford BR, Perry J. The standing heel-rise test for ankle plantar flexion: criterion for normal. *Phys Ther*. 1995;75: 694–698.

2. Jan MH, Chai HM, Lin YF, et al. Effects of age and sex on the results of an ankle plantar-flexor manual muscle test. *Phys Ther*. 2005;85:1078–1084.

Page numbers followed by "*f*" indicate figures, "*t*" indicate tables, and "*b*" indicate boxes.